THE RESCUE.

Wilderness Search and Rescue

Wilderness Search and Rescue

Tim J. Setnicka

Edited by Kenneth Andrasko

Illustrations by Valerie Cohen
and Judith DuBois

APPALACHIAN MOUNTAIN CLUB: BOSTON

FOR JOHN BAZAN

DISCLAIMER

This book is not a complete instructional manual for climbing, wilderness travel, or rescue. It is not meant to replace field training by competent SAR instructors and experience. The author and the Appalachian Mountain Club take no responsibility for the use of this book or any information contained therein. Endorsement of specific equipment is not implied. The opinions and technique presented here are those of the author and do not necessarily represent those of the AMC or its chapters or committees.

Half title page illustration: From Powell's *Canyons of the Colorado*, 1895
Title page photograph: Rescue of climbers caught in storm near summit of Half Dome, Yosemite. *Photo Tim Setnicka*
Contents page illustration: From *Scenes of Wonder and Curiosity in California*, J.M. Hutchings, 1860.

ISBN 0-910146-21-7

GENERAL VIEW OF THE YO-SEMITE VALLEY.
From Open-eta-noo-ah—Inspiration Point—on the Mariposa Trail.

Contents

Editor's Note

RESCUE ACTS OUT A HEROIC MYTH of cheating death and outsmarting the gods. Search and rescue stories are among the most ancient and elemental tales: Old Testament accounts of sages and tribes lost in the desert, the rescue of Helen from Troy, the Quest of the Holy Grail, and the Scarlet Pimpernel saving condemned aristocrats from the Parisian guillotine.

The Romantics saw nature as wild and malevolent, making rescue a heroic adventure against predestination and a victory for the advancing idea of rugged individualism. The mountains were seen as cruel, ugly, and demoniac before Ruskin's time in the middle of the last century, when climbing began in the Alps. Saving someone from them was a noble act, like St. George confronting the dragon. For every tale of valor, however, there was unfortunately one of failure — for every hero a Lord Jim, who abandoned command of a sinking ship full of pilgrims in Conrad's novel of the same name. Like Jim, those who have seen needless death due to personal inaction are haunted by it. Because of these failures of nerve and expertise, books like this one have to be written.

Today rescue in America is pragmatic. It is a classic American expression of the denial of death by means of technology and motion. Americans have always thought that movement, especially West or to Alaska, would solve their problems. The crux of SAR theory is that rescue is a *transportation* problem of rescuers to the victim and the victim to safety. We have also held that the appropriate technology and equipment can solve any difficulty from Vietnam to space travel; hence, hypothermia sarongs, oxygen apparatus, helicopters, and Carolina Moons. Salvation from death is a mainstay of the American Dream of the good life and perpetual youth. Since the mountains are no longer miserable or frightening but instead a place for relaxing and a source of spiritual and physical rejuvenation, the possibility of rescue from them is pretty much taken for granted. The Wilderness is considered a place for recreation, not trial.

In a way our organization of rescue teams and our move toward experiential education encourages wilderness travel in an atmosphere that allows and even encourages failure. If there is a publicized method of bailing people out of trouble, then they tend to swamp more often.

There are still deserts and the great ranges where travellers perish when they make mistakes, but these are becoming rare.

Yosemite, where much of this book was put together, is a fine example of this transformation from wild-eyed adventurous climbing over The Edge to a popular local climbing center. Today, the rescue organization in Yosemite is highly sophisticated, like that in the Alps. In a way this book is the final statement of institutionalization of the rescue process in the Valley: a published book on how to pluck people from Yosemite (and other) walls. The Yosemite rescue crew is the best possible response to the SAR situation there and does a terrific job. The problem is that such a big job needs to be done at all. As a young climber in the late sixties I was unconcerned about rescue, safety, helmets and the like. Climbing was a *personal*, experiential immersion in the natural world and in oneself. Anything that argued against direct contact with the mountains by virtue of its presence in the rucksack or on one's head was undesirable. Now, after the deaths of four close climbing friends in as many years and several close calls myself on Alaskan faces, I recognize the element of *society*, too. Concern for the whole group, not only oneself, is an important element of the climbing and wilderness experience.

One of the reasons climbers celebrate and revere the heroes of rescues, Terray assisting the others down from the rigors of Annapurna or Gary Hemming in his famous rescue on the Dru, is that they act as counterpoint to the ultimate expressions of self that climbing necessitates. Our other heroes, lonely solo climbers like Hermann Buhl, Walter Bonatti, and now Reinhold Messner, perform superhuman feats of will in extreme alpine conditions. While most climbers are awed and moved by the deeds of the supreme soloists, most also wait around for someone to hold the other end of the rope and tell good stories. So, rescue is a strong affirmation of the bonds of society. Usually, of course, it just takes the form of something that needs to be done.

It seems to me — a non-SAR member of the climbing community — that there are two major related problems facing the climbing and rescue world now and for years to come. The first is that rescue has become very technological, and has created a special class of practitioners involved in it for its own sake and for the interesting gear and experiences involved. The result is that most climbers and wilderness travellers know very little about how to get themselves out of trouble. This has happened in the medical world to a far greater extent.

The second problem is that rescue has become a specialized service provided — "free" by a government-appointed agency of an industrial society; or at the user's expense, via insurance or court-ordered payment (very rarely) — for victims who are no longer willing to extricate themselves. If the myth of *self-reliance* that climbing has grown up with and around, the myth of the *Übermenschen* like Terray and Messner, falls away, only its other aspect of *society* will be left. A society of rescuers and rescuees results. So, climbers must initiate strong self-reliance and improvisational skills to continue their own explorations in a climate of independence, yet without sacrificing the newer element of society and compassion needed due to the overpopulation of the wilderness. Rescue is the reiteration of social ties when volunteers perform it, in an era that alternately calls for a sense of community and bureaucratizes life. Yet when rescue becomes institutionalized, like the money-back guaranteed salvation offered by faddish religious cults, then the spiritual quality of personal exploration on the mountain is lost.

We've also got to realize that there is too much *machismo* in our response to climbing deaths. A strong paradox has arisen, as in any dangerous activity: because we must regularly confront our fear of death while climbing through stonefall or forty meters above our last psychological piece of protection, we are unable to respond openly to death when it occurs. Our steeled control prevents us from learning death's lessons

Accidents are system failures. A mishap is an *error* of some sort. It should not be nonchalantly dismissed with some falsely heroic notion of "going for it" and losing. Instead, the technique and assumptions in use must be carefully reexamined. It's not enough to say that "Chauncey would have wanted to go that way" — nobody *really* wants to go. We have to allow the full force of the tragedy to strike home and initiate change.

What emerges from all of this, then, is what might be called the *soft path* of SAR — a decentralized, low technology approach to rescue problems (both within one's own party and on the part of rescue teams) that stresses simple technique and a commitment to finding the answers to all of one's own predicaments. Climbing has moved beyond a fascination with big wall paraphernalia and into a period of exploring the limits of free climbing and of small teams attacking superalpine projects. Likewise, what I see as the "technological imperative" of SAR should be carefully rethought. We cannot relegate the responsibility for protecting ourselves and others solely to advanced tools (as is popular in ice climbing as well as SAR) and simply consider equipment failure an acceptable reason for death or injury. What must be remembered from the pioneering spirit of the American frontier and early American climbing is not the introduction of innovative devices inspired by Yankee ingenuity but instead the development of artful, autonomous climbers and adventurers fully aware of the games which they play and in which they seek their rewards.

A few words about the book. We have attempted a kind of 'Rescue Guide for the Compleat Idiot.' The intent was to produce a logical, somewhat modular handbook that built upon the preceding material and could be easily followed by people with some exposure to standard climbing practices and gear. By relying on conventional equipment, the Yosemite SAR crew has a vast manpower pool available in the climbers that frequent the Valley. Training of support personnel is minimized, and roles become fairly interchangeable. This modular method of recombinable systems also encourages rapid response.

Luckily, most aspects of basic mountaineering are pretty clearly described in some of the standard texts. Avalanches, ice climbing, rockcraft, and wilderness medicine are especially well covered and so only the rescue aspects are treated here as this is not a climbing instruction manual. Read them to supplement this book.

The wilderness and SAR worlds are changing very rapidly now. Much of the gear described in these pages will be replaced by new designs in the near future, though most of the technique will not change appreciably in the same period. One change reflected here is the increasing use of the metric system in the U.S. — and in climbing in particular. English system equivalents are given initially for conventional sizes and lengths, e.g., a 50-meter (165-foot) rope.

Hopefully the increased availability of ways to solve bugaboos in the field through training and information in accessible and entertaining publications will help bring about the ultimate goal of all SAR groups — to be put out of business by a lack of demand for their services.

Cambridge, Massachusetts
August 1980

Preface

THE MERRIAM-WEBSTER dictionary defines the word "tumor" as "A . . . growth arising from existing tissue but growing independently of the normal rate or structural development of such tissue . . ." This book has been an electrical tumor, a small unpretentious electrical impulse in my head which slowly and quietly kept growing and feeding on itself until it became painfully obvious and unstoppable. The project grew so fast that sometimes it was almost out of control, totally dominating my life.

As I cursed and labored over this tumor, John Dill's advice to avoid the one-author-who-knows-all syndrome kept things in perspective. I want to avoid giving anyone that impression by here and now stating that this book is an anthology of thousands of ideas, concepts, and thoughts from hundreds of people. My role as author is defined as a synthesizer, an alchemist throwing ideas and concepts together in hopes of producing a product of higher value than a solo project.

Exactly why I got into this book writing business in the first place is still a great mystery to me. One reason was certainly ignorance of what it takes to turn out a reasonable sentence, much less reams of cohesive paragraphs. Edward Abbey wrote that "We write in order to share, for one thing — to share ideas, discoveries, emotions. Alone, we are close to nothing." Thus Teton climbing rangers Tom Kimbrough and Anne-Marie Rizzi and I spent most of one evening sitting at a bar in a Reno casino drinking 15¢ draft beers and drawing and discussing various rescue systems on cocktail napkins. I still have the napkins, er, notes, in my file but I unfortunately did not write down the name of the casino.

The roots of this book are in the mountains: the Rockies, the Alaska Range, and the Sierras. It is based on the technique that mountain people use to travel comfortably and to successfully achieve their goals. Much of this book is therefore concerned with technique climbers use to locate, reach, treat, and evacuate themselves or others, whether in emergency circumstances or not. At times the book requires and assumes a certain basic knowledge of technique. The chapters break down each component of the total SAR picture and are added together and built on as we go. Thus, descending technique and the use of belay devices and a six carabiner rappel are presented so that when lowering systems are discussed the pieces of the framework are connected together in the reader's mind as well as in the field application.

This is essentially a modular approach to search and rescue: a system built on parts generally known and accepted by those who are familiar with the mountain environment.

The same modular approach is used for discussing search management. The technique for resolving special situations is also discussed in detail but again search management relies on the ability of the searchers to successfully travel and exist in the wilderness environment.

This direct, modular approach is a step back from the rush toward a vast quantity of technological wizardry that often floods our lives with complicated systems for attaining rather simple goals. This method emphasizes simplicity and is readily understood and performed by almost anyone after sufficient training.

This book is not meant to be an encyclopedia of all wilderness search and rescue procedures known to mankind. There are numerous alternatives to the ideas presented here. Many of these tools and much technique need to be changed, expanded, and improved upon if the art of extracting people safely from dangerous situations is to continue to progress.

Another purpose of this straightforward approach to wilderness SAR is to encourage self-reliance: as an individual, a pair, a group, or a team. We usually have the requisite knowledge and equipment to extricate ourselves or members of our group from a situation. Yet in one year alone I had the distasteful job of stuffing over thirty dead humans into olive green plastic body bags. That same year we performed over one hundred more successful extraction operations of people hurt or in trouble in the wilderness. Tragically the vast majority of these situations were not true accidents. During the investigation of each we could see the step-by-step plan which led to disaster. If any one of the many links of that disaster chain had been broken, the accident would not have occurred.

When situations like these continue to occur it is easy to see what happens. An agency is found to be responsible and public pressure demands action. Action means more and more rules, regulations, policies and the times become rapidly more authoritarian, meshing control by myriad governmental bodies. One only has to listen to the intense debate on climbing regulations and policies governing the new Alaskan parks to see why it is so important that each individual be accountable for his actions rather than forcing governing bodies to accept the responsibility.

Fortunately there are two organizations which assure a professional response by trained, skilled personnel. One of these is the Mountain Rescue Association (MRA). The MRA is composed of amazing people — amazing because their search and rescue activities are usually their avocation. They volunteer precious time to participate in search and rescue operations and pay for their expenses out-of-pocket. All of this is for the pleasure of thrashing through manzanita or being exposed to frostbite.

The MRA is a non-profit organization of member teams located around the United States and dedicated to getting other people out of trouble in wild places. It is a group oriented toward field skills. It also organizes, coordinates, and conducts safety and public information programs, and serves as a central organization through which individual members and units can coordinate, communicate, and promote mountain safety and SAR techniques. As my friend Dick Sale (Sierra Madre Search and Rescue) once put it, "We (the MRA) will go any place, at any time, to help anyone, for no charge . . . ." Along with many others, I wish to take my hat off to these folks. They encourage the exchange of ideas and inquiries from all interested people or groups: Mountain Rescue Association, P.O. Box 396, Altadena, CA 91001.

The National Association for Search and Rescue (NASAR) is a non-profit membership organization composed of paid professionals and volunteers who share a common interest in search and rescue of any type. It has well over a thousand member groups and individuals, and as its main goal seeks to provide a forum for these federal, state, local, private, and volunteer members. NASAR is a facilitating organization rather than one equipped to put people into the field. Its many independent members are still the field troops. NASAR invites you to join: NASAR Headquarters, P.O. Box 2123, La Jolla, CA 92038.

For a book like this one, I think it is extremely beneficial to mention specific trade names of equipment. Certainly regional and local approaches to search and rescue problem-solving dictate modifications or changes in what I present. I use trade names for the information and convenience of the reader. Bear in mind that this does not constitute official evaluation or recommendation of one product over another.

It seems that we are forever scratching our heads in order to come up with workable, non-sexist words which are simple to use, such as "rescuepersons" or "layperson." In general, we have used both male and female pronouns here to achieve a balance. Throughout this book the word "victim" is used in its broadest sense to describe the focus of a search or rescue operation: the person who is lost, stranded, sick, or injured. I personally do not feel the word has nasty connotations. Lastly search and rescue is abbreviated to "SAR" throughout this book. The word "rescue" refers to a situation in which others are assisting a "victim" whose location is known. A "search" occurs when the victim's location or her physical state is not known. A "recovery" is the location and evacuation of the body of a fatality.

Acknowledgments

Most of this book comes from conversations, letters, arguments, and personal experiences with countless numbers of people. Some of them I have listed below; I apologize to any I missed. Without these folks there would be no *Wilderness Search and Rescue*.

Four people in particular — John Dill, Valerie Cohen, Ken Andrasko, and Lucinda Mirk — are the corners of the foundation of this effort. John provided long hours of advice and counsel ranging from explaining how pulley systems work to telling me in clear, explicit terms what pieces of garbage he thought certain passages, ideas, and philosophies of mine were.

Valerie (and eventually her husband Michael) was lured into this project by my request for "a few simple illustrations" over three years ago. As the project continued to grow, Valerie agreed to persevere and continued to try to make line drawings out of my scribbled, unreadable sketches.

Ken Andrasko was the person who put together, edited, and re-edited all the various stages and versions of piles of typed pages and stacks of photos into a readable, useable book. This was no easy task, because as Henry Berrey (manager and editor of the Yosemite Natural History Association) once told me, "The problem with your writing, Tim, is that you write like you speak — which is very entertaining, but grammatically horrible!"

Lu Mirk, my ex-fiance, persevered through the entire project, diligently typing draft after unreadable draft. She also put up with living with piles of Xeroxed copies, boxes of slides, and Andrasko and I spreading our work over her entire house for weeks on end.

To these four folks I am eternally grateful, as well as to the following: Steve Medley; Bea Weiss; Jack Gyer; Scott Gordon, U.S.N.; Norman Hicks, U.S.N.; Gary Ostrander, U.S.N.; Robert Beatty, U.S.N. (Ret.); Craig Patterson; Bob Gerhardt; Dick Martin; Bob Howard; Rick Lavalla; George Durkee; Paul Fodor; Tom Vines; John Chew; Dennis Kelley; Lois McCoy; Gene Rose; Chris Andress; Dan Horner; Peter Miles Hart; Ed Leeper; Gerald Fritskie; Sandy Bryson; Jim Brady; Mary Vocelka; Dr. Jeff Folkens, M.D.; Dr. Helen Clyatt, M.D.; Dr. Peter Hackett, M.D.; Dr. James Wurgler, M.D.; Mead Hargis; Charles "Butch" Farabee; Tony Andersen; Pete Thompson; Knox Williams; Bill Clem; Tom Vines; Steve Hudson; Daniel Smith; Dick Sales; Rick Smith; Jean Syrotuck; Bill Syrotuck; Doug Erskine; Bill Wendt; Bill Mattson, U.S.A.F.; Rick Gale; Selene Widemeyer; Ray Smutek; Peter Fitzmaurice; Bryan Swift; Tom Rohr; Bill March; Sandy Dengler; Jack Morehead; Dave Walton; Bill Wade; Judy DuBois; and Margaret Murphy.

My thanks also to those at the Appalachian Mountain Club who worked on the book: Robert Saunders and Arlyn Powell. Mike Fender designed text and cover. Dartmouth Printing set the type and Maple-Vail did the printing and binding.

Prologue:
At Night on
Mt. Watkins

IT WAS A SURPRISINGLY warm afternoon for October in Yosemite Valley, and it felt good to run my usual route along the Merced River trails and roads, to ease the day's worries. I had completed about half of my course and was running near Curry Village when the night supervisor's car pulled dramatically in front of me, forcing me to stop. Before I could say anything, ranger Rick Smith briskly leaped out of the car and said, "You'd better get in. We've got a real problem." He didn't wait for my response.

As I hastily slid into the back seat, I recognized Chris Falkenstein, whom I had known casually for the past two or three years as an excellent local rock climber and summer guide for the Yosemite Mountaineering School. John Dill, a seasonal ranger who made up the other half of the search and rescue division for Yosemite Park, was sitting in the front with Rick. The three began to fill me in on the details of the situation as Rick sped toward headquarters.

Chris and his partner Bob Locke had been climbing a well-known route on the south face of Mt. Watkins, at the eastern end of Yosemite Valley near the beginning of Tenaya Canyon. This difficult climb takes about two or three days to complete, and is rated Grade VI, 5.10, A3. On October 13 the two had walked in to the base of the route, and then climbed two pitches the next day and rappelled down to spend the night. They jumared back up their fixed ropes on the 15th and committed themselves to the face. At about noon, Locke began leading the eighth pitch while Falkenstein belayed from a sloping ledge. He climbed about

South face of Mt. Watkins in Yosemite. *Photo Kenneth Andrasko*   1 ten meters above the ledge, clipped his rope through a fixed piece of protection, and moved up the same distance again before placing two protection nuts of his own. After continuing on about a meter past his last nut, Bob suddenly fell while attempting a hard move. Chris said Locke swung down like a pendulum and immediately ripped out the two nuts he had just placed. He slid down and across the face, almost hitting Falkenstein, who ducked as he flew past. The force of the fall pulled the belay rope through Chris's hands so rapidly that his left one was burned severely.

Finally, after what seemed a long, slow-motion dream, Locke crashed into an inside corner to the left of and slightly above Chris. He hung limp on the rock, barely conscious. Although it all happened in an instant, Chris noticed a dramatic rupture in the rope now taut between them and instantly began lowering Locke the remaining meter or two to the ledge. Just as Chris was grabbing Locke, the remaining two strands of the rope's core broke. Bob plummeted again.

A haul line — a light rope used to pull up sacks containing the food, water, and clothing necessary for multiday climbs and not meant as a safety rope — was casually tied to his harness. Miraculously, it kept him from falling the rest of the distance to the ground, although it was radically abraded in the process. Bob halted a full rope-length down, about 50 meters below Chris's ledge.

Jumaring down the haul line to a point about ten meters above Bob, Chris placed anchors and then continued to him. Locke was hanging, still conscious, from the end of the 9mm rope, so Chris clipped into him and struggled to jumar up to a small ledge barely large enough to lie on. After securing Bob, Falkenstein jumared the remaining 35 meters to the belay station, collected food and clothing, rappelled to Locke and eased him into a sleeping bag. Once he was as comfortable as possible, Chris gathered some gear and made a series of harrowing rappels using a portion of the broken main rope tied to the damaged haul line.

The rough five-kilometer trail to Mirror Lake was covered in record time. Chris called the park dispatcher from a pay phone at exactly 5 P.M. Smith and Dill raced over to Mirror Lake, and picked me up on the way back. Bob's injuries were described as a serious cut on the head, apparent paralysis of the legs, and difficulty in moving his arms. He had complained of pain in his shoulder and back, but was conscious and in reasonably good spirits when Falkenstein left.

It would be dark in less than two hours. We began to discuss rescue and logistical options while driving to headquarters. Mt. Watkins, at 2510 meters (8235 feet), is one of the more remote climbs in the Valley, as there are no roads close to it. The mountain looks like a large scoop of vanilla ice cream with its sheer south face eaten away, leaving the final 325 meters of the face overhanging. No spots to land a helicopter exist near the base, and the start of the climb involves ascending steep rock slabs for a long way. The top of Mt. Watkins is in intermittent forest over broken granite slabs. It seemed possible to land a helicopter on the summit reasonably near the top of the face.

Rescuer rappelling to edge of face to assist in positioning lowering ropes. *This and subsequent photos National Park Service.*

We had to know Bob's exact location on the wall, the estimated vertical distance from it to the top of the face, and the whereabouts of an accurate lowering point on the summit slabs. Fortunately, the park's contract fire helicopter, a Bell B-1, was still in the park. It was decided that John would fly an immediate aerial reconnaissance of Watkins. Smith was to contact the Rescue Coordination Center at Scott Air Force Base in Illinois, and request military helicopter assistance from LeMoore Naval Air Station, about 275 kilometers south of the park. I would begin to assemble equipment and a backup crew at the main rescue cache. Smith pulled into park headquarters at 5:15 P.M., and we immediately commenced our tasks.

Fifteen minutes later, John was airborne in the contract ship. He radioed that the pilot was unable to get close enough to the wall to locate

Bob Locke, but that they had spotted the party's haul bag. John reconfirmed our decision that, based on the terrain, time of day, and Bob's probable location, the fastest way to reach him would be to lower rescuers from the summit.

Rescuers belaying spotters and lowering litter team to site of accident.

At approximately 5:45 P.M. we were notified that the military helicopter would be unable to assist us because of impending darkness. Thus, we would have to use the contract helicopter to move people and supplies to the summit in numerous short flights. By this time Dill was back on the ground, and we evaluated his observations and speculated on several unknowns. The contract ship was the only way to transport the required quantity of personnel and equipment to the top. A quick conference with the pilot, Jim Daugherty, evaluated all pertinent factors: the weather was cool, with very little wind; the moon would be full; and stable weather was predicted. We had just enough light left to establish a safe night helispot. Daugherty, a veteran of Vietnam combat operations, thought for a minute as he looked up toward the gray mass of Watkins and replied, "Let's go for it. I can fly it safely." Without the helicopter, we could not have reached the summit until the next day, and Locke's condition was serious. It was a crucial decision.

Spotlights had been rounded up and along with truck headlights brightened the woods enough to allow us to set up a heliport in the

Valley. Shuttles to the top began right away. With portable spotlights, an adequate summit helispot was secured about a kilometer from what became the rescue site. The B-1 made a round trip in 20-25 minutes and carried a payload of 125-135 kilograms per flight. In five hours, eleven rescue personnel and their equipment were on top. Six of the rescuers were local climbers, guides, or members of the park's standby rescue team on call in Sunnyside campground. The last rescuer was off-loaded on Watkins at 11:30 P.M.

Back at headquarters, another request had been placed through Scott AFB for a CH-130 flare ship to provide illumination. The request was declined on account of fire danger. After more telephone calls, however, the staff at Scott located another light source, a nine-million-candlepower spotlight known as a Carolina Moon, mounted in a U.S. Coast Guard CH-130 based in San Francisco. The Coast Guard was happy to assist and at 10:15 P.M., while rescuers were still being helicoptered in, the CH-130 arrived and began orbiting in the Watkins area at about 2800 meters. Luckily, its crew could talk directly with the coordinators at the rescue site on the park's radio frequency, eliminating some potential communications problems. The CH-130 could circle until dawn, but the Carolina Moon has a limit of about two hours, for it depends on a separate jet fuel source; and, it takes ten or fifteen minutes for the light to warm up sufficiently. We decided to leave the light off until the lowering commenced.

All rescue personnel and equipment were at the summit above Locke's estimated position by 12:15 A.M. Our plan called for two climbers, one an EMT, to be lowered to evaluate his condition, whereupon we would decide to raise him immediately or wait until morning. First, a point directly above him had to be determined. Once the rescuer goes over the edge, significant lateral movement is impossible due to the weight of the ropes and climber and the possibility of damaging the ropes on sharp edges or by rockfall generated by the traverse.

One of the finest local climbers, Dale Bard, rappelled about 30 meters down slabs to the edge of the wall and peered over into the darkness to locate Locke. Radio contact with the CH-130 fired up the Moon and directed it along the wall. Each pass of the ship illuminated the wall for less than a minute. The pilot experimented with different patterns and distances from the face to maximize the length of time and the brightness of the light on the wall.

From this first position Bard estimated he was 70 meters too far west.

A second observer was sent down from a new position while Bard jumared back up the rope. The second rappel was still fifteen meters west. On the third try, Dale reported he was directly over Locke. Without the powerful light of the artificial Moon, it would have been impossible to accurately align the ropes and the rescue would have halted.

Bard was lowered over the edge at 1 A.M. on a two-rope system. He was to establish anchors on a large ledge known to climbers as the Sheraton-Watkins, about 70 meters above Locke. For most of the 400-meter lowering, Dale hung completely free on the ropes, away from the overhanging wall. The CH-130 continued to orbit and intermittently illuminate the face. Dale reached the Sheraton-Watkins, placed a directional anchor to slightly correct his line of descent, and continued the remaining distance to Bob. At 2:48 A.M., after being lowered for an hour and fifteen minutes, Dale radioed brusquely, "He's dead." On top, everything was quiet. Eventually, someone broke the silence: "Damn it."

Dale jumared up to the larger ledge and prepared to spend the night. He had been lowered on a two-rope system, with each rope fed through a carabiner brake backed up by prusik safeties, one rope bearing the load and the other acting as a belay. Slack and tension in the belay line was controlled by Dale via radio. Each of the rope systems was composed of a 365-meter and a 185-meter rope tied together.

Another rescuer, Rick Accomazzo, was sent down to spend the night with Dale. Extra food and clothing as well as equipment needed to retrieve the body the next day accompanied him. Rick reached Dale at 4:40 A.M. The CH-130 and its Carolina Moon departed for San Francisco. It had proved an invaluable asset for the rescue effort.

There was one hour of sleep for all.

We were awakened at 6 A.M. by the familiar sound of Angel 3, a UH-1N helicopter from LeMoore, arriving on schedule with three more rescuers, food, and gear. Recovery operations got underway. On top, a solid Stokes litter was rigged for either horizontal or vertical raising. One 365-meter rope was pulled up and the litter attached to it and lowered in a vertical position to Sheraton-Watkins ledge, guided by the second rope in what was essentially a vertical Tyrolean system. A stand-by plan to lower someone from the top to assist the litter if it hung up on descent was formulated, but all went well.

The guide rope was tied directly to the litter once it descended to the

Sheraton-Watkins, so that both ropes could be used to raise or lower the litter. Next, the Stokes was eased down to Locke's small ledge, while Bard rappelled down separately using 50-meter ropes secured to independent anchors on Sheraton-Watkins. With the litter in a horizontal position, Bard was able to maneuver the body into it by himself and then rerig it for raising in the vertical position. Dale jumared back up to the main ledge, where he and Rick were safe from falling rock loosed by the ropes or litter.

The raising operation completed, the litter and bearer arrive at the top of the face.

Because the wall was overhanging from Locke to the summit, we had decided to raise the litter rather than lower it to the base. This method would not require a litter attendant until near the top, a much safer and less complicated strategy. The lowering would have taken place over ledges covered with loose blocks, exposing the attendant to rock fall. What's more, a much more hazardous and longer carryout requiring additional help would face the SAR crew.

The raising was accomplished with a simple 3:1 pulley rigged on one haul rope with seven to ten people moving it approximately fifteen meters with each pull. The second, belay rope was pulled up at the same rate by six or seven workers using Jumars. Both ropes employed Jumar or prusik safeties, and the belayer used a friction device in case of trouble. When the litter reached the summit slabs, the haul rope became

The crew dismantling the raising rigging and preparing to take the body to the summit helispot.

wedged in a crack. Combined with friction on the slabs, this increased the drag to the point that a rescuer had to rappel 70 meters to the litter and jumar beside it.

The litter raising of about 460 meters took some two and a half hours, ending at 2:30 P.M. Once the litter was lifted well above Sheraton-Watkins, Bard and Accomazzo started rappelling to the ground. Six bearers headed off toward the helispot with the body while the remainder of the crew stayed behind to tear down the ropes and clean up the area. The LeMoore helicopter arrived on schedule as usual at 4:15 P.M. Five round trips were necessary to pick up all gear and personnel, including Bard and Accomazzo, who had reached a one-skid landing zone in Tenaya Canyon. The operation, the longest raising we have done in Yosemite, concluded at 6:30 P.M. on October 16th.

It will probably be a long time before conditions arise again that allow us to undertake such a complex operation at night. Whether or not a Pandora's box was opened with this rescue in the dark is a question constantly raised. Too many things might have gone wrong. The decision to attempt this rescue was not an easy one but was reached after open, honest evaluation of the situation and resources. Somehow, everything was favorable to our plan from the start: perfect weather, immensely skilled pilots, the availability of the Carolina Moon, fine coordination among all participants. This was an operation that moved smoothly from onset to conclusion. While its goal, that of saving the life of an injured, isolated climber, was not realized, it remains a glimpse of the possibilities of fusing training, technology, and decisive action into a coordinated effort capable of performing difficult and dangerous tasks.

Part One
The History and Philosophy of Search and Rescue

"IN ATTEMPTING TO PASS THE CORNER I SLIPPED AND FELL."

1 | Historical Notes

WAY, WAY BACK, before the time of helicopters, mountains presented challenging mental and physical barriers to those who attempted to pass through or live in them. Mountain folk routinely fell victim to natural disasters and were sometimes pulled or carried to safety by comrades or travelers. As long as there have been wanderers and wilderness there have been mountain accidents and rescues. A careful reading of texts and stories preserved from most ancient cultures reveals accounts of heroics and defeat in the face of the elements (often portraying divine or evil forces).

Rescue (usually a form of divine salvation) is a major theme of the Bible. The Old Testament tells of the angels rescuing Lot from Sodom just before its destruction (Genesis 19) about 2000 B.C. Abraham cast out Hagar and Ishmael and the two were at the point of dehydration when they too were rescued by angelic revelation (Genesis 21). The New Testament tells the story of the good Samaritan Luke, a prototype of the EMT who gave aid, care, and transportation to victims encountered in his movements until he could assure them competent care. The concept of the good Samaritan is alive today and is one of the prime factors motivating SAR workers.

Watercolors from China painted during the 4th century B.C. depict men climbing rocks, though for exactly what reason is unclear. Throughout history sojourners have made their way through high mountains with silk or carpet or salt caravans, to wage war, or to make pilgrimages to holy shrines. Hannibal's epic crossing of the Alps in 218

From *The Ascent of the Matterhorn*, Edward Whymper.   13

B.C. is one of the greatest journeys on record. He lost some 18,000 soldiers, 2,000 horses, and several of his famed elephants to the avalanches and steep slopes. His adversaries, the Roman legions, also suffered mightily during their major campaigns among the mountains and Gallic wilderness.

Jesus Christ (in Matthew 18:10-14) tells of a shepherd who leaves his 99 sheep to go and seek and rescue the one that is lost. Since Jesus equates Himself with the good shepherd (John 10), with all the people as His sheep, this passage is interpreted as one source of the idea of unselfish giving of oneself in order to help another in need. That there should be a strong tie between religion and the roots of search and rescue is hardly surprising since the quest for salvation is one of the fundamental principles of most religious traditions.

This ideology of self-sacrifice and assistance to others nurtured the development of any number of institutions devoted to helping and rescuing mountain travelers. In the 10th century A.D. a young man decided on the day before his wedding to give up worldly pleasures, join the church, and spend the rest of his life working for those in need. This man, Bernard of Menthon, by virtue of his personal gifts and service came to be widely known as St. Bernard. By 962 he had founded a monastery by a pass at 2600 meters in the Alps. The Great St. Bernard Hospice, as it became known, served as an alpine lodge and support base for one of the earliest search and rescue organizations, composed of monks who went to the assistance of strangers in trouble. Other hospices were built by the Augustin Order on other mountain routes. Traffic over these passes was heavy; in the 18th century, for example, over 15,000 travelers a year crossed the St. Gotthard Pass. It was not rare to serve 400 meals a day to travelers.

One of the monks, Father Lorenzo, spent many years at the St. Gotthard Hospice and recorded some of the first SAR statistics when in 1783 he reported an average of three to four deaths per annum from avalanches and freezing. The hospices provided early mountain guide services along with a program of preventative SAR. Each winter morning for centuries, a monk or hospice servant would set out to guide travelers down below the pass and then pick up a group to climb back up to the hospice. This practice continued every day from at least the early 1400s until 1885, when the first telephones in Switzerland were installed in the hospices.

The renowned St. Bernard dogs were trained in search and rescue at the St. Bernard Hospice. The number of lives these dogs (and their monk trainers) saved is not known, though it is safe to say it ranges up into the hundreds. This duty was not without hazard. Documents indicate that from 1810 to 1845 avalanches cost twelve monks their lives at just this one hospice. The standard established personally by St. Bernard was assistance to anyone in need: both princes and highwaymen were guided to safety. One monk was killed while attempting to guide a group of Italian smugglers across a remote, untraveled path to avoid detection. Asked why smugglers and criminals were freely helped by the monks, one prior replied, "Our duty is to all travelers. Why they are traveling is no concern of ours." This lack of judgment about the motives of those in trouble largely continues in SAR teams to this day.

Other SAR organizations blossomed during this time. The Duchy of Savoy allowed certain men to be excused from military service to form a group of guides and rescuers known as the Soldiers of the Snow to assist travelers during the winter months.

But it was when modern alpinism — simply, mountaineering practiced for its own sake, for sport — was born in the 18th century in the Chamonix Valley in what is now known as France that SAR groups and related technique began to proliferate. The idea of scaling mountains for personal challenge rather than for reasons of war or business was greatly furthered by a wealthy Genevese named Horace-Benedict de Saussure, who offered a cash reward to the first party to scale Mont Blanc, the highest peak in Europe. Despite the prize it was not until 1775 that the first serious expeditions were launched, and 1786 that the summit was attained.

Both Chamonix and the nascent sport of mountaineering founded there began to attract enthusiastic advocates from among the English and Continental gentry. Local villagers soon found that they could make more money shepherding wealthy clients than safeguarding the more traditional species of sheep on the mountains. With more inexperienced would-be alpinists flocking into the hills in the early 1800s, disasters were inevitable.

One of the first recorded mountaineering accidents involving an alpinist unfolded in August of 1820 when a large contingent attempted to climb Mont Blanc. A small avalanche swept away the entire party of sixteen, killed three guides, and buried most of the other members of the group. Forty-three years later the remains of the three guides were found at the terminus of the glacier, including a compass still in working order. The notorious Matterhorn tragedy of 1865, wherein Edward Whymper watched as four of his ropemates plunged to their death when the rope broke on the way down after the first ascent, was perhaps the most famous climbing accident of all time.

Search and rescue incidents began growing steadily in number, complexity, and diversity. One of the first illustrations depicting a SAR event (other than the Matterhorn incident) — "Incident before reaching the Grand Mulets" — was executed by A.D.H. Brown and published in 1853. It shows climbers assisting a fallen comrade and is the archetypal image of rescue endlessly repeated in magazines, journals, books, and movies.

On May 9, 1823 the King of Sardinia (who then ruled over the Chamonix area) issued a decree proclaiming the founding of the Syndicat des Guides de Chamonix. It consisted of fifty-six articles detailing the responsibilities of the guide in safeguarding his clients, and was an early delineation of professional and moral obligations of rescuers toward all those in danger.

Volunteer SAR and recreational organizations such as the Swiss Alpine Club were formed, in this case in 1863. Each valley had small voluntary rescue teams of accomplished climbers and guides with strong mountain skills and a willingness to risk well-being in order to save others. France, Germany, Switzerland, Austria, and other countries also fostered similar groups affiliated in various ways to their national alpine organizations.

More recently, during the 1920s, specialized groups like the Swiss Parsenndienst established themselves as leaders in avalanche, winter, and ski search and rescue. The Parsenndienst is a solely winter rescue organization that handles 500-600 cases annually. Preventative action and the evacuation of injured skiers are the mainstays of the staff of over 40 patrolers.

The airplane was an American invention, so it was fitting that Americans should be the first to adapt its advantages for mountain flying, expedition support, and rescue. By the mid-thirties pioneering bush pilots in Alaska were regularly taking off on skis from hosed-down grass fields and landing on glaciers. During modern times the use of fixed-wing aircraft and later helicopters became more prevalent in Europe. In 1952 Hermann Geiger, a pilot and mountaineer, began to work planes into rescue missions by landing on glaciers, using the same technique as Alaskan pilots of landing uphill on short and steep slopes and then quickly turning the plane at a right angle to the fall line to keep it from sliding backwards. Geiger soon had a following of pilots who, during the late fifties, began flying helicopters in the mountains. In March, 1960 the Rettungsflugwacht (Swiss Aerial Rescue Guard) was founded, a national organization with over 40 aircraft of various kinds at its disposal. By dialing 11, the Swiss national emergency number, the reporting party can be instantly directed to the correct local rescue unit.

FOG-BOW SEEN FROM THE MATTERHORN ON JULY 14, 1865.

From *The Ascent of the Matterhorn*, Edward Whymper.

While the concept of mountaineering or alpinism was born in the Chamonix valley in the 18th century, it was not until late in the 19th century that it came of age in North America. As the trickle of immigrants to America during the 16th and 17th centuries swelled to a flood, expansion into the wilds westward began. Unlike European geography the American landscape had no immediate huge physical barriers like the Alps that had to be crossed for commerce and economic growth. The Appalachians presented only minor challenges compared to those of the Alps, Rockies, Sierra Nevada, and other higher and more rugged ranges.

In the early 1800s a handful of explorers and scientists ventured west to wander through the Rockies. These early explorers and soldiers were occasionally drawn to climb prominent peaks out of curiosity or for a vantage point rather than for sport. By the mid-1850s these adventurers were joined by surveyors and scientists who likewise attained major summits for secondary reasons.

By 1900 many of the more prominent mountains in the continental U.S. had been climbed by one-time adventurers rather than recreational climbers. Up to the beginning of the 20th century two salient obstacles prevented the widespread emergence of mountaineering. Surprisingly, one reason was that many of these grandiose peaks were too easy, despite their height. The second reason was that the mountains, like so much of America, were still too much of a frontier. It took a major commitment of one's time and effort simply to survive in the American West. As yet there was not an American equivalent of the English gentry flood of wealthy patrons into the Alps in the early 1800s. Climbing was not yet a sport. This was soon to change.

Easy accessibility to wild and remote peaks in North America influenced not only climbing history but also the SAR history of the continent. Because Mount Rainier was not a difficult ascent and was close to Tacoma and Seattle, over thirty parties had reached the summit before the turn of the century. By way of comparison other more typically remote mountains like Longs Peak and the Grand Teton were either climbed late in the 19th century or ascended only once without repeat for many years.

Exactly when the first search or rescue in technical terrain occurred in the U.S. is unclear. Most of the early events were unfortunately body recoveries; many such accounts are preserved in the literature. The first death of a recreational mountaineer in North America was recorded in 1896 in the Canadian Rockies. Phillip Abbot, a young climber with wide-ranging experience in Switzerland, was attempting Mount Lefroy along with other members of a party from the extremely active Appalachian Mountain Club of Boston, responsible for much early exploration in that range. Abbot untied from his rope in order to climb ahead to scout the route. The rest of the party waited below and became worried when they heard a cry from above. Suddenly Abbot flew past them in a hail of rockfall and rolled down the slope out of sight. The fatality raised serious ethical debate about the propriety of the sport for gentlemen for some time.

In July of 1897 one of the early accidents took the life of a Professor McClure, killed while exploring a small cliff during the descent of Mt. Rainier with a party of 200 Mazamas.

A few rescue events are presented below in detail as examples of particularly well-known SAR efforts that illuminate the pressures on authorities to effect rescues, and the intense interest accorded such activities by the public.

Floyd Collins, an unknown Kentucky farmer and avid caver, was trapped in a small cave near Mammoth Cave, Kentucky on January 30, 1925. His internment in Sand Cave for seventeen highly publicized days captivated the nation as much as any event in the history of search and rescue in this country. After only a few days had passed since a dislodged boulder trapped Collins while he was on an exploration of the cave to assess its commercial tour potential, Collins's plight came to symbolize personal tragedy and lonely rugged individualism in the trials of a dirt farmer trying to improve his position through guided tours and then trying to survive a dramatic fight against death.

His story captivated the public interest in a way unmatched by any other similar survival episode, perhaps because of the long unfolding of the rescue efforts and resulting detailed reportage on the man and his life, and the personal qualities that endeared him to reporters and readers alike. He was portrayed as a vibrant man helplessly forced to wait and pray for delivery from death, clinging to his faith and desire to live while volunteer rescue crews worked around the clock overhead to clear a passageway. Following a week of futile work in the confined passage, a cave-in forclosed that option for evacuation and forced rescuers to begin work on a tunnel cut down from above. Hundreds of volunteers emerged from the crowd of an estimated 50,000 spectators and 10,000 cars that mobbed the site on Sunday (and averaged about 2,000 daily), creating a boom town and carnival that presented major law enforcement difficulties.

Media exploitation of the event and the man was unparalleled in the annals of rescue journalism. Although only a few facts surfaced in the two-and-a-half weeks of coverage, voluminous newspaper and radio accounts explored human-interest angles to the story, often liberally mixing fact and fiction and emphasizing those aspects of special interest to their readers: Floyd's vague relationships with a number of women, his family's poverty, local color. Careful manipulation of news kept reader interest in the events high.

A serious lack of leadership and control of the rescue by locals greatly hampered progress until the lieutenant-governor arrived with heavily armed national guardsmen to restore order and transfer leadership to the Red Cross and mining engineers. The population of nearby Cave City quadrupled, and the cave was finally cordoned off by barbed wire and soldiers to allow the work on the new tunnel to continue unabated. All manner of strategies were developed to get to Collins and to keep him warm and well-fed: dogs were sent down the original and other shafts with canteens around their necks in the hope that one might find a way through; banana-oil fumes were blown into the cave and sniffers positioned all through the hills in an effort to locate another entrance; a light bulb was hung around his neck for light and heat. The frustration of being able to pass small objects to the trapped man yet being unable to save him bore heavily on those closest to him throughout the operation.

Floyd Collins was reached by the tunnel excavated from above after eleven days of digging by four-man crews. He was dead. His story continued to be told by reporters, songwriters, lecturers, relatives, authors, and filmmakers for years hence, and furthered the widespread vicarious involvement with the agonizingly slow, graceful death of a simple man. The legend of Floyd Collins's struggle remains the epitome of the fight against death by rescuers and victims alike.

In 1941 George Hopkins, a stunt parachutist, floated down onto the isolated top of 160-meter-tall Devil's Tower in northeastern Wyoming to win a $50 bet. His plan to lower himself on a 300-meter rope failed, unsurprisingly, and some of the best rock climbers in the country sped to the Tower to render assistance. The Goodyear Blimp left Akron, Ohio to do what it could, and a pilot with a ski-equipped plane was ready to land on the top. The rescue became a sensationalistic media event closely followed throughout by a thousand spectators and an untold daily readership. Jack Durrance, with many pioneering climbs in the Tetons and the second ascent of the Tower to his credit, flew in from Dartmouth College and reluctantly roped up with rival Teton climber Paul Petzoldt and six others anxious to be a part of the show.

Hopkins was found on top casually lounging in a pile of food and clothing and camping goods dropped from planes during his five days of enforced solitude. He readily rappelled off the climb with his rescuers, illumined by spotlights, and with them faced a barrage of reporters and publicity once on the ground. It was 1941, in the early years of war in Asia and Europe, and the grand carnival event was no doubt a welcome relief of straightforward heroism in the face of relentless war and economic news.

By 1968 the basic raising and lowering system still in use by the Yosemite SAR team had been worked out. In one of the more remarkable rescues to date, the iconoclastic Warren Harding and his partner Galen Rowell were trapped high on the unclimbed, blank south face of Half Dome during a fall storm. They had been hanging in hammocks for several days in the cold rain and snow, losing strength to the point of being unable to continue either up or down. In a dramatic operation a rescue team was helicoptered to the summit slabs and reigning master (and Harding's archrival) Royal Robbins was lowered over 300 meters through the fog to their sullen bivouac, directing the descent by means of a portable radio. The pair managed to jumar up to safety, though not without difficulty.

Yosemite was the site of a highly publicized climb and near-rescue in 1970. Again the pioneering Warren Harding and Dean Caldwell, both highly experienced in establishing major new routes, moved up an extremely blank section of El Capitan just right of the original Nose route. The unclimbed Wall of the Early Morning Light was some 850 meters high and had been attempted numerous times without success.

Harding wanted to gain sponsorship for an expedition to South America by doing "a truly spectacular climb in Yosemite on our own resources." A plan was formed that included a support team of two professional photographers along with a business manager who was an ex-newspaper reporter. Materially prepared for a long siege of 12-15 days and augmented by the diplomacy of their agents below, the pair drilled around 300 holes for bolts and dowels to make slow progress on the route. They weathered a four-day storm in hammocks of their own design and continued upward at a pace slowed to thirty meters a day at times. The park officials became apprehensive, as no one had ever spent twenty days on a wall before and the weather was unstable.

The situation began to escalate during the storm. Radio reports on the climb began with dramatic lines like, "Warren Harding, well-known Yosemite climber, may be trapped . . ." During the third day of the storm Pete Thompson of the NPS went to the base of the wall with the business manager and asked if the two planned to go up, come down, or request a rescue. The two shouted down, "Going up! Just get this rain stopped!" and composed a note detailing their condition and feelings, immediately dropped to those below.

Conflicting weather predictions kept arriving. According to one a major storm was approaching. Reports from the wall became ominous — the two could not retreat and another storm might place them in jeopardy. Reporters started hungering for more information and interviewing local climbers, NPS officials, and friends of Harding and Caldwell. The NPS decided to send twenty rescuers and all the equipment necessary to rescue the two to the top of El Cap, as a helicopter was available then and the storm was moving into the mountains. Meanwhile Barry Bates, a local climber, rappelled down the face and yelled down to the climbers, who replied that a rescue was "unwanted, unwarranted, and will not be accepted." Bates passed the message on to the NPS planners. The next day headlines screamed variations on "Climbers Refuse Rescue!" and the Air Force helicopter lifted off all but two or three climbers of the rescue team.

The amassed media representatives wanted to fly to the top of El Cap, and after a few high-level phone calls permission to use the Air Force helicopter came through. The NPS by law forbids landing of private or commercial aircraft within park boundaries except in the case of an emergency, so later someone suggested opening the Tioga Road to provide access to within ten kilometers of flat walking of the top of El Cap. More phone calls to higher authorities put pressure on local officials and the road was eventually opened. Local climbers were hired at inflated prices as guides and porters to carry equipment up a trail to the summit, and to act as runners to transport film down to the Valley floor and on to Fresno for processing to meet deadlines. Later, as over a hundred people gathered on top of El Cap, private helicopters were used for aerial coverage as well as to pick up film by lowering a short length of rope from the hovering craft.

During the final days of the event the summit took on the appearance of a boom town. Media personnel huddled in tents surrounded by their hired advisers, porters, and friends. The NPS rangers present established a rope barrier so that in someone's enthusiasm to photograph the scene or the climbers a rock or body would not go hurling down over the edge. Two hookers actively solicited business from the personnel on top, despite the presence of officials! Everyone wanted a piece of the action.

As the final hundred meters were climbed by the pair, the media frenzy increased to a higher pitch. Fixed-wing aircraft and helicopters circled overhead, roaring down the Valley with their long-lens cameras straffing the cliff. Hundreds of tourists watched from the meadows below, lectured by rangers with impromptu interpretative displays and a model of the face. Only twenty meters from the top the two coyly stopped on a small ledge since nightfall was approaching. The excitement mounted. The next morning the pair topped out early in the morning of the twenty-seventh day of the climb, and were proclaimed by the media to have conquered the greatest climb since that of Mount Everest in 1953. The sudden heros now became instant celebrities.

Harding-Caldwell summit press conference after the Dawn Wall climb. *Photo Gene Rose, Fresno Bee*

The climb was artfully orchestrated throughout by the public relations man on the ground. The embarrassed park officials had to talk their way out of an unenviable situation brought on by their well-intended and perfectly reasonable course of action, i.e., preparing for a rescue in case it was necessary, based on the available information —

limited food and water, the long distance left on the climb, predicted storms, and the limited use of a helicopter. All of this rescue preparation made the two climbers instant heros and the cautious NPS officials villains. As it turned out, the storm did not materialize, Harding and Caldwell were much tougher than perhaps even they realized, and the climb was completed.

Soon thereafter noted sports commentator Howard Cosell interviewed Harding on the "ABC Wide World of Sports:" "Warren, what did you really think would happen after the storm continued?" Climbing and popular magazines alike had long articles and interviews and arguments over ethical questions of excessive bolting, managed publicity for climbs, and the decisions by the NPS to begin a rescue and by the climbers to refuse it. Rescue and climbing at once became very big time, reminiscent of the Floyd Collins and Devil's Tower cases.

The accidents of climbers and wilderness wanderers are spread all too liberally through the annals of their climbs and journeys. Many incidents of mountaineering history are famous tales well-known to a wide audience or within the climbing community, stories of tragedy, valor, defeat, and grim success. There is the story told in *The White Spider* of Toni Kurz, his partner dead and frozen in the ropes high above, descending alone with his last strength to the gallery window of the railroad tunnel cut through the Eiger north face, one arm frozen from hanging in slings all the previous night, rappelling to within centimeters of rescuers below until a knot jammed in a carabiner and he was too weak to force it through, gently calling, "I'm finished" and then dying on the spot. And the successive tragedies of the German and Austrian expeditions to Nanga Parbat in which eleven died from exposure in 1934, and another sixteen climbers perished in an avalanche in 1937 in a continuing series of disasters on that peak. The retreat by the American K-2 expedition in 1953 with the seriously ill Gilkey was a classic of endurance and luck in an ultimate struggle against the elements. The list goes on, some accounts of great rescues from certain death, other stories of grisly demise.

Europe has had a full complement of brilliant rescues off of the most notorious faces in the Alps — the Eiger, the Walker Spur of the Grandes Jorasses, the Dru, all the great climbs. Unfortunately a true history of search and rescue has yet to be written, and that task must await another author and time.

During the 19th and early 20th centuries in America rescues were rare and were performed for the most part by party members or guides. But as pressure on the backcountry increased from first sportsmen and climbers and later hikers, kayakers, and sightseers, SAR incidents became more frequent. Often the party was ill-equipped or too inexperienced to carry out self-rescues, so the burden fell upon guiding services, park authorities, and groups of experienced mountaineers. The history of Mt. Rainier National Park, its development of climbing regulations, and its response to SAR needs is perhaps emblematic of SAR progression in this country.

Mt. Rainier, in the state of Washington, was sighted and named in 1792. The 4380-meter summit was first approached in 1857 but the party stopped short of the top, leaving the first complete ascent to Stevens and Van Trump in 1870. Rainier was in sight of large and growing urban populations and as a result tempted both climbers and novices alike. A guide service was started during the 1890s. Large outing clubs and the guides regularly ushered groups of thirty or fifty trampers up and down the mountain. In July of 1897 Professor McClure was killed after falling from a rock. His body was evacuated by members of the group, there being sufficient manpower available.

Other deaths and rescue incidents were reported from time to time, but not on the order that one might expect. In *The Challenge of Rainier* Dee Molenaar writes that from 1857 to 1970 over 20,000 climbers made the summit of the peak. During this time the mountain claimed only seventeen lives, probably due to the ease of the routes taken to the summit. It was not until the 1960s that a serious climber was killed climbing on the mountain.

Body recoveries and rescues in the park required a coordinated effort from guides, rangers, climbers, and (later) the military services and their array of aircraft. This mix of rescue professionals with volunteer climbers, guides, and park employees is one which surfaced in many areas around the country and continues to this day in many cases, though professional SAR teams are on the ascendant.

Qualified professionals for climbing and management jobs were hard to find and keep in the early years at Rainier and most American climbing centers and national parks (i.e., from the late 19th century until after World War II). Occasionally the NPS was able to lure accomplished climbers into its bureaucratic web. At Rainier it wound up with people like William J. Butler, a guide who distinguished himself such that his permanent job was granted by nothing less than a personal proclamation by President Roosevelt in 1936. In the Tetons pioneer climbers Fritiof Fryxell and Phil Smith were hired as seasonal rangers immediately after Grand Teton National Park was established in 1929. In more recent times Wayne Merry, a member of the first ascent party on El Capitan, was hired as a ranger largely due to his technical skills and solid rapport with climbers. But climbers of this caliber were hard to find. Local guides of various stature from Jim Whittaker of Everest fame on down to first-year beginner's class instructors were used time and time again for rescues.

A fine example of this early teamwork came about on Rainier when Delmar Fadden, an ambitious young climber, did not return from a solo winter ascent. The subsequent search and recovery operation ranks with the most strenuous of any SAR operation to date in North America. Along with Bill Butler were a number of the most experienced mountaineers of the region, including Ome Daiber, Joe Halwax, Jack Hossack, and Bob Buschman. As a result of all the publicity about the event, Daiber was often called to lead search and rescue operations. He gradually built up a list of climbers that he could depend on in emergencies and who, in turn, constituted an informal rescue team.

As years passed these volunteers were sought more often. Eventually those involved realized that the number and scale of SAR events in the Pacific Northwest by that time dictated that a more formal rescue organization be developed. In the spring of 1948 the Mountain Rescue Council was officially convened under the sponsorship of the Mountaineers, the Washington Alpine Club, and the Northwest Region of the National Ski Patrol. The organization flourished and branch units sprung up throughout the Northwest. The burden of constant field events was taken off of a few men and distributed among a host of prepared and trained volunteers.

Other rescue units in Colorado, California, and Oregon originated at about this time, cognizant of an underlying need for a national group to promote training, education, and conferences in order to exchange ideas. On June 7, 1959 eleven rescue teams wrote the organizational bylaws of the Mountain Rescue Association. Currently there are over 50 member units and 1500 individual members in the MRA.

Mountain search and rescue activities are of course not limited to the westernmost mountainous national parks. As newer tracts were discovered and frequented for outdoor use it became apparent that the

MRA and similar organizations were of great benefit to local county sheriffs and federal and state land management agencies in assisting with the growing number of SAR calls in their area. SAR problems proliferated with increased access to remote places. Volunteer organizations and auxiliary and reserve sheriff's deputies were introduced to assist in certain types and scales of rescue, especially those of little interest to mountaineers and guides like searches for campers or downed aircraft.

One example of this expansion of volunteer SAR units is the Mountain Rescue Association in California, whose units are distributed mainly along the coast and in Southern California's urban centers. This topography has not figured very heavily in the climbing history of the country but has been of great significance to the development of SAR in America due to its diversity and proximity to a concentrated population. Since Southern Californians are particularly enthusiastic outdoor recreationists, finding, treating, and evacuating those that injure themselves is a full-time job for many county sheriffs and land management agencies.

Fortunately the military, under the National Search and Rescue plan, is obligated to render service to the civilian sector as a secondary function. The MAST program (Military Assistance to Safety and Traffic) was established in 1970 and relies upon Army and Air Force helicopters to provide free ambulance service in rural areas. The program was a huge success and in 1971 it was extended to include mountain SAR missions. Naval Air Station LeMoore in California, for example, has from three to five helos available at all times whose primary mission is military SAR support for the hundreds of Navy aircraft stationed at the base. A secondary mission is civilian search and rescue; LeMoore flies regular missions in the surrounding national parks and forests and state counties. Another function of the station is the transportation of SAR personnel and equipment in military aircraft under the military transport system. Search dogs, ropes, and searchers have been flown around the country in big HC-130s as well as helicopters.

All these resources are available to designated SAR authorities throughout the nation through the Air Force Rescue and Coordination Center in downstate Illinois. The Air Force is legally responsible for the approval and supervision of all military equipment and personnel engaged in inland search and rescue regardless of the branch of service involved. The center has a twenty-four-hour number for a mission coordinator capable of locating the required hardware and specialists. For example, a helicopter with a hoist capability was needed to evacuate two injured climbers off Grand Teton in July, 1979. All local helos were on fire fighting duty in Idaho or other SARs. As a result an Army helo was dispatched from Ft. Carson, Colorado and flew up during the night. It performed the rescue early the next morning at the same hour the local unit would have responded.

Another federal agency with responsibility for carrying out field SAR operations as well as with jurisdiction over coordinating military SAR activities is the U.S. Coast Guard. The Coast Guard is in the Department of Transportation rather than Defense, and is unique in that it is a federal agency specifically devoted to civilian and military search and rescue work in the oceans surrounding the U.S., the Great Lakes, and all other navigable waters. Operations are coordinated out of the Coast Guard Rescue Coordination Centers, in Seattle, San Francisco, and San Diego on the West Coast, for instance. The AFRCC in Illinois and the Coast Guard RCC are in constant communication to interrelate their efforts.

Some 22 of the 50 states have a state agency designated for SAR oversight and deployment. The legal responsibility for rescue activities is generally handed to the county sheriff, who determines the appropriate response and issues requests for military assistance, volunteers, or support from other state agencies.

On federal land there are three types of legal jurisdiction. One is *exclusive jurisdiction*, in which federal law supercedes all state authority — executive, judicial, and legislative — as in Yellowstone and Yosemite national parks. The federal government may choose to utilize certain state statutes like a vehicle, health, or sanitation code, though. In areas of *concurrent jurisdiction* the state and federal governments occupy the land jointly, each with certain law enforcement authority (e.g., Grand Canyon and Grand Teton parks). Mutual aid and agreements of understanding between specific agencies determine the breakdown of service fulfillment. In Grand Teton, for example, the NPS is responsible for extracting injured hikers or climbers from the mountains and the local sheriff's office offers the support functions. This relationship is a result of tradition, interagency agreements, a realistic assessment of resources and manpower, and economics.

The third form of *proprietary jurisdiction* allows the federal government to perform only certain designated functions and enforce certain laws. From the federal viewpoint this is much more restrictive than concurrent jurisdiction, as the state has the bulk of responsibility for making and keeping laws. Until the 1970s Grand Teton was an area of proprietary jurisdiction despite the fact that federal employees performed the vast majority of SAR work. The sheriff's office helped whenever necessary but the NPS was clearly better able to provide professional SAR service.

In new areas of federal involvement such as Southern California the local counties are often better equipped than federal counterparts to manage rescue situations. In Los Angeles County the rate of SAR incidence is so high that a regular unit of professional sheriff's deputies (including paramedics, climbers, SCUBA divers, and so on) works full time on SAR events much in the way a SWAT team handles extreme law enforcement problems. Add to this the fleet of helicopters that L.A. County maintains and a highly skilled and trained SAR group emerges, capable of fast and efficient response to the myriad problems the new urban parks are experiencing. The old "who's in charge of this ledge?" joke and common scenario has taken on a new meaning in a time of overlapping jurisdictions and proficiencies that need to be well-established long before the callout into the field.

I am sure that St. Bernard is looking down at HC-130 aircraft circling overhead and paramedics rappelling out of helicopters and the computers spitting out probability locations of downed airplanes in the oceans at the Coast Guard RCC centers and wondering what he and a few mongrels started so long ago. Oftentimes it seems like there are more people on the telephone coordinating than acting in the field. But every once in a while when that emotional rush occurs when you get back home and cannot sleep because you know you helped someone survive or gave it the best possible effort, all the other endless bureaucracy seems worth it.

In sum, the history of the development of search and rescue capability in the U.S. has been one of a highly regionalized response to growing local problems. National coordination of SAR activities began in the late fifties and was solidified after a decade of implementation by private rescue associations, state agencies, and federal (largely the military and national conservation system land management agencies) offices. The rapid increase in mountain use in the late sixties has led concomitantly to an increase in accidents and rescue operations. The NPS spent over a quarter of a million dollars on SAR in Yosemite National Park alone in

1978. The result has been succinctly summarized by Chris Jones at the end of *Climbing in North America.* "The precedents are clear. Either we bring our affairs into order by taking a greater responsibility for rescues, or the government will want to regulate us. We should never accept payment for rescue work, and we may well have to initiate a rescue fund or insurance scheme. It will be a small price to stay free of permits and certificates." I wholeheartedly agree. It is significant to note that Jones was referring to the relatively homogeneous climbing community. What about casual hikers, tourists, and backpackers, a diverse and unaffiliated group that accounts for the vast majority of SAR operations on the national level? The question of whether or not and exactly how these park users will organize into self-help bodies has been raised by the swollen accident rate. Change of some sort lies not too far ahead, with only its form uncertain.

Early Yosemite rescue. *Photo National Park Service*

BIBLIOGRAPHY

BERNSTEIN, JEREMY. *Ascent: of the Invention of Mountain Climbing and its Practice.* Lincoln, Neb.: University of Nebraska Press, 1979.

BRUCKER, ROGER. "The Death of Floyd Collins." In Mohr, Charles and Sloane, Howard. *Celebrated American Caves.* New Brunswick, N.J.: Rutgers University Press, 1955.

BUHL, HERMANN. *Nanga Parbat Pilgrimage.* London: 1956.

DURRANCE, JACK. "Emergency Ascent of Devils Tower, Wyoming." *Appalachia* 24 (June 1942):123.

FIELD, ERNEST K. "The Devils Tower Episode." *T & T* 276 (December 1941):167.

HALLIDAY, WILLIAM R. *American Caves and Caving.* New York: Harper & Row, 1974.

HARDING, WARREN. "Reflections of a Broken-Down Climber." *Ascent* 1(5)(July 1971):32.

HARRER, HEINRICH. *The White Spider.* 2nd rev. ed. London: Hart-Davis, MacGibbon, 1976.

JONES, CHRIS. *Climbing in North America.* Berkeley, Los Angeles, and London: University of California Press, 1976.

MOLENAAR, DEE. *The Challenge of Rainier.* Seattle: The Mountaineers, 1976.

NEWBY, ERIC. *Great Ascents: A Narrative History of Mountaineering.* New York: Viking Press, 1977.

REINARTZ, KAY F. "Floyd Collins, Hero of Sand Cave." In Sloane, Bruce, ed. *Cavers, Caves, and Caving.* New Brunswick, N.J.: Rutgers University Press, 1977.

ROWELL, GALEN. "South Face of Half Dome." *American Alpine Journal* 17(1971):266.

_____. *The Vertical World of Yosemite.* Berkeley: Wilderness Press, 1974.

SCOTT, DOUG. *Big Wall Climbing.* New York: Oxford University Press, 1974.

"Warren Harding: Interview." *Mountain* 9 (May 1970):15.

2 | The Core Elements of Search and Rescue

WHENEVER A SEARCH or a rescue occurs, it is accompanied by a wealth of confusion, duplication, and what seems like too much complexity, all readily apparent to the untrained eye. A closer examination of this bedlam reveals a structure, an underlying foundation, on which a SAR event is built. Anyone involved in SAR work must study this structure, or at least acknowledge its existence. Failure to do so is like trying to play major league baseball without knowing the rules of the game. There is no place for amateurish George Plimptons in a crisis. It is important that this SAR framework be made known to managers, field workers, and observers, so they may function instantly and efficiently in real situations.

But first a definition: what is SAR? Any operation aimed at helping someone in trouble, someone who cannot solve his or her problem alone, becomes a SAR event. It could be on the South Side of Chicago, on Apollo XIII, or in the middle of the ocean. The problem may or may not involve an injury, but if no one acts, an injury could result. Maybe a hiker is stuck on a ledge; he has no injuries now, but he will die of thirst, starvation, hypothermia, or a fall if no one gives him a hand. Or he may be right on a trail, but injured and unable to move by himself. Or perhaps it is the classic day ski-tourer caught in a storm overnight and ill-prepared. The possibilities are endless, but the common denominator is the same: the victim is isolated and cannot correct the situation alone. Isolation can be either physical (stuck on a ledge) or psychological (unable to walk down a dark trail), and often one sort accompanies the other. Whenever a person lacks the resources to survive very long where he is, and does not have the ability to transport himself safely to a place where he can survive, he is isolated.

Mental isolation is occasionally overlooked but is as important as physical isolation. Some years ago, a man came to visit Yosemite National Park from Latin America. He did not speak English and was alone on the Yosemite Falls trail, a modest, heavily traveled route. It became dark; he was without a light, and didn't know his way. After wandering back and forth on ledges, he couldn't get down, was very frightened, and called for help — in Spanish. His isolation was very real to him, as was his fear, and the "rescue" that ensued was valid. Gene Fear of the Survival Education Association states that survival is eighty percent mental attitude.

SAR, or the process of eliminating the victim's isolation, is a problem of transportation, usually over difficult or unusual terrain. Either the victim must be transported to the solution (e.g., to the hospital for a broken leg), or the solution transported to him (e.g., a warm tent and clothing brought to a hypothermic skier). Rescuers and victims must often move through challenging terrain, so many SAR techniques are specifically designed to meet the demands of the topography. Most of the difficulties unique to mountain SAR begin and end at the trailhead. The structure of this process of eliminating isolation will be addressed first, as a background for the discussion of specific skills.

The Core Elements

All complete SAR operations proceed through four phases, or core elements. The goal is the removal of the victim's isolation through transportation — getting rescuers to the victim, and bringing him back to safety. Each element contains factors common to all four, as well as its own special problems, which will be looked at later. These elements are defined as follows:

1. LOCATE the victim. No help can be offered until the victim is found. The location phase may take only five minutes with a pair of binoculars, or it may take days and be the crux of the problem. This phase is a specialized form of SAR called a *search*, and is rapidly acquiring its own technology and methodology.

2. REACH the victim. This may range from walking to the base of a climb (five minutes), to rappelling halfway down a big wall (several

hours), to being flown into a remote glacier or river and establishing a base camp (several days).

3. STABILIZE the victim. First aid for any injuries must be performed, and his physical comfort and safety assured so that he can be transported. The injuries may be either potential (hypothermia prevented by warm clothes and a candy bar), or they may be actual (broken femur, internal bleeding, or fear).

4. EVACUATE the victim. Again, this may be very simple (leading someone down a trail at night), or extremely difficult and complicated (lowering a litter 800 meters down a vertical wall).

By putting the core elements in chronological order, one can begin to discern the structure of SAR. The starting point is the second after the initial responding person or group has been notified.

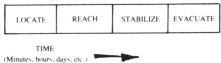

Fig. 2.1 Core elements of a SAR event.

If the size of the block is made to reflect the length of time devoted to a particular phase, a successful search for a high-country ski tourer lost in a sudden snowstorm might look like this:

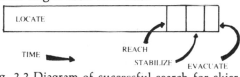

Fig. 2.2 Diagram of successful search for skier.

A search to rescue a cold, wet climber from a cliff might look like this:

Fig. 2.3 Diagram of a technical rescue.

In this broad framework, a search, long or short, is the first phase of any rescue. The search for a person is often highly specialized and complicated, requiring particular knowledge and techniques which dominate the entire operation. If a search is unsuccessful, it may be diagrammed as:

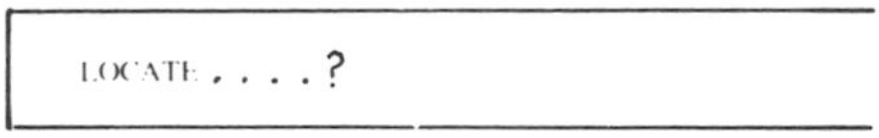

```
┌──────────────────────────────────┐
│  LOCATE . . . . ?                 │
│                                   │
└──────────────────────────────────┘
```

Fig. 2.4 An unsuccessful search.

The four core elements are the basic components of all SAR operations, and it is essential to understand their interrelationship. How one approaches the four phases from a manager's standpoint during an actual operation will be covered next.

Solving the SAR Problem

By keeping the core elements of SAR in mind while carefully analyzing actual SARs, a uniform evolution of steps is noticed, the sum total of which comprises a complete SAR operation. These components are always present, and their order of occurrence is almost always constant. This is true whether each component is only briefly considered and then filed in the back of the mind, or is so complex that each part of the whole must be analyzed with the care and attention to detail characteristic of a space shot. If a SAR manager knows where an operation currently stands, and how to break it down into these problem-solving components, then he has a streamlined and economical procedure. The result, of course, is faster achievement of the goals of SAR — and an earlier success party down at the roadhouse.

In the context of SAR operations, the following components may be identified:

1. *Preplanning.*   Besides having necessary rescue equipment "at the ready," the SAR team must have specified organization and management guidelines. This assures that all concerned know their own roles, as well as who is in charge of particular aspects of managing a situation once a call comes in.

2. *Notification.*   Someone must indicate to the appropriate party that there is a problem or that one is developing. This sounds trivial, but is a frequent source of error.

3. *Planning and Strategy.*   The process of gathering information so that an accurate assessment of the situation can take place must be timely and accurate.

4. *Tactics.*   From the best possible information at hand, the manager outlines options for a solution, including backup plans. These solutions

should be flexible so, if new information arrives, they may be quickly modified.

5. *Operations.* This includes the field phase where the tactical plans are carried out, using specific skills as required.

6. *Suspension.* The operation is finally discontinued, whether or not it is successful, for a multitude of reasons.

7. *Critique.* Total evaluation of participants, methods, and strategies occurs continually throughout the entire operation. A final step, however, complete with documentation, is necessary so that the best and the worst may be articulated and incorporated into everyone's "SAR data file," real or cerebral. This review and analysis should be reflected by appropriate alterations of the preplan, so that learning and improvement of performance take place.

Fig. 2.5 Simplified scheme of SAR components.

Both the core elements and the SAR components occur in chronological order, as well as in a definite sequence, but the components overlap during their development. Planning and strategy continue well after the tactics phase has started, and while the first field teams are initiating action. Naturally, whenever new information or methods are introduced, planning continues. Figure 2.5 diagrams these components along a time scale, in order of occurrence. The order may be interrupted and partially begun again via positive feedback loops, when new information is put into the system, such as the advent of bad weather or the discovery of new clues. The order is constant but the entire system is flexible. Diagramming this for a search may look like Figure 2.6. The core elements are real; the seven SAR components are segments of the total SAR operation perceived from a field manager's point of view. The components are categories which can be used to evaluate performance in solving the central SAR problem of eliminating a person's isolation.

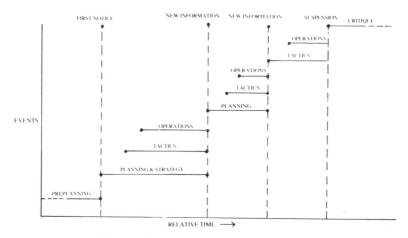

Fig. 2.6 Detailed SAR component scheme.

Time is generally referred to and measured as "speed" (or the lack thereof) in SAR work. Did everyone respond fast enough? Should the hasty team fly or walk? Speed most often appears to be limited by physical factors such as the availability of resources (the helicopter or good skiers), or environmental factors (darkness or rain). From another step back, though, safety is the ultimate, although often hidden, or, worse yet, forgotten factor limiting how soon an operation can be concluded. The operation can proceed well into the planning phase, using any and all ideas and resources available, and all is fine until someone suddenly says "It's not safe," and crash . . . back to the computer or dirt blackboard. No rescuer has ever helped an operation be speedy and efficient by being exposed to unreasonable mental or physical risk. Safety says "yes" or "no" to individual actions as well as to the overall plan.

Webster calls safety "freedom from danger." If we expand that definition to include "freedom from physical or mental danger," it becomes a major concept of SAR theory. Since the degree of safety varies with the skill of the individual, a group's safety depends on the weakest link in the chain. The whole group's performance and freedom from mishap depend on its ability to assist and monitor that weakest link. Safety is based on an individual's skills, attitudes, knowledge of the situation, and the actions of others around him. Because safety is so elastic, despite a large body of rules, it is hard to determine when someone is acting unsafely. The decision that action is unsafe is a reflection of personal training and grasp of the system. For example, if someone is climbing a pitch without protection, is he acting unsafely because of the fact that the pitch is rated 5.6 (medium difficulty)? Not necessarily, if the climber is someone like Dale Bard, who regularly leads 5.11 (extremely difficult) for days on end, and considers 5.6 safe and something he can climb quickly and efficiently. On the other hand, if Dale is climbing in an area which is rated 5.4 amid constant rockfall and loose dirt, and it is raining, he is probably acting without due consideration of safety factors. Often however, especially in alpine conditions of mixed ice and rock, speed *is* safety, as it lessens exposure to objective dangers (rockfall, icefall, weather).

Since safety depends on the individual, anyone engaged in mountain rescue must acquire as many skills and as much experience as possible. A broad background will buttress knowledge and confidence, and will allow one to judge the relative safety of others' actions. Each participant must be able to determine how much compromise is necessary (climbing without protection or skiing with little winter gear in order to go faster), while still maintaining an adequate margin of safety.

After the primary considerations of safety and speed are correlated with available resources and environmental factors, the rescuer turns to secondary factors, cost, efficiency, and training benefits. These secondary factors help build depth in the organization, and recruit membership. The proficiency and team consciousness of the whole unit are enhanced, which tends to increase the safety margin, which in turn improves speed and efficiency.

The successful SAR equation may then be stated as:

$$\text{SAR components} \times \frac{\text{Speed}}{\text{Safety}} = \text{SAR solution}$$

BIBLIOGRAPHY

CHAPTER TWO

FEAR, GENE. *Surviving the Unexpected Wilderness Emergency.* Survival Education Association, 9035 Golden Given Road, Tacoma, WA, 1975.

Part Two
Search
Management

THE TELESCOPE ON THE JOMEIN.

From Whymper's *Ascent of the Matterhorn*

3 | The Basics of Search Management

"THIS IS OUTRAGEOUS," I thought as I walked along. *"We ought to wait until daylight so that we can see something . . ."* The third sapling branch in as many minutes whacked my left shoulder. It was December in the High Sierra: cold, snowing again, fairly miserable.

Earlier in the evening I had talked to Butch Farabee, another Park Service ranger, who had taken a report of a woman overdue on the trail, supposedly well-equipped but nonetheless late in arriving. She had been hiking with her husband on one of the oft-traveled summer trails when darkness had settled in, snow had begun to fall gently, and they had become separated in decreasing visibility on a circuitous treadway.

That was at five o'clock; it was well past that now. Butch had given her a few hours to navigate through the storm to their destination, but there was still no sign of her. "Well, let's send someone out at first light," I suggested, somewhat unenthusiastically. It was a reasonable and standard response to a recurrent situation. Butch had not agreed. He was older and wiser, so after I muffled my impatience and disagreement, the two of us hustled together our gear and struck off down the trail at a brisk pace, into the dark night laced with snow.

Yet another branch slapped me as I stumbled along the edge of the trail, in poor light. We yelled loudly at regular intervals, feeling a little foolish at times. After about three miles of this monotonous routine, we suddenly came across her, right alongside the trail. Except for having become separated, she had done everything correctly — stopped immediately, constructed a makeshift shelter, and built an encouraging

Winter search in northern Presidential Range, New Hampshire. *Photo George Rizer, Boston Globe* fire. She was in fine spirits, and after a few rounds of luscious cocoa, we all packed up and headed back down the trail.

I watched my headlamp make weird, otherworldly shadows on the footprints right in front of me, one after another, and wondered why I had made such an obvious error of judgment. Why should we have waited until daylight? It finally occurred to me that until this point, I had used only what I had considered to be strict logic and subjective feelings to organize my decisions about and methodology for search situations. Clearly there must be other ways to think about these problems, and make more rational decisions on such serious matters. What if she had broken a leg, and we had realized it only late the next day, after a grueling search and a foot of new snow?

The state of the art of search management has been rapidly progressing since the early seventies. Pioneers in the field such as Dennis Kelley, Jon Wartes, Bob Mattson, and the Syrotucks have done considerable research on predicting lost persons' behavior and location, and on methods of efficient detection.

Bill Syrotuck, an experienced search manager and dog handler who synthesized statistical search methods, approached Bill Wade at the beginning of the decade about the possibility of developing a course for the field search manager which refined all extant material into a coherent and digestible form. Wade supported his idea, and gained the sponsorship of the NPS at its H.M. Albright Training Center in Arizona. Numerous other people, many of them members of the National Association for Search and Rescue (NASAR), contributed their own expertise. The outgrowth was a three-day search course first presented in 1972. After critique and expansion, it quickly became one of the most popular in the NPS program.

In 1975, Jim Brady, another instructor at the academy, joined forces with Wade to design a package for instructing course teachers. The product included both instructor and student notebooks, overhead slides, handouts, and 35mm slide shows. By training forty-five core instructors, eight to ten times as many students per year could be exposed to search principles. "Managing the Search Function" is being offered to NPS and other federal, state, local, and volunteer personnel through NASAR, NPS, and junior college programs. Much of the material that follows is contained in that course, and is presented here in a form dictated by considerable field trial and error.

The techniques of wilderness search are not as tangible as the techniques of wilderness rescue. Usually, search techniques are conceptual in nature, and not easily photographed or illustrated. By presenting a step by step general chronology of the events, techniques, and problems associated with managing a search, it is hoped that the methodology of search management will unfold and be clarified. Anyone having more than a passing interest in or with responsibility for managing the search function, as well as any participant in field operations, should study the many current publications that address particular topics in greater depth. Many of these are listed in the bibliography, and are mentioned throughout the text.

Dennis Kelley, author of the classic and seminal *Mountain Search for the Lost Victim* and one of the innovative thinkers of modern search theory and application, has coined a simple phrase which puts the concept of search management into proper perspective: "Search is an emergency." If two preliminary reports arrive simultaneously, one of an overdue hiker, and the other of a climber with a broken leg on an isolated ledge, the search may appear to be less of an emergency, requiring less initial energy than the rescue of the climber with the lower leg injury. This line of reasoning is completely erroneous, however.

During the first week of September in 1974, the ranger in charge of the Tuolumne Meadows area of Yosemite National Park received a telephone call from a supervisor of thirty teenage girls from a private boarding school. The group was on an outing to the Meadows for about a week, and one of its members, Lynn Caldwell, was missing. She was last seen at 9:30 A.M. The supervisor was not overly concerned, but she did want to report the incident. Lynn was regularly being administered psychotherapeutic medication, but did not require constant supervision. She was wearing shorts, a halter top, was barefoot, and had little if any equipment with her. Rick Smith looked at his watch as he took the report: 4:10 P.M., still relatively early. Smith put out a Be On the Lookout For (BOLF) for Lynn over the NPS radio network.

At 10 A.M. the next morning, Smith received a second phone call from the supervisor, who indicated that Lynn still had not returned. Smith made contact with the supervisor in person, and began a series of individual interviews which eventually numbered more than fifty. Besides her physical description and details of her emotional problems, Smith learned that the girl had been seen in the company of a uniformed ranger the previous day. Most of Lynn's friends agreed that she would not hitchhike out of the park, and that she was not having a very good time on the school trip. The question of how she would react without further medication came up frequently, and each person interviewed gave a different opinion. Two more trained interviewers were called in by Smith, who also rebroadcast the BOLF.

Smith was able to locate the ranger that had talked to Lynn. Janet O'Brien was a summer park naturalist who remembered Lynn because she had asked to join a nature walk Janet was leading. The two had talked on a small ridge to the north and west of a prominent granite formation called Lembert Dome, about a half-mile from the ranger station and the lodge where Lynn was staying. After the hike was over, Lynn had mentioned that she was going to the store to get something to drink; that was the last that Janet had seen of her. Another interviewer received a report from the cowboys at the concessionaire's stables that Lynn had been watching the horses there at about 3 or 4 P.M. the previous day. Smith spoke with the cowboys in person, and on a whim decided to walk partway down a trail that ascends the ridge where Lynn and Janet had conversed. A short way down the trail, he found a lipstick container and put it in his pocket. Later in the day, it was definitely identified as one of Lynn's belongings.

This preliminary investigation took about three hours. Based on the clues that had been found thus far, a hasty search was started. Foot, horse, and helicopter search of the Dog Lake-Young Lakes-Tuolumne Meadows region using a dozen personnel turned up one clue: the sighting of a woman matching Lynn's description. When thoroughly investigated, however, she was not Lynn.

At dark, all hasty searchers returned to the Tuolumne Meadows ranger station. Smith decided to initiate a major search effort, even though there was a strong possibility that Lynn had left the vicinity of the Meadows. An overhead team of search specialists was called in from other sections of the park. Plans for the next day were discussed, as a major call of NPS employees and assorted volunteers was initiated.

The strategy for the second day of the search required eighty-five grid searchers to cover an area approximately eight miles square, using a staggered start. Each team of twenty to twenty-five searchers was to mark its flanks with flagging, so that the team following on its left could follow a line. Additional horse patrol and foot patrol units were requested, to search and to interview hikers along trails and to check areas of low probability. Bloodhounds were to start from where the lipstick container had been found in an attempt to pick up a scent trail. The helicopter was to continue to fly an aerial reconnaissance in an attempt to locate clues. In addition, a radio and communications relay point was established on the top of Lembert Dome.

The search was started at 8 A.M. A fifteen-minute interval separated the four different teams of grid searchers. By noon, all teams had reached the base of Ragged Peak and, after a short lunch break, started back toward the road. In the late afternoon, a few barefoot tracks were found in the Delaney Creek drainage, and the search continued. All searchers were out of the field shortly after dark.

A debriefing was held and the difficulty of maintaining straight patterns of search was discussed. The third day's plan was formulated, and consisted of a close-grid search of an area of about six square miles directly east of the land covered on day two. A different tactic of search was to be used, with each team working its own square grid. More search dogs were requested from the state of Washington, and additional helicopter time was to be expended.

At 6 A.M. the hundred-plus searchers were fed and briefed, and were mobilized to their respective stations by 7 A.M. At 11:10 A.M., a sweatshirt belonging to Lynn was found, and at 2:50 P.M., and again at 3:45 P.M., other articles of clothing materialized. Finally, at 4:14 in the afternoon of the third day, Lynn was located. She was exhausted, but otherwise unharmed.

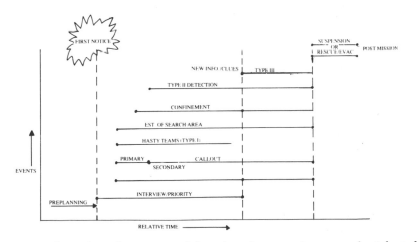

Fig. 3.1 Chronological sequence of functions in managing a search. Adapted from *Managing the Search Function.*

Thanks to the "atmosphere of positive urgency" created by Rick Smith, the woman was found. Was that enough? Was the search managed efficiently?

In thinking about any search, especially in evaluating performance, it is important to be aware of the overall chronological framework which a search follows. In Chapter Two, the general structure of SAR was elucidated; the search framework is illustrated in Figure 3.1. Refer back to this figure periodically to correlate the pieces of the frame that follow.

4   Auldjo's party breakfasting on Mont Blanc, 1827

From a lithograph by J. Auldjo, 1830

BIBLIOGRAPHY

CHAPTER THREE

BRADY, JAMES, ed. *Managing the Search Function — Instructor Manual.* Grand Canyon, Ariz.: National Park Service, September 1978.

KELLEY, DENNIS. *Mountain Search for the Lost Victim.* Montrose, Ca.: pub. by author, 1973.

LaVALLA, RICK, AND WADE, BILL. *A Model for SAR Management.* La Jolla, Ca.: NASAR paper 76-107, 1976.

PARGETER, RICHARD. "Search Management Graphics." NASAR, La Jolla, Ca.: 1978.

WILLIAMS, PAUL. *Rescue Leadership.* Altadena, Ca.: Mountain Rescue Association, 1977.

4 | SAR Preplanning

IN THE ACCOUNT of an overdue hiker presented at the beginning of the last chapter, I made a number of decisions — specifically not to search at night — that seemed reasonable at the time but in the final analysis were ill-advised. Despite a personal bias against nocturnal operations, searching at night is a very productive tactic. While physical preparation for a SAR mission was complete, personnel in good condition, and quality equipment packed and ready to go, not enough thought had been given to search strategy and philosophy: *when* and *how* to go.

SAR preparedness and preplanning involve more than fancy paraphernalia and a notebook of telephone numbers. They must occur on an individual as well as organizational level. The third part of this book addresses the skills necessary to reach the victim, concentrating on technical details. Search skills are often intertwined with rescue skills, in turn related to the requirements and methods of travel in demanding environments. Tracking, ELT direction finding, dog handling and training, ice climbing, and so on are discussed largely from the standpoint of a manager. Both the basic and fine points of each are best left up to respected publications in the field, to master practitioners of the skill, and to experience.

The Preplan

The organizational SAR preplan is generally, unlike most individuals, documented, labeled, flexible, and organized. At least this is the theory. The preplan is an operational guide that, if designed and implemented correctly, will help introduce order to the chaos and furor accompanying

Briefing just before helo rescue. *Photo Blackburn*

the initial notification for help. The search manager and his or her organization are enabled to use the most effective resources in the shortest time to find the subject in a safe and economical manner. The preplan is a combination of search technique, management guidelines, and policies integrated for use in resolving field SAR situations.

To accomplish this purpose, the preplan need not be long and involved. Length and design vary according to the specific requirements of the group. In areas where jurisdiction is held by one primary responsible agency, say in a state or national park, the preplan may be short, even though the problems encountered are acute. As SAR events become more complex bureaucratically (as opposed to technically), usually as a result of overlapping legal responsibilities (county, state, federal), land ownership, and land management, the contents of the preplan tend to become more complicated. The end result should be, however, a preplan that is a flexible, workable document utilizable in any contingency.

If the plan is not useful because it is merely an exercise in creative writing, it should be scrapped and reworked. Remember, the preplan is an intangible rescue cache of sorts, containing the procedures, resources, and authority essential for resolution of life-threatening problems. It should be neat, orderly, well-maintained, and current, periodically reevaluated to insure it continues to provide efficient response.

In order to be a functional document, the plan must be a synthesis of policies, legal requirements, guidelines, assignments, and organizational outlines pertaining to the question of how to realize certain tasks at each step of search management so the ultimate goal — locating the lost person — may be achieved as soon as possible. A good preplan takes effort to write. Revision and change maintain its timeliness and effectiveness.

Writing or editing a preplan requires familiarity with terrain, expected weather, and the cycle of recreational and industrial use, as well as the location, intensity, and social details of these activities — hunting, off-road vehicle use, backpacking. Any available records and a sense of the history of the area may help isolate both what kinds of misadventures have occurred (lost hikers found in one spot in a remote canyon three times, accidents on the winter descent route from a particular climb), and potential future problems (the recent increase of hang gliding off of one set of cliffs, or the sudden popularity of a new shortcut through a high mountain pass). Knowledge of the policies and strategy of adjacent agencies identifies legal responsibility and official management roles in the field. These chains of command and legal requirements, in addition to the dictates of practicality, need be specified in the preplan and supported by adequate documentation. The whereabouts of resources, both human and material, is indicated, along with a delineation of the procedures necessary to obtain them. These resource locator lists will often prove the value of the preplan during an operation.

The considerations addressed in the body of the preplan follow. Their presentation in the plan is up to the individual, but its major tenets are realism, pragmatism, and clarity.

1. *Plan objective or purpose* — to save lives in the most efficient and safe manner.
2. Priority of *resource allocation* — state what is needed, and secure agency agreement that search is life threatening and has agency priority over activity.
3. Specific *agency guidelines* — acceptable landing zones for helicopters during emergencies, public relations, and so on.
4. *Preparedness* — training, standards, minimum staffing, equipment caches.
5. *Organizational tasking* — who does what during an event, command, transport, reserve personnel versus regular staff.
6. *First Notice* — mobilization plan, telephone trees, authorities that must be notified.
7. *Initial responsibility* — who is in charge upon notification, and when does the responsibility change hands?
8. *Investigation* — performed by whom, according to type of incident. What is SAR team's role? Special equipment required?
9. *Priorities and decisions* — what does the crew need to know in order to make decisions? Is it possible to preplan decisions, i.e., if such and such is true, we will do thus and so?
10. *Strategy* — who is involved? Why? At what stages are backups called into play?
11. *Preference for resources* — in what situations are certain resources mandatory (e.g., anyone entering water above the knees must have PFD and wetsuit)?
12. *Callout* — procedures.
13. *Tactics* — whatever is necessary to carry out your strategy.
14. *Clues* — emphasize clue awareness.
15. *Base camp* — logistics of support, preplan phases for small and large, extended missions.

16. *Communications* — internal and external (news media, telephones).
17. *Medical considerations* — both for the subject and the searchers.
18. *Rescue and evacuation* — the rescue is on. What is to be done by whom? Different resources may be essential.
19. *Fatalities* — agency procedures, contacting and cooperating with proper authorities.
20. Mission *suspension or deescalation* — how and when does one decide this?
21. *Demobilization* — how will it occur? Priority of release. Who is responsible?
22. *Documentation and reporting* — what is required?
23. *Critique procedure* — detailed, recorded, and implemented results widely available.
24. *Prevention* — public safety and SAR training programs to act on new ideas.

Meeting and greeting all the resources in the preplan, while not a written requirement, is a fundamental task for the SAR manager. A letter or phone call often substitutes for a personal visit. Knowing who the other person or group is, what it can do, and how it operates often means the difference between successfully putting these resources into play or not. A fine example of this type of relationship is the one developed between Naval Air Station LeMoore and state and federal agencies in the surrounding districts. Much of the helicopter technique outlined in the chapter on that subject was developed by Navy and NPS personnel working in concert. After each practice session, the two groups got together to imbibe and indulge and found out how much they had in common. The SAR folks liked to fly but were a little short on cash for Huey helicopters, and the Navy crew wanted to learn to climb, so we traded training. The results were a total commitment to each other's operation and development of new SAR technique, plus increased efficiency and safety for all groups during real events.

So now this complete, thorough, and neatly typed document (right?) is sitting in its fancy binder on the shelf. How will it be used? For the recent employee or new member to an organization, the geography of the area is unfamiliar and suddenly you have the duty to manage the SAR function there. Most of the time it will not be necessary to work through the preplan step by step when a rescue situation unfolds. Instead, the SAR resources locator or index portion of the plan is consulted. If responsibility for getting things rolling and for managing various aspects of the search is clear to all involved, the question quickly becomes one of planning and applying the talent and material available. What should be commissioned: skiers? overflights? snowmobiles?

Assuming these are realistic resource choices, the problem is where to get them right now. If they are not readily mobilized, certain options and strategies are eliminated. Therefore, the more resources available, the more tactics and coverage can be employed. Hence it is critical to locate all possible sources of equipment and personnel well before a callout occurs.

Human and equipment resources can be divided into those that are readily commandeered, and those not immediately on hand that must come from other agencies over greater distances. Questions about search overhead, medical factors, dogs, livestock, transportation, food, shelter, aircraft, communications, and whatever ought to be addressed in advance. Two of the best resource guides, arranged by location and type of support needed, were published by NASAR: the *Resource Guide for Search and Rescue Training Materials* and the *Official Directory for NASAR*.

In summary, the preplan for a particular organization should reflect the group's goals, needs, most current ideas and policies, and present available resources in a usable document. The value of such an instrument becomes apparent at the first notification of a problem. Besides, think of what great reading it will make on late winter nights!

The Rescue Cache

Once the document is in hand, the second phase of preplanning requires that a certain amount of personal and group equipment be accessible, in order, and ready to go for an instantaneous response. The team gear is usually stored in someone's garage or a building basement at a location known to everyone concerned. The rescue cache in Yosemite was moved around a number of times and finally ended up in the corner of a barn. When the barn burned to the ground in the early seventies, we got to test a lot of heat-treated carabiners. The cache was moved to its own building, a vacant Dodge City-style jail, the kind outlaws used to dynamite their buddies out of, which made breaking in as hard as getting out.

The current Yosemite SAR cache is a six-room affair expanded and reorganized to meet the requirements of the times. The four rooms readily accessible to anyone with a key contain various items all prechecked and immediately usable. The other two rooms are not generally open to perusal because they contain either bodies (the morgue) or equipment in various states of disrepair or development, or gear that simply has not been gone over and logged in since the last event.

The central room houses most of the technical hardware and ropes, since many SAR situations in the park require them. Two 1340-meter ropes, four 370-meter ropes, six 185-meter ropes, and eighteen 50-meter ropes are neatly coiled, bagged in haul sacks, or kept on portable spools ready to go. Next to these hang over 100 miscellaneous pitons, 150 assorted nuts, 200 carabiners, dozens of slings, helmets, radio harnesses, rescue pulleys, edge rollers, Jumars and prusiks, litter prerigs, and eight litters in a variety of designs. Certain prepackaged units like the emergency medical kit, blitz packs, anchor packs, and helicopter sling load kits are also kept here. The idea is that people can charge in and instantly select what is needed from equipment displayed right in front of them or grab a prepackaged kit and roar out of the cache in record time. It seems to work well.

One room adjacent to the technical room is devoted to electronic and surveillance gadgetry, including radios, batteries, rechargeable spot and flood lamps, headlamps, binoculars, a Questar telescope, cameras, a 100-watt loudhailer, line guns, and random bits and pieces of all of the above.

On the other side of the technical room is the winter chamber, draped with ice axes, crampons, ice screws, avalanche equipment, skis, snow flukes, shovels, and what have you.

The fourth room holds soft goods and water rescue gear. All the down and Polarguard sleeping bags, jackets, half bags, raingear, flight suits, and wet suits hang on a rack. A number of tents are stored packed, alongside stoves, pots, pans, dried food, and the sundry items useful for overnight excursions. Eight SCUBA tanks with regulators, masks, fins, and all line this room, yet it manages to serve as a changing room for those going out into the field, who store limited amounts of personal gear in it.

The fifth room is the research and development center, with testing apparatus and tools for designing, modifying, or gluing back together new and abused pieces of equipment. Everything returned from a SAR that needs to be checked for damage is automatically tossed in this room with a unique lock.

The final subdivision of the cache is the morgue, accessed by a separate door. All bodies are temporarily stored in it and processed (fingerprinted, and so on) while awaiting the arrival of the undertaker.

An open porch on the outside of the cache is handy in summer for laying out and organizing gear, and gossiping after hours. In winter or periods of inclement weather it is an absolute must so everyone is not crowding into the cache trying to snare or grab equipment like a 50% off sale at a ladies' lingerie department.

Of course one need not have a six-room building to store equipment. The salient point is to devise an organized, readily accessible facility with adequate security.

THE RUCKSACK IN POSITION.

From *With Camera and Rucksack in the Oberland* by Malby.

BIBLIOGRAPHY

CHAPTER FOUR

BRADY, JAMES, ED. *Managing the Search Function — Instructor Manual.* Grand Canyon, Ariz.: National Park Service, September 1978.

McCOY, LOIS. ED. *PrePlanning the Land Search Organization.* La Jolla, Ca.: NASAR paper 77-1022, 1977.

LaVALLA, RICK, ED. *Resource Guide for Search and Rescue Training Materials.* Tacoma, Wa.: Survival Education Association, 1978.

NOTO, JAMES V. *Official Directory — National Association for Search and Rescue.* La Jolla, Ca.: NASAR, 1978.

SCHNEIDER, ANNE AND STEVEN. *The Climber's Sourcebook.* New York: Anchor Books, 1976.

5 | First Notice

THE INITIAL REPORT of an accident reaches the SAR team in a variety of ways — from a witness who hails a ranger, via a concerned relative's phone call inquiring about a party overdue, through cries for help heard by someone in the area and relayed by phone. *Notification* of a SAR situation should always be considered as a real request for assistance in potentially hazardous circumstances. Regardless of how improbable or unfounded the report appears at the time, a compelling *firehouse response* is essential until SAR personnel have arrived on the scene and determined the accuracy of the information. Firemen responding to an alarm in the stationhouse do not know whether a trash can or an entire apartment complex full of sleeping senior citizens is in flames, so they treat all callouts as potential three-alarm fires. Flashing lights and sirens may not always be the proper approach for SAR work, though. The emphasis instead is on professional performance — immediate, decisive efforts to assess the validity and magnitude of the problem. This might take the form of a decision to send the most experienced searcher and interviewer to talk with the reporting party, or to deploy trackers to secure the area in question until further information is received and a plan of action formed

In the search for Lynn Caldwell detailed in Chapter 3, notification did not present any problems. The management structure of the national park system allows fairly rapid identification of the NPS employee responsible for search and rescue efforts in any area of the park. The ranger in charge was notified of the trip leader's concern for Lynn's

Accident on El Cap. *Photo Kenneth Andrasko* 59

safety almost immediately, when the park dispatcher placed the reporting telephone call through to him.

Relative Urgency Assessment

The relative urgency of a reported situation should be established — if it is not immediately apparent — during the first notice and interview phase. Despite the need for a constant firehouse response to all reports of complications of any kind, some latitude for flexibility exists and should be exercised. There are times when the victim's condition is presumed stable; prudence and concern for the safety of SAR personnel encourage the manager to await the arrival of daylight and more propitious conditions for evacuation. A call from a hiker reporting something like, "Help, my friend has a broken leg and is unconscious at a small lake north of Benson Lake where I left him yesterday in a snow cave" is an example of an obvious emergency. The urgency is clear, and the SAR crew must instantly mobilize and leave for the field on the basis of the information given.

Sketchy or inaccurate reports are much harder to evaluate. They require the construction of a relative urgency index of the situation, based on available knowledge of the area in question correlated with the reported physical and mental condition of the victim, and modified to take into account time and weather factors. Occasionally political sensitivity, bureaucratic or media pressure, or emotionalism enter into consideration.

To help establish and quantify the urgency of a problem, a *relative urgency rating* system has been developed by SAR instructor Bill Wade. In his method one assigns each pertinent factor a value on a scale from one to three, and adds the total number of points compiled. The lower that sum, the more urgent the case. The accompanying table outlines these factors and their range of values.

Table 1.   Relative Urgency Rating Factors

Factor	Factor Value
Subject Profile	
Age	
Very young	1
Very old	1
Other	2-3

Medical condition
    Known or suspected injured or ill   1-2

Medical condition	
Known or suspected injured or ill	1-2
Healthy	3
Known fatality	3
Numbers of subjects	
One alone	1
More than one (unless separation suspected)	2-3

Weather Profile

Existing hazardous weather	1
Predicted hazardous weather, 8 hours or less	1-2
Predicted hazardous weather, more than 8 hours	2
No hazardous weather predicted	3

Equipment Profile

Inadequate for environment	1
Questionable for environment	1-2
Adequate for environment	3

Subject Experience Profile

Not experienced, does not know area	1
Not experienced, knows area	1-2
Experienced, not familiar with area	2
Experienced, knows area	3

Terrain and Hazards Profile

Known hazardous terrain or other hazards	1
Few or no hazards	2-3

History of Incidents in this Area	1-3
Bastard Search	2-3

NOTES: The lower the value of each factor and of the sum of all factors, the more urgent the situation. Considerable elapsed time from when the subject was reported missing and the political sensitivity of the circumstances have the effect of increasing the relative urgency. Reproduced by permission of Bill Wade.

Once one computes the sum of assigned factor values for these eight categories and considers (or places a numbered value on) the implications of elapsed time and political sensitivity, some rough indications of appropriate response are generated.

Table 2.   Appropriate Response to Urgency Ratings

Factor Sum	Response
08-12	Emergency response
13-18	Measured response
19-24	Evaluative response — Should we do anything?
25-27	Search situation or missing person?

The possibility of a *bastard search* — where no victim exists, because the report was inaccurate or the individual has left the area on his own or has been found by another party — is always present. Some years ago in California a mission continued for over eleven days in a major commitment of time, personnel, and money (over $20,000) to search for a middle-aged man reported lost while on a four-day solo hike in the High Sierra. Both his wife, who was eight months pregnant, and his father traveled several hundred kilometers to base camp to press the search effort and consequently spur an emotional commitment to the project from everyone involved. During the last days of the search, the subject's wife knew it was de-escalating but tearfully implored us to continue. Finally, as we were almost into the second full week of searching, a friend of the missing husband received a postcard from him postmarked in Bangor, Maine. Apparently he was alive and well and had simply decided to leave his wife for personal, emotional reasons; his long hiking trip offered him an opportunity to do so. The fugitive husband thought lost in the wilds and nearly given up for dead had been riding a transcontinental bus for the past two weeks!

In the Lynn Caldwell search the question of urgency and appropriate response was not sharply defined. When the report of a missing hiker came into the SAR office, the circumstances seemed to indicate that there was no real cause for alarm. A seventeen-year-old girl not having a good time on a group trip could be expected to try to remedy the situation by wandering off alone, finding new friends, hitchhiking out of the district, or any number of other actions. While she had a known emotional problem, it did not require constant monitoring or supervision according to her supervisor. There were no impending weather changes and most of the afternoon was left for Lynn to safely reappear. Lastly, her supervisor did not display an attitude of great concern, but instead wanted to inform the local authorities of the matter as a routine precaution. This initial report advised the ranger's office of a missing person, not an overdue hiker. Therefore, the SAR team response was a measured one. A standard Be On the Lookout For (BOLF) call was broadcast over the NPS radio frequencies, and patrol rangers talked with hitchhikers and checked campgrounds in the course of their normal duties.

An application of Wade's scale of relative urgency to the Caldwell situation at first notification might have looked something like that presented in the adjacent summary (Table 3).

Table 3. Relative Urgency of Caldwell Situation at First Notification

Factor	Factor Value
Age	3
Medical condition	2
Number of subjects	1
Weather profile	3
Equipment profile	1
Subject experience profile	1
Terrain and hazards profile	3
History of incidents in area	3
Possibility of bastard search	2
Total	19

Thus the measured or passive, evaluative response chosen by the SAR office at first notification, based on a preliminary assessment of the pertinent factors, was consistent with the rough indication of appropriate response noted for a factor sum of 19 in the table preceding this one.

However, when Caldwell's supervisor called on the telephone at 10 A.M. on the second day, Rick Smith knew he had a real problem. She had waited until late morning to call because she had still hoped that Lynn would materialize on her own. The situation was suddenly transformed into a high priority search effort and an exercise in gathering information through interviewing. At this point, the possibility of a bastard search was still prominent and further research was deemed crucial.

During the first few hours of mobilization, Smith spoke to almost twenty people and directed two interviewers to locate and question a number of others that might have some knowledge of the matter.

Several facts surfaced from the statements of witnesses who had seen her the afternoon of her disappearance that suggested the possibility of searching a tract adjacent to those already combed. When Smith checked a trail there, the lipstick case was found, establishing a possible point last seen. All interview information was recorded and transmitted to Smith, who initially acted as the clearinghouse for victim information and details of the mission.

Search briefing during Caldwell operation. *Photo Dick Sale*

The key to successful management of notification and determination of urgency is the concept of firehouse professionalism — careful, immediate response by skilled specialists (trackers, interviewers, pilots) and comprehensive interviews. As Dennis Kelley continually reminds, "Search is a classic mystery — all of the clues are available and the solution reachable if the right questions are asked."

Interviewing

Interviewers with adequate sensitivity training should be employed in the field from the earliest moments of the event in order to establish good rapport with reporting parties, witnesses, and relatives. The interview function must be assigned to someone who appreciates its delicacy and importance and perceives it as his primary role in the search rather than as an allocated duty. The reporting party is usually the first source of information. The job of gathering data necessitates cool, skilled interviewers from the moment of notification and during the chaotic and formative stages of the whole search process. The effort expands from attention to those who brought word of the problem to working with members of the lost subject's group; those who last saw the victim; local sportsmen and officials who know the region intimately; and friends, relatives, and coworkers of the subject.

Tact is essential. After formal information gathering sessions (when basic data are collected and written down), the interviewer should take *mental* notes to promote ease and cooperation on the part of those being interrogated. Go easy; leave cross-examination to the court room. Try to comprehend the emotional state of someone who has just gone through a grueling experience of one sort or another. If you have trouble understanding his point of view, gracefully relinquish the job to someone who can be compassionate. The goal of an interview is to painlessly obtain information from a participant in or witness to a trying incident in order to devise an effective course of action. One minor aside or brief reference may provide a clue so significant that the search might be entirely redirected or even halted as a result of the disclosure. Be as thorough as possible.

A written record of all interviewing is crucial, either taken down during the conversation or reconstructed straightaway. As one occasionally forgets to address an item that later becomes significant, a check list is recommended to insure complete coverage of all major information categories. The lost person report form that follows details salient points within each category. While the list appears interminable, if filled out initially it may preclude the need to recontact interviewees in order to pursue lines of questioning not deemed apropos at an earlier time. With a bit of luck, the victim will miraculously reappear before the form is completed!

Table 4. Lost Person Report Check List

NOTE: File separate report for each person. Detailed answers are needed to identify clues when found in the field. Place "none," "NA" (not applicable), or "unsure" in blanks as appropriate.

PART I: Information critical to immediate decisions and the initiation phases of a search. Record all Part I information at the time of first notice of a lost or overdue person.

Date _____ Time _____
Case incident no. _____ Ranger _____
Report taken by _____ phone _____in person _____
Hours overdue _____
Name of missing person _____
Local address _____local phone _____
Home address _____home phone _____
Nicknames _____Aliases _____

A. Physical   Age _____Race _____
   description: Height _____Weight _____Build _____
                     Hair color _____length _____sideburns _____
                        beard _____balding? _____
                     Eye color _____
                     Facial features, shape _____Complexion _____
                     Any distinguishing marks, scars? _____
                     _____

                     General appearance _____

B. Clothing: Shirt, sweater   style _____color _____
                     Pants   style _____color _____
                     Jacket   style _____color _____
                     Rain gear   style _____color _____
                     Shoes   style _____size _____
                                       sole type _____
                                       is a sample of sole type
                                          available? _____
                                             where _____
                     Head gear   style _____color _____
                     Gloves   style _____color _____
                     Glasses   regular, sun _____style _____
                     Any extra clothes, shoes? _____
                     Scent articles available? _____ where _____

C. Equipment: Pack   style _____brand _____color _____
                     Tent   style _____brand _____color _____
                     Sleeping bag style _____brand _____color _____
                     Food   what _____brands _____amount ____
                     Water   canteen style _____amount _____
                     Flashlight _____Matches_____Knife_____
                     Map _____Compass _____
                     Ice axe _____brand _____covers? ____
                     Snow shoes   type _____ brand _____ binding type _____

Tour skis   brand _____ length _____ color _____
                    binding type _____ binding brand _____
Ski wax   type _____ brands _____ colors _____
Ski poles   type _____ length _____ color _____
                    brand _____
If rental equipment, rental markings? _____
Ropes, hardware _____
Fishing equipment _____ brands _____
Camera _____ brand _____
Money _____ amount _____ credit cards _____
Firearms type _____ brand _____ ammo _____

D. Trip Plans: Going to _____ via _____
                  Purpose _____
                  How long _____ How many in group? _____
                  Group affiliation _____ transportation _____
                  Started at _____ when _____
                  Car located at _____ type _____
                    license _____ verified _____
                  Alternate car at _____ type _____
                    license _____ verified _____
                  Pickup, return time _____ where _____

    All in Group: Name _____ address _____
                    phone _____ car license _____
                  Name _____ address _____
                    phone _____ car license _____
                  Any alternate plans, routes, objectives discussed?

E. Last seen: When _____
                  Where _____
                  By whom _____ present? _____
                    if not, location _____ phone _____
                  Weather _____
                  Going which way _____ How long ago _____
                  Special reason for leaving? _____
                  Unusual comments upon leaving? _____
                  How long overdue _____

F. Experience: Familiar with area _____ how recently _____
                  If not local, experience in what other areas _____

                  Taken outdoor classes _____ where _____
                    when _____

Taken first aid training ＿＿ where ＿＿＿＿＿＿＿＿
　　　　　when ＿＿＿＿＿＿
Been in Scouts ＿＿ where ＿＿＿＿＿ when ＿＿＿
Military service ＿＿＿＿＿＿＿＿＿＿＿＿＿
How much overnight experience? ＿＿＿＿＿＿
Ever been lost before? ＿＿ actions ＿＿＿＿＿＿
Ever go out alone? ＿＿＿＿＿＿＿＿
Stay on trails or go cross country? ＿＿＿＿＿＿
How many long trips before ＿＿＿＿＿
If not regular hiker, general athletic interests and
　　ability ＿＿＿＿＿＿＿＿＿＿＿＿＿＿＿＿

G. Contacts person would make upon reaching civilization:
　　Home address ＿＿＿＿＿＿＿＿＿＿＿＿＿
　　phone ＿＿＿＿＿＿＿＿＿ anyone home? ＿＿＿
　　Local contact ＿＿＿＿＿＿＿＿ phone ＿＿＿
　　Friends ＿＿＿＿＿＿＿＿＿＿ phone ＿＿＿

H. Health:
　　General condition ＿＿＿＿＿＿＿＿＿＿＿＿
　　Any physical handicaps ＿＿＿＿＿＿＿＿＿
　　Any known medical problem ＿＿＿＿＿＿＿
　　　knowledgeable doctor ＿＿＿＿＿＿＿＿＿
　　　　　phone ＿＿＿＿＿＿＿＿＿＿
　　Any known psychological problems ＿＿＿＿＿
　　　knowledgeable person ＿＿＿＿＿＿ phone ＿＿
　　Any known external factors that might have affected sub-
　　ject's behavior (family argument, depression, business
　　problems) ＿＿＿＿＿＿＿＿＿＿＿＿＿＿
　　Taking prescription medication? ＿＿＿＿＿＿
　　　doctor ＿＿＿＿＿＿＿＿＿
　　　consequences of loss ＿＿＿＿＿＿＿＿＿
　　　amount carried ＿＿＿＿＿＿＿＿
　　Eyesight without glasses ＿＿＿＿＿ spares? ＿＿

I. Actions taken so far:
　　By (friends, family) ＿＿＿＿＿＿＿＿＿＿＿
　　＿＿＿＿＿＿＿＿＿＿＿＿＿＿＿＿＿＿＿＿
　　＿＿＿＿＿＿＿＿＿＿＿＿＿＿＿＿＿＿＿＿
　　Actions taken ＿＿＿＿＿＿＿＿＿＿＿＿＿＿
　　＿＿＿＿＿＿＿＿＿＿＿＿＿＿＿＿＿＿＿＿
　　＿＿＿＿＿＿＿＿＿＿＿＿＿＿＿＿＿＿＿＿
　　When ＿＿＿＿＿＿＿＿＿＿＿＿＿＿＿＿＿
　　＿＿＿＿＿＿＿＿＿＿＿＿＿＿＿＿＿＿＿＿
　　＿＿＿＿＿＿＿＿＿＿＿＿＿＿＿＿＿＿＿＿

PART II: Information that may be significant later in the mission. Can be obtained after initial actions are taken and further information on the subject is necessary.

A. Personality habits:

Smoke _____ how often _____ what _____
                brand _____
Drink _____ brand _____
Drugs _____
Hobbies, interests (fishing, flowers, climbing,
        photography) _____
Works for spare money _____
Outgoing or quiet; likes groups or lonely _____
Evidence of leadership _____
Ever in trouble with law? _____ now? _____
Hitchhike often _____ accept rides _____
Feelings toward grownups _____ hippies _____
Any current family or love problems? _____
Religion _____ serious? _____
What does person believe in? _____
What does person value most? _____
Who is person closest to in family _____
                        in general _____
Where born and raised? _____
Any history of depression, running away? _____
Status in school _____ draft _____
Who last talked at length to person? _____
        where _____ subject _____
Any recent letter? _____
Give up easily or keep going? _____
Will person hole up and wait or keep moving? _____

B. For children:

Afraid of dogs? _____ horses? _____
Afraid of dark? _____
What training regarding what to do when lost? _____
What are actions when hurt? Cry? Carry on? _____
Talk to strangers; accept rides? _____
Active type or lethargic? _____

C. For groups overdue:

Any personality clashes in group? _____
Any strong leader types not actually the leader? _____

What is competitive spirit of group? _____
What would be actions if separated? _____
Any persons especially close friends? _____
What is experience of leader and rest of group? _____

D. Family (to prevent press problems):
      Father's occupation _____
      Parents separated or similar problem _____
      Family's desire to employ special assistance _____
      Name, address, phone of father, mother, husband, wife, son,
      daughter to notify if found in good condition (give most appropriate
      kin for information or contact when found)
      Name _____ address _____
      phone _____ relationship _____
      Person to notify if found in very poor condition or dead (should be
      friend, relative, or minister of next-of-kin)
      Name _____ address _____
      phone _____ relationship _____

Appropriate Response Determination

After first notification has arrived and a determination of relative
urgency has been made, the next decision faced by the SAR manager is
what type of response is suitable for the situation at that time. Usually
this question is pondered while the interview process continues.

Three broad categories of response are possible: 1) an emergency
response, 2) a measured response, and 3) an evaluative response —
should we do anything yet?

In many ways the *emergency response* is the easiest to choose, as one
is convinced that someone will die or be seriously injured if help does
not arrive directly. While the safety of rescuers is considered the primary
concern, the margin of safety may be fairly narrow and a perceptible
amount of risk involved in the necessary response. Speed is only slightly
less significant than safety on a hypothetical response factor scale at this
time, for a lethargic field mobilization may quite realistically result in
loss of life.

An emergency response differs from a measured response only in
terms of speed and with regard to the number of personnel initially committed to the field. In an emergency, a *blitz* or *hasty team* is immediately
whisked to the accident or search site. This group is composed of a

minimum number of rescuers who are extremely experienced, carry little gear, and head straight for the victim. Support teams follow, bringing additional ropes, I.V. fluid, and whatever else is requested over the radio by the blitz team once on the scene.

A *measured response* is appropriate when the information on hand is insufficient to dictate the exact outline of a SAR action plan. Complete mobilization and deployment of personnel to what is ultimately an incorrect route or location results in unnecessary hazards, logistical complications, and slow reaction times. Thus it may be prudent to dispatch two rescuers to evaluate the best route to a ledge or into the point last seen while the main contingent awaits their report back at base camp. A response of this kind definitely commits SAR personnel to the field, but emphasizes team safety and efficiency at the expense of speed in reaching the victim. Experienced searchers often suggest resting until daylight rather than working through the night, or waiting for a complete synopsis of the situation incorporating all pertinent factors to insure an efficient and secure operation once underway.

An *evaluative response* occurs when the reported problem is unconfirmed or seems likely to resolve itself. The SAR manager asks whether it is necessary to do anything at all, and is required to make very difficult decisions based on fragmentary information. Overreaction always seems justifiable; underreaction always appears inexcusable. Consequently, the natural internal and external group pressure for action of some sort means that the option of waiting for further developments is usually overlooked. It may, however, be a legitimate response to very uncertain, relatively harmless circumstances.

The answer to the question of proper action in a vague situation is contingent upon how long the manager is willing to wait due to environmental concerns (snowstorm, mudslide, nightfall) or the eventual arrival of more accurate information, and how serious the problem sounds in terms of past SAR experience in that area and current conditions. If daylight will allow direct observation of the victims and provide pertinent facts unavailable thus far, then a strong argument exists for waiting until dawn. Remember, the report and evaluation brought in by a third party may well prove incorrect. But, it may be *either* too dramatic or too understated a description of the realities of the event underway, and one or another factor may have been altered in the meantime.

Therefore every report, no matter how innocuous sounding, must be considered bona fide and evoke an earnest reply until it is unequivocally clear that the problem is nonexistent, has solved itself, or cannot be resolved without the SAR team's participation. In an evaluative response, SAR personnel may or may not be committed to the field, but they are actively investigating the reported mishap.

Callout

As the most suitable response is being chosen, regardless of what sort it will be, a preliminary plan of action is synthesized from the information gathered by any officials on the scene, interviewers, blitz teams, and calls to other concerned agencies and groups. A *callout* of field personnel is also initiated. Its structure is dictated by the preplan and most often relies on telephone trees that require each team member to call specified other members.

In the case of the Lynn Caldwell search, the first day of the operation was consumed by interviews and hasty searches. By 1 P.M. an immediate measured response was indicated by an assessment of all variables and a radio callout mobilized local NPS employees. Hasty teams were sent into the field to survey areas thought to have a high probability of victim presence. All new bits of information acquired during the day were pursued by readjustment of the hasty search plan. But by nightfall no additional facts or clues had emerged, although some of the potential search tracts had been eliminated by the blitz crews. No confinement scouts had been placed in the field to seal off exit drainages, trails, and the like. All searchers returned to base camp after completing their assignments.

Theoretically, callout is composed of two steps. The primary response can be measured in minutes, while the secondary, less critical reaction consumes hours and may proceed in escalating stages according to need.

Primary callout consists of direct communication with other agencies likely to become involved in the operation: the county sheriff's office, the state fish and game department, a branch of the military. Most importantly, contact with the organization charged with legal responsibility for search and rescue in the region must take place. From the moment any field response is contemplated, the SAR manager must inform local authorities of all actions, yet not at the expense of slowed reaction time. He uses the interagency liaison pathways already outlined in the preplan. Cooperation among organizations is often overlooked in the primary stage of notification because of pressures within the responding group to act and mobilize into the field as soon as possible.

Certainly intergroup callouts are the foundation of any SAR response. The sooner searchers are in the woods and meadows, the faster the confinement phase can begin while planning and clue detection continue. Be certain the callout procedure is standardized for all potential participating agencies and groups.

The *secondary callout* is performed as soon as it is feasible. Its functions include preparing public information links to the appropriate agency offices and the news media, establishing liaison with local administrators removed from field operations, calling in additional SAR personnel to observe and train, and starting to recruit resources for the search effort. By maximizing information flow and training opportunities, the secondary callout invests resources like time, knowledge, and personnel into the SAR team in order to increase the benefits from the entire operation.

The SAR resource and personnel locator portion of the preplan proves its value during the callout process. Prior mutual aid agreements, insurance coverage, allocation of transportation costs, arrangements for landing site, and so on ad nauseam should all be already understood by all parties. All that need be done by the mission manager is to call and give a brief description of the situation to the requisite officer of a particular group after identifying himself as liaison for the agency in charge. Give the team leader some indication of what skills are sought, the number of teams and team members desired, and which other units are responding to the general callout. Include current weather conditions along highway and air transportation routes to base camp, and predicted weather for and ground conditions of the search sector. Recommend personal equipment and specialized group gear required for these conditions. Explain exactly where the teams should report and who they should contact upon arrival. Offer a phone number they can call every few hours while enroute to ascertain if the search is still underway, to spare them the frustration of madly driving to the mountains only to find that the event has already concluded. Public radio broadcasts on specified local stations or calls to their own communications headquarters can serve admirably as means of calling off a search.

Give a realistic estimate of how long searchers will be away from home. Volunteers in particular need to know how much time off from their jobs will be required. Be honest — if the circumstances suggest a week-long search then say so, even though it will complicate the mobilization process. Also estimate any unusual costs (food, lodging, equipment) that may not have been anticipated. This way, when the mission is over in two days and they receive a sandwich, a beer, and a tank of gas, they will be eternally grateful. Honest, pragmatic evaluations of need during callout translate into closer knit organizations and plenty of help the next time it is needed.

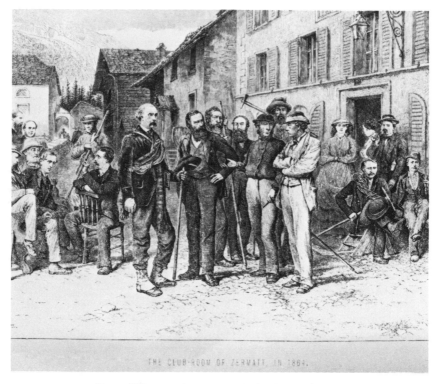

THE CLUB-ROOM OF ZERMATT, IN 1864.

From Whymper's *Ascent of the Matterhorn*.

BIBLIOGRAPHY

CHAPTER FIVE

DORAN, JEFF. "Guidelines for Information Gathering." No further publisher's data.

KELLEY, DENNIS. *Mountain Search for the Lost Victim*. Montrose, Ca.: pub. by author, 1973.

KRIGBAUM, DOTTIE. *Explorer Search and Rescue*. An ESAR Information Unit. Western Region Explorer Search and Rescue, 1111 NE 195th, Seattle, WA 98155.

HARDY, RICHARD E., AND CULL, JOHN C. consulting eds. *Applied Psychology in Law Enforcement and Corrections*. Springfield, Ill.: Bannerstone House, 1973.

6 | Planning and Strategy

AS THE FIRST stages of response are being formulated and enacted from fragments of raw information (verified or not), the next logical step is the construction of a plan of action. Planning is nothing more (or anything less!) than choosing one plan from among a host of known, realistic options. Determining the basic plan is straightforward, but further divining the most suitable choice from among a multitude of discrete actions distinguishes the truly competent SAR leader.

The Planning of a Search Mission

Planning is a critical step in the solution of a SAR problem and one almost always only hastily acknowledged, especially in the case of rescues. The impetus to act instantly without reflection upon receiving notification that someone is in pain or danger stifles good judgment. A manager may not pause long enough to consider whether going up or down is faster, or whether walking may be more efficient than flying. Vast quantities of time, effort, and money could have been saved any number of times had more thought been given to the planning stage of an operation.

Planning Data

Information obtained by the combination and evaluation of all knowledge and conjecture about an incident constitutes the *planning data*. The task of assembling this body of facts and theories is facilitated by dividing the activity into four broad subject areas.

Search party returning to base of Mt. Washington after searching for lost campers. *AP Wirephoto*

1. Information about the *victim* obtained from sources other than witnesses: companions, friends, and relatives.

2. Information about the *incident* from witnesses.

3. Information about *environmental* factors: local geography, weather, and SAR history.

4. Information about the availability of *SAR resources* and their respective time frames.

These four categories can be further delineated into a series of distinct questions and concerns that must be addressed in order to amass comprehensive planning data. The table that follows presents a representative though incomplete compilation of sources of information on a mishap.

Table 5.   Sources of Planning Data

1. Information About the Victim

Reporting party:	Detain or keep on phone; get phone number, identification, location, auto, photos, maps; return to scene; where staying?
Reconnaissance:	Need Questar, geographical viewpoints, loudhailer, hand signals, helo, Polaroid; use backcountry crew or blitz team.
Automobile:	Returned? equipment, notes, maps; leave note to "call ranger."
Home:	Returned? equipment, notes, maps; leave note to "call ranger."
Place of work:	Returned? equipment, notes, maps; leave note to "call ranger."
Friends, relatives, coworkers:	Returned? plans, physical and mental condition, habits, drugs.
Registration cards:	Returned? plans, experience, equipment, who to contact.
Registration cards:	Contact other parties which may have seen subject.
Wilderness permits:	Contact other parties which may have seen subject or know subject's plans, address.
On scene:	Locate track, equipment.

Clues:	Spot candy wrapper, dog scent articles.
Wanted posters:	Mailed to wilderness permit holders in same area, posted at trailheads and in stores.
Trailheads:	Interview hikers.
Visitor center:	Interview staff, display wanted posters.
Summit registers:	Check for subject and possible witnesses.
Bus drivers:	Let subject out where? make announcement on bus.
Local medical facilities:	Interview staff, check local records.
Local law enforcement:	Separate the overdue from the emergency.
Campgrounds:	Check registers, fee receipts.
Weather Records:	Local and regional records.

2. Information About Incident

What happened?	Fill out lost person report check list. Overdue, cries for help, crime, slipping, stuck, cold, thirsty, fallen, injured, dead, symptoms, walking wounded, equipment and personnel on scene, instructions by and to victim, reasons why overdue.
Where?	Show maps, photos to witnesses for accuracy. On ground, third class, fifth class, how far up or down, what climb, what pitch, in water, on bank, what trail, where last seen, headed in which direction, landmarks, distance, type of terrain, route taken before accident, afterwards, washed downstream, how long did witness take to get out? car parked, was he staying there? Search point last seen; if possible have witness locate it on ground as well as on map.
When?	Last seen, supposed to return, injured, ran out of water, symptoms appeared, fresh tracks or old, storm hit (match itinerary to weather).
Who?	Name, age, sex, weight, marks. Witness, passers by, companions, backcountry personnel in area.
Why?	Family problems, drugs, avalanche, rock fall, illness.

3. Environmental Information

Weather forecast: See if favorable to spend the night, three-day storm, lightning, wet rock, rising water.

Marginal Forecast: Call upwind county sheriff or FAA flight service station.

Daylight: Check dawn and dusk tables in newspapers, almanacs.

Moonlight: Find out when it rises at the specific locale, what phase, enough to walk or fly by?

Temperatures: Ascertain valley floor and rim and highlands temperatures; take differences into account.

Snow, water conditions: Anticipate changes with time of day and temperature; find out high tides, avalanche conditions.

Rescue reports: Study local files.

SAR data file: Study terrain assessments, practices, aerial photos, rescue routes, past rescue histories.

Photographs: Sort through SAR photo file, aerials, guide books, magazines; contact agencies.

Maps: Borrow from mountain shops, USGS, USFS, BLM, other parks and agencies, sportsmen.

Guide books, knowledgeable people: Contact those who live nearby, ski schools, avalanche and forestry workers, hunters, mining companies.

Terrain analysis: Find out if sloping or level, barriers, escape routes, confusion factors, possible short cuts, natural attractions, passes or river gorges.

4. Information About SAR Resource Availability

SAR preplan: Consult resource locator sector, means of notification and callout.

Check current status of resources, necessary permissions.

Activate telephone trees.

Time frame: Estimate period of need honestly.

Calculate travel time and organize travel arrangements.

Find out if limitations on resource use or time in field.

Politics: Determine if political situation has altered, effects on use of resources and timing.

Base camp: Organize number and person for arriving personnel to call and meet; speedy field deployment factors.

Exhaustive data collection in these four data categories allows the generation of reliable information upon which to devise a comprehensive search plan. Informed opinions and facts encourage the discovery of clues to the subject's detectability (how easily he can be and will allow himself to be seen), his capacity for survival (whether he is adequately prepared both psychologically and physically), his elapsed time overdue (whether he failed to communicate a return place and date), and most importantly his last known location. The point last seen (PLS) is the mandatory focal point in the field for hasty search team and confinement tactics, and the spot used to project distances and paths of travel and to coordinate a complete survey for field clues.

The planning reveals the basic search data required by hasty teams rushed to the field: a name to shout, a shoe print to identify, the color and type of clothing and equipment to notice, and other clues like cigarettes, candy, and habits to keep in mind. Radio contact with the blitz crews allows the manager the flexibility to gracefully shift strategies and search locales as new information is generated by the deliberate quest for relevant data.

A major search effort evolved in the Caldwell case because it was not known whether or not she had left Tuolumne Meadows, and the hasty teams had not found any clues in their quick passes through the area. The turn of the trail where Smith had found the lipstick container became the PLS for the formal search, as it was the only spot that provided tangible evidence that Lynn had been there sometime during her visit. The forested area behind Lembert Dome was suspect, as the statements of the cowboys and of ranger Janet O'Brien complemented each other in indicating her movement in roughly that direction. Thus the blitz teams were redirected to sweep the trail and forest there.

Organizational Structure

At this critical point in the initiation of a search, an organizational management framework must be constructed. Successful search management depends upon the efficient and effective utilization of available and potential resources applied to the problem at hand. Proper organization helps channel, apply, regroup, and evaluate resources to concentrate efforts, avoid redundancy, and promote rapid recovery of the lost party. The particulars of each incident dictate exactly how much formal field and support structure must arise.

There are, however, five major *organizational functions* (rather than specific jobs) common to every search management method, regardless of the size of the mission. The complexity of large operations demands that these functions be broken down into itemized activities performed by workers directly responsible for them. But in any search the manager should fully consider how each function is being fulfilled. These five functions are command, planning, operations, support services, and communications (Fig. 6.1).

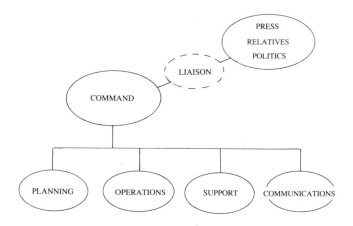

Fig. 6.1 Organizational functions for a search.

The *command function* is fulfilled by one leader, although he or she will most likely have several assistants and advisers. He has overall responsibility for the mission, and reaches key decisions on strategy, resource allocation and acquisition, tactics implementation and redeployment, media relations, and most other significant aspects of the mission. Naturally the leader should be the most experienced and sagacious available, and not necessarily the highest or senior officer.

The *planning function* too often evaporates as soon as any reasonable plan emerges, especially in seemingly uncomplicated matters. Yet strategic and tactical maneuvers have to be developed for contingencies and the gathering of data directed. Planning is perhaps the single most important function, as prodigious manpower can be misdirected for days in the wrong valley or management can be unaware of the logistical limitations of tactics it is considering because of miscalculations by the plans unit. Accurate answers to basic questions insure the efficiency of the whole effort.

The *operations* facet of search management oversees field workers and allocates resources as the need arises. Operations finds helicopter rides for ambush teams, and coordinates air, road, and water activities with ground searchers on a platoon-by-platoon basis. The dictates of the plans and command teams are realized by the actions of operations.

The *support* branch of the mission management attends to the needs of all search personnel both in the field and in the office. Food, shelter, special equipment, supply, and maintenance are provided by support, which also establishes, administers, and breaks down base camp. Without a solid breakfast for workers provided right on time, the entire operation may be stalled for several hours.

The last function is *communications*, maintaining the nervous system of any mission. Anything used to disseminate information — photocopy machines, radios, relay stations, telephones, runners — is handled by those in charge of this wing of the SAR structure.

Further discussion of just what jobs are subsumed within each function in different scale operations is the province of widely available works like Kelley's *Mountain Search for the Lost Victim*, and federal guidelines like the *Fireline Notebook* published by the Department of Agriculture. Organizational charts are provided in these texts. As a search grows in size, most of the tasks involved are apparent to the manager. His main challenge is to keep all five functions in mind at all times, to avoid emphasizing one or another such that an omission will generate problems in the days or weeks ahead.

By way of example the organizational diagram for the Caldwell search is exactly that already given in figure 6.1, with the slight addition of a group coordinator for volunteers who attended to the needs of the supplemental manpower that streamed in from outside the park.

Each of the five functions was managed by an NPS employee brought in from duties elsewhere within the park with the exception of command, retained by Smith since he was the ranger normally in charge of the search area. The concept of an overhead team has been used for years in fire control management, yet its application to search and rescue is largely unexplored. No doubt advances will be made in the first part of this decade. Certain elements, in particular support functions for food, shelter, and aircraft, are almost directly transferable to search and rescue work; only minor adaptations seem obligatory for communications, command, and operations. It is in the realm of planning that major revisions of fire overhead practices are essential, but experienced practitioners are available in most regions. Identifying and locating them for inclusion in the preplan must of course occur well in advance of an operation. Overhead team training, both theoretical and on-the-job, is mandatory. The concept of an overhead team has been introduced into SAR work with great success and should be considered a profitable though sophisticated management tool.

Search Strategy

Assuming the search underway is not of the bastard variety (without a victim still on the scene) and the hasty teams have not discovered the victim although they may have found clues, the planning data collected thus far should begin to isolate a region with distinct geographic boundaries. *Strategy*, as it relates to search theory, is the process of establishing a probable search area most likely to contain the subject. The term *tactics* refers to the explicit methods used to deploy search resources into that area to search for the victim or clues to his whereabouts.

The immediate concern for the search director is swift establishment of the boundaries of a probable search area, to focus efforts on a limited universe. This is accomplished by setting up a perimeter around the tract that cannot be perforated by the victim without his passage being detected. Optimally the search area is kept as small as possible to keep the scale of the search small. Its size is largely dependent on time in most instances: the time available to the subject to travel away from the PLS, and the time required by searchers to cover the terrain found in that area.

A fleet mobilization and confinement defines the search area, helps increase the probability of clue and victim detection, and decreases the quantities of requisite resources: personnel, food, gas, dogs, press liaisons. This, in turn, reduces logistical and command complexity and total operation cost.

Determination of Search Area

There are four basic means of establishing a probable search area: the theoretical, statistical, subjective, and Mattson methods. All of these set boundaries around a zone dependent upon the point last seen (PLS). If the PLS is relatively inaccurate, the probable search area is not likely to contain the victim. The need for precise field location of the PLS cannot be overemphasized. In most cases it is best to physically take the reporting party back to the exact spot. If it is found, enormous amounts of time and frustration may be saved; if it is not, the mission takes on a different tone. A tentative or vague PLS broadens the search.

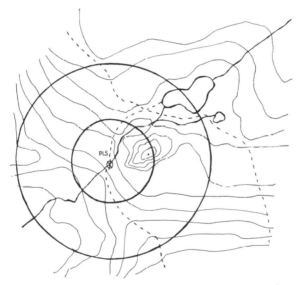

Fig. 6.2 Estimated theoretical search area and the importance of confinement. A 1.0km radius of travel from the PLS results in a 3.1km² search area; a 3.0km radius produces a 28.2km² search area.

The Theoretical Method   The probable search area is generated in this method by the use of tables that express the area as a function of distance traveled by the lost subject. This necessitates reliable determination of the PLS. The area's boundary is a circle drawn on the map centered on the PLS. The length of its radius is the maximum distance the victim could have journeyed in that terrain in the time elapsed since he was spotted at the PLS. This theoretical distance is a straight line ignoring barriers to travel. For example, one kilometer traveled from the point last seen translates into a search area of 3.1 square kilometers (Fig. 6.2), and three kilometers potentially hiked by the subject produces a search area of 28.3 square kilometers. These distances are read and adjusted from charts such as those constructed by Gordon Waddell and reproduced in *Mountain Search for the Lost Victim.* Adjustments include consideration of pertinent factors: elevation loss or gain, victim backcountry experience and physical condition, terrain, weather, snow conditions.

Once this revised distance is calculated, it is used as the radius of a circle drawn on the map around the PLS (Fig. 6.3). Then features like lakes, trails, steep embankments, and so on are evaluated and the search area begins to be articulated, leading naturally to subdivision into manageable search segments bounded by topographic landmarks.

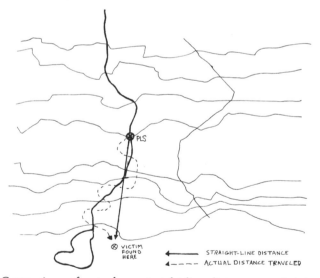

Fig. 6.3 Comparison of actual vs. straight-line distance traveled from PLS.

The Statistical Method   Case studies of the behavior of persons in the wilds provide the data for the statistical method. Calculations of how far individuals were found (in straight-line distance) from the PLS have been made and assembled. The subjects may have actually walked or skied infinitely farther in their peregrinations, but only the resultant straight-line distance is of concern in this technique. Despite its title, the statistical method is obviously approximate and subject to exceptions. The computed distances are best utilized to plot zones of probability of success.

The pioneering work in statistical search area description and lost victim behavior by Bill and Jean Syrotuck is the subject of four extremely interesting and detailed publications by them of considerable interest to anyone involved in SAR work. Only a few basic examples are presented here, to serve as an introduction to the Syrotucks' technique and its myriad potential applications in the field.

Table 6 presents data on case studies of twelve searches. The percentage of the lost victims found (alive or dead) within 0.3-kilometer increment ranges in straight-line distance from the PLS is given in table 7. Although the number of cases is quite small and hence statistically not entirely reliable, these percentages give some indication of the probability of finding a subject in each zone.

Table 6. Distance Subject Found from PLS in Twelve Case Studies

Subject	Distance found from PLS
1	0.12 kilometers
2	0.19 kilometers
3	0.40 kilometers
4	0.48 kilometers
5	0.56 kilometers
6	0.72 kilometers
median	0.76 kilometers
7	0.80 kilometers
8	0.80 kilometers
9	0.88 kilometers
10	1.04 kilometers
11	1.12 kilometers
12	1.44 kilometers

Source: Adapted from course materials developed by Gene Fear from data by William Syrotuck; used by permission. Data originally expressed in miles.

The median distance within the entire range of cases is the value below and above which there are an equal number of values. The laws of statistical probability hold that a lost subject will be found closer to the median distance than to any other value within the range. The median distance for the twelve case studies is calculated by interpolating a value from the sixth and seventh distances in ascending order, 0.72 and 0.80 kilometers respectively. The median is 0.76 kilometers.

Table 7.   Percentage of Subjects Found in Distance Ranges from PLS

Distance Range From PLS	Number of Persons Found	Percentage Found in This Range	Cumulative Percentage Found in Progressive Ranges
0.00-0.32 kilometers	2	16.6%	16.6%
0.32-0.64 kilometers	3	25.0%	41.6%
0.64-0.96 kilometers	4	33.3%	74.9%
0.96-1.28 kilometers	2	16.6%	91.5%
1.28-1.60 kilometers	1	8.3%	99.8%

Notes: Data originally expressed in miles; 1.60 kilometers equals 1.00 miles. Percentages found by dividing number of persons found in range by total number of persons. Taken from course materials developed by Gene Fear from data by William Syrotuck; used by permission.

By drawing a line through the point last seen, the various zones of probability of victim location are identified when the line is properly calibrated and circles drawn through those points. One can predict the odds of the subject's being in a certain sector by inserting the percentage zones on both sides of the median distance point along the line. If a 25% chance of finding the victim in a certain zone (or the *probability of area* (POA)) is desired then a zone determined by two circles centered on the PLS should be drawn on the map. Because there are twelve cases in the sample under discussion, the three subjects found closest to the median distance (numbers 6, 7, and 8) constitute 25% of the total. If the distance between subjects 6 and 8 is computed (0.80km-0.72km=0.08km) and the difference split and graphed on either side of the median, then a zone with a POA of 25% is fashioned: the area between two circles centered on the PLS passing through these two points equidistant from the median. Statistically, a search of this zone should reveal the subject three out of twelve times, or 25%.

If a one-in-four chance of success is unacceptable, then a zone of any other success ratio can be computed and inscribed on the map. A 75% zone of 0.92 kilometers in width can be centered around on the PLS; nine of twelve victims in the sample were found within this zone. Thus 75% of the time a lost hunter or birder will be discovered within two circles with a distance of 0.92 kilometers between them drawn centered on the PLS and equidistant from the median.

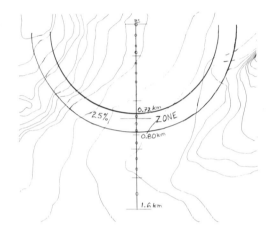

Fig. 6.4 Search zone shape. The area in which 3 of 12 subjects (25%) are found forms a 360° zone of this shape (if no known direction of travel) in which searchers have a 25% probability of finding the subject. Courtesy of Bill Wade.

Naturally the inclination is to devise a probable search area with the highest probability of attaining the goal sought. The limitations arise when the search area chosen is far too large for the six or seven searchers available and a stormfront is about to come in over the coastal range. At this point, deft application of the statistical approach improves the odds of success for hasty teams immediately directed to the most promising tracts. Several theoretical tools are available to assist the search manager in the construction of a victim profile and a probable search area. They are introduced in the broad array of articles and booklets listed in the bibliographies for this chapter and adjacent ones; see especially the aforementioned "How to Estimate Hiking Time" by Gordon Waddell, and *Analysis of Lost Person Behavior* and *A Statistical Analysis of Lost Persons in Wilderness Areas*, two books by William Syrotuck.

In *Analysis of Lost Person Behavior*, Syrotuck published tables based on over two hundred case studies of searches, mostly from Washington and New York states. The data were organized into six categories: small children (ages 1-6), children (ages 6-12), hunters, hikers, miscellaneous adults, and the elderly. Each individual's behavior was quantified, the distance traveled from the PLS was calculated, and the results were plotted with consideration for the type of terrain encountered, either flat or hilly.

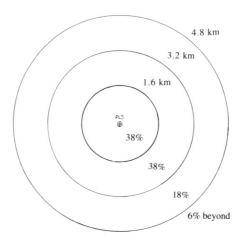

Fig. 6.5 Percentage distribution of lost children (6-12) found at different distances from PLS on flat terrain. From "Statistical Analysis of Lost Persons and Report" by William Syrotuck.

Syrotuck computed probability tables from the data generated by the twenty-two cases in the category of lost children 6-12 years of age. Figure 6.5 illustrates the percentage of subjects found within each zone of distance from the PLS on flat terrain. The results for hilly or mountainous country are shown in figure 6.6.

The delineation of probability zones was based on the assumption that the probability of finding a lost subject within any one zone is equal to the percentage of real victims found within it. For example, if 75% of lost children were eventually discovered within an area between 0.3 and 3.5 kilometers (0.2 and 2.2 miles) from the PLS, then one can infer that the search force has a 75% probability of detecting a lost child within this zone. Figures 6.7 and 6.8 illustrate the Syrotuck findings for flat and hilly terrain.

Fig. 6.6 Percentage distributions of
lost children (6-12) from PLS found
on hilly terrain. 30% found within
1.6km; 33% used travel aids.
Adapted from William Syrotuck.

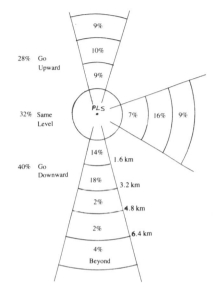

In August of 1976, seven-year-old Christopher Peterson was camping
with his family in a popular campground on the shore of a lake in the
high country of the Sierra Nevada mountains. Chris left the group for a
moment and walked to the family car to retrieve a box of cereal. When
he failed to return after some time had elapsed his family became concerned and notified campground personnel. A contract helicopter in the
vicinity and a foot patrol were unable to divine his whereabouts after
about two hours of surveillance and trail checks. Additional sweeps over
the surrounding country by the helicopter continued while the ground
effort was intensifying.

Syrotuck's probability tables on subject behavior indicated that there
was a 40% chance he would go downhill, and a 50% probability he would
be found between 3.4 kilometers downhill and 0.8 kilometers uphill
from the PLS. The 75% zone was calculated and it suggested he would
travel a maximum of 6.4 kilometers downward and 3.2 kilometer upward. The lake, however, essentially eliminated any upward movement.
Two rescuers were jumped ahead about 6 kilometers and began to walk
back until they came upon the boy, found by some hikers less than 2
kilometers from the point last seen. The search was over in less than
four hours. The boy admitted seeing and waving to the helicopter, but
its occupants apparently never noticed him.

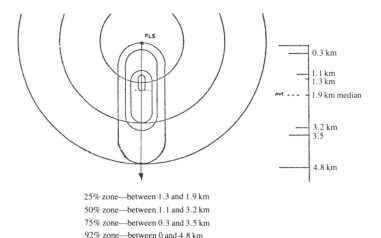

25% zone—between 1.3 and 1.9 km
50% zone—between 1.1 and 3.2 km
75% zone—between 0.3 and 3.5 km
92% zone—between 0 and 4.8 km

Fig. 6.7 Probability of finding lost children (6-12) in certain zones on flat terrain along a known direction of travel (arrow). If direction not known, the area would be between concentric circles around the PLS. From *Analysis of Lost Persons' Behavior* by W. and J. Syrotuck.

The Subjective Method   The third means of deciding upon a probable search area is the subjective method, the distillation of a broad spectrum of factors somewhat less objective than the ones employed in the first two modes. Historical data, intuition, the location of natural barriers and clues, and consideration of the physical and mental limitations of the subject are all taken into account. Data of this sort are often more arguably intangible than those generated in the first two procedures. As a result, a strong personality may prevail in the absence of agreement. Nonetheless, this tool has proven invaluable on a number of occasions, especially where an absence of a firm PLS hinders the application of theoretical data. The indispensability of a solid historical perspective on the cycle of accidents in a locale is demonstrated by the following example.

Tenaya Canyon in Yosemite park is the scene of three or four SAR incidents each year which follow now-classic lines of progression. Someone plans to trek along the Snow Creek trail to Yosemite Valley from the Tioga road up in Tuolumne Meadows. He starts off about three-and-a-half kilometers from the mouth of the canyon on the trail which, if one follows it correctly, skirts the edge of Tenaya Canyon before dropping down into the forest and eventually into the Valley. Unfortunately, the path traverses vast, open slabs with a clear view of the precipitous back side of Half Dome. The hiker always thinks he is proceeding in the wrong direction because he is walking east instead of south, becomes worried and impatient, and walks down the slabs into the canyon proper.

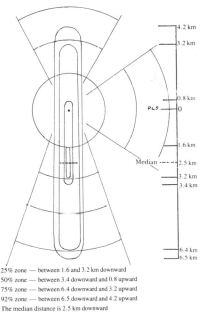

Fig. 6.8 Percentage zones of lost children (6-12) found on hilly or mountainous terrain. From *Analysis of Lost Persons' Behavior* by W. and J. Syrotuck.

25% zone — between 1.6 and 3.2 km downward
50% zone — between 3.4 downward and 0.8 upward
75% zone — between 6.4 downward and 3.2 upward
92% zone — between 6.5 downward and 4.2 upward
The median distance is 2.5 km downward

All goes well for several kilometers until the canyon walls close down to form a deep inner gorge. A technical climbing traverse manages to force a way through it. The other option available to the hiker is to rappel fifteen meters down to the streambed and then, if the creek is dry, work downstream until it is possible to exit from the inner gorge into Yosemite Valley. The latter route takes about three to four times as long as traveling along the trail. Once the rappel site is reached it is usually late in the afternoon. The hiker had planned only a day trip and is tired, has eaten his lunch, and does not feel strong enough to walk back. He begins to wander around until dark, when he builds a fire and waits for help if he had the foresight to carry matches along on the walk. So whenever someone reports a friend overdue on this trip, the SAR crew knows where the person is 90% of the time due to the strikingly similar histories of past cases.

Thus the subjective method uses experienced searchers' personal data analysis, logical reasoning, and wild speculation on a number of variables to define a probable search area.

The Mattson Method   A fourth way of establishing a probable search area was generated as an outgrowth of decision-making studies conducted by Lt. Col. Robert Mattson of the U.S. Air Force. Bob used the concept of synergy and the dynamics of group consensus to elicit a search area proposal from search managers. The Mattson method helps document and rationalize an unpredictable procedure that has been the time-honored system of search area conjecture: two or three people stand over a map and employ what is now known as the subjective method to decide where to look for someone. Everyone, regardless of rank, experience, or training, offers equal input into the democratic process that is the heart of this technique. The calculations involved are rudimentary, and require no case history studies or probability tables.

The search boss divides up the options of probable search areas or routes of victim travel and labels each (Fig. 6.9). Every evaluator is briefed on the information and facts on hand. Relying on this intelligence, each team member assigns a percentage of importance to each choice based on his or her feelings, experience, and education, singling out the most likely search areas. All that is required is that each evaluator's percentages total 100%, regardless of how they are distributed. The worksheets (Table 8) are filled out confidentially, handed in, and combined and averaged by the search manager. These composite percentages determine the probability of area (POA) of each search area or route choice.

The Mattson group consensus method balances subjective and objective information and knowledge, and allows for equal input from all evaluators without the prejudicial influence of dominant personalities. It encourages the use of all available data and all three other search area determination methods. Its emphasis is on calculating the probability of subject presence in a particular tract of wilds as a means of deciding how to organize a coherent plan of attack that faithfully reflects all objective and subjective observations. A very fine system indeed!

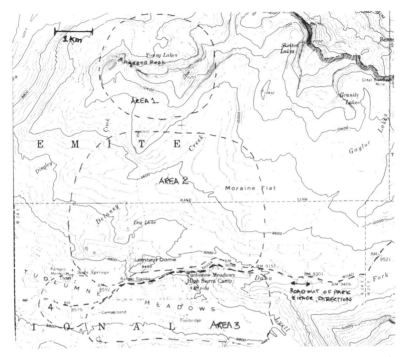

Fig. 6.9 Establishing search area by Mattson method for Caldwell search.

Table 8.   Mattson Method Worksheet

Evaluator	Area or Route				
	1	2	3	4	Total
Smith	10%	55%	5%	30%	100%
Anderson	15%	35%	10%	40%	100%
Setnicka	15%	40%	15%	30%	100%
Koegler	25%	25%	25%	25%	100%
Ewing	15%	25%	10%	50%	100%
Total	80	180	65	175	
Average	16%	36%	13%	35%	

Notes: Each evaluator's line must total 100%.
For the average, total all the percentages for each area and divide that sum by the number of evaluators.

The probable search area in the Lynn Caldwell mission evolved as follows: Theoretically, she could have easily walked fifteen or twenty kilometers down two or three different trail networks. The vast Tuolumne Meadows could have been crossed and the lodgepole pine forest entered at almost any point. But most of those interviewed thought she was barefoot. Hasty teams failed to find any trace of her passage in the Meadows or on the trails. If Lynn had wandered down one of the paths, most likely she would have come upon any number of backpackers able to offer instructions or aid in the event she was injured or only needed food and clothes to spend the night. Were this the case, she would have reappeared in the Meadows or been seen during the day. So the theoretical travel distance on the trails was discounted.

How far she could have traveled through the thick lodgepole pine in the region was an important question not easily answered. The majority of the forested country culminates in bare rock outcroppings like Ragged Peak, or spreads north through the narrow patches at lower elevations. However these connecting fingers of forest house the trails in the vicinity, so Lynn would have come across one at some point and been intercepted by hikers.

Search manager at operations base for Caldwell search. *Photo Dick Sale*

Use of the statistical method was impossible, as Bill Syrotuck's work was still in the initial stages and unavailable. There was, however, a statistical and historical source that could be called upon in the form of district ranger Herb Ewing, who had spent most of his life around the Meadows. He could remember a good half-dozen cases over the years where people had become lost near the west side of Lembert Dome. They had always been found or had reoriented themselves once they had wandered to the northeast side of the peak.

The subjective view contributed the observations that a natural barrier existed to the north in Ragged Peak and its ridge line; that Lynn would have been detected or found her way had she reentered the familiar, popular part of Tuolumne Meadows; and that the Tioga Road provided a similar recognizable boundary to the south that enhanced both detection and reorientation. The only truly wild, unbounded terrain was the forest to the east.

Final determination of the search plan took the form of group consensus in an open forum. Stronger personalities dominated but discussions were positive and evaluative. The end result was agreement on a search area of approximately twenty square kilometers commencing at the Tioga Road and spreading north to Ragged Peak. Roughly eighty-five searchers, including a majority of volunteers, were mobilized by a secondary callout. Bloodhounds were requested for deployment to the point last seen.

As the preceding examples of defining a probable search area illustrate, the process normally identifies two or three plots of varying sorts of terrain. From a practical viewpoint it is more effective to break up an area into manageable units that maximize the use of the available types of searchers or clue finders. If trained dogs or troops of Boy Scouts or only a few untrained employees will be on the scene, then certain tactics become preferable to others. Conceptually, search area segmentation is logical in light of Dennis Kelley's binary search theory.

Binary search theory is founded on the notion that by rapid elimination of portions of a finite search area due to a lack of clues, the size of the total area is reduced and resources can be concentrated in the remaining segments. This in turn increases the probability of detecting clues and the lost person. Binary search theory depends upon clue location by means of *sign cutting* — traversing or encircling a relatively limited topographic feature or tract in an effort to intersect or "cut" tracks and evidence. Searchers must therefore be especially clue conscious in any movement through the search area, and seek hints of subject passage at points (creek beds, passes, notches) with the greatest likelihood of sign detection. Selective sampling of the parcel in question is the order of the day rather than thorough grid searching with a 99% coverage (Fig. 6.10). The binary approach is either/or, yes or no: either some clue is found and attention continues in that segment, or the plot is eliminated from consideration as the crews push on to other tracts.

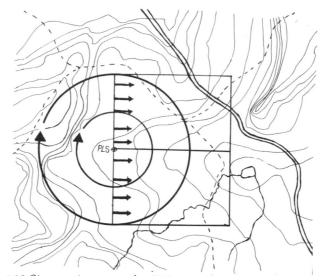

Fig. 6.10 Sign cutting around a PLS compared with grid searching.

In a sense, sign cutting is related to the introduction of hasty teams to an area to rapidly cover certain likely routes of travel, although it occurs at any number of stages in the search. The idea behind both tactics is to seek more definitive information about where and how to launch a comprehensive search effort by trying to either find the victim right off or identify some point he passed through. Sign cutters estimate a probable travel route or start with the PLS. Then, by studying the map or knowing the terrain, assemble a quick set of patterns they can walk in the field that will probably intersect the victim's path at some point. Theoretically they will notice signs of passage and thereby pick up the trail or at least eliminate that area from further consideration.

An example of binary search (Fig. 6.11) shows a sixteen-element search area investigated by a maximum of four sign-cutting teams. The swift passes by the teams unearthed evidence of passage at several points, indicating square eleven as a good prospect for a more detailed search using grid technique. Normal grid methods would require eight teams of ten searchers or eighty personnel for that same plot. Sign cutters (trackers in this case) work in pairs; in this example eight trackers are necessary. Thus in terms of efficient use of limited manpower, the binary method is laudable.

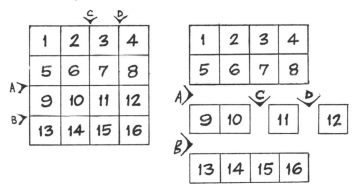

Fig. 6.11 Binary search theory in a hypothetical search. Vast portions of the search area are quickly ignored. Team A found tracks along border of 7 and 11 leading toward 12. Team B found nothing. C found evidence near 11. D found nothing. Therefore 11 looks promising and a grid search is directed toward there. Used by permission from *Mountain Search for the Lost Victim* by Dennis Kelley.

A final argument for a sampling method of this sort is time. Time is critical in any search effort, as a laborious search can in effect kill a victim. While the grid search is exhaustive, it is not nearly as fast as other means of area coverage that provide a probability of detection of clues or the victim only somewhat decreased. The upcoming chapter on tactics addresses this point in greater detail.

The purpose of splitting a probable search area up into segments, as stated earlier, is to allow application of the principles of binary search theory. Subdivision encourages the use of complementary search tactics in these segments, depending upon what is called for in each type of terrain. The use of natural barriers and the invocation of a historical perspective lending insight from other events in the region usually results in a realistic segment size for the kind and number of resources at the manager's disposal. The presence of few or no natural barriers forces reliance on compass bearings, string lines, or plastic flagging to divide up the real estate. A child missing from a small group during a cold spell in fall necessitates a more urgent response; sign cutting may prove invaluable.

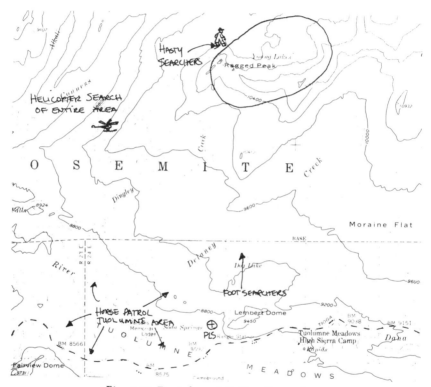

Fig. 6.12 First day of Caldwell search.

From the standpoint of binary search theory the first day of the Caldwell search was strictly a hasty search of areas thought to have a high probability of victim location. Foot and horse patrols and a reconnaissance by helicopter proved unsuccessful (Fig. 6.12). The only clue discovered was a false sighting up by Young Lakes.

On the second day a smaller, more distinct area was laid out and more thorough search methods were employed (Fig. 6.13). The PLS was worked by bloodhounds in the absence of any footprints or a visible trail. One important clue was netted: footprints heading generally north and east. It was not clear, however, that they matched Lynn's foot size. Trackers were sent in that direction the next day to try to follow the trail.

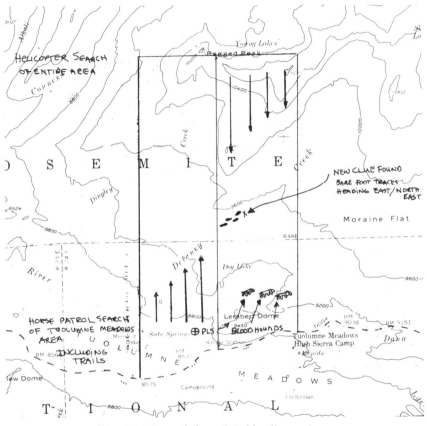

Fig. 6.13 Second day of Caldwell search.

The morning of the third day of the search (Fig. 6.14) delineated an even tighter search area. Lynn's sweatshirt was found early that morning. As long as segments were checked and eliminated and additional clues, few as they were, kept appearing, the search area was whittled down to manageable size. Either a plot yielded positive information or it was considered negative and discarded from consideration.

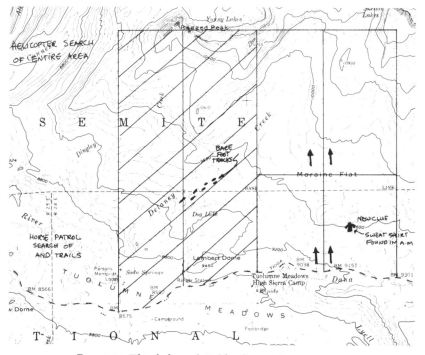

Fig. 6.14 Third day of Caldwell search — morning.

When the sweatshirt was recovered, additional resources including scent dogs were mustered and sent into that point to press the grid search (Fig. 6.15). The dogs located two other pieces of clothing and were closing in on Lynn when one of the grid lines happened upon her. From the first hasty searches to the closed grid work, a large area was constantly reduced to more diminished units until the subject was found.

In the use of binary theory, the priority of segment search and the resource concentration in each plot can be decided by use of one or a combination of the same methods used to choose the probable search area. Naturally it is best to begin to search all segments at once rather than to direct all resources to one likely tract. Rather the preferred option is a broad attack with a variety of tactics using ground searchers, dogs, and air support applied to all the search area segments according to the established probabilities of area assigned to each.

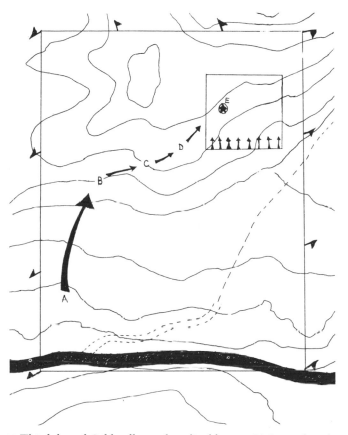

Fig. 6.15 Third day of Caldwell search — final hours. A) Sweatshirt found 11:10 A.M. B) More clothing found 3:45 P.M. C) and D) More clothing found. E) Grid searchers find Lynn at 4:14 P.M. Dogs only slightly behind.

BIBLIOGRAPHY

CHAPTER SIX

ANDERSON, R.E., AND BRISKEN, A.F. *Experiments with a Geostationary Satellite.* La Jolla, Ca.: NASAR Search and Rescue Technology Series, 1976, pp. 76-105.

FEAR, GENE. *Surviving the Unexpected Wilderness Emergency.* Survival Education Association, 9035 Golden Given Road, Tacoma, WA, 1975.

JACINTO, MARVIN. *Coordination of Volunteer Search and Rescue Units.* La Jolla, Ca.: NASAR paper 76-108.

MATTSON, ROBERT J. *Establishing Search Priorities.* No further publisher's data.

McCOY, LOIS. "Land Search Organization," *Search and Rescue Magazine,* Fall 1974, pp. 8-33.

McDONALD, GREG. *Volunteers — Success or Failure.* La Jolla, Ca.: NASAR paper 77-1022, 1977.

RUBY, S.M. *Use of Aerial Photography for Pre-Search.* La Jolla, Ca.: NASAR paper 76-106, 1976.

SYROTUCK, WILLIAM. *Outline for Strategy and Tactics.* 1976. No further publisher's data.

SYROTUCK, WILLIAM. *An Introduction to Land Search Probabilities and Calculations.* Westmoreland, N.Y.: Arner Publications, 1975.

SYROTUCK, WILLIAM. *A Statistical Analysis of Lost Persons in Wilderness Areas, Number Two.* Westmoreland, N.Y.: Arner Publications, 1974.

SYROTUCK, WILLIAM. *Statistical Analysis of Lost Persons and Reports.* June 1978. No further publisher's data.

SYROTUCK, WILLIAM. *Outline for Strategy and Tactics.* 1976. No further publisher's data.

WADDELL, GORDON. "How to Estimate Hiking Time," *Summit,* September 1968.

WADE, BILL. *The Role of the Management Team in a Large Search.* La Jolla, Ca.: NASAR paper 76-103. 1976.

WILLIAMS, PAUL. *Rescue Leadership.* Altadena, Ca.: Mountain Rescue Association, 1977.

"Consulting Murray." From *Switzerland and England* by Lunn.

7 | Tactics

TACTICS ARE THE methods used to deploy a variety of resources to the field problem to carry out the planned strategy for a particular search area. All resources, including those operating outside of the search area (interviewers, agency personnel), are basically clue finders that attempt to orient the search effort by discovering information pertinent to the problem.

Clue Finding

As the search manager begins to receive and digest the various bits and pieces of information called *clues*, he attempts to solve the question of victim location by ordering actions designed to uncover additional clues from the leads suggested by existing ones. Dennis Kelley calls search a "classic mystery," one solvable by "looking for clues and not the victim." He refers to the lost person as the "ultimate clue!"

Dennis continues by saying that the victim is a signal generator who continually sends clues to receivers — the searchers. The receivers must be tuned to the signals sent their way. The ongoing condition of *clue awareness* by searchers is learned through training and experience. Sometimes the clue finding process involves pinpointing one clue. Other times it focuses on receiving and separating many clue signals and then attempting to home in on only one type. Kelley lists four broad categories of ways a victim's clues may reach searchers: 1) physical evidence — a footprint, 2) recorded information — a trail register or wilderness permit, 3) people — a witness or relative, and 4) events — cries for help. Some of these signals are easily received because they are obvious. More often clues are only discernible by trained personnel programmed to perceive clues. Hence a popular axiom holds that trained, clue-aware searchers are the best qualified clue receivers in the field.

There are more clues than victims. Searchers who look for clues rather than the victim increase the odds of quickly assembling the pieces of the jigsaw puzzle. An absence of clues specifies where the victim is not and furthers progress via binary search methodology. Clue seeking is a continuous, ongoing process that never stops until the victim is found. No clue should ever be discarded or minimized, and no one person can adequately gather all facts and clues.

Six broad categories of clue finders are available:

1. Search dogs — bloodhounds, air scent, and tracking dogs;

2. Professional human trackers — Border Patrol agents or other trained personnel;

3. Trained ground searchers — grid searchers and hasty teams;

4. Investigators — skilled professionals to examine evidence in the field and follow up on leads from interviews;

5. Electronic and mechanical aids — aircraft emergency locator transmitters (ELTs), long-range listening devices and so on; and

6. Aircraft — fixed wing, helicopters, and satellites.

Each type of clue finder and related technique has advantages and drawbacks. In order to apply any one of them effectively to the problem at hand, accurate evaluation of its means of operation and requirements must take place if not detailed in the SAR preplan. For example, it is almost impossible to rely on search dogs introduced after human trackers have systematically trampled the woods. Ideally dogs and trackers should survey different segments of the search area rather than confuse each other. On the other hand, helicopters, fixed wing aircraft, and ELT equipment usually complement one another well if coordinated correctly, and their use does not affect ground search personnel.

The application of SAR clue finders to the field operation is the backbone of the search framework. How and where should these clue finders be distributed in the field? What strategy and tactics need be applied?

Confinement of the Search Area

As a probable search area evolves the SAR manager begins to establish a perimeter around that area and lost person. The idea is that the victim will not be able to pass through the surrounding ring of searchers without being detected, thereby lessening the likelihood of an enlarged search area.

Confinement is a form of passive search dependent on limiting subject mobility. It removes vast regions from consideration by virtue of assuring that the subject cannot enter them. A heavy reliance on the lay of the land is the best way to devise a succinct and easily implemented confinement strategy. Any natural feature that tends to inhibit or channel travel offers potential for controlling the lost party's movement and spotting him. Since gulleys, riverbeds, ridges, and meadows allow rapid progress they are logical avenues of victim mobility. Conversely, prominent cliffs, dense forest, deep gorges, and major water bodies restrict movement and can serve as perfect vantage points for confinement scouts.

In field applications, confinement requires an emergency response rushing some rescuers off while the data gathering and planning phases commence and continue. If the team waited until the majority of the facts were known, the real value of confinement would be negated. The boundaries of the search area already would be greatly enlarged due to the longer elapsed time of unrestricted victim roaming. A counterargument holds that as time passes the subject is more likely to find his way back to camp or to stumble upon some sign of civilization. While this frequently occurs, search area confinement assumes that the victim probably will not reorient himself on his own. What is more, further traumatic or psychological injury or environmental injury (dehydration, hypothermia) is possible and its probability of occurence increases with time.

The tactical phase of search management is entered once confinement personnel are deployed. Up to this point few SAR workers have gone into the probable search area to look for the subject. The data gathering process is now underway though, and a preliminary search plan has been synthesized and priority search segments drawn on the map. Finally searchers are ushered into the field to close off and encircle the area deemed most significant. Field technique requires trained, clue-conscious wilderness users who are skilled in living in the environment under scrutiny and can comfortably concentrate not on the mechanics of movement through it but instead on discerning clues.

Thus the first phase of confinement involves determining (from familiarity with the terrain, the study of maps and photographs, interviews, and the use of overflights) topographic barriers and detection and attraction lookout points. By leapfrogging ambush teams ahead of the victim's suspected direction of travel, the manager closes off avenues of escape from the area. These stationary teams sit and wait for the lost person or observe him as he moves away from their position. Hasty teams may accompany the confinement units and move back down the trail toward the PLS or areas of high probability of victim or clue location. The perimeter watchers hold their ground to interview hikers and show photographs of the subject, and keep watch in case he slips by the hasty teams by using another route or traveling in darkness or bad weather. Searchers can also show photos and alert other wilderness users to be on the lookout for the victim.

Photo Tim Setnicka

Late one February during a snowstorm, Lon Trixon, about eighteen years old, took a wrong turn while attempting to traverse from one ski run to another at a major Western ski area. He was soon lost. His friends reported him missing at 5 P.M., saying they had last seen Trixon at 2 P.M. that afternoon. At 5:45 P.M. several hasty teams of professional ski patrollers started sign cutting along contours from the highest point on the mountain accessible by chairlift.

About fifteen minutes later one team found a single pair of ski tracks heading away from the ski area. It began following the tracks as another team continued to contour around the peak and scout for other signs in case the trail that had been found did not lead to Lon.

The tracks headed down into a creek drainage. The search leader decided to send a hasty confinement team up an old road in order to construct a perimeter around Trixon. If these confinement skiers progressed beyond where Trixon could see them, it was theorized that he would probably notice their fresh tracks and follow them downhill to safety.

About 8:30 P.M. the first team of hasty trackers caught up with Trixon, who had not yet reached the road. He was unharmed but wet, cold, and tired. The confinement team was only a few minutes away and because of its trajectory would have seen his path imminently had the first team not been so fast or had it lost the trail. The concept of instantly deploying clue-conscious hasty trackers and confinement skiers paid off admirably on this particular stormy night.

Posting surveillance or attraction lookouts is another confinement technique. The *surveillance lookout* is assigned a strategic location with visual command of the search area. He studies terrain for any signs of the victim approaching the perimeter, such as a campfire or a lone hiker. *Attraction methods*, including the use of smoke, flares, lights, sirens, flashing mirrors, and loudspeakers, solicit the willing victim's attention and draw him toward the source of the commotion. Lookouts can also help direct team movement and provide base camp with status reports. Careful choice of lookout spots allows a multiplicity of services to be rendered.

Aircraft are obvious tools available for attraction work, as evinced by the Michael Parker search. Michael, age ten, was camping with a large church group in the Sierra backcountry. He got into an argument with several members of his party such that the counselor had to restore harmony. The following day he asked those he had disagreed with if they would join him on a hike down a creek drainage. The others decided against it. Michael left the camp alone and was disoriented shortly thereafter. He spent the night huddled against a gigantic boulder.

When Michael had not reappeared by early evening of the first day, the counselors requested assistance and searched the immediate vicinity in the dark with members of the group. Soon after daybreak the next morning a helicopter began flying in search teams and dogs in a series of relay flights. Michael heard the repetitious drones, spotted the helicopter, and walked toward its apparent landing zone right into camp late in the afternoon.

If the search will entail multiday operations, all search personnel should be made aware of this before they arrive at base camp. In this way they will be prepared with both sufficient equipment and adequate employer notification to spend the time in the field demanded by the situation. In some types of terrain like the dense forests of the Pacific Northwest, attraction and lookout station use is ineffective. Instead long, flagged string lines are actually laid out between trees to create artificial boundaries. In some cases tags are placed on the string at intervals with signs labeled "Search Base" containing an arrow pointing to safety. In lieu of a continuous line one can install brightly colored plastic surveyor's tape tied to branches. Every so often a sign may be added giving directions to base or a road. Both of these measures work well to segment search areas.

Confinement by air is possible, although aircraft usually find greatest use in hasty searches. However snowfields and bare rock ridges covered with fresh snow have been checked by air for signs of transgression, eliminating huge portions of a potential search area. Confinement ends only when the total search effort has been halted.

Simultaneous with the introduction of confinement crews is the dissemination of blitz teams. These pairs or trios canvass features of high probability like drainages, waterfalls, mine shafts, and derelict buildings and follow known or suspected routes of travel in search of signs.

Trackers can begin to sign cut along a predetermined perimeter while the lookouts and road blocks are being established. Constricted passages or places that provide the only realistic course of movement through a region are called *track traps* and should be checked for tracks even if the trackers have no footwear description. All tracks found should be noted and documented. When it is learned that the victim left his hiking boots at home and wore a pair of tennis shoes, the new clue will already have been checked. In large search areas or ones difficult to cover due to insufficient manpower, dense undergrowth, or whatever, these track traps and logical travel routes should be frequently revisited in case the trackers cut sign before the subject staggers through the trap.

It is interesting to note that few confinement methods other than assuming restricted movement due to natural barriers were brought into play for the Caldwell search. Figure 7.1 demonstrates a possible confinement strategy for the second day of that mission. Some of the confinement functions of the tactics shown there were subsumed by other tactics, namely the early helicopter overflights and blitz team checking of the Young Lakes district and trail, but neither of these actions persisted throughout the operation.

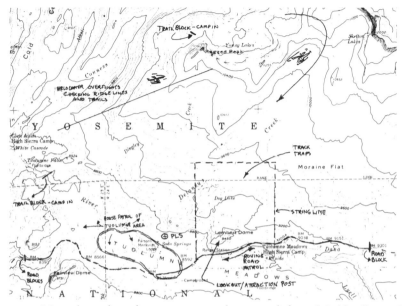

Fig. 7.1 Hypothetical confinement tactics for second day of Caldwell search.

Briefing and Debriefing

When auxiliary SAR group members actually arrive on site a formal briefing should take place. Often hours or even a full day has transpired since they were contacted by phone and called out to the scene.

The purpose of a *briefing* is to summarize the situation past and present, and to provide any information that will help orient new personnel to all environmental and strategic facets of the problem. The briefing details mission organizational structure and specifies the jobs a person or group has been assigned. For this reason a face-to-face talk with all assembled field personnel is ideal. If numbers or staggered schedules prevent this, team leaders may have to be briefed separately and relied upon to pass the information on to their respective crews. Because of individual differences in sorting, weighting, and remembering information, some facts and emphasis may be altered in the process of transferral to the rank and file. Any time a unit returns to the field, even if there is no appreciable mission or job change, another short briefing is in order. It serves as a fine opportunity to rejuvenate the crew's enthusiasm and to let everyone know how much his efforts are appreciated. There should be adequate time during briefing for questions and comments to be aired, to insure that all have a chance to contribute ideas and suggestions and that no details are overlooked.

Briefing during Caldwell search. *Photo Dick Sale*

Numerous items of information must be passed on to field teams during briefing. A photocopied subject information form with complete physical and psychological profiles and current search status handed out to every searcher is the most reliable means of conveying requisite facts. Photos, sketches, tracings of boot prints, or descriptions of other possible clues can be distributed at this time if copies are not available for all. Team assignments should be unequivocally clear and drawn on maps given out or uniformly corrected. Any safety considerations or hazards should be discussed and located, and procedures for working around or through them agreed upon. Written team assignments are distributed to the team leaders, emphasizing the time frame for job completion. The debriefing process should be outlined as well.

The history of the search should be summarized, noting the interrelationships of all groups and agencies involved. Radio call numbers and procedures and communication networks ought to be spelled out. Discussion of unusual equipment needs and of the most recent weather forecast takes place if necessary. The location of family and relatives and of the press contact is given; any media representatives are introduced.

Lastly, transportation plans for movement to and from the base camp are organized on a team basis. Any special safety precautions for helicopters or watercraft in use need reiteration.

Daily debriefing is more difficult, as everyone is tired from the physical and mental stress of concentration on finding clues and maneuvering through knee-deep snow or prickly krummholz. Consulting with the team leader or the plans office for a solid debriefing session may be considered a chore.

Debriefing is a complete interview with and interrogation of a team's field search units in order to gain a thorough understanding of all evidence and activities encountered during the day. Ideally this takes the form of a comfortable one-to-one chat with each team leader or searcher. In practice, of course, the debriefing transpires on a picnic table at base camp under the dim light of a Coleman lantern while everyone is struggling to stay awake.

The debrief is organized to collect, record, and exchange information on what happened while a specific team was in the field in order to assess its effectiveness. The exact terrain traversed is drawn out on a master planning and tactics map. An estimate of the percentage of coverage is drawn in and the number of sweeps noted. Any clues collected are described and their finders' names and whereabouts included, and the clues plotted on the main map. Barriers to progress are revealed and decisions are made to circumvent or manage them the next day. Feedback on the search bosses and strategy should be solicited. How was the timing of unit coordination? Would other tactics prove more productive? Is tomorrow's projected plan realistic?

The debriefing, like the briefing, is another clue to the search mystery. When it is documented and appropriately filed it is available for review at a later date. Both sessions are synergistic attempts to communicate maximum amounts of data and ideas between those involved in actively managing the search and those working in the field. They should be an integral, ongoing part of the operation until its final stages.

The Three Types of Search Tactics

Hasty and confinement teams are generally the first personnel in the field. Blitz teams are an immediate attempt to solve the problem by a rapid response to the best information available a short time after notification. Their introduction is a practical application of binary search theory as they help isolate tracts that do *not* contain the victim or his clues. By scouring paths and track traps, traversing danger zones, trail running, cutting sign, walking through drainages, and scouting features with a SAR event history, they offer instantaneous perusal of high probability areas. This effort is known as a *Type I detection phase* of applying resources to the field during the tactical stages of a mission.

The second detection phase commences while blitz teams pursue their goals. The *Type II phase* concentrates on a relatively fast, efficient search of locales of high probability using methods that produce the highest results per hour. The tactics involved include the use of search dogs, wide search patterns flown by aircraft, and open grid sweep searches.

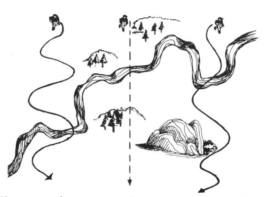

Fig. 7.2 Type II open grid sweep search in open country with wide spacing to cover area quickly. Compass holder in center keeps flankers in line. Adapted from Jon Wartes.

A Type II open grid sweep search (Fig. 7.2) utilizes teams made up of three to seven searchers. The individuals are widely spaced, usually one to two hundred meters or more depending on the terrain or the density of vegetation. A team member in the center has a compass and keeps the group headed on the correct bearing. Other members act as flankers and move randomly back and forth looking for clues. Each team's search area is normally vast and without carefully defined boundaries at this point. An open grid search might take the form of teams dropped into the headwaters of a drainage to sweep down on either side of the stream for five or ten kilometers (Fig. 7.3).

In contrast with the open, approximate character of the Type II search is the Type III detection mode implemented within a closed area. *Type III grids* are segments of the search area split up via articulated boundaries and scoured with an emphasis on producing a high probability of detection in capturing clues (Fig. 7.4). Dogs, foot searchers, and aircraft can all be used in an intense closed grid search effort of this sort. Artificial boundaries marked in the field by string, surveyor's tape, or toilet paper are replicated on the master map and the results noted. A typical Type III action is comprised of some thirty searchers walking in a line six meters apart for the full length and breadth of their assigned plot.

Fig. 7.3 Type II open grid search along a stream, which acts as a control line.

The three phases and methods of detection are distinguished by the increasing probability of detection along with greatly increased time of implementation as the mode moves from Type I to Type III. If hasty teams check apparent hazards, adequately perform their sign cutting and tracking, and survey possible victim attractions, either the victim is most likely not within the designated search area or a more thorough method of detection is mandatory.

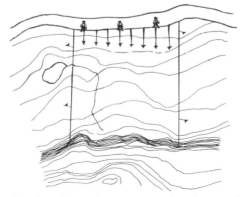

Fig. 7.4 Type III closed grid search. Last resort for object with low detectability (e.g., firearm casing). Spacing about 3-10 meters between searchers. Adapted from Jon Wartes.

From a tactical perspective, the Lynn Caldwell search proceeded as follows. A hasty team search by foot, horse, and flying patrols was launched on the first day in a move to swiftly locate Lynn or more tangible evidence of her activities. Trails were swept by teams consisting of one or two rescuers and roughly 65 square kilometers were studied by helicopter. A reported sighting of Lynn near Young Lakes was countered by three two-man teams flown in to verify the report. The sighting was valid but the individual noticed was not Lynn.

Type III wide-spaced closed grid searching for clues during Caldwell search. *Photo Dick Sale.*

The second day's tactics were planned before a firm count of available ground searchers was possible. About eighty-five eventually arrived ready for field duty, the majority trained SAR personnel. To search the 20-square-kilometer area they were divided into four teams averaging twenty members each. The managers felt that a two-kilometer-long grid line of searchers would be virtually impossible to control. To combat confusion, the search bosses chose to stagger the start of the four teams by fifteen minutes. The first team marked both flanks as it proceeded on a compass bearing to approximate a straight line. The second team followed hard on the first team's west flank and removed its surveyor's tape as it went. The second team in turn flagged its west flank for the third party and so on.

By means of this configuration, the average theoretical distance between searchers was about twenty meters. Each team member tried to travel in a straight line and yell appropriate commands ("Stop," "Close up," "Thin out") when the line became too ragged or something had to be more carefully investigated. By about noon of the second day, the teams reached the base of Ragged Peak, shifted around to the east, and used the same staggered start to move south. Just after dusk the wave of searchers lapped onto the Tioga Road, completing a variation of a Type III closed grid search.

Throughout the second day bloodhounds worked the Lembert Dome slabs and forest but were unable to discover a scent trail. The helicopter continued its aerial survey, and two teams of three searchers studied both sides of the Tioga Road east from the Lembert Dome parking lot for ten kilometers for any sign Lynn might have crossed the road. Other small lakes and popular day-hike trails well out of the search area and any hikers near them were canvassed by four supplementary two-member teams. The only clue generated by the entire day's effort was unearthed late in the afternoon along the Delaney Creek drainage. Two or three unconnected footprints had been spotted. Lynn was thought to be barefoot.

That night during the debriefing the four team leaders complained that it was exceedingly awkward to stay in line and on a true north-south bearing due to the density of the lodgepole pine. Another tactic was needed. The bloodhounds, it was learned, had been recalled to their home base due to another emergency.

A plan for the upcoming day emerged. A tract immediately adjacent to the second day's search area would be divided into four segments and each team would be responsible for negotiating a straight-line grid in one section, rather than all four working in unison. The boundaries of each segment were to be established at first light by small teams using compass bearings and flagging. Replacement search dogs had been requested from Washington state but would not arrive until midday at best. Helicopter overflights were scheduled to continue, along with perusal of selected features outside the search area. Trackers were to begin tracking if possible from the barefoot prints found in the Delaney Creek watershed.

By 7 A.M. all searchers were at their respective starting points and the third day of the Caldwell search began. As fate would have it, Janet O'Brien, the last person to talk with Lynn three days earlier, found her lying next to a log in one of the four new search grids at 4:14 P.M. that afternoon. Lynn did not cry out when she saw Janet approaching. Janet only said "Hi, Lynn" and sat down and gave her a big hug. Lynn was exhausted and dehydrated but in good condition otherwise. Lynn later said she was largely immobile after the second day and had to tread around in circles at night to keep warm. She had torn up her clothing to fashion an arrow pointing to her position. When the helicopter flew overhead she had waved but its occupants unfortunately did not notice her.

Luckily, Lynn was found alive and well. The Yosemite and assisting SAR units learned a tremendous amount from the mistakes made on this complex operation. Four years later, after additional learning experiences and a rapid progression of the state of the art of search management, another search occurred that took a rather different course. But first discussion of another management tool is in order before that story is told.

Janet O'Brien talks with Lynn Caldwell after she was found. *Photo Dick Sale*

Probability of Locating Clues or the Victim

After the first day of any search, if not sooner, the question of performance arises. How well are the tactics in use surveying the search area?

This concern for determining an efficiency quotient of the odds of finding the subject in a certain area with particular tactics leads to generation of the *probability of detection*. It is related to the probability of a victim's presence in a search area and is calculated with the following equation:

$$Pa \times Pd = Ps$$

where *Pa* is a value that gives a priority to the search area segment;

Pd is a value given to the ability of the resources to detect the subject or clues, and

Ps is the product of the two, used to measure success.

Chapter 6 investigated methods of establishing the probability of victim presence in a search area both initially and when the area is divided into search area segments. Now the means of measuring how well given resources are being applied and predicting how well others would work will be discussed. These tools can facilitate the redistribution of resources as the search area increases or decreases in response to the appearance of new clues or the failure of tactics in play. The decision of when to suspend a mission is made more rational as well, and easier to justify to higher authorities, friends, relatives, and media representatives.

Somewhat in parallel with the Syrotucks' work on composing probable search areas by reliance on historical and experimental data, Jon Wartes has experimentally developed ways to compute the chances of clue detection by grid searchers. Wartes's data are relied upon to calculate *Pd* (the ability of resources to detect the subject) in the probability of detection formula presented above. Two qualifications should be stated right away. First, Type III closed grid searching is the third and final search technique invoked, when other tactics have proved unsuccessful. Second, Wartes's work does *not* establish universal figures for closed grid search in all kinds of terrain. His studies were conducted in the thick underbrush of the Pacific Northwest, and must be used with this in mind. In a sparse desert, for instance, these figures might be inaccurate, although experiments conducted in Colorado largely supported his conclusions.

There were four explicit preconditions in Wartes's work: 1) trained Explorer (EASR) Scouts, 2) the moderately dense underbrush of the Northwest, 3) searches for objects of varying size but representative of search clues, and 4) twelve daylight and eight nighttime tests. One other point bears mention. Wartes's data were collected and presented in English system units, expressed as efficiency per square mile. The original data have been converted to metric measurements here, complemented by formulas for both metric and English measurements where appropriate.

Wartes ran six six-man teams through his experiment. He found that it took three-and-a-half hours for them to search 2.5 square kilometers (1.0 square mile), and that the probability of detection varied inversely with the distance between searchers in a line. The *Pd* or odds of finding clues or the victim was determined from these field tests and is offered in table 9.

Table 9

Results of Wartes's Search Grid Efficiency Experiments

Spacing	Searchers	Hours		Total Searcher-Hours	Pd
30 meters	53	× 3.5	=	185.5	50%
18 meters	88	× 3.5	=	308	70%
6 meters	264	× 3.5	=	924	90%

NOTES: *Pd* is the probability of detecting a clue or victim with the tactic in use in a particular type of terrain (the dense underbrush of the Pacific Northwest). Results are given for a search of 2.5 square kilometers (1.0 square mile). Used by permission of Jon Wartes.

To calculate the *Pd* for searcher spacings other than those shown in this table, use the formula

$$Pd = 100 - (1.6 \times m)$$

where *m* is the spacing between searchers in meters; or the English system equivalent

$$Pd = 100 - (0.5 \times f)$$

where *f* is the spacing between searchers in feet.

For example, the *Pd* for grid searchers spaced 12 meters apart is reckoned as follows.

$$Pd = 100 - (1.6 \times 12)$$
$$Pd = 100 - 19.2$$
$$Pd = 80.8$$
$$Pd = 81\%$$

The higher the desired *Pd*, the greater the amount of time necessary to accomplish the search. Thus grid searching can be very inefficient when there is a limited time frame for victim survival. If evidence or a body is sought, then perhaps the added time and expense can be justified. This is clearly not the case when a sixty-four-year-old cross country skier has been lost for six hours and a cold, dark night is rapidly falling.

Expanding on this basic formula, it is possible to calculate the results of a multipartite search effort. Remember that all *Pd*'s are hypothetical, with the exception of those derived from Jon Wartes's data for the Northwest. His data may be applicable to other types of terrain. But until someone performs similar experiments in local conditions to create detection probabilities the best one can do is make an educated *Pd* guess, relying on the resources (helicopter crew, dog handlers, team leaders) to compose performance estimates for the conditions experienced.

Suppose a search for a lost person has continued for two full days. Thus far there have been very few encouraging developments: few clues, no victim to date, destabilizing weather, and searchers who want to go home. The manager, however, is legally and morally responsible for solving the mystery. The question becomes whether or not and when to terminate the mission. The boss has depended upon open grid searchers and tracking dogs in separate segments of the search area, with a number of reconnaissance flights over another tract. After consulting with and debriefing the ground troops and helo crew, the following estimated detection probabilities are obtained:

$$\text{Open grid:} \quad Pd = 60\%$$
$$\text{Search dogs:} \quad Pd = 75\%$$
$$\text{Helicopter:} \quad Pd = 40\%$$

To compute total search area coverage thus far, use the formula below.

$$Pd_{final} = 1 - (a \times b \times c)$$

where $a = 1 - (Pd \text{ first coverage})$
$b = 1 - (Pd \text{ second coverage})$
$c = 1 - (Pd \text{ third coverage})$

In this particular search

$a = 1 - (0.40)$	$b = 1 - (0.75)$	$c = 1 - (0.60)$
$a = 0.60$	$b = 0.25$	$c = 0.40$

therefore
$$Pd_{final} = 1 - (0.60 \times 0.25 \times 0.40)$$
$$Pd_{final} = 1 - (0.06)$$
$$Pd_{final} = 0.94$$
$$Pd_{final} = 94\%$$

To date, the search action has surveyed the search area with a 94% chance of success in finding either clue or victim. Practically speaking, with a Pd this high some reevaluation of the dimensions of the region being considered and of victim survivability is in order.

Using Wartes's data or other local estimates one can compute the number of searchers required for any type of operation. Say it was possible to round up 35 trained Mountain Rescue Association (MRA) members for a grid search, but they were available for only eight hours of work in the field. How large an area can they canvass with what probability of detection? The search manager should decide what success rate is desired. Although the search boss might prefer a 99.9% *Pd*, a more realistic *Pd* of 70% is chosen. Wartes's experiments reveal that a *Pd* of 70% necessitates 88 searchers working 3.5 hours to cover 2.5 square kilometers when spaced 18 meters apart. The following equation is evolved, relying upon the total number of hours that the searchers are available: 35 workers × 8 hours = 280 man-hours.

$$\frac{\text{man-hours required}}{\text{man-hours available}} = \frac{2.5 \text{km}^2}{x} \quad \text{or} \quad \frac{\text{man-hours required}}{\text{man-hours available}} = \frac{1.0 \text{ mile}^2}{x}$$

$$\frac{308 \text{ hours}}{280 \text{ hours}} = \frac{2.5 \text{km}^2}{x} \quad \text{or} \quad \frac{308 \text{ hours}}{280 \text{ hours}} = \frac{1.0 \text{ mile}^2}{x}$$

$$x = 2.3 \text{km}^2 \quad \text{or} \qquad\qquad x = 0.91 \text{ mile}^2$$

Now the search boss has an estimate of how large an area can be searched by available grid personnel. This will, in turn, help him decide whether to increase or decrease his *Pd*, and which tracts will benefit the most by the introduction of additional manpower. The computation may suggest a surplus of or need for supplemental resources of one sort or another.

Tactical Applications

Calculations of this sort assist the manager in the selection and application of different types of resources, too. For example, suppose Sandy Bryson, a member of the WOOF SAR Dog Unit in California, arrives on the scene with her trained search dog. After consultations and inspection of the search area terrain she reckons that she and her dog can range through 2.5 square kilometers (1.0 square miles) in six hours with a *Pd* of 75%. How many grid searchers would she and her canine replace if the *Pd* is held constant? Since the data for a *Pd* of 75% are not readily available from Wartes's chart, one must find out how far apart grid searchers need be to produce a *Pd* of 75%. Insert the known information into the *Pd* formula and solve for *m*.

$$Pd = 100 - (1.6 \times m) \quad \text{or} \quad Pd = 100 - (0.5 \times f)$$

Or it is possible to derive a general formula for spacing (*m*, in meters or *f*, in feet) as follows.

$$m = \frac{100 - Pd}{1.6} \quad \text{or} \quad f = \frac{100 - Pd}{0.5}$$

$$m = \frac{100 - 75}{1.6} \quad \text{or} \quad f = \frac{100 - 75}{0.5}$$

$$m = 15 \text{ meters} \quad \text{or} \quad f = 50 \text{ feet}$$

So grid searchers need a spacing of 15 meters to canvass 2.5 square kilometers with a *Pd* of 75%. How many searchers does one sweep of this area demand? One side of 2.5 square kilometers is 1.6 kilometers long or 1600 meters. Similarly, a perfect square mile has two sides 1.0 miles or 5280 feet long. Use the formula:

$$\frac{\text{length of grid search line}}{\text{searcher spacing}} = \text{number of searchers required}$$

$$\frac{1600 \text{ meters}}{15\text{m spacing}} = 106 \text{ searchers} \quad \text{or} \quad \frac{5280 \text{ feet}}{50 \text{ foot spacing}} = 106 \text{ searchers}$$

Therefore it would take 106 searchers 3.5 hours to cover 2.5 square kilometers, compiling a sum total of 371 man-hours.

Amazingly, one trained search dog can patrol a tract in six hours that it would take 106 workers 370 man-hours to comb with the same probability of detection. Information of this kind greatly aids the search manager's struggle to plan a mission and allocate precious resources.

The fact that the detection capability of different resources varies draws attention to the concept that repeated sweeps of a segment with wide spacing between rescuers yield better results than a single pass with close spacing (Fig. 7.5). Searchers tend to feel uncomfortable about broad spacing both while in the field and while mapping strategy and choosing tactics. No one wants to miss clues or the subject because of excess room between searchers. For this reason the concept of wide spacing and multiple sweeps is one which is not readily accepted by managers despite statistical proof of its advantages (Table 10).

Fig. 7.5 Spacing, thoroughness, and efficiency in grid searches. Wide spacing is more efficient, less thorough, relatively fast and covers much more area. Close spacing is less efficient, very thorough, very slow, and covers less area. From Jon Wartes.

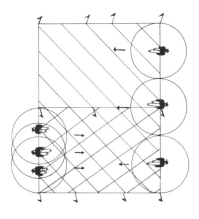

Table 10

Effectiveness of Multiple Grid Sweeps

Spacing	Sweep 1	Sweep 2	Sweep 3	Sweep 4	Sweep 5
30 meters	50%	75%	87.5%	93.7%	96.9%
18 meters	70%	91%	97.3%	99.2%	99.8%
6 meters	90%	99%	99.9%	99.9%	99.9%

SOURCE: Data adapted from work by Jon Wartes. Used by permission.

Grid searching becomes a more effective tool when spacing wider than what was thought essential is utilized, as the speed of coverage of a given area is noticeably increased. With a finite number of workers the team can traverse more plots by broadening the distance between members, as each person scouts more area per unit of time. One positive benefit of a faster search pace is the enhanced odds of encountering a conscious victim capable of responding to attraction stimuli, thereby ending the whole operation at the earliest possible moment. Then everyone can move on to the next critical stage of the mission: the victory party!

Jon Wartes has drawn attention to the broad array of misconceptions and old wives' tales rampant in SAR circles about grid searching and search in general. Commonly expressed fallacies include the notion that an area should be searched only once as it is wasteful to range across it a second time, and the idea that one should search with an emphasis on thoroughness, such that one can be certain that the subject is not in the tract covered. Both of these vague feelings of course translate tactically into closely spaced grid searches.

Actually, both theory and experience demonstrate the efficacy of the loose grid search and of continuous rotation of teams among segments rather than repeated sweeps by a tight grid line. A strategy of this sort relies heavily on well-marked segment boundaries. If successive teams start into the tract from different sides or angles each time, without concern for staggering the rough lines walked by the individuals in each team, complete coverage is virtually assured (as demonstrated by table 10).

A search manager must select only a few tactics from the innumerable potential variations in order to maximize his search efficiency. Success is dependent upon the odds that the victim is located within the designated search area and the probability that the field resources will find him or his clues. Simply put:

$$P_{success} = P_{area} \times P_{detection}$$

In applying tactics remember the order of the three basic types of detection: hasty teams first, open grid search methods second, and closed grid modes (Type III) last.

Tactical Summary: The Orin Sample Search

The search for Orin Sample, age seven, was a classic demonstration of textbook strategy and tactics admirably activated for a search emergency. It took place some four years after the three-day organizational and tactical challenges of the Lynn Caldwell search and reflected advances in search theory and practice.

Orin and his family were enjoying a summer camping vacation and were on their way back home to New Mexico. They stopped at a popular campground along the Tioga Road in the Sierra high country not far from the site of the Caldwell operation. It was mid-June and the sunny weather had been stable for weeks.

Orin and his younger sister were playing near their campsite. After a few hours, Orin started to wander off on his own. His sister told him he had better not and that he should return to the family with her. Very sternly he told her, "No, I'm going to look for pine cones." By that time it was about 6 P.M. When there was no sign of Orin by 7 P.M., his father called for assistance, mobilizing the entire campground clientele to thrash through the woods nearby. The first park staff arrived on the scene at 7:30 P.M. and began interviewing the family and all the other campers. A gentleman surfaced who said he saw a young boy matching Orin's description meandering onshore against the flow of Porcupine Creek around 6:30 P.M. The spot indicated was less than two kilometers north of the campground (Fig. 7.6).

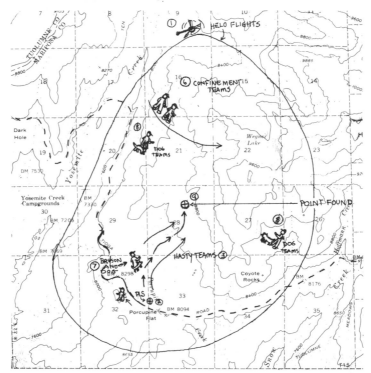

Fig. 7.6 Orin Sample search tactics. Confinement and hasty teams were immediately deployed, and dog teams brought in as soon as possible.

At 7:45 P.M. a helicopter operating about ten air minutes away was ordered into the air on a fast hasty search of the vicinity even though it was already getting dark. The elderly man who had last seen Orin was asked to show the rangers the exact whereabouts of the PLS on the east bank and the boy's direction of travel. They marked and secured the spot and proceeded upstream in Orin's wake, cutting sign for tracks or evidence. Another blitz team hastened up along the west side of Porcupine Creek and continued to trace its left or east fork. Sandy Bryson and her search dog had been working in the Tuolumne region and were drawn into the maneuvers by the search boss. The helicopter was able to execute only a very scattered series of passes over the drainage before it was forced back to base due to darkness.

Supplemental park search troops were recruited by radio and upon arrival at 9:30 P.M. were split into two teams. One headed west and the other east, cutting sign along the abandoned grade of the old Tioga Road passing near the campground in case Orin had strolled back downstream to the road or tentsites. Several concerned campers had volunteered to help and been asked to canvass everyone in the campground. Four hikers agreed they had definitely seen Orin traveling upstream beyond the point where the first witness had pinpointed Orin's PLS. Two old timers who had fished local waters for over forty years accurately evaluated the terrain for the planning team, highlighting track traps and the twists and secrets of the stream's course. A two-ranger vehicle patrol cruised the main highway on the off chance that Orin might intersect it.

The topography of Porcupine Creek readily lent itself to natural containment. A rock ridge running north and south to the east of the creek served as a logical search area boundary and barrier to Orin's movement, and the main road bordered the area on the south and west. A minor stream offered a boundary though not a barrier to the north. Confinement personnel could walk this watercourse and maintain a tight perimeter.

Since the hasty air and ground searches and the sweep searches along the creek had not been successful, Bob Johnson, the operations leader, decided at 11 P.M. to call all workers back to base to let the watershed cool down from searcher scents. All personnel were to be out by 3 A.M. The dog team was to advance upstream from the PLS shortly before dawn. Two other dog teams would be ferried in by helicopter and would follow suit.

Sandy Bryson relied upon a number of scent articles preserved specifically for her dog's use. As she and her dog progressed toward the headwaters in the early morning light, grid lines were scribed on a map for an intensive closed grid search and teams were composed and briefed. These Type III searchers were to be deployed right after the two new dog teams were ushered into the field. Confinement personnel hiked in to patrol the north boundary stream. The contract helicopter started flying a loose pattern above the entire search area.

At 7:35 A.M. Sandy and her dog Hobo found Orin. He was in good condition, very cheerful and talkative, and seemed little worse for wear. Everyone rallied around the campground to a huge, festive breakfast and the beginning of a good day, realizing that this was precisely how the whole process was supposed to work. Orin did not find the pine cones he had sought, but Johnson and company did find him.

A variety of changes in strategy and tactics had been implemented in the years since the Caldwell search. The now-entrenched concept of a firehouse response upon notification insured that the incident was to be treated as an emergency. Confinement, interviews, clue awareness, evidence preservation, and the invocation of *several* blitz teams all began simultaneously and continued through the night. Planning and interviewing kept pace to facilitate the more intense sweep and grid searches just getting underway when the boy was found. A few touches of luck — the coincidental presence of both a helicopter and a search dog team — eased the logistical and tactical burdens. The result was a classic execution of the basic principles of search management, enabling rapid recovery of the "ultimate clue" — Orin Sample, found alive and well just twelve hours after being reported missing.

Orin Sample reunited with his parents just after he was found. *Photo National Park Service*

BIBLIOGRAPHY

CHAPTER SEVEN

BRYSON, SANDY. *Search and Rescue Dog Training.* Pacific Grove, Ca.: The Boxwood Press, 1976.

DARTANNER, W.L., AND GORDON, B.E. "ELT Search," *Search and Rescue Magazine,* Fall 1976, pp. 13-16.

DORAN, JEFF. *The A.B.C.'s of Dogs in Search and Rescue.* La Jolla, Ca.: NASAR paper 77-1015, 1977.

FEAR, GENE. *Surviving the Unexpected — Curriculum Guide.* Tacoma, Wa.: Survival Education Association, 1978.

KEARNEY, JACK. "How to Teach Yourself Tracking Techniques," *Search and Rescue Magazine,* Fall 1975. pp. 5-9.

KEARNEY, JACK. "Teach Yourself Tracking, Part II," *Search and Rescue Magazine,* Fall 1975, pp. 11-18.

KELLEY, DENNIS. *Mountain Search for the Lost Victim.* Montrose, Ca.: pub. by author, 1973.

McCOY, LOIS. "Man Tracking," *Search and Rescue Magazine,* Summer 1975, pp. 20-26.

RESNIK, H.L.P., AND RUBEN, HARVEY L. EDS. *Emergency Psychiatric Care: The Management of Mental Health Crisis.* Bowie, Md.: Charles Press Publishing, 1975.

RENGSTORF, BILL, WARTES, JON. "The Use of String Lines for Subject Confinement, Search Area Segmentation, and Grid Sweep Control," *Search and Rescue Magazine,* Winter 1973, pp. 7-17.

SYROTUCK, WILLIAM. *Some Grid Search Techniques for Locating Lost Individuals in Wilderness Areas.* Westmoreland, N.Y.: Arner Publications, 1974.

SYROTUCK, WILLIAM. *Outline for Strategy and Tactics.* 1976. No further publisher's data.

WARTES, JON. *An Experimental Analysis of Grid Sweep Searching.* Woodinville, Wa.: Western Region Explorer Search and Rescue, 1974.

WARTES, JON. *An ESAR Information Unit,* Woodinville, Wa.: Western Region Explorer Search and Rescue, 1975.

WARTES, JON. *Explorer Search and Rescue Team Member and Team Training Manual.* Woodinville, Wa.: Western Region Explorer Search and Rescue, 1976.

WARTES, JON. *New Concepts in Sweep Searching: The Evidence Favoring Non-Thorough Methods.* 1975. No further publisher's data.

WARTES, JON. *The Taylor Mountain Evidence Search.* Woodinville, Wa.: Western Region Explorer Search and Rescue, 1975.

8 | Victim Evacuation and Mission Suspension and Critique

THE SEARCH IS now in full swing. Helicopters are flying, ground trackers are cutting sign, and dogs are working from the point last seen. Type I detection blitz teams have uncovered nothing substantial so the search boss has begun to implement Type II tactics and enlarge the base camp. A sudden burst of good news comes over the radio: an advance team has located the lost boy in a newly added segment of the search area, on prominent cliffs above a river gorge. However, the boy is immobile on a narrow ledge with a compound fracture of the lower leg. The reporting pair of rescuers has requested that a technical rock team equipped with a field medical kit assist in the rescue, and has recommended evacuation with a Stokes litter.

Evacuation

Hopefully rescue and evacuation plans have already been germinated. Consequently the boss selects one of the hypothetical options only briefly considered up to this point, and sets it into motion to initiate the next phase of the mission. If contingency strategies have not been outlined then the management is not planning far enough ahead. An evacuation plan must be developed as soon as rescuers are committed to the field.

Most well-organized SAR teams have members who are multi-qualified and perform technical mountaineering, whitewater, cave, surf, or whatever type of rescue is called for by the situation. Both the team and its individual members solicit advanced and broad training because

Presidential Range evacuation. *Photo George Bellerose*

it is exciting and simply part of the job. The onus is on the mission manager to be certain the necessary skillholders are participating in the search or are on standby alert, have access to requisite equipment, and can be instantly transferred and transported from a grid search role to a rescue operation. The field technique for reaching and evacuating victims in unusual environments forms the last part of this book. The administrative and strategic concerns of the team or mission manager are presented here.

The means of reaching and evacuating a subject fall into five broad categories:

1. Hiking in to or traversing or making a Tyrolean over to him,
2. Climbing or skiing down to him,
3. Going up to the subject in some fashion,
4. Operating from the air over the victim, or
5. Combining any of the above, and in special situations, caving, kayaking, tunneling and so on.

Experience and preplanning are invaluable guides to unraveling transportation alternatives. During the evaluation process be certain to consider questions like the following.

1. How long will it take to walk or fly or roller skate to the scene?
2. What kind of resources and equipment are available, and how many skilled and unskilled personnel are needed to carry them?
3. How many people will plan A require, versus a plan B that requires more time to orchestrate but is less labor intensive?
4. How quickly does the victim need to be extricated from his or her predicament?
5. How far is it to the scene via different routes? How fast can each be traveled under the present conditions?
6. Can the searchers continue effectively through the night, or should they retire until dawn?
7. What if the weather closes in and the helicopter cannot fly?
8. Should plans A and B be put into effect simultaneously?

The list is endless, or so it seems in the heat of action. The brief compilation here only underscores the importance of conception of an evacuation and rescue plan at an early point in the operation. The plan is formulated around the best information available with regard to the condition of the subject. The victim will be: 1) alive and well and cooperative, 2) alive and not critically injured but in need of first and second aid, 3) critically injured, 4) found dead, or 5) or not easily reachable or removable in one of the above conditions. How would each of these situations be managed? Try to canvass the options of rescue and evacuation in the very initial stages of an operation, in the midst of decisions about dog teams and ground searchers. A rough survey will highlight obvious tactical impossibilities and further focus the entire event, allowing rapid response to any situation that develops.

Suspension of the Search

Not all searches are successful. At the other end of the spectrum of final stages of a search from evacuation is the decision to halt the operation. When does the manager resolve the operational crisis by calling home all the field teams?

The act of suspension is simple — a short message is broadcast over the radio net. But the process of arriving at that verdict is one of the hardest and most important decisions the search manager will ever make. There is always a nagging doubt that the victim might have fallen and been hurt, and cannot respond to or see the field crews. While this scenario is not very likely, it occurs frequently enough to remain a possibility that plagues rescue team members, especially those with the power to continue or suspend the mission.

The decision to terminate a search is centered around two questions: Is the victim dead or alive, and is the search area the correct one? The answers to these questions are obviously not absolute. By methodically considering the various elements of the search and its circumstances, the search boss can attempt to rationally resolve the dilemma.

1. Is there any evidence that the subject is not in the search area (i.e., the Pa) because he or she is a runaway, emotionally unstable, or suicidal? Has the possibility of a misunderstanding between the "lost" person and the reporting party been thoroughly explored?

2. How effectively has the area been searched (i.e., what is the Pd)? Was the search plan executed in an organized manner with a high degree of accuracy and consistency? What probability of detection was achieved? Would another overflight or grid search be appropriate, or would it be of marginal utility? Remember that effectiveness should not be measured in the number of days the search has consumed.

3. How low is the probability that the subject is still alive? The U.S. Coast Guard's data, for example, have shown that people have repeatedly survived far longer than was thought possible. A general rule

of thumb for predicting survival is to multiply the time frame felt realistic for survival of a particular person in specific conditions times *three*. Search theorists have produced a body of data that greatly enhances the manager's ability to make such predictions. Tables of time frames for survival based on case histories of hypothermia, windchill, dehydration, water immersion, and so on are available in works like Kelley's *Mountain Search for the Lost Victim* and Fear's *Surviving the Unexpected Wilderness Emergency*.

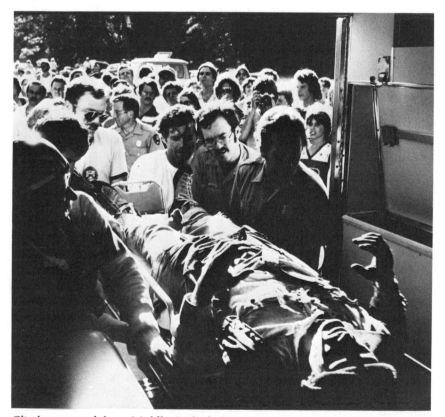

Climber rescued from Middle Cathedral Rock, Yosemite. *Photo Tim Setnicka*

4. Do the hazards of the search terrain, weather, and other environmental factors endangering searchers warrant termination? Mental or physical fatigue can introduce the same sorts of dangers to rescuers. If

worker jeopardy is the result of fatigue, should fresh teams be called in?

5. Are there unresolved clues — a shirt, a partial track, a fingerprint — which will soon be identified? What effect will they have on the search? Are they worth waiting for?

6. Is political, family, or media influence exerting counterpressure to continue the search even though other factors encourage termination? A situation of this sort is very difficult to manage rationally.

7. Have resources been depleted or diverted to other areas, thereby decreasing field effectiveness? Should other resources be sought elsewhere, despite the time and expense involved?

8. Have environmental factors drastically reduced the field effectiveness of resources? Should teams continue to battle the elements, or wait, or be withdrawn?

9. Has economics entered into the decision to terminate the operation? The U.S. Coast Guard places the value of human life at $250,000; should the local organization do the same?

10. Are there any other more intuitive reasons — gut feelings, bad karma, organizational pressure — that encourage termination? Factors in this final category are perhaps hardest of all to justify and articulate to those pressing for continuation of the mission.

The decision to suspend a mission obviously involves a combination of these factors. It is possible to use a Mattson-like approach and perform a weighting of factors by each participant, but it would be awkward to tell a father, "Well, we all got together and voted and we're going home tomorrow." A markedly factual, reasoned evaluation eases the difficulties. Group consensus can be tallied with the use of the format shown in table 11.

Table 11

Determination of Group Consensus on Search Termination

Factors	For	Against	Rank	Decision
Survivability	____	____	____	____
Pa	____	____	____	____
Pd	____	____	____	____
(List others)	____	____	____	____
	____	____	____	____

A third, middle-of-the-road option is available however. In between the choices of continuation with a full-scale operation and complete termination is the option of a *limited continuous search*. A compromise of this sort assuages the search boss's feelings of guilt about an unfulfilled responsibility and a failed mission, and accedes to emotional pleas by the parents to continue. With an ongoing, low-level search the *mission* can be suspended but not the *search*. The case remains open. If any additional clues are found, the manager is in much better posture to take action than if he had totally ceased the operation.

Limited continuous search technique includes overflights, patrols into the search area by trained personnel, distribution of signs and posters to anyone entering the area and acting in effect as an untrained searcher, training sessions held there, and invitations to other groups to train with the local team in the search area. If the option of a limited continuous search is chosen, the search boss must suspend the mission and debrief for a final time all involved in the operation. Full plans for the new limited search must be developed and implemented while demobilization takes place.

Demobilization

The search is over. Successful or curtailed due to extenuating circumstances, the operation must suddenly cease and desist. The process of releasing resources and equipment after a search is finished is *not* the mirror image of the way they were mobilized (Fig. 8.1). Information on the places of origin, methods of travel, travel times, and so on of all resources should have been collected upon their arrival at the search base. Relying on this information, the plans personnel should have drawn up a formal demobilization plan before the end of the first day. As an operation intensifies, the plan is edited and amended as necessary.

A written demobilization plan should be required on any large search, a function of the plans and support crew. Orchestrating demobilization takes teamwork due to the complex nature of providing a small army with food, shelter, and transportation home. Staffing for the function varies as required: a few coordinators on the first day of a search working part time, and a large percentage of the planning and operations teams on the last day. A solid demobilization plan is decidedly cost effective for it helps cluster scheduling and logistical needs. When long travel times are anticipated, try to keep everyone busy in base camp rather than milling around or heading off on his own until logistical priorities and transportation have been arranged and confirmed. Everyone is assured of a safe trip home in this way.

The demobilization plan details responsibilities for plan initiation, establishes a chain of command for moving resources from one point to any other, and specifies who delivers which services during this process. Resource release priorities must be in accordance with each agency's procedures, and should correlate with the needs of the plans chief and the search boss. Inclusion of these limitations and procedures in the demobilization plan lessens the potential for conflicts of interest. Late-night release or travel is to be avoided if possible.

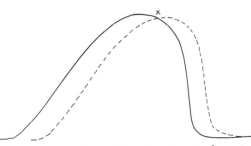

Fig. 8.1 Demobilization curve. Demobilization is not the mirror image of mobilization. Mission suspension point is marked.

The purpose of addressing demobilization in a coordinated, detail-conscious fashion is to guarantee a smooth check-out and release phase. Usually, a large number of tired searchers anxious to return home are released within a short period of time. A demobilization plan helps get everyone on the correct bus or airplane or in a carpool with a minimum of frustration and elapsed time.

Postmission

Well after the demobilization plan has terminated the operation and the troops have left the area, the postmission duties are addressed. The only field activity at this point might be a continuous limited search, if that option has been selected. The *postmission* requirements fall into two categories: a review, and a critique of the operation.

The agency or group in charge *reviews* the inner workings of the mission, successful or not, from start to finish. This assessment begins with a determination of why or how the search incident occurred, and how it might have been prevented or limited in seriousness. It continues by focusing on the initial stages of response to the event, the tactics and strategy effected, and the efficiency of the entire project. The idea is to study the history of the event, and illuminate which aspects went smoothly and which provided problems of a temporary or continuing nature.

All information should be compiled into one file during the postmission evaluation process. A format for discussion and documentation of the event is settled upon by the search managers. A somewhat random cross-section of participants in the mission other than those normally required to be in attendance — agency heads, pilots, search team members from other regions, dog handlers — is assembled. All attendants are issued a mission report or the equivalent. The report should have been submitted to each member of the critique board (if the preplan calls for use of such a board) far enough in advance to allow him or her time to read the paper and isolate questions to be raised. A chairman is appointed and charged with presiding over the meeting. The entire search plan and resultant actions are examined, starting with the preplan and moving on to organization, strategy, tactics, equipment, and special problems. The investigation should query in depth, to identify policy or practice in need of revision.

In the wake of the review comes the second part of postmission activities — a *critique* of the event. Sound out the assembled rank-and-file for diverse opinions and perspectives not always present in a local group's managerial meeting. Was all evidence and information properly identified, separated, investigated, and correlated? Could timing and coordination have been improved? A form and checklist for the review and critique, compiled from critiques of previous field events, may speed progress and encourage complete coverage of pertinent topics. Improvements rather than faults should be the watchword of the meeting, to promote an atmosphere of open, positive information exchange.

A final mission report with attached criticism and recommendations is the goal of the postmission inquiry. Press releases should be written and sent to appropriate media representatives. Optimally these statements explain the causes of the incident, give adequate credit to all involved units, and emphasize preventative safety messages without becoming overbearing. Prompt letters of appreciation to individuals and units are warranted and will further ties among members of the SAR community. The last postmission task is to implement the recommendations and changes in the preplan and equipment. Tomorrow or the next day the whole process will begin all over again. . . .

Of all the steps in the cycle of SAR work, this final critical analysis is the one most often casually performed or ignored entirely. There are an infinite number of reasons why this happens. Experience has shown that a considerable quantity of valuable information is lost as a result of incomplete critiques. New ideas mean new methods. Without the ideas, born of poor judgment in the field or sudden insight, the state of the art will stagnate.

Remember to keep critique sessions democratic and nondestructive. *Everyone*, regardless of real or imagined status, has something to offer. Write down each speculation, idea, or theory. What seems implausible today might be the key element of an innovative reorganization in a week or a month.

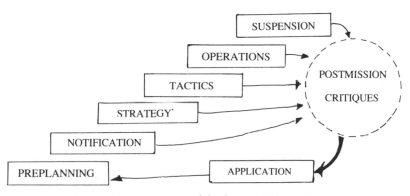

Fig. 8.2 Synergistic model of postmission critique.

The performance of the team should be compared against the ideal, no matter how fleeting and imaginary that goal appears. Questions that do not challenge traditional performance criteria need to be raised nonetheless: Was it dangerous? Were the risks worthwhile? Were certain actions too slow or too fast?

Critiques allow the team to throw an idea into a synergetic model of evaluation (Fig. 8.2) that digests, dissects, examines, rejects, rebuilds, or adds onto the seed. The final product of a thorough, open-ended critique that encourages the free flow of ideas is often spectacular. Use all available evaluative tools to investigate the full SAR cycle in order to reach, treat, and evacuate people in need faster and safer.

The value of a hard-nosed inquiry into the mechanics of a SAR event is demonstrated by the story of a rescue that took place a few years ago. It happened during one of those midwinter periods of warm weather not uncommon in the Sierra. Six local Yosemite hikers climbed Half Dome (2700 meters) via the popular eleven-kilometer trail to the summit. They intended to spend the night there with minimal gear of poor quality. The weather prediction was favorable. Unfortunately the day went sour and winter rapidly returned in the form of a turbulent snowstorm. As they had no ropes along, the summit campers could not make their way down the 300-meter slab of slick granite leading off the crest.

On the morning of the following day, when some of the party did not arrive at work, they were reported overdue. The initial report took a few hours to reach the search and rescue office as it was not considered threatening — six hikers equipped to spend the night were late in returning. The SAR crew was confident that they had been slowed down by the poor weather but would reappear shortly. Our confidence in this hypothetical scenario was so complete that we did not even send someone down the road to study the cap of Half Dome with binoculars. This would have been easily accomplished from the driver's seat of a car. Further supporting our scenario was the fact that the weather was clearing again. However the six never arrived that day.

The snow began to fall once again. Upon training a powerful telescope on the summit, an observer immediately noticed a signal for help. The weather was further deteriorating. The team manager decided to call the closest naval air station to secure the assistance of a military helicopter. By the time it landed in Yosemite Valley some two hours later, it was impossible to locate the huge mass of Half Dome through the cloud and snow.

The rescue effort quickly assumed the form of a major ground operation. By its later stages about forty-five field personnel fought through fresh knee-deep powder on snowshoes up a trail considered a pleasant stroll in normal conditions. Base camps were established at regular intervals up the trail to act as staging grounds for movement of large stocks of equipment and supplies ferried in expedition style. Rather suddenly, just as the ground teams approached the summit slabs, the storm cleared momentarily, allowing the helicopter to evacuate the trapped campers.

All were cold but not suffering from any major discomfort or injuries.

The mistakes made in our response to this situation became painfully clear during the critique held after the mission. The initial report was received by only one park employee, who did not pass on the information to all SAR unit members. As a result, no commitments or plans were synthesized for the next day. The situation was not adequately assessed and not considered from a *worst possible case* perspective. The ensuing delays caused the victims to spend an extra night out in the storm; they could have been reached the first day with a calculated response. No functional callout lists were on hand, and chaos reigned supreme at the rescue cache with forty-five rescuers all trying to ready gear and stay dry at the same time. No team leaders had been assigned to the first parties into the field, precipitating an immediate problem when some members became separated and turned back due to insufficient physical conditioning. Not much thought was given to avalanche danger even though all workers had to cross slopes of high risk. Virtually every headlamp failed because the batteries were not the alkaline ones best suited to cold weather use. The list continued on and on.

The outgrowth of this embarrassing episode was evolution in unit preplanning and organization. A porch was built onto the cache so equipment could be issued in an orderly fashion by a quartermaster and rescuers could stay out of the elements. A more flexible callout method was developed and introduced. The SAR preplan was revised such that certain key staff were always notified of situations as they were reported, rather than leaving all decisions about proper response to one or two individuals in the dispatch and SAR offices. Alternative rescue routes were charted and a SAR photograph file begun for use in planning. Personal skills of all staff were noted in a manpower inventory along with each person's availability, to help minimize the physical effort and expertise required of the initial rescue team. And now operation and team leaders were to be the first workers chosen for any mission, regardless of size, to cure the leadership vacuum in the first stages of a field action.

This one critique drastically altered the theory and practice of search and rescue in Yosemite. Unfortunately it took a fiasco to stimulate change and an awareness of limitations, but the negative feedback generated by the ineffectiveness of the operation was converted into unit maturation.

Ethan Allen Crawford carrying an exhausted woman off of Mt. Washington, New Hampshire in the 1830s. From *Lucy Crawford's History of the White Mountains.*

BIBLIOGRAPHY

CHAPTER EIGHT

FEAR, GENE, AND LAVALLA, RICK. *PSAR Preventative Search and Rescue.* La Jolla, Ca.: NASAR paper 77-1017, 1977.

FEAR, GENE. *Survival/Disaster and Basic Outdoor Comfort Graphics.* Tacoma, Wa.: Survival Education Association, 1978.

FEAR, GENE. *Surviving the Unexpected — Curriculum Guide.* Tacoma, Wa.: Survival Education Association, 1974.

KELLEY, DENNIS. *The 250,000 Message.* La Jolla, Ca.: NASAR paper 76-108, 1976.

LAVALLA, RICK, ed. *Resource Guide for Search and Rescue Training Materials.* Tacoma, Wa.: Survival Education Association, 1978.

LAVALLA, RICK, AND WADE, BILL. *A Model for SAR Management.* La Jolla, Ca.: NASAR paper 76-112, 1976.

PATTERSON, CRAIG. *Mountain Wilderness Survival.* Berkeley, Ca.: And/Or Press, Inc., 1979.

9 | Administrative Considerations

Documentation

ACCURATE DOCUMENTATION of all aspects of a search effort in a retrievable form is essential and may prove a godsend if legal complications arise. Some governing agencies specify their data uses and requirements in agency forms and manuals. In general, though, the SAR office can never collect too much information about an operation, assuming adequate staff time to correlate and file data during and after the action. While cartons of papers can always be discarded, it is almost impossible to generate accurate records after the fact.

In some circumstances legal requirements dictate that records be kept during any search. Depending on the outcome of the search, the SAR management may end up in court defending its actions. An extreme example of the importance of documentation is a death in the field of a victim or rescuer. All of a sudden the times, dates, and places of events and exact actions and reasoning of all personnel become of paramount significance, regardless of the absence of criminal intent.

Any investigative process is furthered by diligent recording of information. At first notification someone no doubt started writing down who is reporting what, at what time, and to whom. If not, he or she had better start soon! An explicitly named recorder is essential. As the interview and interrogation phase unfolds, information is recorded so that the incipient search can be gracefully parlayed into a full-scale operation or a limited action with different tactics.

Rescuing controlled substances from airplane crash in High Sierra. *Photo L. Lefkowitz*

The taxing decision to terminate a search is made more efficiently and wisely if sufficient data illustrating every activity for the duration of the event have been collected. These records facilitate an exhaustive critique — which tactics progressed smoothly, which fared poorly and why. The road to field action improvement passes through thorough documentation of all critique suggestions and findings and on to revision of the preplan.

Documentation is a continuous process. A *chronological log* of all events entered as they occur is the foundation of SAR record keeping, and is usually kept by the dispatcher or someone assigned data recording as a primary duty. Team briefing and debriefing reports and all tactical maps drawn during the operation, especially the master map, should be saved along with all incoming communications data (e.g., weather changes). The mission log should reflect major decisions and tactical changes, and include when and where they were made and by whom.

The *final mission report* is composed in part of all these documents. A narrative of the entire operation provides the main structure of the report and is built upon the details of the mission log, indicating the resources used and their cost, compensation (if any was paid) and the total number and type of hours expended during the exercise. The critique record should present any media coverage or articles as well as recommendations that surfaced, and it should be filed as part of the final report. Copies of the report may be shared with participating or interested groups and agencies. Lastly, the preplan is amended as necessary and follow-up preventative measures are carried out — warnings are issued, signs placed or changed, newspaper articles written, additional training organized, and so on.

Aside from local team organizational needs, there are broader interests served by accurate reportage of SAR incidents. Cumulative data are the fundamental grist for analytic tools. How much money is spent on search and rescue annually in the state or the nation? How many SAR missions are undertaken per annum? What is the average victim profile for a certain activity? How can educational efforts reach and affect these potential victims and prevent accidents? When someone does become lost or injured, what does he or she do, where does he go, and where can he be found?

NASAR formed a group to address these questions. Air Force SAR instructor and theorist Bob Mattson chaired a committee for the development and design of a SAR data collection system. Along with

Jon Gunson of the Summit County, Colorado SAR unit; Stan Bush, president of the Colorado Search and Rescue Board; and other experienced professionals, Mattson developed a *standardized SAR event form* applicable to local, state, and national levels to secure a data base. Dennis Kelley, Jon Wartes, and Jean and Bill Syrotuck's works arose in part from this information and proved the value of data collection. Still, a more universal approach was needed. Some three-and-a-half years and five revised drafts later, the best possible form for the production of data for all levels of use emerged.

The form is a two-sided, one-page, multiple choice questionnaire easily completed in fifteen minutes. A SAR team can either adopt it without change or include it as an addendum and complement to local requirements. NASAR, the Mountain Rescue Association, and federal land management agencies are adopting this form to encourage interchangeability of data and to limit the paperwork burden on the reporting unit. NASAR is coordinating the project; interested parties are encouraged to contact it for more precise information and copies of the most current form. National and state data bases are becoming established and their information and spin-off studies will be helping field search managers relatively soon.

Investigation of Death or Serious Injury

Investigation of serious injuries and accidental death is one of the least enjoyable but most important aspects of SAR. As is the case with most investigative work, the investigator is presented with a set of circumstances for which he must find a cause or explanation. The detailed study of the event and evidence is the legal responsibility of trained public officials — coroners, medical examiners, or law enforcement officers, depending on the location and nature of the mishap. Most states require a coroner's investigation of all accidental deaths and deaths not attended by a physician.

A thorough inquest fulfills the legal requirements of the state and the moral obligations to family and friends, and from a SAR standpoint, perhaps provides answers to questions about safety and prevention. The exact details of the death inquiry process vary widely from state to state and county to county. There are, however, some important guidelines for SAR team members as well as anyone else investigating a death or significant injury.

The first responsibility of someone arriving on the scene of an accident is to decide if the person is, in fact, dead or critically hurt. This most often means the victim must be touched or moved. Go ahead! The concept of not touching anyone or altering the accident scene does not apply until someone decides the victim is actually dead; only then does one back off and avoid disturbing the surroundings. Remember, only certain officials and doctors can legally pronounce someone dead; hence first aid measures are continued all the way to the hospital. But in remote situations SAR actions are governed by a decision that the victim is dead or alive. It involves making a crucial unofficial determination, like it or not.

Investigation of a climbing fatality from cut rope during free jumar. *Photo Kenneth Andrasko*

If the injured party is alive, do whatever is necessary to stabilize and evacuate him. During this process, try to notice any evidence from or clues to the accident. If anything is in danger of being lost, destroyed, or moved, note this and preserve the information by writing it down and photographing the objects before recovering them.

As soon as the victim is removed or officially pronounced dead, secure the area surrounding the incident and body. Establish physical barriers by placing a rope or string around the scene or by posting guards to insure that the curious or the official do not casually wander in and out of this location. If any item within the area is threatened by wind or movement, capture it at any cost even if this means picking it up and bagging it. First, write down whatever was observed and where, and take especial pains to record any disturbances, intentional or not, the SAR team members might have caused to the scene. Failure to report this could lead to nasty accusations of destroying evidence and acting beyond one's authority. If alone, stay at the scene until a passerby can be sent for the authorities.

State laws concerning who does the official investigation vary, although generally a coroner, deputy coroner, or medical examiner is charged with this work. In some states medical investigation takes precedence over criminal investigation and the medical examiner is in total command of the site; the body can be moved only at his word. Often SAR personnel are required to assist his investigation under his direction.

To prepare for the medical examiner, if there is time, sit down and record all observations and actions prior to his arrival. Usually someone in your group will be required to make a statement, so be ready to offer one as accurate and detailed as possible. If the entire scene is in danger of disappearing, say during a snowstorm or flash flood, meticulously photograph and sketch the relationship of objects with the body and collect everything possible. If a radio is in use, contact the proper authorities to notify them of the situation and ask for advice on how to proceed.

Unless directed to do so, do not search an obviously deceased person for identification. It really does not matter if the body found is the one being sought, as all must be processed in the same manner. Generally clues like clothing, sex, hair color, overall condition of the body, and so on indicate whether or not it is the reported victim. If you do find a wallet or piece of positive identification, think twice about mentioning specifics like names over the radio system. Notification of next of kin must take place before the general public and news media are alerted. The identification must be cross-checked and rechecked until it is positive and unqualified. Many folks monitor rescue and police frequencies and any number of people listen to radios within your own network. Imagine the anguish caused by incorrect reporting of the death of a child, or by hearing of your own child's death via the local radio news broadcast. Both examples actually occurred.

The topic of sensitivity culminates in the painful act of making *the* telephone call, or worse, knocking at someone's door. Telling a parent that someone he or she created and watched grow and develop or is intimately involved with is dead touches the very deepest human emotions. Reactions to this news are almost always unpredictable. Try to plan for the worst possible emergencies, whether medical or emotional, and rehearse your actions. Be as sensitive and supportive as possible.

Often the plan suddenly changes though. My boss and I once headed over to a campsite to tell a large family that the oldest boy had just drowned. It was his job to inform them, and we discussed what would be said. As we pulled up, the anxious parents ran over to my side of the car and the mother swung open the door just as I started to get out and gasped, "He's dead, isn't he!" All I could do was to put my arms around her and nod my head. She immediately collapsed but did not faint before I could explain the circumstances or say anything at all. Have a plan, but do not expect it to work: be prepared for the unimaginable.

If notification must be made over the telephone, one way of helping to insure a disaster does not compound itself is to call the local police department. Request that an officer go over to the house and simply inform those involved that a serious accident has occurred and that they will be receiving a telephone call from you. The police should be asked to stand by while the call is put through and the incident explained. A better technique is to have the local police check around with neighbors to see if a clergyman, relative, or close friend is available to be with the family. Inquire if the person being contacted has any known medical problems that might suddenly erupt and plan for this contingency. These complications dictate that identification and death be firmly established before notification is considered.

A great many states require an autopsy — a medical examination to determine the exact biological cause of death — for any unattended death regardless of circumstances. At the coroner's or medical examiner's word, the body is removed to the local morgue.

During the coroner's official investigation, every clue is photographed and eventually seized and held either as evidence or impounded property. Schematic and representational drawings are made and witnesses interviewed and often reinterviewed. The procedure follows common practice for criminal investigation, using professionals to seek and analyze clues and evidence laypersons might miss.

An intensive investigation of a climbing accident occurred in the spring of 1978 in Yosemite National Park that exemplifies the potential complexity of this process. A park visitor had walked up to the base of El Capitan to photograph some climbers doing a classic route known as the Nose. One of the groups of climbers he was photographing was about 300 meters directly above him on the face. The photographer alternated between taking photos of this team and a second one lower down and to the west on the same wall. As he peered up through his telephoto lens at the higher group, he suddenly found it impossible to focus. In an instant he realized why — all three climbers were falling.

Before he could take two steps backward, the three climbers and their equipment hit the ground about ten meters away from him. All were killed upon impact. What in the world happened? How could three climbers fall to their death simultaneously? A cut rope? A belay anchor failure? Equipment malfunction or failure?

The subsequent investigation was one of the most complete and extensive in Yosemite's history. It was directed by Chris Andress and John Dill, both park rangers with complementary technical training: Chris is a seasoned criminal and death investigator, and John an experienced technical climber and ex-physicist with a keen eye for analysis. Over 400 hours of work went into the initial report, and follow-up studies continue today.

The first NPS employees on the scene, Dick Martin and Jim Lee, identified and retained witnesses while they examined the climbers. It was painfully apparent all three were dead. The area was roped off and left untouched until the primary investigators (Chris and John) arrived at the scene. The incident took on an even more ominous air when a hefty rattlesnake crawled out from underneath some brush onto the bodies, refused to leave, and had to be removed.

Photographs were taken of all evidence as found ("in situ") from a variety of vantage points so that months later the position of the clues and bodies could be readily reexamined. A new clue or bit of evidence might turn up and redirect the investigation, especially in cases of apparent suicides or accidental deaths. In unwitnessed events, the coroner's report or other information could transform proceedings into a homicide investigation.

Upon obtaining an exhaustive photographic record, rescuers made sketches complete with precise measurements between and descriptions of items impounded, capturing the image of the total scene.

Then all equipment and all film taken at the scene were seized and held as evidence or impounded property; eventually everything was turned over to the owners or next of kin. Items found on the talus at the base of El Cap included a partially opened pocketknife, a perlon sling, three broken and stressed carabiners, a roll of film from one of the victim's cameras, and most importantly half of a broken bolt hanger. The climbers' harnesses were examined, photographed, cut off of the bodies, and held in evidence. A thorough Type III grid search of the immediate area was conducted for stray clues. After the bodies were removed by three litter teams, a final search for clues concentrated in the area where they had come to rest.

Examining gear to document and recreate the accident. *Photo Kenneth Andrasko*

As the investigation of the scene continued, three rangers began taking witness statements. "Cooperating individuals" who knew the climbers, their plans, or other related information about the incident also made statements. A climbing friend of the three made the positive identification at the morgue, as all three victims were from out of state. Over two dozen people were interviewed and reinterviewed over the next week.

The preliminary results of the investigation led to a chilling reconstruction of probable events precipitating the tragedy. The climbers were rappelling off the climb after a three-day attempt on the wall; all three were found with their rappel harnesses on and intact. No one had rappelled off the end of the rope. Their rappel ropes were still hanging high above the bodies and statements of witnesses confirmed that they were descending when the incident occurred. All climbing iron was put away in the haul bag and all three water bottles were empty. Thus the broken bolt hanger was the key. Something had gone wrong at the rappel station.

The partially exposed roll of film retrieved from the climbers' camera was developed and showed them rappelling down to the station from which all fell moments later.

Eventually a model of the station was constructed from the evidence. It looked bombproof and consisted of two 9x50mm (⅜x2'') bolts, one placed directly above the other. A bolt hanger was screwed onto each bolt. The hangers were linked together with heavy chain, and a large chain link to run the rappel ropes through was crimped to the bottom hanger. The configuration of the equipment suggested that no one had rappelled off the end of the rope, so apparently one or two of them were standing in slings clipped directly to the top bolt hanger. The haul bags and remaining climber or two were connected to the station by a nylon sling wrapped *around* the chain between the two bolt hangers. No one was directly connected to the bottom hanger, probably because they wanted to keep the large chain link clear in order to facilitate pulling their rappel ropes through it.

For reasons still not clear, the top bolt hanger was fatigued even though it was relatively new and had been on the wall less than a year. Once this weakened upper hanger broke, everyone was completely detached from the wall. The hanger may have failed from the combined weight of the climbers and haul bag, although it held long enough for the third climber to add his weight to the anchor and completely unclip his rappel rig from the ropes. If they had been secured to both hangers, they might have had a second chance.

Additional evidence, however, suggests that the anchors may have been shock-loaded before breaking. The knife found on the ground with the blade partially open plus close examination of a cut (not smashed) nylon sling strongly imply that a sling holding one or both haul bags had to be cut due to entanglement. Hence the bags may have fallen suddenly and loaded the system. The haul line for the bags was found tightly wrapped around one of the climber's boots marred by rope burns, suggesting the possibility. It is unlikely the haul rope would have made the burns while everything was falling together. A loop of the haul rope probably caught the boot as the bags were cut free.

The anchors were photographed a day later from a distance of about six meters. Because the bolts are not on any route, six days passed before climbers rappelled from the top of El Capitan and removed and replaced the faulty station. Why did the relatively new hanger break?

During the next week a climber and consulting metallurgical engineer called and offered his services, a stroke of luck to say the least. He was given all the bolts and hangers and examined them with an electron microscope. A comparison test was made on a computer-simulated model of the hanger. The tests confirmed our provisional theory that the hanger had been cracked and weakened prior to total failure. The hairline cracks were probably next to the rock and not noticeable. The analysis showed that the hanger, with probably less than twenty rappels off of it, could have broken with as little downward force as 230 kilograms, roughly the weight of three climbers and their gear.

The details of this puzzling bolt hanger failure are still being investigated. The theory that most satisfactorily explains the failure is centered around a phenomenon known to metallurgists as *post-plating* or *hydrogen embrittlement.* Steel and other alloys above a certain critical hardness for each metal may fail under uncharacteristically low loads (stress) due to the brittleness introduced by the hardening procedure or by hydrogen atoms in the environment. When metals are plated to protect against corrosion, they are dipped in an acid bath to clean the surface and assure adequate bonding of the plating alloy. If all of the acid is not removed after the bath by proper and sustained baking, it may tend to introduce significant numbers of hydrogen atoms into the alloy. Hydrogen embrittlement in a bolt hanger is furthered by environmental factors like localized stress and cracking due to pounding during or improper placement. (This process and bolt problems in general are discussed more fully in the section on bolts in Chapter 15, Anchor Points).

Fortunately, the problem has been brought to light and a number of concerned climbers and manufacturers are working on it. A solution is feasible since there are alloys (although more expensive) that are not subject to this phenomenon, and the elimination of the plating process largely prevents hydrogen contamination. Careful controls on the part of manufacturers and awareness by climbers and SAR personnel can combine to remove questionable equipment from the market and the cliffs, promote research, and encourage proper use. This problem was, in part, illuminated by the solid investigative technique applied immediately, which not only preserved evidence before the investigators even knew anything about embrittlement and its implications, but also encouraged the interest of consultants around the country. They, in turn, assisted by volunteering their time, energy, and expertise to study the problem and propose solutions.

One outcome of this triple death was the issuance of warnings to the Yosemite climbing community that problems had arisen with bolt hangers, and that they should not rely on fixed bolts without backups if at all possible. Numerous letters to the editors of and articles for climbing magazines were generated that underscored the problem and spurred discussion and bolt replacement programs in climbing areas all over the country. SAR teams have a responsibility to seek the cause of accidents and take steps toward their prevention whenever possible. Public education programs and efforts to collect and return broken and possibly defective gear to manufacturers are two means toward this end. The relatively high incidence of failed bolt hangers, most of one design, reported in the space of a year or so has led to elimination of the plating process, a positive response on the part of manufacturers. No doubt other detailed investigations will uncover equally profound insights into the methods and equipment of climbers.

Relations with Victim Relatives and Friends

One of the more delicate challenges of SAR team leaders is liaison with the friends and relatives of the lost subject. Great reserves of emotional sensitivity and political acumen are required of the team member who undertakes this task. Assign one person with a gift for crisis management to this responsibility regardless of whether or not those concerned are present at the search base. Ideally good personal rapport between the liaison and the worried parties can be nurtured so that they will have an acquaintance to call with questions rather than a random telephone number. The family liaison must be someone who actively desires the job and does not want to be doing something else more glamorous. If the liaison rushes off with a new grid team, problems will arise.

Should family or friends arrive at the search base, it is imperative that all searchers be made aware of their presence. Otherwise the potential exists for a devastating casual radio or camp conversation overheard by a visitor. If they insist on remaining at base camp for an extended period, give them something to do. Do not let them wander aimlessly. The father of a missing hiker in one search was put to work stuffing and sealing envelopes containing flyers about his son; he kept occupied and greatly aided the project. Likewise, companions of an injured or lost hiker can be mobilized to collect firewood or clear snags from an evacuation route along with several compassionate crew members to move them away from the scene somewhat and distract their attention. Explain to them the intricacies of field work. Relatives are especially helpful if present to boost morale on both sides when a search team drags in from a hard day's work. Avoid raising expectations, but mask overly negative assessments too. Try to fabricate a realistic impression of the obstacles the crews and subject are encountering. The Yosemite team has loaded a relative into a helicopter and flown her over the search area on a few occasions to provide a firsthand look at the complicated terrain. This can be a very persuasive experience for a person not attuned to the rigors of backcountry travel.

If family members must face press conferences, assist them in preparing a statement or relaxing before the encounter. In short, offer wide-ranging support in the form of honest, accurate information and encouragement any time difficulties arise. The wishes of loved ones should be respected even though at times they may seem harsh, uneducated, emotional, or impatient.

Media Relations

Liaison with media representatives encompasses many of the delicacies of managing victim friends and relatives. Again, the responsibility should fall on one talented individual attentive to the sensitivity of the job. Someone with a working knowledge of law, agency procedures, interpersonal skills, and search principles and technique is a perfect candidate. Prior experience interacting with print and broadcast journalists is an asset, as they can be alternately helpful and hostile. The media determine the public's perspective on this particular event and on SAR teams in general, so artful cultivation of professional relations with them is mandatory.

Only the press liaison officer distributes press releases and information about the incident. No one else offers statements, observations, or holds interviews without direct clearance from the overall search manager. Tight regulation of press relations insures diplomatic and accurate information dissemination; a field worker may not yet know that the subject is the daughter of the Mexican or Haitian consul. It may be advantageous to include the press liaison in briefing and debriefing sessions, and to have press releases written and ready for distribution when the phone calls and press arrivals commence. Be honest and skirt speculation on facts or figures. By having an idea ahead of time what an interviewer would like to know, the liaison can solicit additional information or obtain clearance on the release of facts or documents by discussing the answers with the appropriate officials. Constant invocation of answers like, "We do not have any information about that at this time" and "I am not at liberty to disclose . . ." does not foster ties with the press, even though these may be honest replies. The liaison has to do his homework and be prepared.

A positive relationship with the press may prove advantageous to the search in one way or another. Attention drawn to the event may reach someone with valuable information that could change the direction of the mission or even curtail it. One search in the Sierra, mentioned earlier, was terminated after almost two solid weeks of intensive effort when a friend of the subject noticed the search news in the papers, discovered her friend was the man sought, and called the SAR office to say she had just received a postcard from the missing party posted in Bangor, Maine! Favorable coverage promotes safety messages, attracts donations and potential SAR personnel, and may generate resources not previously considered. Some positive effect on the annual SAR budget may be noticed as an added bonus.

If the lost person is a celebrity or has political connections, media relations may be intense. A seasoned expert spokesman from within one's own agency ought to be drafted for the role in a case of this sort, to prevent political interference or minimize its effect on field actions and to guard against costly slips of the tongue.

The guidelines outlined for managing relatives apply to the media — honesty, directness, no speculation, and positiveness. Remember that when a reporter presses hard questions or, through some independent research, uncovers some facts about the current mission or previous ones, he is just doing his job — getting the details of the story as he sees it. His work is most likely *not* a personal vendetta against local SAR or agency officials or policies. A sense of humor and coolness under fire are invaluable skills for liaison work of any kind.

Base Camp Administration

The fabrication and administration of a well-run base camp is a valuable skill developed in training courses given by local, state, and federal fire fighting agencies. A base camp provides the staging area for personnel and equipment and their logistical support — toilet paper, dry clothing, and the "three hots and a cot." The base camp is also the home of the central nervous system of the search in the plans, communication, command, operations, and support facilities.

Design and construction of a large base camp (for fifty rescuers or more) is best left to an expert borrowed from one of the wildland fire fighting agencies if at all possible. Once someone within the team serves as understudy and masters the details, he can be the primary resource for this complex task. Each base camp operation will have peculiar needs and quirks, but some generalizations are possible. Day and night sleeping areas, command quarters, and heliport and helispot sites should be separated as much as the terrain allows. The supply, kitchen, garbage, latrine (chemical toilets *not* pit latrines are recommended) and aircraft and vehicle fuel dumps need ready access to a serviceable road. The distances between two activity sites is a function of the limitations of the base camp location and the number of search personnel using the camp.

A schematic drawing illustrating relationships among the various components of a base camp is presented as figure 9.1.

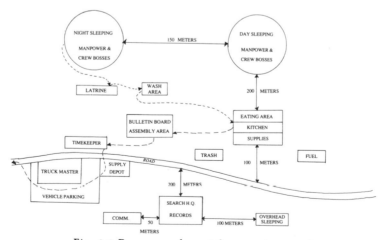

Fig. 9.1 Base camp layout for a major search.

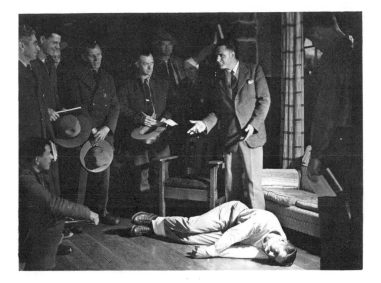

FBI special agent showing Yosemite rangers how it's done. *Photo National Park Service archives.*

BIBLIOGRAPHY

CHAPTER NINE

HARDY, RICHARD E., AND CULL, JOHN C. CONSULTING EDS. *Applied Psychology in Law Enforcement and Corrections.* Springfield, Ill.: Bannerstone House, 1973.

HOLMES, T.H. AND RAHE, R.H. "The Social Readjustment Rating Scale," *Journal of Psychosomatic Research* 11 (1967): 213-218.

McGEE, RICHARD K. *Crisis Intervention in the Community.* Baltimore: University Park Press, 1974.

RESNIK, H.L.P., AND RUBEN, HARVEY L. EDS. *Emergency Psychiatric Care: The Management of Mental Health Crisis.* Bowie, Md.: Charles Press Publishing, 1975.

U.S. DEPARTMENT OF AGRICULTURE, FOREST SERVICE. *Fireline Handbook.* Stock Number 001-001-00397-2 Washington, D.C.: U.S. Government Printing Office, 1975.

U.S. DEPARTMENT OF INTERIOR, BUREAU OF LAND MANAGEMENT. *Fire Control Field Reference Handbook — Alaska.* Alaska State Office, 555 Cordova St., Anchorage, AK

WADE, BILL. *The Role of the Management Team in a Large Search.* La Jolla, Ca.: NASAR paper 76-103, 1976.

Part Three
Tools

Mock rescue by early Yosemite rangers. *Photo National Park Service archives*

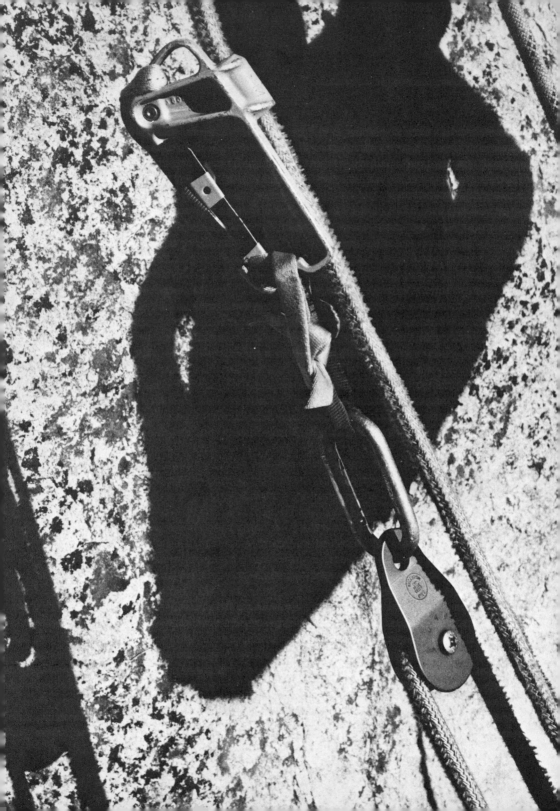

10 | Ropes

THE FIRST TIME I did a real climb — that is, one with a climbing partner other than a paid guide who shepherds a class of twelve through basic knots and a top-roped climb at the end of the day — I tagged along with Pete Thompson. Pete's a great guy, real good-sized, with a set jaw and straightforward ways. We got along famously.

It was a classic early morning Yosemite start, about eleven A.M. We met over at the park's rescue cache, a five-room former jail housing even the most greedy climber's dream — an almost unlimited amount of first-class climbing equipment hanging on the walls, just about begging to be borrowed. As we were racking up all the hardware we'd temporarily liberated, I noticed that Pete did not take down one of the cache ropes. This seemed a bit odd to me, as I had already casually examined by the touch method the braiding pattern of at least half of the numerous ropes on display there, fingered the radio sets and oxygen units a bit, and tried the gate action on a baker's dozen shiny, anodized orange carabiners.

After the mandatory desperate bushwhack a good ten minutes to the foot of the climb, we stopped to sort gear and rope up by some tall, sharp-edged flakes. This appeared to be the route. At one point in the proceedings, while I anxiously copied whatever he did, Pete noticed that I was standing on what would eventually be his end of the rope.

"Ah, Tim, could you please get off of my rope," was the polite request.

"Oh, sorry, no problem," I replied, and remembered that he had insisted on carrying it, and uncoiling it once at the cliff.

Photo Kenneth Andrasko

As Pete began to lead the first pitch, from up about three meters or so he glanced down at his belayer trying hard to perform his critical role, and once again standing on the rope. "Get off the rope."

"Oh, sorry!"

Pete finished the pitch, and pulled up slack rope in order to put me on belay. I was nervously contemplating my first few moves when the rope pulled tight under my foot, nearly knocking me off balance. "Get OFF the rope!!" A small projectile went flying just past me, striking the ground authoritatively not a meter away. Just from whence and how it came to pass wasn't clear.

"Yeah, well, ah, sorry."

After reaching the end of the pitch, with some difficulty, I scrambled onto the compact belay ledge. I was tired and it was hot at midday, so I didn't notice where my feet were until, "God DAMN IT — Get OFF the rope!" was yelled directly into my ear, the way the Keystone Kops in silent films used to yell into the throat of those old crank telephones that were screwed onto the wall.

At this point, Pete took some time to point out with great vigor and with some rather dramatic and explicit gestures the reasons for not standing, jumping, sitting, walking, dancing, cramponing, or performing any other activity on the rope that might compromise its strength and decrease the rope's life. Not only did our lives while climbing often depend on the rope, but my life in particular *directly* depended on my not standing on his rope one more time! I pretty much picked up the drift of his concern at that point.

Ropes have been applied to any variety of tasks for a long time. Some of the oldest were found in Egyptian tombs and date from about 5300 years ago. These prototype ropes were made by twisting papyrus reeds together. Early man also fashioned ropes by rubbing plant fibers with one another, adhering them by friction and resin. American Indians braided horse hair into cords. Plant fibers were the basis of hemp and manila ropes until the 1940s, when synthetic ropes became commercially available.

In 1928, DuPont industries began basic research programs to investigate the possibilities of developing artificial substitutes for natural raw materials. In 1930, DuPont research teams discovered synthetic polymers that could be formed into filaments both tough and elastic.

Some of the products eventually developed from this polymer family are known today as polypropylene, polyester, and nylon.

In 1946, "Belaying the Leader," a seminal work on the theory of belaying (protecting climbers by the use of the rope) by R. Leonard and A. Wexler, was published in the *Sierra Club Bulletin*. It publicized the design and use of a new type of climbing rope perfected during the war and made from a material called nylon. This synthetic allowed a rope to absorb energy by stretching instead of breaking when a climber fell. The early design of these ropes was a three-strand laid or twisted construction commonly referred to as a mountain lay rope, or mountain nylon. The brand made by Columbia called Goldline became standard. These ropes gradually replaced the natural manila fiber ropes.

During the 1950s, cavers began experimenting with improved technique in order to explore virgin caves as yet untrammeled due in part to the fact that they involved vertical descents of up to 350 meters. Numerous mountaineering skills were adopted and refined, including the use of mountain lay rope. For cavers, however, a rope design that increases spinning by a climber during rappelling or ascending, and that stretches considerably under low loads (body weight) like any laid rope, creates major problems during long drops and ascents.

A southeastern U.S. caver, Bill Cuddington, sought and eventually found a rope strong enough, with minimal spin, and commercially available in that part of the country. The rope became known as Samson rope after its manufacturer, and had a braid-on-braid construction. It remained popular until the late sixties, when another design with the brand name Bluewater appeared on the scene; it had a parallel fiber core of continuous strands, largely eliminating stretch under body-weight loads.

In 1969, the commercial mill producing Bluewater decided to end that operation. A small coterie of cavers bought the production equipment, and began marketing a Bluewater II line. This was the major caving cord until 1967, when Pigeon Mountain Industries (PMI) commenced production of caving rope. These two firms remain the leaders.

While caving rope was being refined, several different designs of climbing rope were being developed and marketed in Europe, until recently virtually always more progressive than the U.S. in terms of technical mountain equipment. As climbing became increasingly popular here, these vastly superior ropes were regularly imported despite their significantly higher price. The European manufacturers are still the largest volume makers of climbing rope in the world.

The distinctions between climbing and caving rope designs are significant. Each offers valuable assets to SAR work. Climbing ropes have relatively low abrasion resistance and a high energy absorption capacity, while caving ropes offer high abrasion resistance and a very low ability to absorb energy. These are the two major factors to be considered when using either rope.

Materials in Rope Construction

Ropes made from natural fibers like manila are worth mentioning in passing, although their use in search and rescue is very limited, even nonexistent. The greatest drawbacks include their tendency to rot with age, and, even when new, their very low ratio of strength to weight. For example, the best grade of manila would have to be about 50 millimeters in diameter and weigh over two and a half times as much as an 11mm nylon climbing rope in order to equal that rope's breaking strength of roughly 2270 kilograms. Nylon's energy absorption capacity is about eight times that of manila rope and twenty-seven times greater than steel cable. What is more, manila ropes have very low resistance to abrasion.

Three key groups of synthetic materials compose ropes prevalent in SAR work. These are polypropylene, polyesters, and nylon.

Polypropylene, along with polyethylene, is the lightest of the three. Ropes made from this synthetic float, and are not weakened by nor do they absorb water, leading to their use in water sports. They resist deterioration by most chemicals and have fair resistance to abrasion and flexing. They do, however, have a relatively low breaking strength and a reasonably high rate of deterioration from excessive exposure to sunlight, and an energy absorption capacity of only three-fifths that of nylon. Heat damages polypropylene readily. Thus, polypropylene is generally avoided for technical rope work, except for non-life-dependent applications, for example sling-load ropes for helicopter support. Expeditions have increasingly relied on polypropylene for fixed ropes in response to its low cost, low stretch, light weight, and resistance to freezing, since it absorbs little water. Wind and rock abrade it at an alarming rate, however, and ultraviolet rays deteriorate it rapidly at high altitude.

Polyester has been given the trademark Dacron by DuPont, and Terylene by ICI Limited in England. Polyester ropes and webbing have excellent resistance to damage from abrasion and flexing, and relatively high breaking strengths with low stretch. Water, chemical, sunlight, and high temperature injury are all well resisted. Until the value of caving rope was demonstrated, Dacron ropes dominated rescue work where a low-stretch rope was necessary. Because of polyester's high resistance to acids, marginal strength loss when wet, and low moisture regain, it is ideal for use in caving equipment and ropes. "However . . . if acid is allowed to dry on webbing, it will concentrate and damage polyester when approximately 80%. It should also be remembered that the energy absorption capacity of polyester is generally lower than that of nylon due to its lower elongation properties."[1] Polyester does resist attack by acids unless in concentrations above 80%. A 10% solution of an alkali like caustic soda dramatically damages polyester, however, and can result in a loss of strength of at least 60% within a few weeks of exposure to it.[2]

Nylon is a generic term for a material, and like its European counterparts Perlon (German) and Grilon (Swiss), is polymide synthetic resin made by numerous manufacturers. In general, nylon is about 17% lighter than polyester but rates about the same in flexure, and resistance to abrasion, ultraviolet light, and chemicals. Nylon is rated slightly above polyester in elongation and breaking strength while under a continuous load (tensile strength), and suffers at least a 10-20% (and possibly 30%) loss in breaking strength when wet. The higher elongation and energy absorption does make nylon an excellent material for dynamic loading applications, a major reason why nylon is the major component of mountaineering ropes today. Its drawbacks include its liability to attack by acids and its noticeable loss of strength when wet or frozen, the result of its high moisture absorption. An electrolyte like battery acid severely damages nylon rope or webbing. "In general the majority of the damage was done within the first fifteen minutes. Washing nylon tape which has had acid on it is futile. All nylon gear which has had acid on should be discarded as even the smallest amount of electrolyte can do immense damage. The important thing to note is that very little physical sign of damage was obvious, except for hardening of the web."[3]

[1]"Troll Tape and Slings," Troll Products booklet, Oldham (England), n.d. (circa 1977), p.3.
[2]Ibid., p.5.
[3]Ibid., p.4.

In direct reference to nylon webbing, a booklet by Troll Products states[4] that

> natural 'loom-state' nylon webbing loses only 0.5% of its strength after a 252 hour Xenotest estimated to be equivalent to 300 hours 'English' summer sun, whilst dyed tapes lose over 4% or more. Tapes dyed with fluorescent dyes may have a frightening 66% loss in strength after similar exposure (and this, one assumes, applies to the sheaths of ropes treated in the same way, though U.V. inhibitors obviously lessen this effect). Conversely, it is interesting to note that the shrinkage resulting from normal dyeing processes often reduces the strength of the tape by as much as 10%, whilst increasing retail prices by up to 50%. This rather incredible situation . . . seems to be totally ignored by the climbing public who apparently prefer colourful gear to maximum safety.

While there are infinite variations in type, form, and specific qualities of nylon, two primary melts are utilized in the manufacture of nylon ropes: Nylon 6 and Nylon 6.6. Both have similar properties. Nylon 6.6 has a slightly higher melting point (250°C, 482° F) and a higher softening point (230° C, 446° F) compared to Nylon 6's melting (215° C, 419° F) and softening point (160° C, 320° F). Most hawser-laid ropes are made from Nylon 6.6, and kernmantle ropes from Nylon 6, which the German trademark as Perlon.

General Designs of Climbing Rope

A number of different types of nylon ropes are associated with SAR work, determined by their means of construction. Once the basic Nylon 6.6 melt is produced, it is heated and extruded through tiny holes to form hairlike fibers stretched, cooled, and formed into yarns. Most climbing and caving ropes contain continuous fiber yarns throughout the entire length of the rope, devoid of splices. These continuous weave yarns may be combined together in laid (twisted) or braided designs for rope.

Hawser-Laid Rope, usually just referred to as laid rope, consists of three twisted strands, each composed of large, twisted yarns in turn spun from smaller continuous yarns. This configuration necessitates that each of these fibers be exposed on the surface at some point along the length of the rope, subjecting each to abrasion and other damage.

One of the first laid mountain ropes was white Columbia nylon, still in use in the early sixties. A gold rope manufactured by Plymouth and

---

[4]Ibid., p.6.

known as Goldline is now the most popular and common climbing brand in the U.S., although others are available. Laid rope designed for mountaineering use (a hard mountain lay) is generally stiffer than other types, and tends to stiffen more with use. A corollary is that one has to be very careful in tying knots in the rope, and be sure to back up each knot, especially inherently loose knots like the bowline. Other disadvantages include the fact that stiff ropes are harder to stack and handle. The twisted construction translates into accelerated spinning on rappels and potentially more rope salads and kinking when the rope runs through a friction system. Lastly, laid ropes create more friction from their rippled surface and therefore more heat when moving over rock or carabiners.

On the positive side, a laid rope is easier to inspect for wear and damage than a kernmantle because it can be twisted apart and visibly examined. Laid ropes are generally stretchier than other types of climbing rope because they can untwist slightly under force, in addition to the

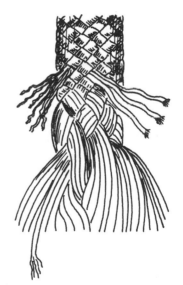

Fig. 10.2 Kernmantle rope construction.

Fig. 10.1 Laid rope construction.

stretch that the nylon material undergoes. This elongation by un-
twisting, however, does not necessarily mean that this design is stronger
than other types. Because of the right construction in the hard lay of
mountain ropes, though, they are generally more resistant to abrasion
than braided or kernmantle ones.

Kernmantle Rope is a European two-component design long the
principal one in use on the Continent. The kern, a high-strength inner
core, is covered by an outer, braided protective sheath called the mantle
(or mantel). The core can be made of parallel filaments or filaments
spiraled into cords. Each bundle of woven fibers in the core usually runs
the entire length of the rope. Contrary to some opinions and to the
traditional criticism of kernmantle, experience suggests that it is very
difficult to damage the core without obviously disrupting the sheath
weave. One possible exception is localized tensile stress and compression
at a knot or over an edge (say a carabiner), producing a shear component; hawsers are equally unlikely to evince this sort of injury. This
possibility of hidden core injury is still a controversial subject and open
to much discussion. The braided nature of the sheath makes a kernmantle rope much easier to use than most other types. It has a softer feel than
Goldline and makes tighter, therefore potentially safer, knots. Kernmantle has minimal elongation (about 2-4%) under low loads like body
weight, a highly desirable trait for tension technique, rappelling and
jumaring, Tyroleans and hauling, but under high loads kernmantle
stretches, as much as 40-70% at rupture depending on the specific
design. The sheath contributes about one-third of the total strength of
the line. Thus, considerable damage to the mantle seriously compromises a rope's reliability, and requires that it be retired. It is possible
to study damaged, retired ropes by dissecting them and examining the
effect of a sheath injury on the core, gaining some evaluative powers in
this way.

Braided Rope is constructed by weaving rope filaments together
uniformly, much like braiding someone's hair, without a sheath and core
construction. This type of rope is characterized by feeling softer than
and testing not quite as strong as a kernmantle of the same diameter, and
is more subject to abrasion due to this fluidity.

Braid-On-Braid Often you will hear the term "braid-on-braid" used
to describe a rope, usually American-made and most likely a special
order item. The rope is really a variant of the sheath and core kernmantle
design. The Yosemite rescue cache's long ropes (550 meters and 2000

meters) are of this type and are 13mm in diameter, with a breaking strength up around 2700 kilograms. These ropes can be obtained from most large cordage dealers, and are a good compromise in workability and cost between Goldline and the more expensive kernmantle mountaineering ropes. A disadvantage of braid-on-braid rope is its great stretch under normal loads. In addition, the soft sheath means a lower resistance to abrasion than a standard climbing rope.

Caving Ropes are specially designed lines featuring low stretch, high strength, and high resistance to fraying and wear. These ropes are of kernmantle design manufactured from a variety of Nylon 6.6 that produces a higher breaking strength than climbing ropes, from 2270 to 3170 kilograms depending upon the brand. They have a low tendency to spin on long free rappels, and do not bounce during ascents back to the surface or summit.

The extremely high resistance of these ropes to abrasion was demonstrated by a series of tests initiated by Kyle Isenhart, and reported in his paper "Abrasion Testing of Ropes and Slings," presented at the 1977 National Speleological Society convention. A unique testing apparatus was invented. A small, low-speed (36 cycles per minute) engine with an eccentric arm with a Jumar ascender attached gripped a length of test rope with a 26 kilogram weight hung over a 90° steel edge. Each revolution of the eccentric arm rubbed the rope against the metal edge. The results of the test are presented in the accompanying table.

Table 12

Results Of Abrasion Test On Ropes

Rope Type	Cycles	Comments
11mm Edelrid Classic	76	sheath penetration
11.8mm (7/16″) Goldline	230	8 out of 24 main strands broken
Bluewater II	243	sheath penetration
Bluewater III	279	sheath penetration
PMI	560	sheath penetration

Many of these ropes come in roughly 11mm diameters and have very high tensile strengths. Therefore, they provide more than adequate safety margin in SAR work if used correctly. Smaller sized ropes, such as 9mm ones, are frequently carried for rappelling — they are lightweight, small, and still perfectly acceptable in strength for this purpose.

What Makes a Superior Climbing and Rescue Rope?

Since the basic element in any technical rescue (assuming cable is not involved) is the rope, one of the first considerations must be the strength of particular ropes. Taken by itself, this factor is *not*, however, a sufficient indicator of the most desirable rope for mountain search and rescue.

Nylon, and possibly Dacron, are generally considered the only realistic choices for rescue ropes, as they are available, and have a high strength-to-weight ratio for a given diameter.

Table 13

Generalized Static Breaking Strength Of Rope Materials

Diameter	Material	Static Breaking Strength[1]
11.8mm (7/16″)	Manila	715 kg
11.8mm (7/16″)	Polypropelene	1600 kg
11mm	Polyester (Dacron)	2270 kg
11mm	Nylon (Perlon, etc.)	2270 kg
11mm	Nylon (non-stretch caving)	2270-3170 kg[2]

[1]Haas, Frank, *Knowing the Ropes* (reprinted from *Sail* magazine), available from Columbian Rope Co., Auburn, N.Y., no date.
[2]Product information, PMI and Bluewater Ltd.

The design of climbing and caving ropes takes into consideration a number of other, often more important, factors than how much force it takes to break a rope.[5] For example, a rope's fall-holding capability is extremely important. How many test falls can a rope consistently hold before it breaks? How about its ability to absorb energy over an edge (working capacity over an edge, WCOE)? What is the energy absorption capacity before the rope stretches and breaks? What are the handling characteristics (via a flexibility test according to the British Standard), and abrasion resistance? Its knotability? For these as well as other reasons, the static breaking strength of a rope alone does not give a true

[5]The table of test figures on rope models produced by Helmut Microys in his excellent article "Climbing Ropes" in *AAJ* 1977 is useful for examining a variety of rope properties for the models listed.

picture of the rope's performance and limitations. Yosemite SAR has purchased a particular brand at one time or another simply because it does not kink too much, and holds knots well, even though it has a lower breaking strength than another brand. Commercial climbing ropes come in a variety of diameters, from 9mm double ropes or haul lines, to 10.3, 10.4, 10.5, 11.0, 11.1, and so on, up to Goldline at 11.8mm (7/16'').

Rope Management and Etiquette

It is extremely important for all SAR personnel to understand a few basic concepts about rope handling and management. The overall goal is to maximize the life of the rope as well as the life of the person dangling from the end of it. With this in mind, everyone takes pains to avoid jumping, walking, sitting, cramponing, or skiing on a rope.

Dragging a rope on the ground allows small dirt particles to become imbedded in the sheath, work their way into the core, and slowly cut fibers. Do not leave a rope under tension for any extended period of time unless absolutely necessary. Remove all knots as soon as possible and try to avoid overloading a knot at all costs.

A wet or cold rope is demonstrably weaker, and up to 40% heavier, than a normal one. Researchers conducting static breaking strength tests on iced ropes at -45° C discovered a reduction of about 30% for these ropes. In tests performed by Edelweiss ropes, their ropes rated at three or four standard UIAA falls held only *one or none at all* after they had absorbed 37% of their own weight of sprinkled water. German Alpine Club tests prior to 1974 suggested that wet and wet-cold ropes (saturated and stored in a refrigerator) would in general hold fewer (as many as three less!) UIAA falls than when dry, and that some ropes specifically marketed as resistant to water absorption held two falls less than in the manufacturer's tests.[6] A wet rope is harder to handle, and a frozen one really impossible, introducing some additional safety concerns. Prusiks and the various mechanical ascenders are markedly less efficient on wet or frozen ropes, and may fail to work at all. For winter climbing and rescue, the advantages of the water resistant ropes now available are obvious, if they are indeed effective.

A rope thrown into the back of a pickup or into the trunk of a car may be exposed to sharp objects and chemicals. Nylon is very resistant to gasoline, grease, and oil, but a soiled rope should be washed. Improper

[6]Microys, Helmut, "Climbing Ropes," *American Alpine Journal* vol. 21 no. 1: 142-43.

washing will harm a rope (see Rope Care). Prolonged exposure to sun (especially ultraviolet rays, more prevalent at high altitude) has been shown to have a detrimental effect on cordage. High temperatures (120° C, 250° F and above) will damage rope *very* quickly, so it is dangerous to dry a rope by a campfire. A more common heat damage problem occurs when a rope runs through a brake or rappel system too quickly, for friction creates heat. This is one reason why gloves should not be worn during a rappel. If hands heat up or burn, imagine the heat building up in the carabiner brake — probably approaching a level detrimental to the rope — the weak link theory again.

Nylon moving across nylon will melt through the stationary piece in an incredibly short period of time (Figs. 10.3-10.5). Beware when running a prusik over a static, larger diameter rope. During one experiment, a 13 millimeter prusik holding a pulley slipped three centimeters at 680 kilograms of force (kiloponds) on an overloaded Z-rig hauling system. Immediately the prusik partially melted onto the 11mm rope, damaging it severely. A permanent dimple appeared, and the sheath fused with the core.

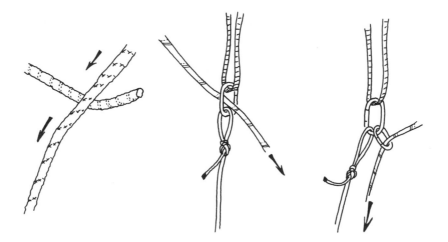

Fig. 10.3 Avoid nylon running across nylon.   Fig. 10.4 Another nylon across nylon situation to avoid.   Fig. 10.5 Correct way.

Heat injury likewise transpires when rappel ropes are pulled too swiftly or incorrectly (e.g., when twisted together or dragged down despite heavy friction) through rappel anchors or around tree trunks (Fig. 10.6). Damage is especially likely if the anchor is made of nylon. This sort of damage can occur quickly.

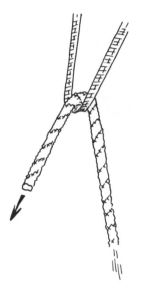

Fig. 10.6 Avoid heat damage from pulling too quickly.

Try to prevent kinking from occuring while coiling a rope. *Stack a rope* (uncoil and pile it loosely on the ground, keeping track of one end on top and one on the bottom of the stack) rather than feeding it from a coil. This prevents the rope management style that Pete Thompson aptly describes as "a direct hit on a spaghetti factory," during the Sicilian campaign. If a rope is stressed while it is kinked, severe damage may occur, and the rope needlessly ruined.

A rope is cut much more easily when under tension than when it is slack, another point worth bearing in mind. Sharp or even rough edges can tear a loaded rope to shreds, especially if the rope moves back and forth or even continuously (as in hauling) over the irregularity. If the potential problem is spotted in time, the solution is fundamental. Pad the rope, support the line above the hazard (say, via a directional sling in a tree), or round off the sharpness with a hammer. More on edge management later, in the chapter on raising systems.

If a missile falls on the rope, or the line catches a significant fall, is subjected to excessive heat or chemical exposure, or if any other aberration is suspected, inspect the rope immediately, and seek advice before you reuse it. Mark a questionable section by tying a loop around it and adding a tag with an explanatory note.

Padding a rope. *Photo Kenneth Andrasko*

Rope Care

Ropes can be periodically washed to remove the build-up of dirt inside the sheath. Care must be taken to insure that mechanical cutting or fraying from the washing machine's agitator does not occur during the washing process. Pigeon Mountain Industries markets a rope washer, a short length of modified pipe connectable to any standard faucet. In-numerable pin holes within the pipe force the water to circulate around and scrub the rope as it is fed through the washer by hand, centimeters at a time.

Exactly how to *wash* a rope, at what temperature, and with which chemicals or soaps (if any) is a question eliciting considerable opinion and little agreement. The cooler the water, the less chance of damage; using no soap or additive at all avoids the risk of chemical injury. The recommended maximum temperature for washing rope along with chemicals marketed as safe for nylon is 40° C. Any temperature above this stiffens the rope and holds in dirt. Check directly with the manufacturer about the specific procedures advised for a nylon rope if in doubt, or consult a reference like the *Handbook of Textile Manufacture*. Some folks dry ropes in the sun, others dry them outside away from direct sunlight, and still another faction advocates use of a dryer with temperature adjustment, maintained at the setting for "cool." For machine washing (and drying, if you are so inclined), *chaining* a rope helps prevent it from becoming unbelievably tangled (Fig. 10.7).

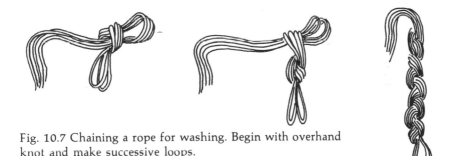

Fig. 10.7 Chaining a rope for washing. Begin with overhand knot and make successive loops.

Since most SAR caches contain many lengths, types, and colors of ropes, it is handy to hang each rope on a wooden peg carrying its own recorded history of use card (Fig. 10.8). If obvious damage has occured from a fall or noticeable abrasion, tie the uncertain spot into a knot and label the rope something like, "Do not use until checked." Do this right away at the rescue scene. Never place the rope back on the rack or in a blitz team ready-pack until it has been examined. More often than not, ropes are retired due to use and abuse sustained over a long period of time. For this reason, each rope ought to be permanently marked on one or both of the flat, fused ends by melting a number into it with a metal stamp. No confusion can arise among ropes of the same color with very different lengths and histories. After every operation or climb, the date and function of each rope is briefly outlined on its adjoining history card. The card also notes date of purchase, and the date the rope was put into service. The card, of course, never goes into the field, but remains faithfully back in the cache.

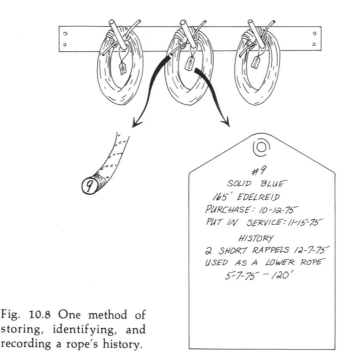

Fig. 10.8 One method of storing, identifying, and recording a rope's history.

Longer ropes are marked in increments by pieces of electrical tape about 13 millimeters wide that contrast with the rope's hue. During field work, these markings regularly abrade off. The idea of dyeing the rope incrementally sounds great, but obtaining a safe dye without nylon eaters like crysillic acid is difficult. The best formula found thus far is military parachute marking dye, apparently free of long-term hidden side effects on nylon.

Checking a Rope for Damage

The most persistent criticism of employing kernmantle and braided rope in rescue work instead of laid rope stems from the belief that they are impossible to check for damage. A laid rope can be twisted apart and inspected internally, unlike kernmantle. One school of thought holds that kernmantle rope is far superior in design, feel, manageability, strength, and safety, not only for climbing but also for rescue. Although the core of a kernmantle rope cannot be seen, students of the controversy now seem to agree that it is impossible to damage the kern without injuring the mantle. Larry Penberthy, in his *MSR Newsletter* for May,

Fig. 10.9 External appearance of a rope when damaged internally.

Fig. 10.10 Internal appearance of a rope showing broken strands.

1972, mentions that he has tried to hurt the core without leaving impact marks but was thwarted. *Check a kernmantle* rope by carefully inspecting the sheath while the rope is being coiled. At the same time, be aware of how the rope feels as it runs through the fingers. Immediately note and tie off any lumps or depressions (Fig. 10.10). Harm to the core consists of filament or yarn breakage and slight retraction. If enough strands rupture, a localized reduction of the diameter of the rope results in a depression that can be felt or even seen. Check any suspected areas further by pulling them under tension (the weight of one person standing on a Jumar or prusik tensioning system is about maximum) (Fig. 10.11), to emphasize the dimple by separating the broken strands and

Fig. 10.11 A rope under mild tension from a Jumar and étrier may show internal damage that can be seen or felt.

enlarging the dip. If there is a clearly noticeable difference in diameter, the rope should be honorably retired on the spot, despite the sacrifice.

Many standard climbing ropes are quite soft, however, and will occasionally retain an indentation after an impact or under normal use, despite an absence of trauma to the core. One way to differentiate between temporary softness and actual, permanent damage is to patiently inspect the sheath for abnormalities. As mentioned earlier, a great deal can be learned about internal damage by cutting open a suspect kernmantle everywhere the sheath is abraded or indented. What seems like certain core damage may, in fact, be limited to the mantle. Whenever in doubt, though, retire it!

After ropes have been in action for some time, say around half of their expected lifetime, especially if lots of rappelling or hauling has taken place, most develop fuzz as the sheath or surface wears. Softer ropes are particularly prone to this condition, which does not seriously affect a rope's strength until the wear is excessive. On the positive side, friction is increased in belaying.

Larry Penberthy, of Mountain Safety Research, Inc., has originated a handy way to determine the retirement time of a rope with a history devoid of obvious trauma. Fuzz arises on the surface of a rope as individual filaments are broken. By examining the base of each strand with a magnifying aid, one can estimate the ratio of cut to uncut filaments. When this ratio becomes 50/50 for a relatively large strand sample (say for eight of twenty-four strands), the rope has lost 30% of its original rating and should be retired (Fig. 10.12). This method discounts major leader falls or other serious damage (overtensioning, ultraviolet light deterioration, chemical exposure) hidden beneath the smooth exterior of a relatively new rope. Knowledge of the rope's history complements physical examination.

Fig. 10.12 Penberthy method of assessing when to retire rope: when ratio of broken to good filaments is 50/50.

The above methods may all be invalid if the rope has been exposed even briefly to chemical damage from bleaches, and battery, sulfuric, hydrochloric, or nitric acids. The rope need be retired, rather than risk someone's life.

Exactly when a rope should be taken out of action when it has never been traumatized is the subject of much speculation. A report by the AROVA-Mammut rope factory (summarized in the March 1975 issue of *Summit*, and in Microys's fine "Climbing Ropes" article) offers the following results of their research. Ropes were tested in the field (in addition to the tests at the factory) by climbers who reported their ascents, difficulties, weather conditions, length of climbs, falls, so on. The test ropes were returned to the factory at specified intervals (50 hours, 100 hours, 200 hours) of use. In the Mammut test, a climbing day encompassed an average of 5.5 hours on the rock. Test rope data demonstrated that weight of the rope per meter increases (0.2% per climbing day), total rope length decreases slightly, rigidity increases (1.2% per climbing day), and the static breaking strength decreases per day of use. In addition, the average maximum working capacity goes down by 0.5% each day. If the averages of the test results are interpolated, a new rope is good for about ninety days or about 495 hours of climbing. At that point, it should be discarded even if it looks new. Unsurprisingly, the test showed high data dispersion and variance within each test, with results covering a wide range of possible values. All of this suggests that the personal care a climber gives his or her rope is still a major factor.

Dr. Kosmath of Austria holds that the length of time (in climbing hours) that a rope should be used is directly related to its UIAA fall rating. The assumption, as yet unproved, is that the working capacity over an edge (WCOE) increases with the number of UIAA falls that can be held by a rope. The rough estimates given appear in the adjacent table.[7]

Table 14

Theoretical Relationship Between
Fall Rating And Rope Life

Number of UIAA Falls Held	Expected Rope Life
2	50 HOURS
4	200 HOURS
6	400 HOURS

Experienced mountain guides, according to one, use stiffness, bumpiness, fuzziness, and fadedness of a rope to judge how long it should be used. Not exactly scientific, this is the traditional assessment method: the general feel and appearance (unless someone did something terrible

[7] "Notes on Equipment," *Off Belay*, June 1975.

to it) tells when it is time to retire it to hanging food out of trees so the bears won't get it.

This pretty much sums up the way rope life is usually determined. Unfortunately, "bumpiness" and "fuzziness" are not exactly precise terms carefully quantified. The newer, more rational methods of rope life analysis are yet to be in vogue, and may not be any more realistic and helpful than the artful, studied conclusions of a competent rope user who has nursed a rope through all sorts of vicious climbs and knows precisely what missiles, insults, and calamities have befallen it. Don't just use one way or the other — the art of careful management and complete knowledge of your ropes should not be dispensed with in favor of the science of strict calculation. A climber or rescuer needs mastery of both art and science at all times.

Royal Robbins recently wrote that "the preponderance of evidence (i.e., the lack of a single instance of a rope weakened through use, breaking in use) indicates that climbers never overestimate the life of their climbing ropes."[8] This observation adds a little perspective. Again, the fundamental rule is retire when in doubt.

Coiling and Stacking Ropes

Coiling a rope is performed in a few simple ways, depending on the climber's location and needs. Two methods are illustrated in figures 10.13 and 10.14. When a rope is uncoiled, it is generally stacked or "flaked out" loosely in a broad, random pile. Make note of the whereabouts of the top end and the bottom end of the stack. Stacking theoretically insures tangle-free feeding of the rope.

Fig. 10.13 Coiling a 50-meter rope.

[8]Robbins, Royal, "Climbing Rope Myths," *Summit*, February/March 1979; a well-worked, challenging article reviewing several prominent myths of rope use.

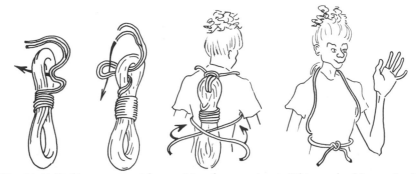

Fig. 10.14 Coiling a rope with provision for carrying it. This method leaves both ends available at once, preferable for alpine climbing and glacier travel.

Complications arise with ropes longer than the normal 46 or 50 meter lengths. You can cheat a little on 92 and 125 meter lengths by coiling them half from each end, as if they were shorter, and then carrying them together. This gets a bit tougher for the 185 meter and even longer lengths, because of the increased bulk. To solve this problem and make transporting more comfortable, the Yosemite SAR crew stacks them into packs and haul sacks.

Fig. 10.15 Stacking a rope, leaving top and bottom ends available.

One person holds the sack open and the other just stacks the rope into it. Both ends are left out. Upon reaching the rescue site, the rope is fed directly out of the sack without unpacking. Since both ends are exposed, they can be tied off or clipped into the anchor instantly. The longest rope we have managed in Yosemite is a full 1340 meters, kept on a factory spool. Once at the site, the spool is suspended from a tree or rock outcrop on a pipe, and fed out as needed. As ropes are pulled in, they are restacked directly into the pack, or fed back onto the spool, eliminating some potentially monumental snarls. The ropes stay cleaner this way, and suffer less damage than they would lying on the ground.

Nylon Webbing

The other form that nylon takes for mountaineering purposes is flat nylon webbing, sometimes called flat rope. Its properties are similar to those indicated for nylon rope earlier in this chapter. There are two broad design categories, flat and tubular. Both types are flat in appearance; however, if a piece of tubular webbing is viewed in cross section, it is actually hollow. Closed-tube webbing is tubular stock sewn flat, for rigidity. Tubular webbing is usually stronger and more flexible than flat webbing, its major advantages.

Tubular webbing, in turn, is constructed from two very different designs: spiral structure and chain structure. While spiral is strong, chain structure is extremely susceptible to abrasion damage from sharp edges or even carabiner gates and threads (on locking models), concentrated at the chained edge. If the chain is pulled out or cut, the webbing tends to begin unraveling and may fail. Both types look the same, unfortunately, until the tube is opened and flattened out. If the crease forms a distinct disconformity at the edge, where a chain stitch joins the ribs together, then it is a chain structure. The spiral variety has no such stitch and has continuous ribs. Tightly woven spiral weave is preferred and most resistant to abrasion. Loosely woven weaves should be avoided, while tight chain structured webbing is acceptable but not optimal.[9]

Some sizes, uses, and strengths of webbing are compared in the accompanying table. Polyester webbing is also available for caving, due to its resistance to acids and moisture, but its poor elongation properties preclude its introduction into mountaineering.

---

[9]"All About Tubular Nylon," *Off Belay* 43:13, from an article by Don Davison, Jr. in the National Speleological Society *News*, June 1978.

Stacking a rope in a rucksack to manage it. *Photo Kenneth Andrasko*

The same rules of rope care and management apply to webbing, with the exception that as webbing does not have the kernmantle construction, surface wear should be taken more seriously — there is no protective sheath. Flat webbing may wear faster than rope in some situations, due to its large surface area. Any knots tied in webbing (customarily, the ring bend or grapevine) ought to be checked quite frequently. This is slippery stuff, and tends to untie or loosen itself when not under tension. Knots slip through themselves if the free ends are too short, so be sure to leave plenty of tail on any knot, about eight centimeters.

Table 15

Overview Of Nylon Webbing

Size	Type	Use	Approximate Tensile Strength in Kilograms
13mm (½")	Tubular	Hero Loops	720-820kg[1]
14mm (9/16")	Flat	Hero Loops	680kg[2]
14mm (9/16")	Tubular, Heavy Duty	Runners, Sub-Aiders	1000-1270kg[1]
25mm (1")	Flat	Etriers	1360-1600kg[1]
25mm (1")	Tubular	Rappel Seats Swami Belt Runners Chest Harness	1800-2000kg[1]
50mm (2")	Tubular	Swami Belt	2700kg

[1]Great Pacific Iron Works Catalog, 1976
[2]John Howard Co. Catalog, 1976

Some other points to consider. Webbing slings used in a running belay should be able to withstand the 1200 kilogram force of a fall factor of two, where the fall distance equals twice the length of rope in play. Almost double this force could act on the sling holding the fall (admittedly rare), suggesting that runners ought to be capable of holding 2400kg. Standard 25mm tubular webbing tied into a sling with a water knot (resulting in a strength loss of some 25-40%) passing over a carabiner would yield a final strength roughly equal to the 2000kg strength of the original material, rather less than the 2400kg figure deemed ideal. Additional losses of strength due to wetness, at 20-30%; abrasion (10% cut strands realizes a 20% loss, and 30% cut reduces strength by about 40%), about 20%; and sunlight, say 4%, add up to a 44-54% reduction before considering knot strength, and loss over an edge![10]

[10]"Troll Tape and Slings," pp. 8-20.

Hence, the cumulative effects of wear and unfavorable conditions culminate in serious reductions of safety margin, and underscore the need for new, carefully monitored, high quality webbing slings. Most of these factors, happily, do not often come into play at once. Sewn slings are stronger than knotted ones, if sewn with heavy nylon thread with a fairly high stitch count per centimeter. Frequent inspection and a harsh rejection policy seem mandatory. Thus, the motto for ropes and webbing in mountaineering and rescue remains: when in doubt, toss it out!

THE BERGSCHRUND ON THE DENT BLANCHE IN 1865

BIBLIOGRAPHY

CHAPTER TEN

BLUE WATER, LTD. *Product Catalog.* Fort Lauderdale, Fla. n.d.

BORWICK, G.R. "Mountaineering Ropes," *Off Belay* 15 (June 1974): pp. 2-7.

COOK, J. GORDON. *Handbook of Textile Fibers, Vol. II.* Watford, England: Merrow Publishing Company, n.d.

CORDAGE GROUP, THE. *Rope Technical Data.* Technical Circular, Columbia Rope Co., Auburn, NY, 1977.

EDELRID-WERK. *Product Information.* West Germany, 1977.

GREAT PACIFIC IRONWORKS, THE. *Equipment Catalog.* P.O. Box 150, Ventura, Ca, n.d.

HASS, FRANK J. "Knowing the Ropes," reprinted from *Sail* magazine. Auburn, N.Y.: The Cordage Group, n.d.

HUDSON, STEVE, AND VINES, TOM. "The Development and Design of Static Caving/Rescue Rope," *Search and Rescue Magazine,* Summer 1979.

ISENHART, KYLE. "Abrasion Testing of Ropes and Slings," paper presented at the 1977 National Speleological Society meeting, Vertical Section Session.

JOHN HOWARD COMPANY. *Nylon Products Catalog.* 1224 East Edna Place, Covina, CA, n.d.

MICROYS, HELMUT. "Climbing Ropes," *American Alpine Club Journal,* vol. 21, no. 1 (1977): 130-147.

PENBERTHY, LARRY. "Climbing Ropes," *Mountain Safety Research Newsletter,* May 1972, pp. 6-8.

PENBERTHY, LARRY. "Some Facts about Nylon for Ropes," *Summit,* January/February 1971, pp. 14-15.

PIGEON MOUNTAIN INDUSTRIES. *Product Catalog.* P.O. Box 803, Lafayette, GA 30728, 1977.

ROBBINS, ROYAL. "Climbing Rope Myths," *Summit,* February/March 1979, p. 92.

SCHMIDLIN, H.V. *Preparation and Dyeing of Synthetic Fibers.* London: Chapman Hall, 1965.

SCOTT, DOUG. *Big Wall Climbing.* New York: Oxford University Press, 1974.

TISO, GRAHAM, "Equipment Notes," *Mountain* 20 (March 1979): 37-39.

WHEELOCK, WALT. *Ropes, Knots, and Slings for Climbers.* Glendale, Ca.: La Siesta Press, 1967.

11 | Knots

COWBOYS AND PACKERS aren't exactly outgoing sorts. Like climbers, futures commodity brokers, or any other highly competitive subculture, cowboys have their own special clothes, equipment, hair styles, lingo, and attitudes. All of this must be well understood in order to communicate with them.

Thus far in my crash equestrian course, the old cowhands hadn't responded to me. A wide range of subtle inquiries into their habits, pasts, and bathing patterns had been coyly launched at them during breaks in the training. Yet my mild anthropological interest remained unsatisfied. I was beginning to think I'd have to go out and get some red bandannas and country/western songbooks.

It was about three and a half weeks into the six-week course. We were rounding up some stray pack horses and mules from a grazing area tucked back in a canyon. Walt Castle, a fiftyish master cowboy who looked like he'd just fallen down off of a Marlboro billboard and was still brushing off the dust, wheeled and dodged his old roan with a brilliant grace that suggested a long youth spent out on the range. Watching him rope was, for me, like observing a gifted climber do a tremendously hard boulder problem — it looked so smooth and easy. Walt took the time to cover a few roping and packing basics with us. We talked about cowboy knots, and he demonstrated, with considerable flair, some special ones for packing and work in the corral.

After this impressive performance, Walt strolled over toward me and said, "Setnicka, you're a climber — can you think of any knot used in

Prusik knot. *Photo Mead Hargis*   *193* climbing that might be useful for improvising a halter for this pinto here? A bowline? Sure, c'mon up here and show us."

I had always been eager to do well in classes of any kind, by means of enthusiasm, flirtation, bringing in the right kinds of apples, or even studying. So I jumped at this sudden favorable development in cowboy/climber relations. Strutting up, glad at last that there was some common ground between the two groups, I took the rope from Walt. With a flash of hand, evincing the pride and pizzazz of a pizza maker in Little Italy performing for the Saturday night crowd, I tied a bowline around the horse's neck.

Stepping back, I was rather pleased with my performance for the class. With visions of gigantic World Champion Rodeo Cowboy silver belt buckles shimmering before my eyes, I casually asked, "How's that?"

"Oh, that's fine," drawled Walt, "except for one problem." He quickly pulled on the rope and showed how the knot would soon kill a horse if it didn't let him get away first. Everyone else laughed, while I managed a smile. Walt had clearly made his point — some knots useful in one situation will get you into trouble in another. And so the diplomatic rift between cowboys and climbers sadly continues to this day.

When discussing knots in any group of climbers, cavers, cowfolk, or sailors, it quickly becomes apparent that everyone has his or her own favorites culled from years of training and experience. The knots used in SAR activities, though, should be the safest and strongest possible, and they should be known to most, if not to all, participants in an event. In short, some degree of standardization is desirable, so that anyone looking at a particular rigging system will know if something is tied incorrectly or with a weak knot. Simplicity in the numbers of knots used will help achieve this goal. And while exotic knots show a great deal of skill on the part of the person tying them, they do not offset the safety margin gained when everyone is familiar with a simpler, more uniform system.

But a few words of warning before continuing. We must not fall into the trap of "the myth of knot strength," most recently restated by Royal Robbins in the February/March, 1979 issue of *Summit* magazine. While it is of interest how strong one knot is versus another, it is important to realize that knots do not break, at least not on the testing machines in laboratories. Climbers simply are not found at the bottom of crevasses and caves with broken knots protruding from their harnesses.

In considering what sorts of knots to use, strength certainly cannot be discounted, but it should not be the sole point of knot selection. Ease of tying, the chance of working itself loose, ease of untying after loading, ease of being taught to others, and allowance of quick inspection to see if it is tied correctly are all pertinent factors. So with these other features of knots to consider, start but do not end your search for the perfect knot by considering some relative knot strengths. Many of these knots directly reflect climbing influences and needs, and are based on the figure of eight family of knots.

Table 16

Relative Strength of Knots for Single Kernmantle Rope[1]

No knot: 100%

Figure of eight: 75% to 80%

Bowline: 70% to 75%

Double fisherman's: 65% to 70%

Water knot (overhand follow through): 60% to 70%

Fisherman's: 60% to 65%

Clove Hitch: 60% to 65%

Overhand: 60% to 65%

Two half hitches[2]: 60% to 70% (tested over 16mm diameter ring)

Square knot[2]: 43% to 47%

Gordian knot: information not available at this time

[1]Microys, Helmut, "Climbing Ropes," *American Alpine Journal* 51 (1977): 140.
[2]"Rope Technical Data," brochure by the Cordage Group, Division of Columbian Rope Company, Auburn, New York (March, 1977).

It is important to remember that smaller diameter sizes of nylon are liable to slip without breaking when tied to form any knot.

Overhand Follow-Through, Ring Bend, or Water Knot

The overhand follow through (Fig. 11.1) or water knot is used for tying together the ends of flat or tubular webbing, as in making a swami belt or a runner. The figure of eight knot's multiple bends tend not to lie smoothly enough to make as efficient a knot as a simple follow through. The overhand follow through works well on flat webbing, but pay attention and avoid any short ends; flat webbing is extremely slippery, and under tension a short end can easily slip through the knot. Make the knot neat, with no twists in the webbing. Hold the knot and pull each of the four ends tight, one at a time, repeating until the knot is snug. Leave six or seven centimeters of free end if possible. Put body weight on the sling to tighten it, and check your knot frequently. Some climbers sew or tape the ends to the main sling loop.

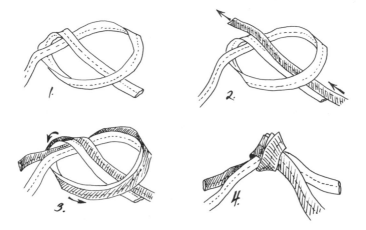

Fig. 11.1 Overhand follow-through.

Figure of Eight Family of Knots

The figure of eight and its derivatives form the basic rescue knot in the Yosemite SAR system. They are the fundamental climbing knots of the Valley, having largely replaced the bowlines. There are a number of reasons for this. A figure of eight is stronger than a bowline. It is a tighter knot, whereas the bowline is an inherently loose knot, able to free itself more easily unless one uses a special tie-off for the free end. The

Fig. 11.2 Two ways to tie a figure of eight knot: left is wrong, right is correct and about 8% stronger.

eight's small, symmetrical arcs are easy to inspect, line up, and keep neat, thereby maintaining the knot's strength, and the simplicity of the knot makes visual inspection straightforward. A very fine knot indeed, but be sure to tie it correctly, as illustrated in Fig. 11.2. The difference in strength may be as high as 8 to 10% for kernmantle ropes.

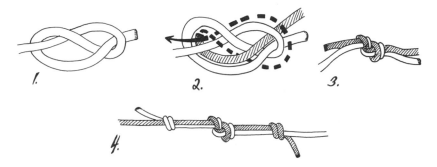

Fig. 11.3 Figure of eight follow-through with double fisherman's tie-off.

Figure of Eight Follow-Through

This variation (also called a double figure of eight) is used to tie together ropes of equal or nearly equal diameters (say 9mm and 11mm), as in rappelling or in a series (Fig. 11.3). A tie-off knot is generally used to secure the end for an added margin of safety. A variation is used to tie the end of the climbing rope into one's swami belt or harness (Fig. 11.4).

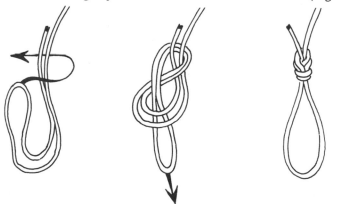

Fig. 11.4 Figure of eight on a bight.

Figure Eight on a Bight

This knot is used to make a loop in the middle of any length of rope (Fig. 11.5). It is easier for most people to tie this than a butterfly knot. The knot can be tied near the end of the rope if a loop is needed, and is stronger than a simple overhand knot. It is readily untied after being tightened and loaded.

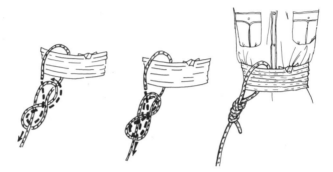

Fig. 11.5 Figure of eight follow-through tied into a swami belt.

Fig. 11.6 Simple overhand on a bight.

Overhand Loop on a Bight

If you incorrectly tie a figure of eight, this is what you get (Fig. 11.6). It is still useful, though a weaker knot than a figure of eight, and very hard to untie after being loaded.

Simple Bowline

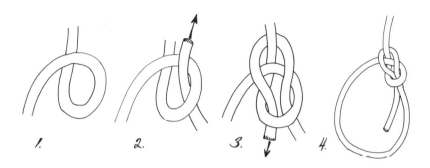

Fig. 11.7 Simple bowline.

This is still the standard climbing knot in many parts of the world (Fig. 11.7). Easy to tie, but it must be tied off or backed up in some manner to insure that it will not loosen while not under tension. Feeding the free end back through the eye of the knot works well as a safety, as in figure 11.11. It is not a problem to untie after loading. If the loop is formed wrong, then the result is no knot at all. It is also possible to tie the knot incorrectly, reducing its strength by about half (Fig. 11.9).

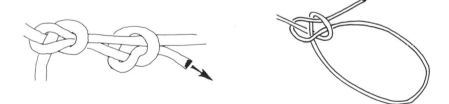

Fig. 11.8 Simple bowline with overhand safety. A double fisherman's knot can also be used as tie-off.

Fig. 11.9 Incorrectly tied bowline.

Double Knotted or High Strength Bowline

By doubling the eye loop of a bowline, one can increase the strength of the knot by as much as 5% (Fig. 11.10). The free end is tied off with an overhand knot, or by tucking the end back through the eye (Fig. 11.11).

Fig. 11.10 Double knotted or high-strength bowline. Must be tied off.

Fig. 11.11 Bowline tied off.

Double Loop Bowline

Another name for this knot is bowline on a bight (Fig. 11.12), and it is tied a bit differently from a standard bowline. It is very useful for setting up the multiple point, self-equalizing anchors discussed later in the chapters on anchors. Make sure a slip knot is not accidentally tied in place of the correct knot.

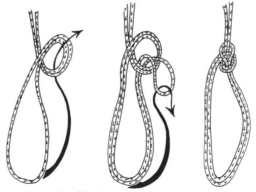

Fig. 11.12 Double loop bowline tied on a bight.

Triple Loop Bowline

This knot (Fig. 11.13) is easily tied by forming a simple bowline with a bight of rope. A chest harness and seat sling may be made by tying this knot carefully, or it can be used to clip into two or more anchor points, though not in a self-equalizing manner.

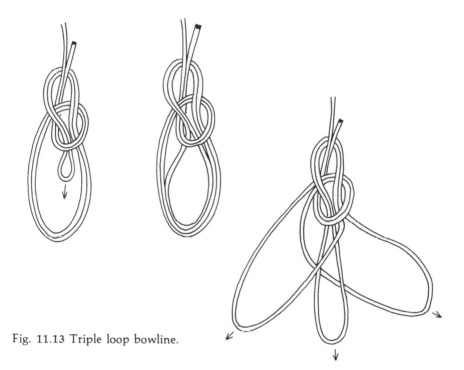

Fig. 11.13 Triple loop bowline.

Bowline on a Coil

With this knot (Fig. 11.14), you can tie or make a quick equivalent of a swami belt tie-in by using several (three or four) wraps of a rope around your waist. This is also the most popular knot for rigging a litter at its rails, as it allows for an adjustment once the litter line is loaded.

Fig. 11.14 Bowline on a coil.

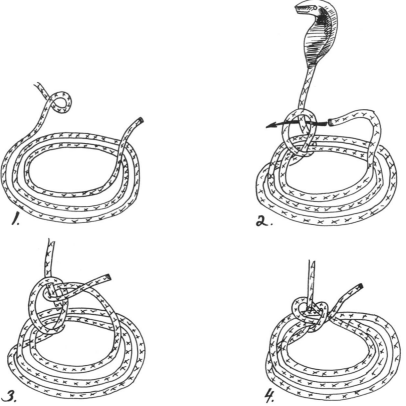

Double Fisherman's Knot

Some climbers use a double fisherman's knot (Fig. 11.15) to join together their rappel ropes. This knot is strong enough for this purpose, but because it has tighter arcs than a figure of eight follow through, it is a much harder knot to untie after loading. Tying only half of it is a popular way to form a tie-off, say to back up a bowline. It stays tied better than a simple overhand, another advantage. The fisherman's is also preferred over a figure of eight for joining together two ropes of unequal diameters.

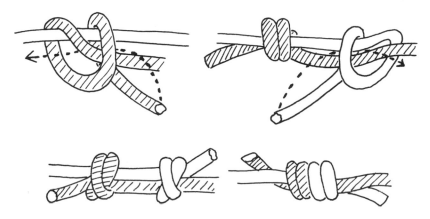

Fig. 11.15 Double fisherman's knot.

Prusik Knot

Named for its inventor, Dr. Karl Prusik's knot (Fig. 11.16) has many uses in SAR work. This is certainly one of the finest knots to use when ascending a rope without mechanical devices. As a safety during rapelling, and as a safety tie-off while raising or lowering ropes, it works beautifully. More on these uses in later chapters.

Fig. 11.16 Simple prusik knot.

The easiest way to make the knot is from a meter length of ¼", 5, 6, or 7mm, or 5/16" rope tied to form a sling. If used on kernmantle or braided rope, then the prusik should be made of laid rope. The opposite is true if secured to 7/16" Goldline. Usually a two-wrap prusik will create adequate friction, but sometimes a third wrap will be required in wet, icy, or muddy conditions. The idea is to use the friction caused by the textural differences between laid and kernmantle surfaces to bind them together under a load. The knot works well, but under extreme forces (over 500 kg) it deforms and may begin to damage itself and the main rope.

If the main rope is a laid rope, a "left handed" prusik may be tied which, under marginal conditions such as icing, will not hold as well as a "right handed" knot (Fig. 11.17). The strands of the rope encourage slipping by the downward direction of their twist. This problem usually does not exist on a braided or kernmantle rope, due to the uniform weave of the sheath.

Fig. 11.17 Left-handed prusik. When loaded in direction of arrow it may slip along twists of rope.

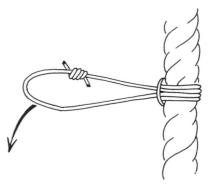

Bachmann Knot

This knot serves the same function as a prusik but has the added advantage of having a handle, making loosening and moving the knot a bit easier. The knot is made from a prusik loop or regular climbing sling and a standard carabiner (Fig. 11.18). The carabiner is held next to the standing rope with the prusik loop clipped through it and then doubled around it and the rope three or four times. Take care that pressure is not placed against the gate side of the carabiner, especially when unattended. Another potential problem surfaces when the carabiner and not the prusik loop is loaded, for the knot will jam and slip.

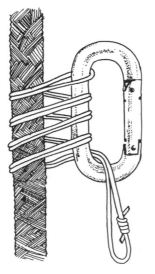

Fig. 11.18 Bachmann knot.

Clove Hitch

A clove hitch (Fig. 11.19) works well when you would like to adjust the tension or length of a rope frequently. It is not meant to be used as a tie-off, nor in lieu of an anchor knot such as a figure of eight. Use care in tying the knot, because it could open the gate of a carabiner (Fig. 11.20); or, if loaded suddenly while loose it could slip through itself and burn the rope.

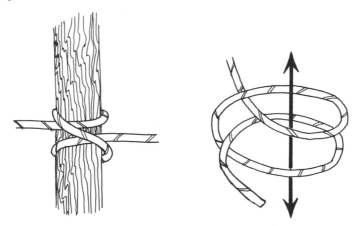

Fig. 11.19 Clove hitch.

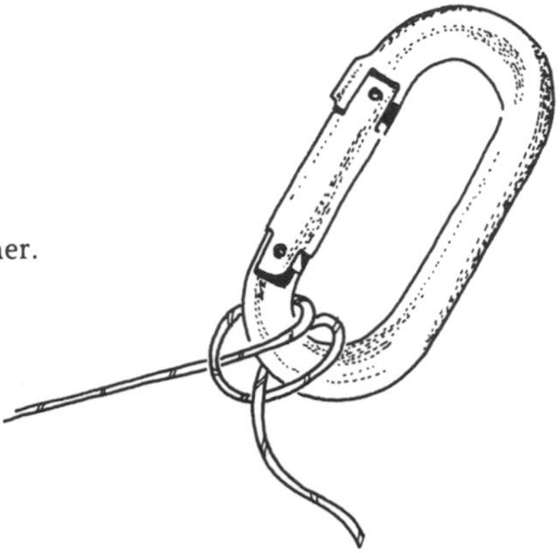

Fig. 11.20 Clove hitch on carabiner.

Girth Hitch

When you are tying a sling into your waist harness or around something and you do not want to use a carabiner, this knot (Fig. 11.21) is fast and simple. It is almost impossible to untie accidentally. Tie it exactly like a prusik, but stop after one wrap. Also known as a lark's foot.

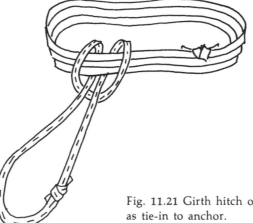

Fig. 11.21 Girth hitch on swami belt as tie-in to anchor.

Other specialized knots are illustrated and explained in the appropriate sections of the chapters that follow.

Yosemite climber, 1954. Note rope through belt loops. *Photo National Park Service*

BIBLIOGRAPHY

CHAPTER ELEVEN

ALEITH, R.C. *Bergsteigen: Basic Rock Climbing.* rev. ed. New York: Charles Scribners Sons, 1975.

SMITH, PHIL. *Knots for Mountaineering.* Published by author, 1975.

SMUTEK, RAY. "Brake Bar Rappels — an Analysis," *Off Belay*, February 1972, pp. 33-39.

WHEELOCK, WALT. *Ropes, Knots, and Slings for Climbers.* Glendale, Ca.: La Siesta Press, 1967.

12 | Harnesses and Seat Slings

MIKE LALONE is a good aid climber and a nice guy, so he was not above helping out a neophyte like me. We climbed together regularly one spring, mostly aid routes, as I was particularly keen on training for wall climbs and didn't know any better. It was a classic alpine partnership for awhile, a little like that of Layton Kor and Pat Ament, or Warren Harding or Fred Beckey and Galen Rowell: he led all the hard and dangerous pitches, while I told jokes and SAR "war stories," took over on the straightforward stuff, and brought all the food.

On another boringly perfect warm morning that July, we started up my first substantial aid route, a real trial at last. The pitches leading up to the crux, an awkward and thin pitch that Mike was going to lead, were downright enjoyable. I figured I'd pretty much licked this aid business. The steepness of the wall beneath the crux allowed only a hanging belay, suspended from two good pins and a nut lodged behind a fin-like loose flake that, combined with the clean, sparkling sweep of quartz crystals in smooth granite, made me feel we were skin diving in the tepid waters off Aruba.

I wore my smooth-soled, light climbing shoes of canvas and rubber called EB's, designed to be flexible for free climbing, as I didn't have a decent pair of stiffer aid boots. When I journeyed out to buy them, everyone heartily recommended fitting them two or three sizes smaller than what I would normally wear. Naturally I wanted to climb well and be one of the guys, so I bought mine the full three sizes smaller than usual. This insured that I was in constant pain from the moment I began

Forrest harness. *Photo Kenneth Andrasko*

struggling to force them on, a pain that continued until we finished a climb. This had, of course, been one of the reasons for doing only short routes up to this point. Somehow I just figured that it was part of the fun of climbing.

Mike was out about three meters on the crux pitch by the time I had completely settled into my belay, hanging from the pins in my light ripstop nylon belay seat. It had taken about four hours to reach this last difficult pitch. We were aiding up a giant dihedral in the middle of a beautiful white granite wall, similar in design to a reflector oven; we were positioned just about where the batch of biscuits goes. Since the sun had heated the air to well above normal body temperature even without the constraints of my Japanese-foot-binding rubber EB's, I was hallucinating about SCUBA diving rather than climbing.

"Hurry up, will you!," I yelled up. Mike smiled and waved, ever the compassionate and understanding leader.

My feet were starting to feel like they were literally on fire. I was sitting in my belay seat facing the wall, with both feet spread wide against the rock. Whenever my feet shouted for relief, I set my knees against the wall (no knee pads, of course) until they became unbearable, whereupon I returned to standing in aid slings with feet pressed against the wall. It was some kind of sadomasochistic rhythm method, founded on abstinence, pain, and momentary pleasure.

Mike was moving efficiently, but we were short on pins. He had to constantly drop back down and pull out the ones behind him in order to keep moving up the crack. My feet got hotter and hotter, we both got drier and drier, and even my toes began to swell voluminously.

"Hurry up, god damn it!," I yelled periodically. Mike would smile and wave pleasantly. Finally, after over an hour, he was at the belay station at the end of the pitch. My feet were screaming. At that point, he looked down. "Are your feet and knees still hurting?," he called down seriously, in a touching way, a leader concerned for his partner's safety and well being.

"Just hurry up and get off, will you!," I vigorously suggested. He was bigger and better than me; there wasn't much more I could do.

"Try sitting sideways with your feet parallel to the rock," he intoned casually. Suddenly, the agony of the last hours disappeared! I felt like I could have hung there all day as the blood rushed back to my feet.

"Why didn't you tell me this earlier?," I yelled back, as soon as my throat could produce sounds again, and muttered a whole host of other comments under my breath.

"I wanted you to remember it," he smiled back. I would have killed him with repeated blows from the blunt instrument in my hammer holster, but we were forty-five meters apart. I did remember the lesson.

Simply put, any ascending or descending for any distance or length of time requires the support of a seat harness or belay seat and knowledge of how to use it. Many enjoy using a chest harness as well. All of these prevent constriction of the diaphragm and encourage stability.

Climbers sometimes use 25mm (1″) or 50mm tubular webbing wrapped around the waist three to six times and tied off with a ring bend or follow-through knot, a simple overhand knot followed back through. This is called a *swami belt*, and was developed in Yosemite by TM Herbert and Yvon Chouinard. While it does provide a secure means of attaching the rope to the body (via a double figure of eight or double knotted bowline tied around the swami), it may not provide for safe distribution of force in a hard fall. It is very uncomfortable to hang from without additional support, and after as little as fifteen minutes may restrict breathing and eventually lead to unconsciousness. For these reasons, many variations of seat harnesses can be made from standard climbing runners or webbing to augment or replace the swami.

The thigh loop (Fig. 12.1) is fine for low angle rappelling, but should be clipped into a waist loop or swami to insure it will not come off the leg in the event of a fall.

Fig. 12.1 Thigh loop.

The figure of eight seat harness (Fig. 12.2) is formed by twisting a standard runner a half turn, after putting one leg through it. It also should be clipped to the swami belt, to keep it from falling down around the knees each time the system loses tension. Furthermore, by clipping it into a swami, you are insured against coming out of it if you fall upside down, as in a rappel mishap.

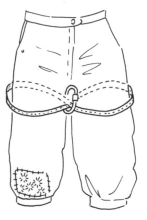

Fig. 12.2 Figure eight seat.

A *diaper sling* (Fig. 12.3) is made from a slightly longer runner than that used for the figure of eight. It is very comfortable but has been known to help turn a falling climber upside down if tied with a low center of gravity. It also could slip off if the climber suddenly were inverted unless it had been clipped to the swami belt.

Fig. 12.3 Diaper seat.

The double sit sling (Fig. 12.4) is made by stepping into a doubled sling which has been crossed in the front. One loop is dropped in back, pulled between the legs, and clipped up to the front with a carabiner. This is also quite comfortable.

Fig. 12.4 Double sit sling harness.

A seat harness can easily be made from a standard swami belt (Fig. 12.5). Wrap the swami around your waist once, then tie a simple overhand knot. Both ends are dropped down between the legs, separated, and next brought up behind each leg. One end is brought over in front from either side, and a simple follow-through or ring bend knot finishes the harness.

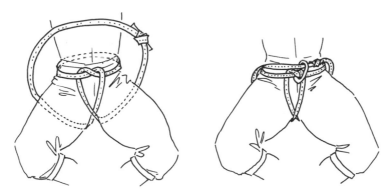

Fig. 12.5 Swami seat harness.

There are also a number of commercially made seat or sit harnesses. The *Whillans harness* (Fig. 12.6), developed by English hard man Don Whillans along with Troll Products, is a very popular one. The harness is loose fitting while one is walking or climbing, but when sitting or jumaring or caught in a fall, the rope automatically snugs up the harness into a comfortable position. The buckling system's slip is rated in excess of 1800kg, and the minimum strength of the webbing subject to a full force is over 2300kg; the stitching has a stronger rating than the webbing in a pure tension test. For SAR work, or whenever it is not possible for each person to be tied into the end of a rope, a small length of webbing or nylon rope should be tied between the two waist loops of the harness in order to back up the buckle in case of failure or slippage.

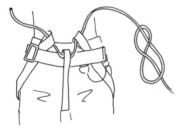

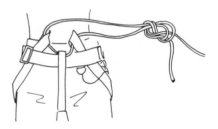

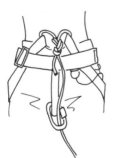

Fig. 12.6 Tying into Whillans harness with end of rope. For rescue work a short piece of webbing can be substituted for the rope to tie harness together, allowing flexibility to move around without the rope as tie-in.

There have been several reports of the thinner, 19mm crotch piece of the newer model Whillans breaking or ripping out during severe falls (including a 30m fall from the Exit Cracks on the Eiger north face during the second winter solo ascent, by Ivan Ghirandini in March, 1978). For this reason, it is prudent to back up that critical piece with another 19 or 25mm piece that follows it around and is then sewn or tied. On rappels, this piece alone attaches the climber to the mountain. Another recommended adaptation for rappels is to quickly clip an extra carabiner through the carabiner in the crotch piece (clipped to the rappel rope or descending ring) and the buckled waist strap. This back up is equally worthwhile if the harness webbing is at all worn on any model.

Other commercially produced seat harnesses include the REI (Fig. 12.7), Millet (Fig. 12.8), and the Forrest (Fig. 12.9) leg loop and swami combination. The Forrest harness is a comfortable one which comes in two parts and is designed to distribute the force of a fall to the thighs as well as to the waist. The waist belt is wide nylon webbing (either 50 or 75mm), and has greater tensile strength than any modern climbing rope (3800kg). It is tied together in front with a 25mm piece of tubular webbing, or rope. The leg loops are held in place by tying the climbing rope through them and the tubular waist tie-in with a figure of eight knot, or by passing the waist tie-in around the leg loops too. This harness allows very unrestricted movement, and is very comfortable. The loops must be large enough, though, to allow for heavy wool knickers and wind pants for winter climbing.

Fig. 12.7 REI seat harness.

Fig. 12.8 Millet seat harness.

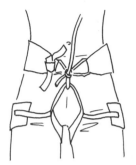

Fig. 12.9 Forrest harness, older model.

A chest harness is generally unnecessary for rappelling, but it may be used for ascending and crevasse travel according to one's particular ascending method and experience. A number of variations can be instantly produced from available webbing during any climb or SAR operation, as illustrated in figures 12.10, 12.11, and 12.12. There are chest harnesses made by quality manufacturers like Edelrid, Troll (Fig. 12.13), and Millet, all more comfortable than the improvised variety due to their wider webbing and adjustability.

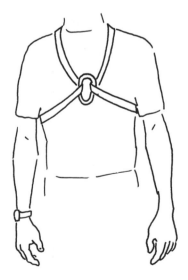

Fig. 12.10 Chest harness made from runner. May or may not be crossed in back.

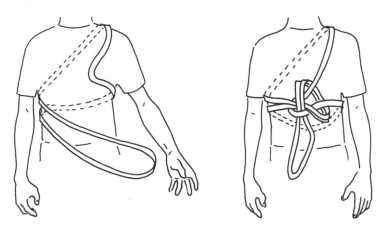

Fig. 12.11 Parisian baudrier harness.

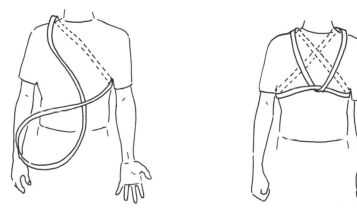

Fig. 12.12 Simple cross-shoulder harness.

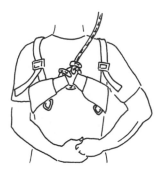

Fig. 12.13 Troll Europa chest harness.

A caution about all harnesses: it is important to inspect your gear regularly because it is subject to the same damage as any nylon rope or webbing or polyester caving equipment, as indicated in the chapter on ropes. Age, use, abrasion, and some chemicals can severely weaken the materials, so one must keep an eye out for and retire any worn or old harnesses.

BIBLIOGRAPHY

CHAPTER TWELVE

FOREST MOUNTAINEERING. *Product Catalog.* Denver, Colo., n.d.

LAVALLA, RICK, ED. *Resource Guide for Search and Rescue Training Materials.* Tacoma, Wa.: Survival Education Association, 1978.

MARCH, BILL. *Improvised Techniques in Mountain Rescue.* England: Jacobean Press, Ltd., n.d.

MARCH, BILL. *Modern Rope Techniques in Mountaineering.* 2d ed. Manchester, Eng.: Acerone Press, 1976.

MAY, W.G. *Mountain Search and Rescue Techniques.* Boulder, Colo.: Rocky Mountain Rescue Group, 1973.

RECREATION EQUIPMENT, INC. *Product Catalog,* 1977. P.O. Box 21685, Seattle, WA 98111, 1977.

SCOTT, DOUG. *Big Wall Climbing.* New York: Oxford University Press, 1974.

RESCUE FROM A CREVASSE.

13 | Ascending Technique

I HAD ALWAYS wanted to climb the Lost Arrow, a striking and famous rock pinnacle that is separated from the main Valley wall high above Yosemite Falls. The climb is spectacular and combines easy free climbing with fine aid work. To reach the base of the spire, one has to grind up to the Valley rim, and rappel two rope lengths into the notch between the pinnacle and the main wall. Once on top, either a rappel back into the notch or a Tyrolean over to the main wall gets you home.

A party of five of us finally broke free from work and roared off to do the Arrow. Bob Howard and I were to swing leads and the rest would jumar. The climb is usually done in two short pitches with a final long one. As it turned out, I had to clean the last pitch, so I rigged my Jumars after Bob led the pitch. The first dozen meters or so went briskly, until I came to a short traverse, somewhat unanticipated and not within my experience. I cleaned the first two points of protection by clipping both Jumars ahead of them and then slowly letting myself swing down over to and below the next point, jumaring up, reaching back and unclipping the rope.

This worked beautifully and relaxed my apprehension. No problem. When I came to the third point and began to put weight onto the top Jumar above the fixed piton, before I could unclip the bottom Jumar it was yanked up and jammed into the piton. So I transferred weight back to the bottom Jumar and thought about the whole thing awhile.

Every time I placed weight on the Jumar above the piton, the bottom Jumar would jam. So I'd struggle around trying to unclip the bottom

Double jumaring rescue off of Half Dome. *Photo Tim Setnicka*   *221*

Jumar, which finally worked, but I couldn't attach it above the piton because to do so I'd have to let go of the rope and go careening across the rock to the next station. This desperate seesaw action continued until I thought the rope would wear threadbare or saw through the carabiner on the pin.

Suggestions from the ledge below were solicited, but as I couldn't see the gallery, it turned into something like a Jumar instruction class taught by Louis Braille. After an hour of a circus high-wire act, I finally regained composure, cleaned the pitch, and resuscitated my ego on top. Obviously I hadn't taken the time beforehand to practice or get briefed on cleaning traverses or other technique that I figured I knew. Had the weather been foul, or the day closer to night, the general humor of my situation would have dissipated instantly. One of the experienced climbers along later told me, "It's good for you — it will make you a better person and climber." I seem to remember that phrase being employed by my parents every time I had to have my teeth drilled by the dentist. "It's good for you. . . ."

SAR personnel use a variety of means for traveling across technical terrain, i.e., any situation in which ropes are used for ascending, descending, traversing, or belaying any person or object.

Non-Mechanical Ascenders

Free climbing (using hands and feet for support rather than the rope or artificial aids) is a non-mechanical method of ascent. Climbing in technical terrain may mean nothing more than free climbing 5.8 for a few moves, or cramponing across an ice couloir to a stranded climber. Whatever your particular needs, there are numerous books on how to climb rock, snow, and ice. Reading and studying are only a start, however. Experience has shown that no matter what the specific situation, when it comes time for a search or rescue involving a special activity, a regular practitioner generally has the edge over someone with little field experience. As in most sports, speed, efficiency, and proficiency come only after much time and effort and a lot of mistakes. Practicing forces us to constantly examine, evaluate, change, and improve. Competent climbers make competent SAR personnel.

"Soft Mechanical" Ascenders

Free or non-mechanical ascending is done directly, with the rope used only as a safety. Mechanical ascending devices, on the other hand, are clamped onto a fixed, static rope, and they fully support the ascender's weight. These rope clamps can be classified into two broad categories, "soft" and "hard."

The *soft ascender* is usually a simple knot formed out of a small sling rope, or a knot used in conjunction with a carabiner. Earlier (in Chapter 11) we mentioned the prusik loop and the Bachmann knot, two of the most popular soft ascenders.

Hedden (Kreuzklem) Knot

This is a simple figure of eight knot, tied over and around the static rope. It is easy to loosen after the load has been removed.

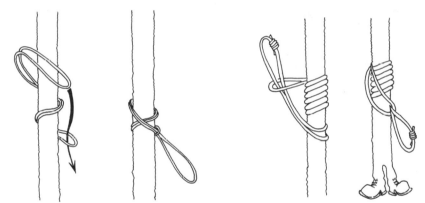

Fig. 13.1 Kreuzklem knot.   Fig. 13.2 Klemheist knot.

Klemheist Knot

The Klemheist knot is formed by wrapping the sling rope around the static rope and then simply feeding it back through itself. It can be tied with one hand. You may vary it by tying in a carabiner, which provides a convenient handle; this makes loosening the knot very easy. It is also known as the Headon knot.

Penberthy Knot

The Penberthy knot consists of a single short length of rope wrapped spirally around a static rope. The short rope is tied off with a bowline, and then both ends are tied off with your favorite follow through, figure of eight, or double fisherman's knot.

Ascending with prusik knots.
Photo Kenneth Andrasko

All of these ascending knots are useful as safeties or planned weak points in raising and lowering systems. If jammed, these knots can be cut while carrying a load, unlike mechanical ascenders, unless they have been rigged with webbing or sling rope. Soft ascenders may be used around more than one rope simultaneously, not true for a mechanical ascender. Finally, these knots may be easily tied in the field from standard climbing equipment. Being familiar with them and their applications may help you get around unforeseen circumstances or improper planning that might otherwise require the use of a mechanical rope clamp.

Hard Ascenders

A *hard ascender* is any mechanical device specifically designed to be used as a rope clamp. Jumar ascenders, Hiebeler clamps, Clog, CMI, and Gibbs ascenders are all examples of hard mechanical ascenders in use today. Their popularity varies greatly from one region of the country to the next.

Some of the reasons hard mechanical ascenders are so popular are that they are easy to use; they can be released and moved up the rope instantly; and, they usually provide uniform performance. If they do slip, however, there is no easy way (if any) to increase their holding power.

Also, hard ascenders may not be as strong as the soft ascenders, depending on the quality and size of the alloy used and the conditions in which they are deployed. This strength consideration is one reason why prusik loops rather than the old Jumars are generally used as safeties on raising and lowering lines in Yosemite.

Fig. 13.3 Penberthy knot.

The *Jumar* ascenders are the most popular in the American climbing community, especially for use on dry rope. They were invented in the early fifties in Switzerland by Adolf Jusi and Walter Marti for ascending ropes to the nests of eagles as part of Jusi's government bird banding job. So common are Jumars on the American climbing scene that the generic verb for using any mechanical ascender is "to jumar."

This device is a cast aluminum alloy frame with a spring-loaded tooth and cam in it. When the Jumar is slid up the rope, the cam allows it to move freely, but as soon as any downward pull occurs, the cam instantly tightens on the rope. Jumars work on rope from 7 to 14mm diameter. A pair of Jumars can easily be operated by one hand, including clipping them on and off the rope; such maneuvers may be necessary when passing a point of protection.

When one chooses to use Jumars, he must consider the relatively low breaking strength ascribed to the old style blue or gray models by the manufacturer (about 160 kg, with no shock loading recommended). The new yellow model has been greatly strengthened by design changes, and is factory tested to 680 kg before it leaves the plant. The Jumar does tend to slip under icy, muddy, or wet conditions, although the new model has larger teeth to combat this limitation.

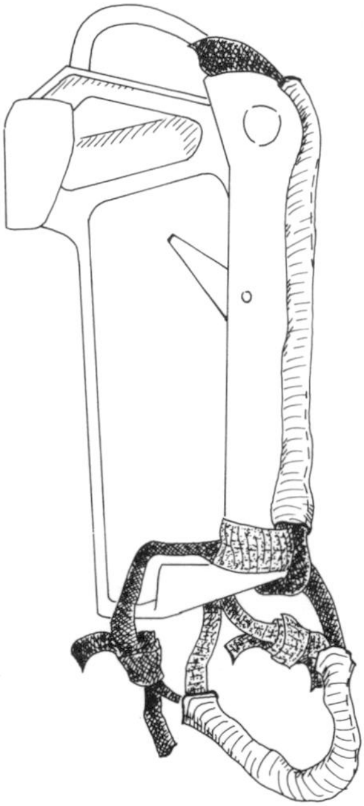

Fig. 13.4 Jumar ascender rigged with safety slings at top and bottom.

The cast aluminum frame is brittle, and can crack or break if dropped or suddenly force loaded. A safety margin against frame breakage can be introduced by rigging it with 14mm (9/16'') heavy duty tubular nylon webbing. The webbing provides two places of attachment to the Jumar instead of one. It also prevents lateral torque from developing when a carabiner is clipped directly into the handle of the frame and twisted, or when one is clipped into the top eye of the Jumar (adding the additional danger of the carabiner slipping down and accidentally opening the cam). This webbing also provides an extra advantage if the Jumar becomes jammed under a load — the webbing may be cut to free the rope and the Jumar. The method shown in figure 13.4 is best.

One of the most frequently heard complaints about Jumars is their potential for twisting or torquing off the rope. This is most likely to occur during a traverse, when the Jumar's path is lateral while the climber's weight pulls downward, causing the cam and gate to torque against the rope. The problem gets increasingly serious as the angle between the Jumar and the rope approaches 90°. To help prevent this rotation, a carabiner should be clipped onto the rope and into the Jumar's 14mm safety slings (Fig. 13.5).

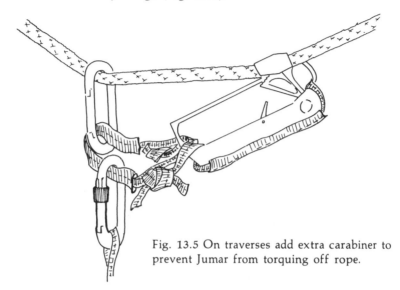

Fig. 13.5 On traverses add extra carabiner to prevent Jumar from torquing off rope.

Placing a Jumar on a rope, especially if the rope runs transversely or hangs free, must be done with care to insure that the cam is fully locked in place with the safety engaged. This is especially critical on the new yellow model, with its extra tooth on the safety that locks the cam open.

Another type of mechanical ascender similar in design to the Jumar is the *Clog*, which comes in two models. The standard ascender features a stainless steel spring-loaded cam in a high strength frame made of heavy sheet aluminum. The safety for the cam is a carabiner placed in a hole in the frame below the cam, so that the ascender can be removed only by choice. This carabiner is also the point of attachment for the climber's harness or étriers. Occasionally one must unclip this safety carabiner to get the rope in or out of the ascender, in order to pass it around a piton. This process is not only time consuming, but it is also potentially dangerous, for the remaining ascender is the only point of attachment to the rope unless one is tied into it directly. Also, there is no handle on this model, so hands take a beating on low-angle rock. The small size of this unit makes it light enough to carry along as an emergency piece of equipment. Figures 13.6 and 13.7 illustrate two Clog models.

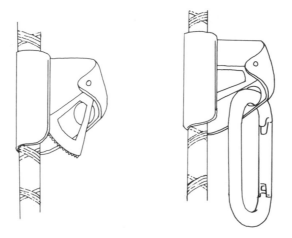

Fig. 13.6 Clog ascenders: open for attachment on left, and ready to use on right. Carabiner is the safety.

More popular is the newer Clog Expedition ascender. This model is a close cousin in appearance to a Jumar, and similar to the first Clog model except it has a handle large enough to accept heavy winter mittens. The Clog's frame is 3mm (⅛″) formed aluminum plate (rated at 400 kg by the manufacturer), which eliminates the brittleness of the cast metal construction of the Jumar. The cam is stainless steel, spring-loaded, and features a safety release to insure that the cam will not come off the rope.

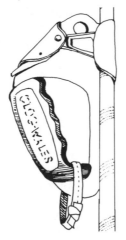

Fig. 13.7 Clog expedition ascender. Rig like Jumar if desired.

Some of the earlier models of this ascender had a hole in the base for a bottom carabiner attachment, but it was found that carabiners twist and load the ascender sideways, creating lateral torque and greatly stressing the gate. This ascender, like the Jumar, requires reinforcing loops of webbing into which the bottom carabiners are clipped. The newer model Clog does not have a bottom carabiner hole.

Hiebeler clamps utilize a system whereby a spring-loaded safety lever allows the rope to move freely through the ascender when unweighted, but without a cam. As soon as a load is placed on the ascender's lever, it automatically pivots and squeezes against the rope as the entire ascender bends. A disadvantage of this clamp is that lateral or twisting force may cause it to pop off the rope. However, this is prevented in part by the spring-loaded safety lever. These rope clamps are more popular in Europe, as they work well on icy ropes. They are seldom seen in the United States, as they are not considered very strong, despite the figures shown in the test tables.

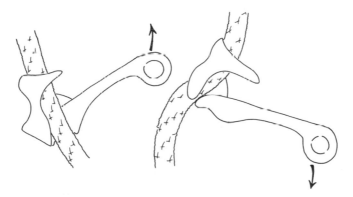

Fig. 13.8 Hiebeler clamps. Unloaded (left) and loaded (right).

The *Gibbs* ascender is one of the strongest available on the commercial market today. The manufacturer tests each ascender to 450 kg before shipment, but other tests indicate that the Gibbs is good to 900 kg without breaking the rope. The strength of the Gibbs comes from a simple design utilizing strong materials (a 3mm aluminum alloy frame with a 15mm-thick aluminum cam held in place by a heavy duty pin). It is a simple machine that is disassembled and then reassembled around a rope of 12mm diameter or less. The U-shaped frame holds a non-spring- or spring-loaded cam (depending on the model) which, when loaded, forces the cam against the rope. This direct loading of the cam by weighting is the major reason why a Gibbs works well on icy, wet, or gritty ropes. The non-spring-loaded model Gibbs may be rigged as a self-following belay between Jumars or as a safety on a lowering rope. Gibbses may also be rigged on feet and knees, enabling a person to ascend a free standing rope by using his legs rather than his arms to move the ascenders. This technique is very fast, but its use is largely restricted to cavers.

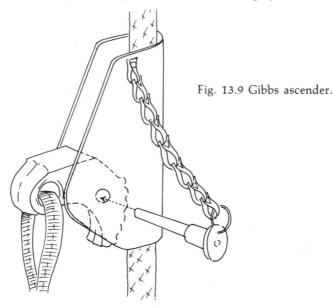

Fig. 13.9 Gibbs ascender.

Another consideration in using a Gibbs is that it generally takes two hands to remove it and replace it on the rope. This can be time consuming when one is cleaning protection from a pitch. The Gibbs also lacks a handle, so that one may have difficulty moving it on a rope pressed against the rock face. It is also possible to place the cam on the rope upside down. The cam still holds to a degree, but with more loading it will suddenly slip, usually damaging the rope severely. The same is true if the frame is put on the rope upside down. A further question is whether or not the cam will jam open during a sudden fall when used as a self belay. This fear is largely alleviated if a 25 or 30cm length of webbing is tied between the eye of the cam and one's tie-in. This additional slack gives the Gibbs a chance to work when suddenly loaded. However, whenever the Gibbs falls down the rope at the same speed (or faster) than a falling climber, say on low-angle terrain, the Gibbs will not catch.

The old and new style Gibbses differ in the tooth design of the cam. If a 570 kg force is placed on a new Gibbs, the rope is damaged very little. The same force placed on an old style Gibbs, however, does significant damage to the rope, usually to the point where it must be retired. The difference is that the older Gibbs has a square tooth configuration with a coarser finish, whereas the newer model features a rounded tooth profile and smoother finish. The older cam can easily be exchanged for the new one. The newest model is spring-loaded to prevent it from sliding down the rope when unweighted, a serious drawback of the standard model when ascending steep pitches. The Gibbs is an excellent tool for mountain SAR as well as for personal use for caving and climbing, especially on expeditions.

The newest entrants into the ascender line-up are the two *CMI* models. The CMI 5000 ascender looks very much like a Jumar but is made from anodized, extruded alloy and is much stronger. Its chief drawbacks (somewhat minor) are the fact that sharp edges in the handle hurt the hand when one hangs from the ascender on steep pitches; the handle is too small to easily accommodate heavy mittens for expedition and cold weather use; and, the safety release is located above the cam, making it awkward to use with one hand. The very latest model is the compact CMI Shorti ascender, pocket-sized and weighing only 320 grams per pair. It was designed as a lightweight alternative to standard ascenders, ideal for glacial travel, field rescue operations, and other applications where the bulk and weight of the others is unnecessary. There is an optional double safety that may encourage its use in SAR work. As yet, the Shorti has not been on the market long enough for any realistic appraisal of its value in the field.

The important point to remember in using any mechanical device is that it can break down at any time. Knowing the strengths, advantages, and idiosyncrasies of each type will insure safe use.

Ascending by Soft Ascenders

Occasionally it will be necessary to ascend a rope in an unexpected emergency without access to mechanical ascenders. This may be accomplished by using one of the soft aids already discussed. As a general rule, ascents using knots are slower than those using mechanical ascenders. However, the system may be as strong or stronger than some mechanical aids. Some of these soft ascending systems are shown in the following figures, depending on how many ascending knots are necessary.

Fig. 13.10 Ascending by one prusik. Also used to unjam prusik on rappel.

Preparing the Mechanical Ascending System

Setting up your own personalized system takes a little time and should be done prior to going on an actual operation. The two most important items are leg slings or *stirrups* for your feet (usually called *étriers* when designed as a webbing ladder for direct aid climbing), and a seat or body harness. The stirrups enable you to stand on one ascender while the unweighted one is moved up the rope. The seat harness allows one rest at will during the ascent. Occasionally a chest harness is used as well to rest the arms. See figures 3.10 to 3.12.

Ascending Stirrups and Étriers

Stirrups which are designed only for ascending (as opposed to the type used for direct aid climbing) can be made from 8mm, 9mm, or 11mm rope, or from standard 25mm (1″) flat nylon webbing. Most people seem to prefer the flat webbing, as it is fairly comfortable to stand in. A slip knot or an ankle hitch (a girth knot, or lark's foot) is tied at the foot end, and the other end is connected to the ascender.

Fig. 13.11 Ascending by two prusiks.

Fig. 13.12 Ascending by three prusiks, one to each foot and a chest harness.

Fig. 13.13 Ascending by three prusiks, one to each foot and a seat sling.

A more versatile stirrup system can be fabricated by tying nylon ladders or étriers, used for aid climbing as well as ascending. There are two basic ways to make étriers, and the standard material again is 25mm flat nylon webbing, although heavy duty 14mm (9/16'') tubular webbing is sometimes used in order to reduce bulk.

The first design features a *Frost knot* (after Tom Frost of Yosemite fame), and requires between six and seven meters of webbing. The Frost knot is tied first, and then a simple overhand knot is used to form each successive step. The top step should be as small as possible, but not so small that it is extremely difficult to place a foot in it. Each step down is increased in size, the lowest being the largest. Getting the correct length of material is tricky and it is important that the steps (usually four or even five) are set a comfortable distance apart.

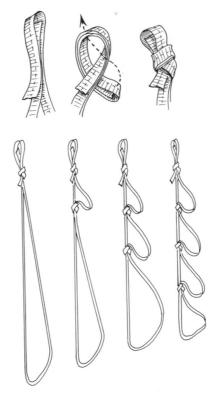

Fig. 13.14 One method of tying étriers, using Frost knot at top.

The second étrier design uses only overhand knots in about the same length of material. The first overhand knot is tied on a bight in the middle of the webbing and should leave about a five centimeter loop. This loop is for a carabiner, similar to the loop made by the Frost knot. The steps are formed by tying successive overhand knots down the ladder. Any material left after the last knot is simply cut off. This method is much easier to adjust to the correct step length (Fig. 13.15).

Fig. 13.15 Second method of tying étriers, including a subaider on right.

As you tie each step with either of these methods, pull up about 10cm of webbing on one side before tying the knot. This excess forms the rung portion of the step and insures that the step will be open when the étriers are under tension.

For a real multipurpose system, make a set of sub-étriers (or sub-aiders, as they are often called) to go along with standard étriers. These are nothing more than short étriers made out of heavy duty 14mm or 12mm tubular webbing. The heavy duty type is preferable, because it is strong enough for emergency sling use.

Fig. 13.16 Right-handed Jumar, étrier, and subaider. Use either one locking or two carabiners with reversed gates to attach étrier to Jumar.

The steps of the sub-aiders should match those of the étriers in order to wind up with two separate sets of étriers to greatly speed progress on aid routes. You can rest comfortably, placing weight evenly on each stirrup, or can tuck one foot under your seat in a good resting position.

For the following discussion, we'll assume the use of Jumar ascenders tied with safeties, but any ascender could be substituted. Tie a piece of practice rope in a tree so that it hangs free. If the system is set up for ascending a free standing rope (where your body doesn't touch the wall — the most strenuous sort), then minor adjustments will enable you to climb vertical or lower angled walls quite efficiently after some practice. It is best to practice free, vertical, and low-angle ascents. The system is adjusted merely by adding or subtracting carabiners.

First, set up a seat sling or harness. Some sort of support around your hips or legs will allow you to sit down while hanging on Jumars, to rest without using your arms for support. A belay seat (30 by 70cm of light ripstop nylon sewn to twill tape, for hanging belays) is useful while

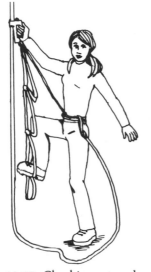

Fig. 13.17 Checking step length. Reach high with Jumar and step high at same time, and adjust length of étrier (and girth hitch around foot) with small sling as necessary so it is tight. Girth hitch other foot in next higher step in other étrier, adding same length small sling if used on the other one.

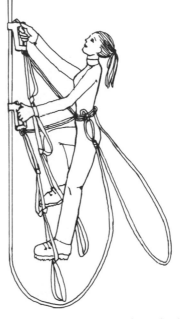

Fig. 13.18 Attach slings from both Jumars to waist harness, and clip a loop of rope to harness as well. As you ascend, clip in new loops, releasing and untying old loops.

hanging from Jumars to rest or clean a pitch. A chest harness can be tied or a commercial one used if deemed necessary to ease the strain on the arms. This is less desirable than a seat harness, though, because one usually has a pack, hardware racks, and other paraphernalia hanging around chest and back, making clipping in and out of the harness difficult. Thin, supple leather gloves with the fingertips cut off save wear and tear on the hands while using ascenders on big walls.

Backup ascender safeties may be used in addition to the main ascenders. A prusik or similar loop can be placed above the lower Jumar,

Jumaring up overhanging pitch in a belay seat for comfort. Glove is used to protect hand. *Photo Tim Setnicka*

or an additional ascender such as a Gibbs can be used between the two main ones. These safeties are tied directly to the seat harness. This provides an added margin of safety, but also adds at least a third more complication to the system, and may actually nullify the increased safety margin due to entanglement and confusion over which sling does what. Practice builds a different kind of safety margin. Confidence, speed, and efficiency are nutured, producing the soundest safety margin of all in the long run. Keep each system simple, and know it intimately.

By now you are probably ready to start ascending, so clip yourself to both ascenders with either slings or sub-aiders, and check to see whether the step lengths are correct (Fig. 13.17). Next, set up a *daisy chain* by tying or sewing webbing (usually heavy duty 14mm) in a series of loops in the design of a miniature étrier, or use a chain of single carabiners (Fig. 13.19). The daisy chain is tied into your harness and then clipped into the upper ascender at a distance not longer than an arm's length. The idea is to slide the upper ascender upwards in order to sit down comfortably at any time (Fig. 13.20). If the wall doesn't overhang, you can press your feet on it to aid the ascent. A daisy chain or sling on a chest harness

Fig. 13.19 Full Jumar ascending system, including daisy chain tie-ins to seat harness.

Fig. 13.20 Ascending in comfort with daisy chain adjusted properly.

can be clipped in too, if it suddenly seems prudent. Resting saves time in the long run. There are several methods of keeping your feet in the étriers, as shown in figures 13.21 to 13.24.

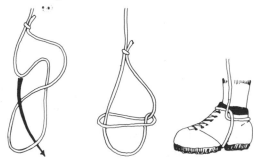

Fig. 13.21 Stirrup method of tying ascending sling to foot.

Fig. 13.22 Figure of eight method.

Fig. 13.23 Girth hitch.

Fig. 13.24 Rubber band method, made from old tire inner tubes.

Once you have reached the victim during a rescue, it is easiest to function by hanging from this ascending system. If the victim is hanging or on a small ledge without much working room, this is especially true. One trick to make it easier to work around a victim is to run the stirrups through your swami belt or seat harness, to help maintain balance and to keep the stirrups from pressing against the victim.

Frequently it is possible to effect a self-rescue by using nothing more than mechanical ascenders and some ingenuity. The simultaneous or *double ascender system* is a good method (Fig. 13.25). If a climber's injury prevents him from holding onto an ascender, it is easy for his partner to jumar ahead of him, either on the same rope or on a separate one. The partner rigs a sling or piece of cord to the top of the victim's ascender. At the victim's request, the partner simply pulls up on the cord and moves the Jumar up the rope. The basic system remains the same for both climbers (daisy chain, seat, and optional chest harness), and each can tie off to the other for a belay or clip into a loop of the rope on which he is jumaring.

Double jumaring rescue. *Photo Tim Setnicka*

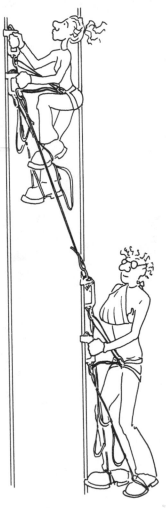

Fig. 13.25 Double jumaring. Top person pulls up one of subject's Jumars for him as required.

Solo ascending is possible if the injured climber rigs three Gibbs ascenders to his seat harness, knee, and foot. His uninjured arm moves the seat harness Gibbs, and the leg moves itself. The Gibbses make this type of ascent possible because they are not spring-loaded, but placing and replacing the Gibbses on a rope (say when passing a knot) may be a bit tricky with one hand.

Fig. 13.26 Using three Gibbs ascenders to ascend.

Fig. 13.28 A special strap easily attaches Gibbs to knee.

Fig. 13.27 Two methods of attaching Gibbs ascender to foot.

Along with climbing books, refer to caving works to get an idea how cavers solve problems like ascending over 300 meters of free hanging rope. Experiment a little — everyone has his or her own system worked out.

Jumaring accident on west face of El Cap. Rope was cut by moderate rock edge as climber reached the anchor after a free jumar up several rope lengths. *Photo Kenneth Andrasko*

BIBLIOGRAPHY

CHAPTER THIRTEEN

AMENT, PAT. *Rock Wise: Reflections, Safety, and Technique in Rock Climbing.* Boulder, Colo.: March Press, 1978.

GIBBS PRODUCTS COMPANY. *Product Catalog.* 854 Padley St., Salt Lake City, UT 84108, 1978.

HARDING, WARREN. *Downward Bound: A Mad Guide to Rock Climbing.* Englewood Cliffs, N.J.: Prentice-Hall, 1975.

JUMAR CORPORATION. *Product Catalog.* CH-3713, Reichenbach, Switzerland, n.d.

MONTGOMERY, NED R. *Single Rope Techniques.* Broadway, N.S.W. Australia: Sydney Speleological Society, 1977.

OWENS, GARY. "A Vertical Caver Looks at Ascending Safety," *Off Belay,* August 1975, pp. 12-15.

SMUTEK, RAY, ED. *Jumars. Off Belay* Report Series, Renton, Wa.: 1979.

THRUN, ROBERT. *Prusiking.* Huntsville, Ala.: National Speleological Society, 1977.

VILLIN, GARY J. "More on Using Jumars," *Off Belay* 9 (June 1973): 3-4.

14 | Descending Technique

IN MAY OF 1979, a classic rappel accident occurred on El Capitan. It was the perfect enactment of one of every climber's worst fears, the subject of frequent gallows humor. After completing about a third of a Grade VI route and deciding to call off their attempt, two climbers set about orchestrating the long descent.

On one of the projected series of a half-dozen or so rappels down a bolt rappel route — in which the anchor stations are 40 or 50 meters apart on rather blank granite — the lead climber found his shirt caught in the descending rig. He was over 300 meters above the talus slope; it was very hot; and, his shirt had the audacity to entangle with the rope and carabiners. Hanging in mid-air, the frustration transforming into desperation, he yanked and cursed, and decided the shirt had to be cut free.

As the wall was nearly vertical, the climber placed one tiny, wired nut behind a small expanding flake in order to stand in étriers (small ladders of webbing) and maneuver. He pulled out his knife, brought along specifically for this sort of emergency (and for the blocks of cheese), and hacked at the cotton shirt. An immediate shock hit him when he saw the two rappel ropes fly off up the face like a loosed slingshot! The taut ropes had been touched by the knife and instantly cut. He realized that he was hanging from a single mediocre nut lodged behind a loose flake. The wind blew the ropes out of reach. It was really hot. Understandably distraught, he yelled for help, echoed by his equally isolated partner, who felt he could not descend the rappel route on the shortened ropes.

Jim Bridwell preparing to rappel 300 meters to Camp V on El Cap during major big wall rescue. *Photo National Park Service*

Rescue personnel arrived on the scene. They set up the Questar telescope and studied the climbers' position. By yelling instructions up to them through a bullhorn, the SAR crew calmed them down, located the next anchor point, and talked them out of their predicament. The solitary nut in question was no doubt retired to a life of leisure and a position of special reverence, having performed yeoman service.

Accidents in North American Mountaineering, published late each spring by the American Alpine Club, details and analyzes mountain safety incidents of the previous year in Canada and the U.S. Since 1951, over a hundred rappelling accidents have been reported, and fully 42% of the total reported mishaps occurred on the descent (with 51% on the ascent, and 6% unknown). It is tragic and ironic that so many accidents occur on the way down, very often after the technical difficulties have been surmounted. This is especially true in expedition and serious alpine climbing, when exhaustion is a prominent factor. Experienced climbers (i.e., ones who have had their wits altered by malfunctions of some sort while on rappel in grisly circumstances) often walk or downclimb much longer routes rather than rappel directly.

Descending can be accomplished by many different means, with downclimbing being the simplest from an equipment standpoint. *Downclimbing* is largely self-evident. Basically, the lead climber climbs down a route chosen ahead of time from a good vantage point or improvised on the way down. His progress is protected in the same manner as on the ascent, by placing slings and nuts — especially on traverses — to safeguard the second. While the leader has a top rope (i.e., is belayed from above), the second downclimbs in circumstances similar to those facing a leader, with the possibility of taking a leader fall. In a party of mixed technical ability, the strongest climber usually goes last. Other parties leapfrog leads in conventional fashion, or climb continuously on easy terrain.

In the latter case, the leader places protection as he moves, and continues climbing when the rope (often shortened, as in glacial travel) comes taut on the second. When the leader runs out of protection pieces to place, the second is belayed and joins him, to either take over the lead with the accumulated rack of hardware, or replenish the leader's supply. Practice downclimbing at every opportunity, so that its odd rhythm, balance, and faith all become second nature.

Rick Reider going over the edge of El Cap during rescue. Note belay rope and gloves. *Photo National Park Service*

Rappelling is the primary means of descending technical rock or ice. It is performed on one or two anchored ropes. One can simply slow his descent by the friction of the ropes over his body. The classic Dulfer technique is the fundamental rappel, and should be learned first. Face into the rock straddling the rappel rope, pass it behind the right thigh to the outside, back up the chest and over the left shoulder, and down across the back to the right side of the waist. The right hand acts as the brake on the tail of the rope; the rope can be held loosely, or drawn across the front of the body to increase friction or stop. Meanwhile, the left hand guides the standing part of the rope above the rappeller and separates the strands (if two ropes are in use) to facilitate pulling the ropes down when the ground or the next anchor station is reached.

Be certain for any rappel that no compromises are made anywhere in the system. All of the climber's weight is on the anchor, so resident slings should be backed up with a new one, pins should be tested and redriven or backed up if necessary, and trees very carefully assessed. At least while all but the last member of the party rappels, backup anchors should be placed and used. Be liberal with the use of sling material — it's very inexpensive relative to the possible cost of anchor failure.

Generally, it is easier and safer to use mechanical friction devices. There are three main ways a climber rigs a rappel: the brake bar and carabiner system, the simple carabiner brake system, and the descending ring system. Those familiar with caving know about the "whale's tail" and related rappel racks for specific descending uses, with some application for SAR work.

After deciding what type of seat harness best suits your needs following trial and error sessions, the next step is to choose a rappel device.

Brake Bar System

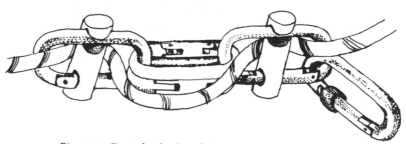

Fig. 14.1 Basic brake bar friction arrangement.

The *brake bar* and carabiner system is popular in many areas in North America. It consists of a solid aluminum bar placed on a standard oval carabiner. The rappel ropes run through the carabiner and over the bar in order to create friction. There are two types of brake bars, depending on whether the slot is straight or diagonal.

Fig. 14.2 Types of brake bars in cross section: straight (left) and diagonal (right).

The use and safety of brake bars is controversial and worth discussing. They are very fast to set up and easy for rappelling, and simplify passing knots in a lowering system. The bars have adequate strength for rappelling and related SAR work.

Brake bars are, however, another specialized piece of climbing equipment to carry along. Their biggest disadvantage is the stress they place on the gate of the carabiner upon which they ride. A carabiner is designed to be loaded along its long major axis with the gate closed. This is how it is tested and rated for strength. The gate and hinge system are a carabiner's major weak points, and can withstand only minimal lateral pressure or torque relative to the carabiner's overall strength (Fig. 14.3).

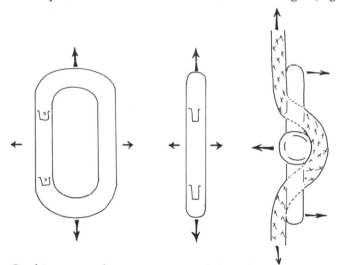

Fig. 14.3 Carabiner strength rating is measured along the strong vertical or long axis. Carabiner is very weak along the short axis.

Problems can occur if a brake bar's width is slightly larger than the width of the carabiner. A large lateral loading force along the minor axis is produced against the gate when the system is loaded, as on a rappel, and the carabiner could weaken or fail (Fig. 14.4).

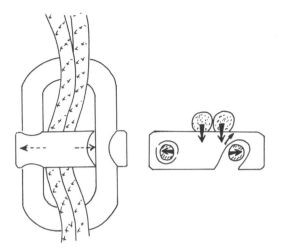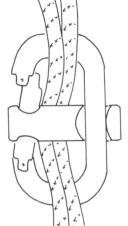

Fig. 14.4 A tight-fitting brake bar transfers the force to the weak axis of the carabiner and may cause it to fail.

Fig. 14.5 If brake bar holes are too large, carabiner gate may open during rappel. It is also possible to clip a rope into the brake bar and carabiner upside down, causing immediate failure when loaded.

If the holes in a brake bar are too large for the carabiner in use, the bar can work itself down to the gate, and the gate could partially work open during a rappel. The rappel rope might then extricate itself through the gate or decrease the carabiner's strength because of the open gate. A snug-fitting brake bar corrects this problem. Be sure to keep the carabiner's gate away (or up) from the rappeller or load.

It is possible, especially with the diagonally slotted bars, to clip the rope in upside down. Placing weight on the rappel rope immediately forces the gate open. A straight-slotted brake bar usually will not allow this to happen, because it does not stay closed in an upside down position. The straight-slotted brake bars do, however, open unexpectedly on occasion when not under tension, say when a climber is on a ledge big enough to stand on and is moving around tying in. Unless a backup prusik knot or Jumar is on the rope, the rappeller will suddenly find himself decidedly unaffiliated with the rope.

Brake bars are safe if used correctly, but they should be backed up by an ascending device or knot and checked frequently. One may improvise a brake bar by using a hammer or piton across a biner if there are not enough carabiners to go around.

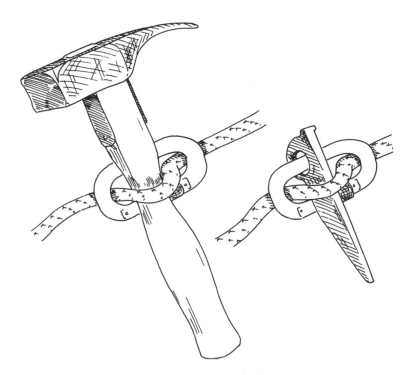

Fig. 14.6 Improvised brake bars.

Simple Carabiner System

The most popular rappel system in use in Yosemite is the *six carabiner brake system*, which utilizes only standard carabiners. The carabiners are attached in pairs with gates reversed from each other. The two brake carabiners are clipped on with the gates opposed. As a result, this system is extremely resistant to any lateral force against a carabiner gate. No extra brake bars or descending rings need be carried to make the system work. And because the brake carabiners are clipped in, they cannot flip off the carabiners they ride on when not under tension. Oval carabiners work best. Accidents have occurred due to mistakes made while setting up or adjusting the system. Always use sets of two carabiners with gates reversed or opposed, and be certain that you can construct the system properly under any circumstances (Fig. 14.8). Try it, for example, in the shower with the lights out and with soapy hands.

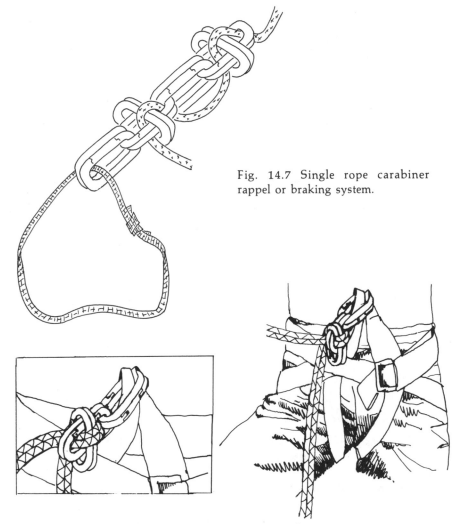

Fig. 14.7 Single rope carabiner rappel or braking system.

Fig. 14.8 Double rope rappel or brake system.

Descending Rings

Another excellent descending device is the *figure eight descending ring* available commercially from many manufacturers, including Clog, CMI, SMC, and Russ Anderson, to name a few. These rings are extremely strong; some can withstand forces over 2700 kg with little if any

Free rappel. *Photo Mead Hargis*

deformation. One must be wary of the small radius created when the rappel rope below one is wrapped around the waist of the ring to cause more friction. It is easy to create a dangerous situation in which nylon runs against nylon. Be sure to keep the tail of the rope straight down below you, and do not let it stray in your lower feeding hand up toward the standing rope (anchored above) coming out of the ring. The rope in the ring can readjust into a girth hitch and lock in place. These rings are speedily set up, and more than one rescue group uses them for rappelling out of helicopters.

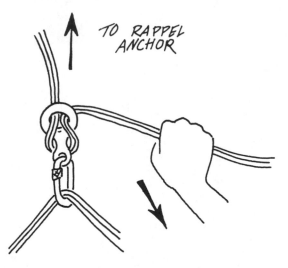

Fig. 14.9 Figure eight ring in use on double rope rappel.

A figure eight ring cannot fall off a rope when unloaded, unlike a brake bar. The small hole in the ring serves admirably as a belaying device, and works the same way as a Sticht plate. The new SMC eight ring is specially designed to be used for belaying in this manner, and works the best of all on fuzzy 11mm, muddy, or icy ropes.

By the way, one can rappel with a Sticht belay plate, but only slowly. Nylon melts at about 250°C, and damage to the sheath may result, as there is insufficient metal to dissipate the continual buildup of heat. There is also considerable serious kinking. Innumerable other European belay and rappel devices exist, like the Bankl plate, a rappel ring of sorts that keeps the ropes separated and prevents kinking and twisting.

Other Devices

Other specialized descending devices include those cavers have developed for their incredibly long vertical descents: gadgets like "whale's tails" and rappel racks. These mechanisms have application in SAR work, too.

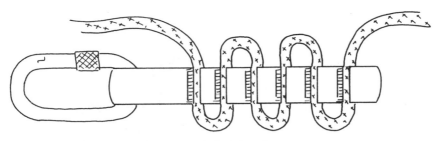

Fig. 14.10 Whale's tail.

A *whale's tail* is a solid piece of machined alloy which has a number of slots cut in it. The rope is allowed to run back and forth through these slots to increase or decrease the amount of friction. The tail reportedly has good heat dissipation, tempered by the disadvantage that the rope could pop out of the openings while slack. Rocky Mountain Rescue Group has developed a brake plate for their lowering systems which uses this same design for the friction source. More on their system in Chapter 18.

The *rappel rack* is nothing more than a U-shaped extended frame that supports many brake bars in series. The rappel rack evolved to assist cavers in adding or subtracting rappel friction as they descended long (over 300 meters!) free rappels (without touching the rock). When you first go over a rock lip on a long rappel, the weight of the rope below helps pull against the friction device. Only one or two brake bars, or a simple wrap on the descending ring, is necessary. As you descend, however, and gradually lose the weight of the rope below, your brake system becomes less and less efficient. The trick now is to increase brake friction while hanging 200 meters down on a free standing rope. With the whale's tail or rappel rack this is relatively easy to accomplish: one can place the rope through an additional slot in the whale's tail or clip the rope exiting from the highest brake bar into another brake bar below it.

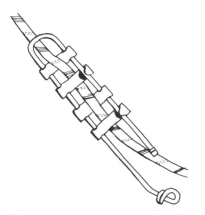

Fig. 14.11 Brake bar rappel rack.

Fig. 14.12 Rappel rack in use. Brake bars can be flipped on and off easily while in use.

These gadgets are not only useful for individual descending, but lend themselves to use as friction devices in lowering systems. Their advantages include greater flexibility in adding or subtracting friction, and easy knot passing. The disadvantage, however, of the carabiner rack is the increased possibility that brake bars could pop off. And a slack rope could come out of a slot in the whale's tail.

Descending Safety

For a stable rappel, the load should be transferred below the waist, not onto the swami belt. This can be accomplished by varying one of the rappel harnesses described earlier. It also helps eliminate the possibility of hanging upside down from the rappel harness, were one to trip or fall over backwards (Fig. 14.13).

Reider reaching Camp V after a largely free 300-meter rappel. *Photo National Park Service*

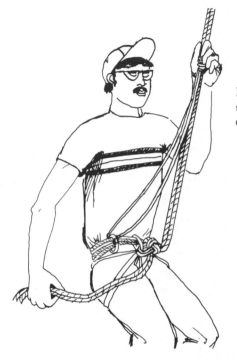

Fig. 14.13 Basic six-carabiner rappel system with prusik safety and figure of eight seat harness.

Whatever system you use for rappelling, it is a good idea to engage a prusik backup or the equivalent. This is a controversial issue. More than one person has started rappelling too fast, fallen, and not been stopped by the prusik safety. Invariably, prusik failure stems from a knot kept too loose, not wrapped with enough turns to hold properly, or unconsciously held by the guide hand during the fall. Therefore, the prusik simply melted as the climber fell, sometimes completely through. However, if used correctly, the prusik is a convenient backup that allows one to stop easily during descent to make adjustments, or saves the climber if the rappel harness fails. A Gibbs ascender or Jumar may also be used as a backup, and is perhaps even more efficient than a prusik.

Some additional comments about using prusiks as safeties during rappelling are in order. For use with 11mm kernmantle rope, 6mm (¼'') or 8mm (5/16″) soft-lay Goldline works well as a prusik loop when wrapped three times around both ropes (on a double rope rappel). Make sure that, whatever prusik material is used, it is small enough in diameter (relative to the rappel rope) and will have high enough friction to grab effectively. Double check that the knot will not be out of arm's reach, were you to hang by the prusik alone, so that you can comfortably set and release the prusik at will. As you rappel, keep your non-braking hand over the prusik. The knot should be kept somewhat loose.

If the prusik does jam unexpectedly, make sure you clip a loop of the free rope below you into your swami belt or rappel harness, wrap the rappel ropes around your leg, or place a Jumar tied into your swami on the rope above — do one of these things *before* you release your braking hand. If the prusik is stubborn, try "popping" it with one hand while you release as much weight as possible from it with the other hand by pulling up. If the angle of the wall is too steep, trap the rope (you're still clipped in, remember?) between the insteps of your feet and stand up in order to relieve the prusik of part of your weight. Naturally, cutting the prusik by blows from a hammer or with a knife will solve the problem. If all else fails, a second prusik can be carried in a pocket, improvised from a sling and a carabiner joined by a Bachmann knot, sent down from above (no, not by spiritual forces . . .), or pulled up from below. Affix this second prusik knot below the jammed one and use it for a foot sling to unweight the upper one. Or try tying a foot loop in the rope with an overhand knot and standing in this loop while freeing the jammed prusik. For comfort during such acrobatics, especially if you are wearing only a swami belt for the rappel, try a *baboon sit* (Fig. 14.15).

But why bother with all this? Rescue personnel should carry mechanical ascenders of some sort on any SAR event, even when it seems unlikely they will be needed — or at least should have them readily available. Basically, become intimate with whatever system you prefer, and with how it operates under all possible conditions. Sometimes a basic body rappel is safest, say during a stormy winter climb at dusk when fatigue and the cold combine to encumber hands and impair thinking. Learn a system perfectly and stick with it.

After all, there's nothing like a long, slow moonlit rappel from a dubious anchor or an equipment snafu halfway down a big, blank face during a snowstorm to encourage a climber to hang up his EB's and read trashy novels on the beach for the rest of his days.

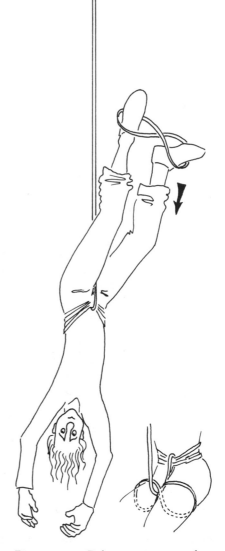

Fig. 14.14 One method of unjamming stuck prusik while on rappel.

Fig. 14.15 Baboon sit to take pressure off abdomen. Figure of eight seat made from a sling is passed over both legs while upside down. Sit up and relax.

"We saw a toe—it seemed to belong to Moore—we saw Reynaud a flying body"

BIBLIOGRAPHY

CHAPTER FOURTEEN

SKY GENIE DESCENT CENTRAL, INC. *Product Catalog.* P.O. Box 6405, Fort Smith, AR, n.d.

SMUTEK, RAY. "Brake Bar Rappels — an Analysis," *Off Belay,* February 1972, pp. 33-39.

SMUTEK, RAY. "The Questionable Prusik Safety," *Off Belay* 30 (December 1976): 14.

SPROULL, CHUCK, "More on Brake Bars and Carabiners." *Off Belay* 10, (August 1973): 30.

U.S. FOREST SERVICE, REGION SIX. *Rappeller's Training Guide.* Unpublished lesson plans for training source, U.S. Forest Service, 1976.

15 | Anchor Points

I HAD JUST turned into Yosemite Valley and was rounding a curve when a number of Park Service vehicles, including the SAR van, appeared along the side of the road, parked in a cluster. A friend of mine told me what was going on. "Two climbers hurt up in the Spires Gulley ... the first part of the rescue team is on its way up now. That's all I know."

I ran back to my van, grabbed my technical gear, and instantly caught up with the rescue group, lumbering under heavy packs. Cries for help had been heard by a visitor who, quite by chance, had flagged down the Chief Park Ranger, no less. As soon as Jack Morehead got out of his car, he heard cries as well, picked up his radio, and started up the gulley. The two injured climbers, separated on different ledges, were located, and he called the situation in to the central dispatcher.

An injured male climber was spotted at the top of the gulley, up about three pitches of third class climbing on wet, mungy, dirty rock. Right away a woman draped in technical gear, his partner, was found at the base of the chute. She was attended to first, after a preliminary patient assessment indicated a possible broken pelvis, among other injuries. Apparently she had downclimbed without any protection that far in order to attract attention. She and her partner had started up what they thought was a modest climb, but had gotten off route. He led high on the first pitch, fell, and pulled out all of his protection before hitting both her and a rough ledge. She was swiftly evacuated by a carry-out team after the second wave of rescuers arrived. In order to lower him — suffering from a spinal injury — in a litter, three different lowering stations

Bolts tied off for rappel anchor. *Photo Mead Hargis*   265 were established. Each anchor included at least one bolt placement in addition to several nuts or pitons. The last station required the placement of two bolts. Once the anchors were set up, the litter and two attendants were summarily lowered and he was carried out. End of rescue; everyone was okay.

Two years later, during the same month, cries for help again alerted climbers in the same area. Once again, a woman and her male partner had gotten into trouble. They had attempted the very same route and, like the previous party, had strayed onto difficult terrain that had forced the leader off. So we ran up the talus and found both at the top of the gulley. This time, the woman had a broken leg and had to be lowered in a litter, but we figured it would be no problem, as we had placed good bolts in the requisite spots two years earlier.

I radioed down to Bob Howard, a plumber who was also an excellent climber, at the bottom, two-bolt station. "Are you set yet? Those bolts should still be good."

"Not really," Bob radioed back.

"Why not?"

"Well, I just pulled them both out with my fingers." I was not to worry at all about the bolts, however, as Bob had them safely stowed away in his pocket.

Conventional Anchor Points

Any anchor point, no matter how good it looks, especially if a bolt or a fixed point of protection, should be carefully checked and its placement thought about before use. The bolts that came out after two years were placed in a gulley on relatively low angle rock, where the freezing and thawing action of snow and rain simply enlarged their holes.

A rock, piton, tree, boulder, chockstone, rock horn, or auto bumper becomes an *anchor point* when it is used in some manner to hold or stabilize any part of the rescue system. The theory of establishing the best possible anchor is grounded in broad experience in a variety of situations and terrain and in the provision of a solid backup to form a multiple point anchor.

A number of separate points can be linked together to form an *anchor system*. How many and what kind of points are included varies with the circumstances and from the experience of one SAR group to another.

Natural features such as trees, blocks, and chockstones — the primary and most desirable type of anchor — are sometimes overlooked. By using these permanent natural anchor points, one can usually avoid damaging the rock with bolt and piton and can establish a secure anchor in much less time (Fig. 15.1). Imagination and experience help immeasurably in locating these points.

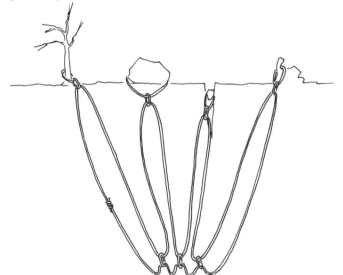

Fig. 15.1 Self-equalizing anchor system using natural anchor points.

Most of us tend to think in terms of artificial anchor points: pitons, nuts, and occasionally bolts are placed or pounded into the rock. *Pitons* in particular are the old standby. They are relatively quick to insert, and are extremely strong if placed correctly. Their strength can be tested in various ways, such as by gently tapping the piton and listening for a clear, high-pitched ring. The ascending pitch that a piton makes going into the rock may indicate a strong placement, but this is not always true, e.g., when the pin is too large or too small for the crack. Another test is to begin to remove the pin by sideward blows with a blunt hammer (on the shaft, not the eye) to see how firmly it is held. Redrive it with a few firm blows after the test. A partially driven pin can be tied off with narrow webbing or perlon to increase its strength by preventing leverage (Fig. 15.2). It is possible, however, to overdrive a piton and weaken the steel (most likely at its eye), or to loosen its fit by continuing to hammer after it refuses to go in any farther and begins to move from side to side with each blow. Likewise, a piton is damaged by driving it in up to its eye and continuing to hammer, out of fear or misjudgment, until the eye starts to deform. Overdriving also widens the crack unnecessarily, increasing the chance of rockfall from thin flakes and inhibiting later placements. Very poor technique indeed!

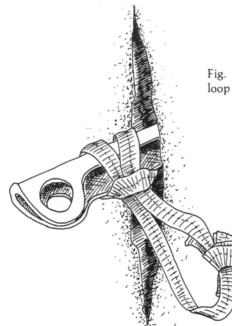

Fig. 15.2 Piton tied off with hero loop to place load closer to the rock.

The use of artificial climbing *nuts* or *chocks* is the rule rather than the exception now, and there is no reason not to rely on them in mountain rescue. They are customarily faster and easier to place and remove than pitons and often can be used where pitons cannot. One of their big advantages is that they have less tendency to destroy or loosen the rock. Types of nut placements are infinitely variable, adding to the skill and fun. Their use in rescue work requires confidence and dexterity, garnered from experience.

All resident pitons must be tested before trusted, and they should be removed if unsatisfactory, as they lend a false sense of security. Resident nuts need scrutiny as well, as they often were lodged in a poor position when someone struggled to remove them (either intentionally or in a

Natural anchor. *Photo Kenneth Andrasko*

fall); under a load, they might fail. Old slings break frequently, due to the rapid aging of nylon in sunlight and storm, so thread your own slings and remove questionable ones left in place. Often it is possible to simply slip in your own nuts next to the resident ones, thereby avoiding uncertainties. Another possibility is to feed a sling completely around the chock as a backup, in case the fixed sling breaks. Solid piton and nut placement is not the sort of thing one learns from a book, and is far beyond the scope of this one.

Potentially the strongest method of establishing an anchor point is via the *tensionless anchor* (Fig. 15.3). The rope is merely wrapped around a tree or other object a number of times and the end tied or clipped back on itself. The knot is not under tension and is introduced only to secure the end. Therefore, the anchor is as strong as the rope, barring any surprises from sharp rock edges or small diameter trees. This method is not a regular in rescue work, but is greatly favored by cavers.

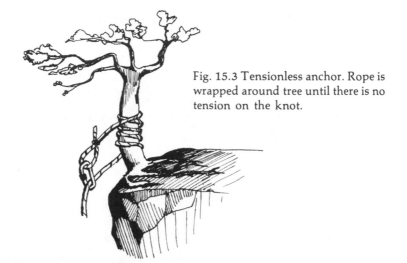

Fig. 15.3 Tensionless anchor. Rope is wrapped around tree until there is no tension on the knot.

Bolt Anchors

The last type of anchor point is the *bolt*. Its use is far more serious, because it permanently disfigures the rock, is not easily removed, and cannot be reused. Bolts are clearly a last resort, when safety dictates additional security. Be cognizant of local ethics regarding their use.

Bolts are placed by drilling a hole in the rock, pounding the bolt stud into the hole, or in some cases screwing it into a lead casing, and then attaching to the stud a hanger of some sort that will accept a carabiner. Placement of a bolt usually takes far longer than any other protection type mentioned, but it is valid if nothing else will insure safety and success. Their employment should always be a conscious, reasoned decision, however, after other options have been thoroughly explored within the time constraints.

In softer rock like limestone, sandstone, or gypsum, the Star Dryvin or the Rawl Lok/Bolt is the preferred. The Star Dryvin features a core much like a nail driven into a cylindrical lead sleeve set in a drilled hole (Fig. 15.4). The length of the nail and hole varies according to the softness of the rock, softer stone requiring longer nails. Be sure to put the hanger under the sleeve's flange, not just beneath the nail head.

These bolts are weaker than other types, and should be used only as a last resort, with backup anchors if at all possible.

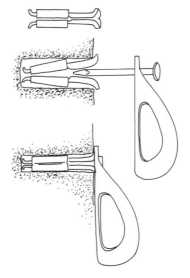

Fig. 15.4 Star Dryvin bolt.

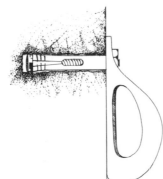

Fig. 15.5 Rawl Lok/Bolt.

In southern Utah, in Zion National Park and elsewhere, the Rawl Lok/Bolt (Fig. 15.5) is frequently chosen for use in the soft sandstone. The ⅜x1⅞" (9x47mm) or the ⅜x3" (9x76mm) sizes are most popular. First, a hole is drilled with a fluted masonry drill, and the bolt is tapped into the hole. The design of the bolt forces a small cone-shaped wedge of metal up toward the nut as the hex nut is tightened down with a wrench. This wedge splits the cylindrical metal sheath, pressing it against the rock.

For harder rock like granite or quartzite, the Rawl-Drive bolt (Fig. 15.6) prevails. A two- or three-flute drill in a steel holder makes the initial hole. This incision should be drilled with care, for the holding power of this type of bolt is derived from pressure exerted by the compression of the bolt's flukes. Avoid tilting the drill in any way.

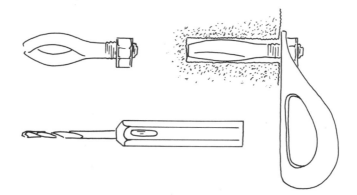

Fig. 15.6 Two-flute stud type Rawl-Drive bolt.

The hole should be at the very least three millimeters longer than the stem of the bolt to prevent bottoming out and bending. If the stud sticks out of the hole, subsequent parties may pound on and weaken it. The hanger is placed on the expansion bolt stud and the nut tightened on finger-tight. The fully prepared stud is then normally tapped into the hole with the flukes aligned in the same plane as the expected pull. Do not hit the nut during the driving process. Rather, strike the top of the stud, causing the end to be peened over, thus preventing the nut from unscrewing. Overdriving a bolt only weakens it; simply tap lightly until it is snugly in place. Remember, the hanger is placed on the stud before it is driven into the hole.

Standard stud size is ¼x1½'' or 2'' (6x38mm) for hard granite. Two bolts is traditionally the minimum for a belay station on hard granite. The 6mm diameter stud plug style bolts (Fig. 15.7) are not recommended. If there is some doubt as to whether or not the hanger can be removed after use without ruining the threads of the bolt, leave it in place. Otherwise a second hole will have to be drilled for a new bolt.

Self-driving bolts (Fig. 15.8) drill their own holes by means of a toothed case. As a result, a separate drill and holder need not be carried.

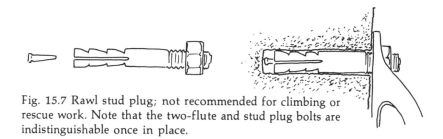

Fig. 15.7 Rawl stud plug; not recommended for climbing or rescue work. Note that the two-flute and stud plug bolts are indistinguishable once in place.

This trait has led to their popularity in the Rockies, and in areas with soft rock. A driver is screwed firmly into the casing and pounded with a hammer. When the casing has cut about two millimeters beneath the surface, it is removed and the expander plug reinserted into the cavity. The casing is hammered home, until flush with the rock surface. A bolt slipped through a hanger screws into the casing. The act of setting the casing drives a screw or pin into the center of the drill unit, expanding and holding it in place.

As to which type of bolt to use in particular circumstances, find out what is standard among local climbers, or install one of the longer or larger diameter models if in doubt. Ed Leeper, in his 1977 catalog, suggests that, "If the hole drills in less than ten minutes, then a different type of bolt should be used."

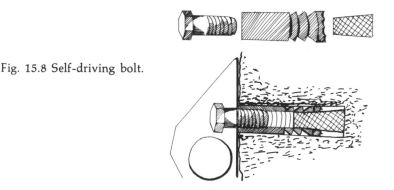

Fig. 15.8 Self-driving bolt.

Regardless of the type of bolt, a *hanger* is invariably introduced so a carabiner or a piece of webbing (much less reliable) can be attached securely to the bolt. One must remember that a bolt is adequate when a force is applied at 90° to its axis, but is very weak (and may be pulled out with a claw hammer) if the force occurs as an outward pull (Fig. 15.9). For this reason, the Leeper, SMC, or similarly designed hangers (Fig. 15.10), with a right angle bend and an eye close to the rock yet allowing deployment of any design carabiner, are highly recommended.

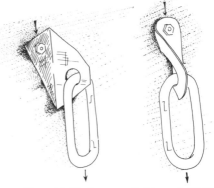

Fig. 15.9 Downward force applies torque to bolt in this type of hanger; not recommended.

Fig. 15.10 Leeper (left) and SMC (right) hangers insure that load is transferred to bolt as sheer force and not torque.

They achieve the correct transfer of force to the bolt. Hangers like those made by Longware may also be used, but if placed incorrectly may torque out. Rounded inner edges on the hanger's eye help prevent webbing from being cut.

Aluminum or other lightweight metal hangers should be avoided. The soft metal variety can bend or have their holes enlarged by the intermittent movement of weight of the kind that is normal during belaying, jumaring, or rappelling.

Inspect any existing bolt before clipping into it, but whatever you do, *do not* pound or hammer on bolts to test them! Clipping a carabiner and sling to the hanger and yanking it sharply once or twice should be enough to indicate especially poor placements. If a bolt is in too shallow a hole, this will be apparent. If the bolt is bent or twisted or otherwise deformed, remove it by prying. Never "chop" a bolt by beating back and forth until the stud breaks, as this leaves an unusable hole plugged with metal. Rawl type bolts have been known to pull out of granite by hand only two years after placement in low angle rock, due to freezing and thawing. The trick is to select a good location for placement — vertical and dry (Figs. 15.11 and 15.12) — and to artfully place the bolt and hanger without damaging either with misguided hammer blows or by overdriving the bolt or nut, distorting the hanger's base (Fig. 15.13).

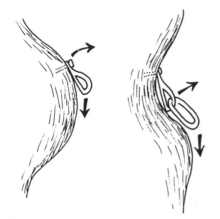

Fig. 15.11 Poor bolt placement locations.

Fig. 15.12 Correct placement: force is 90° to bolt.

Fig. 15.13 Another poor placement, where overdriving is fatiguing the hanger. Adapted from Ed Leeper.

Torque or drive only until snug. Non-hardening epoxy smeared around but not in the hole during placement seems to prolong bolt life by insulating the hole from water. Take along a couple of extra hangers and nuts, too, especially on a route with lots of bolts in place, as hangers are occasionally absent.

How strong is a bolt? Manufacturers' tests usually give a shear force maximum breaking strength of between 900 and 1350 kilograms. Independent testers like hardware (and hanger) manufacturer Ed Leeper have given different values, considerably lower. The tests are usually conducted by placing a bolt in concrete or granite, and applying force parallel to the surface until the bolt fails.

Some of the tests in granite show a failure range of between only 420 and 840 kilograms of shear force. It is important to emphasize that the bolts placed for climbing are produced for other functions, largely for construction or masonry work in rock and concrete. Climbers have adopted them for their own purposes, but manufacturers do not recommend them for climbing or any application where a person's life may depend on one or two.

Night rescue. *Photo Tim Setnicka*

A major factor in failure seems to be whether the force is exerted on the threads or on the solid shaft below. The optimum hanger placement is one in which the threads extend in just beneath the top of the hanger face, so that any force applied on the hanger is not taken on the threads. This type of placement is hard to achieve in the field and difficult to check in a fixed bolt. Hence, a bolt driven too deep into the hole can be as bad as one which is too shallow. One manufacturer calculates the thread strength on a 4:1 safety margin, resulting in a maximum force rating of 180 kilograms! Clearly, good placement is an absolute necessity and is governed by experience, as in piton and nut use.

As Craig Patterson once generalized about bolt use, we are really still in the first generation of bolt, hanger, and related technology. Improvements have been made, but it is worth noting that some of the bolts and hangers which Salathé placed on the Lost Arrow in the late 1940s are still good today, while a bolt hanger failed in less than a year on El Capitan in more recent times and killed three climbers who apparently had not backed it up.

BIBLIOGRAPHY

CHAPTER FIFTEEN

ALEITH, R.C. *Bergsteigen: Basic Rock Climbing.* rev. ed. New York: Charles Scribners Sons, 1975.

FERBER, PEGGY ED. *Mountaineering, the Freedom of the Hills.* 3d ed. Seattle: The Mountaineers, 1969.

GREAT PACIFIC IRONWORKS, THE. *Equipment Catalog.* P.O. Box 150, Ventura, CA, n.d.

LEEPER, ED. "An Epidemic of Broken Bolts," *Summit,* June/July 1977, pp. 8-13.

LEEPER, ED. *Product Catalog.* Boulder, Colo. 1977.

RAWLPLUG COMPANY. *Product Catalog.* New Rochelle, N.Y., n.d.

RED HEAD. *Product Catalog.* ITT Phillips Drill Company, Michigan City, IN 46360, n.d.

ROBBINS, ROYAL. *Advanced Rockcraft.* Glendale, Ca.: La Siesta Press, 1973.

ROBBINS, ROYAL. *Basic Rockcraft.* Glendale, Ca.: 1973.

SCHNEIDER, ANNE AND STEVEN. *The Climber's Sourcebook.* New York: Anchor Books, 1976.

STANNARD, JOHN. "Table F Chouinard Climbing Webbing" and "Table G Webbing Uses and Lengths," in *Clean Climbing.* No further publisher's data.

16 | Anchor Systems

AFTER EACH ANCHOR point has been placed and evaluated, the question of how to tie them together into a system needs to be addressed. While it is common to oversimplify the design and construction of anchor systems, one must carefully study the relationships among the anchor points and within the entire system. A climber experienced in anchor placement visualizes the expected load, direction of pull, and necessary equipment *before* he actually begins to set up his chocks and slings. Only then does he place them, with an eye for safety, speed, and economy if he has the luxury of several potential anchor points to choose from. No two anchors have the same strength, so when there are many being used, the system must be tied together, utilizing the strength of all points equally. No one point should be subjected to the majority of the stress.

There are many ways to self-equalize an anchor system. The use of all sorts of multiloop bowlines and related knots is clever and works fine, but the system illustrated in figure 16.1 is simple and easy to construct. One point to remember is, before you tie off the loop, pull enough webbing or rope to the central point of attachment for the rest of the system from between each pair of anchor points. At least one additional carabiner is then clipped into the *inside* of the sling loop as a safety, i.e., just clipped once through the large sling at one of the bottom loops. Otherwise, it is conceivable that, as is the case with the two-point system shown in figure 16.2, with the failure of all but one anchor the carabiners clipped to the chock or piton anchors could slip through the

Setting up self-equalizing anchor system. *Photo Kenneth Andrasko*   279 other carabiners and allow total anchor failure. With only two anchor points, this is not at all fatuous hypothesizing, but quite likely if one anchor point failed and connection with the system was via carabiners clipped over the doubled sling and not through it. With just two anchor points, you can get away with using just one carabiner and still have it perform as a safety.

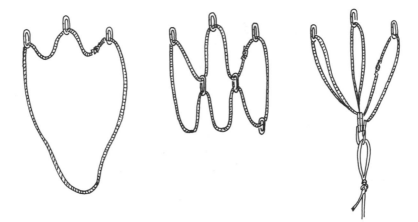

Fig. 16.1 Simple self-equalizing system. Note one carabiner attached inside the loop.

The third self-equalizer is really not self-equalizing — at least not in the way the first two are — but it is fast and without complication if the material is available. Individual loops from separate anchors are clipped together at a common point (Fig. 16.3). All loops must be tied as closely as possible to the correct length before loading the rig. This method merits mention as it is frequently composed for rappel anchors.

A fourth popular self-equalizing system is used in the Tetons. It utilizes a bowline on a bight, and is demonstrated in figure 16.4. Once tied, the loops are effortlessly adjusted into one main loop, clipped into the smaller loop by carabiners. If you prefer, you can use a figure of eight knot on a bight instead of a bowline, but this is harder to adjust.

For any self-equalizing anchor, one must carefully assess the direction from which the expected pull and resulting load will come. If the system has to shift too much in one direction, it may not be truly self-equalizing; perhaps only one point will in actuality take the load. Considerable friction of slings on rock (or snow) might develop due to the low angle of the rock holding the anchor points, or due to frozen or stiff webbing. This would greatly reduce the system's ability to equalize efficiently.

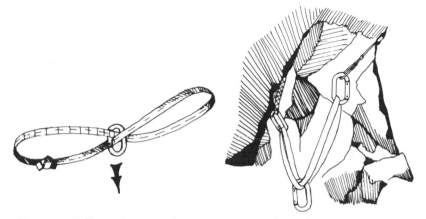

Fig. 16.2 Self-equalizing anchor using one carabiner between two points.

Regardless of the self-equalizing system chosen, there is an additional consideration that minimizes stress on the entire rigging. The angles traced by the slings connecting any two anchor points need be made as small as possible (Fig. 16.5). The resulting force or load on a single point (T_1) is equal to the force ratio multiplied by the force load on the system.

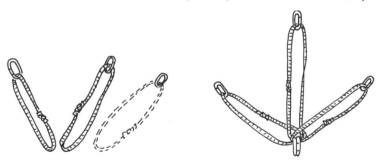

Fig. 16.3 Pseudo self-equalizing anchor. Each sling is tied to a central point.

A small angle of, say, 15° means that the force on the sling material on each side of the angle is approximately equal to half of the weight of the load. As the sling angle between anchor points increases, the resulting forces likewise are dramatically multiplied. Consider the following examples.

Table 17

Relationship Between Anchor Tension and Load

If Angle A is:	The Resulting Force Ratio is:	
175°	11.47	
150°	1.93	
120°	1.6	
90°	.71	Approximately 2:3
60°	.58	
45°	.54	Approximately 1:2
30°	.52	
15°	.50	

A more detailed discussion of rope and anchor point tension is given in Chapter 20, Tyrolean and Rope Tensioning Systems.

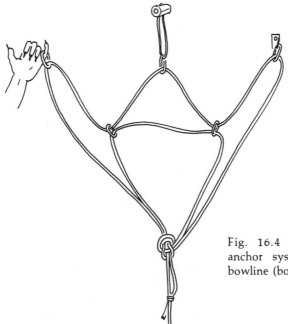

Fig. 16.4 Tetons self-equalizing anchor system using a two-loop bowline (bowline on a bight).

Obviously, we can largely dictate the angle As in our system by a bit of planning and by using plenty of rope or webbing when linking system components together. By minimizing the angles we decrease the strain and greatly enhance the safety margin. As a general rule of thumb for a two, three, or more point equalizing anchor, make all of the angle As 90° or less, a condition instantly estimable in the field.

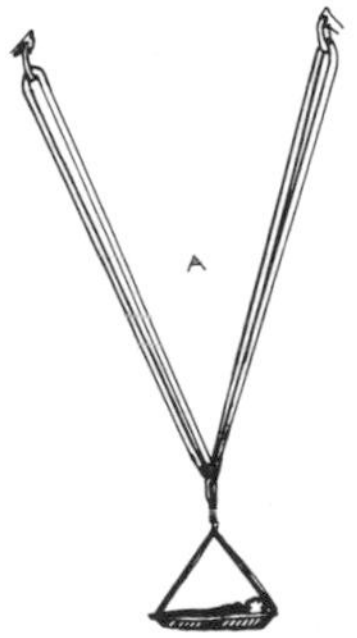

Fig. 16.5 Stress on slings and anchors. Angle A should be less than 90° if possible.

The next question is; How many anchors are needed? The safest, most infallible anchor arrangement for a lowering system includes four independent self-equalizing anchor configurations: one for each brake on each of the lowering ropes, and one for each belayer. This arrangement assumes a choice of solid, available anchors; the barest minimum would be one huge tree or block. Note that qualifier "huge." Too many times loose blocks or apparently secure trees have failed as belay or rappel anchors, with serious or rather embarrassing consequences.

For a mechanical advantage pulley raising system, one needs a minimum of two or three independent anchors in order to separate the hauling rope from the belay rope, and to provide prusik safeties in the appropriate locations.

Belaying

Devising a reliable anchor for a belay stance is an art all its own. Numerous treatises have been generated on the subject since the earliest days of climbing, when the simple maxims of, "The leader never falls" and, "Pass the rope around any available block" superseded further thought on the matter. Luckily, excellent descriptions have been written, especially in Royal Robbins's two instructional books and in *Freedom of the Hills*, though the last is a bit dated. Study them, and practice. The very basics of belaying are as follows.

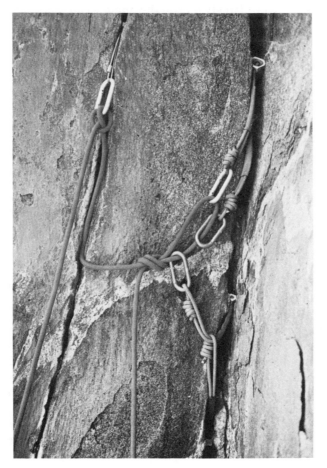

Multipoint anchor. *Photo Mead Hargis*

Fashion a unidirectional, bombproof *anchor*, usually self-equalized, that will keep the belayer from being jerked in any direction should a fall occur. The first step in this process is to envision the probable direction of pull for any sort of fall that might transpire. A leader, for instance, introduces a downward pull upon falling, until he has established a protection point that will hold the significant forces generated. So, if he has a couple of mediocre points in place, the eventual load on the belayer may still be from below if the nuts pull out on his way by. Once good protection is in place, the pull is upward or sideward. In any event, the anchors ought to be tight enough that the belayer scarcely moves at all when misfortune strikes. Hence, anchors for both upward and downward pulls are required.

Self-equalized anchor. *Photo Mead Hargis*

Proper *location* of the belay stance is about half of the struggle. Ideally, the stance provides adequate holds or horizontal ledge space for solid foot bracing, or allows one to sit on or behind a large flake or lip or tree. The belayer then assumes the position with the greatest holding capacity, bracing legs, feet, and hips appropriately in ways that will resist force without damaging the body and causing belay failure by pain. Stopping early at a good stance is faster and safer than proceeding a few meters farther.

Often the body's contortions to prepare for a downward pull, as when a second climbs up to the leader or someone rappels down on belay, have to change when the projected pull changes, e.g., when the erstwhile second swings leads and climbs above the belayer toward the next stance a pitch higher. In sum, the belayer continually assesses the probability and consequences of a fall, and alters the belay as necessary. An adroit belayer squirms around a good deal, constantly studying the play of the rope in the entire protection system, flipping it around flakes that might snag it, communicating with the leader or second, bracing in the best possible manner whenever a fall seems imminent, calling out reassurances or telling jokes to keep up morale, and preparing to haul the gear or clean the pitch. However, the belayer should never remove or unclip from the anchors or take the climber off belay without indicating this to him and allowing him to tie into the rock or ice independently beforehand, as best possible.

The final element in the belay system, after proper anchors and position, is *friction*. The belayer passes the active rope (to the climber) around his hips and holds both the inactive and active ends with both hands at about his navel (Fig. 16.6). One hand, usually his stronger, is the braking hand, and is never removed from the rope. It remains ever ready to increase friction by preventing the rope from slipping around his waist and by instantly wrapping it farther around him. This is an involuntary process; whenever the force of a fall exceeds the maximum a belayer can hold, the rope slips and the friction of his dynamic belay absorbs energy until the fall is checked. The other hand, usually the left, is the guiding hand that feels the tension on the rope and takes in or lets out rope according to what that tension tells him. By lightly pulling on the rope, without dislodging his partner, he can tell approximately where on the pitch the climber is, and whether or not to adjust the amount of slack rope. Most climbers always use the same, stronger hand as the braking hand to avoid the confusion of changing back and forth between the two roles.

To take up slack (often in response to the call, "Rope!" or, "Up rope"), the belayer retains his grip on the rope with his braking hand and reaches forward along the active part of the rope to the climber with his guide hand until his arm is extended. He then pulls in the rope, allowing it to slide around behind his back and be simultaneously pulled by the braking hand, which moves forward with it until the braking hand moves up just below the guide hand (Fig. 16.7). It then gives the inactive rope to the guide hand, which momentarily holds both parts while the brake hand slides back along the rope (Fig. 16.8) to its original position at the waist and again holds it tightly. Lastly, the guide hand stretches forward once again and regrabs the rope in order to pull it up and repeat the cycle (Fig. 16.9). At no time does the brake hand let go of the rope.

Sequence shown is for right-handed climbers, and can be reversed for lefties.

Fig. 16.6 Belaying. Left hand pulls up rope as right hand moves forward.

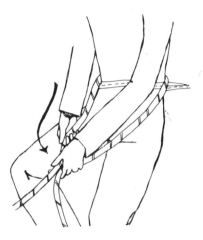

Fig. 16.7 Right hand gives rope to left hand.

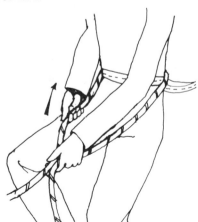

Fig. 16.8 Right hand slides back to regrip rope by waist, without letting go.

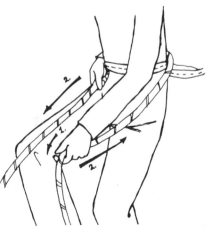

Fig. 16.9 Left hand releases rope and slides forward to regrip rope to pull up again, while right hand pulls forward to give rope to left again.

The rope goes around the waist or above the hips to sustain the extreme loads generated by leader falls. Often, the wide webbing of a harness or swami belt helps distribute the pressure and lessen the chance of burns. Supple, lightweight leather gloves are worn by many belayers. Usually the tie-in to the anchors (slings, or the rope tied with a figure of eight on a bight) is used to prevent the rope from sliding off the body in the event of a fall. For top roping, when the load would come from below, the belay rope normally passes over the tie-in. A leader is belayed with the rope under the tie-in if the rope also passes through a protection point and carabiner on its way to the climber, insuring an upward pull. The safest course in all circumstances is to clip the belay rope routinely through one or more carabiners on the waist loop to forestall its repositioning in a fall of any kind.

The sequence of *verbal calls* between belayer and climber is concise. When the belayer is ready to protect the climber, he yells, "On belay!" This is followed by the climber retorting, "Climbing!" just as he begins, rejoined by a signal by the belayer that he realizes this: "Climb." If the climber wants more slack in the rope, regardless of whether he is above or below the belayer, he calls, "Slack," and when he is a trifle concerned about the amount of loose rope that has accumulated, he shouts, "Rope!" meaning take up the slack. "Tension!" is an indication that things are getting a bit dicey, and a tight pull by the belayer would help out on a bulge or a tension traverse. Whenever any sort of projectile is loosed on the masses below, "Rock!!!" is shouted energetically. Finally, when the climber reaches a safe spot and ties into protection there, he yells, "Off belay" to the belayer, who replies with a banality of some sort, or the more proper call, "Belay off." Most of the other calls used in climbing are unprintable.

A variety of *mechanical belaying devices* have been introduced in recent years. The Sticht belay plate (Fig. 16.10) and the figure eight descending rings, used either as in rappelling or with the rope inserted through the small eye (like the Sticht), thereby producing considerably more friction (Fig. 16.11), can be used to belay. The rope is forced through the hole in either one, and then clipped to a locking or to doubled, reversed carabiners, in turn clipped to the waist harness or to a sling around an unquestionable anchor. A light cord on the device about 10 to 15 centimeters long is clipped to the safety biner to prevent it from travelling too far from it and not coming into play fast enough. In the event of a fall, the normally parallel standing and active ends of the rope are pulled apart by the belayer to form a wide angle, jamming the device up against the carabiners and preventing slippage of the rope. Both hands are employed in roughly the same braking and guiding rope positions as in hip belays, though the full sequence is more awkward with a device. One place the mechanical devices have found favor is on big wall climbs, wherein time consuming aid pitches and the multiday nature of the climbs encourages dozing by flesh-and-blood belayers. The devices add an element of at least psychological security in these circumstances.

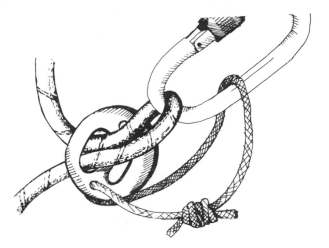

Fig. 16.10 Sticht plate in use as belaying device.

While the use of mechanical devices (especially the figure eight descending rings) has become common on climbs and to a lesser extent rescues, they have been criticized for their tendency to lock immediately and give static belays (as opposed to dynamic delays that gradually, over several meters, increase friction on the rope). Climbing manufacturer Ed Leeper in particular has urged climbers in print not to use mechanical belay devices with his equipment or in any situation in which the load will be transferred to protection hardware, as the larger loads a belayer can hold with the devices can overload hardware and software. This is a valid point, for regular hip belays and hands do slip under high loads, and, like prusik safeties deliberately weaker than the anchors in lowering systems, act as weak links that slip enough to prevent ultimately serious anchor failure.

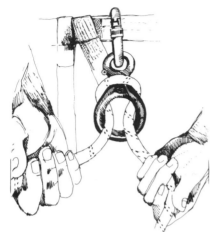 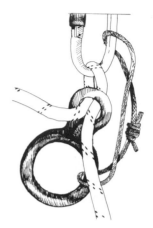

Fig. 16.11 Figure eight ring as friction device for lowerings.

Fig. 16.12 Figure eight ring as belaying device, with small eye in use (preferable over use of large eye for belaying).

Over the past few years, a great deal of concern over current belaying technique has been evinced and published. A number of innovative belaying methods have been proposed, including the Munter or Italian hitch, Saxon crosses, and floating carabiner belays. The bibliography for this chapter includes a representative sample of this debate. As yet, none of these methods have been widely accepted for rescue work — though individual climbers are experimenting with them — because of their obvious limitations of stress on anchors, high friction on ropes in nylon-on-nylon situations, and their newness and uncertain performance under field conditions.

Lastly, in terms of basic belaying technique, when a serious fall does occur and the climber must be tied off in order for him to rig a baboon sit or prusiks because he is injured or because the belayer must move from his stance for one reason or another (say, to throw down a second rope), the technique shown in figure 16.13 works best.

This is only the most succinct summary of a complex and hotly debated subject far beyond the province of this book. Be sure to perfect all of this and other basic belaying skills such that they are second sense, if not for any other reason than because it is the single most controversial point of technique likely to arise between two highly verbal partners on a climb!

Belaying, tight against anchor. *Photo Mead Hargis*

Anchor Expertise

Anchor design and systemic construction are best performed by those with the most climbing and rescue experience. Everyone, however, should take time to scrutinize the system and recognize how and where it was set up, questioning, if necessary, whoever installed it.

During one of the more spectacular rescues off the face of El Capitan in Yosemite in recent times, the role of technical expertise was graphically demonstrated. The top of El Cap, especially near the edge, is far from flat. Rather, it slopes back quite a ways in stair-step layers of exfoliating granite, steep and slippery enough that one must be careful walking around on it, as the next stop down would be the Valley floor. Half Dome, in contrast, is much leveler where the climbing routes top out, and is salted with large broken blocks of rock. During rescues, these chunks are speedily tied off for secure anchors. Finding anchor points and suitable cracks is much harder on El Cap, although a few sizable trees and bushes have managed to survive there.

Fig. 16.13 Tying off a fallen leader or second to render assistance.

Lloyd Price and a few others were hunting around for anchor points since the trees were not exactly well situated for our purposes. I helped carry some bulky gear down from the helispot and was gone for a few minutes. When I got back, the anchors were set, fully self-equalized, and about to be tied together. I looked around and found that all five anchor systems were either natural vegetation or adroitly placed nuts. No pitons or bolts had been resorted to anywhere.

We completed the 350 meter raising operation, after lowering one brave soul down to the ledge and raising him with the injured climber, without a hitch. In four or five hours, it was all over. The many anchors were removed and no holes, cracks, or chips had been made in the rock. No lasting sign of a major rescue was left, a fine tribute to the style, ethics, and environmental awareness of everyone involved.

BIBLIOGRAPHY

CHAPTER SIXTEEN

CHISNALL, ROBERT. "In Search of a Better Belay," *Off Belay* 47 (October 1979): 15-18.

FERBER, PEGGY, ED. *Mountaineering, the Freedom of the Hills.* 3d ed. Seattle: The Mountaineers, 1969.

LEEPER, ED. "Belaying — The European Connection," *Summit,* August-September 1979.

LEONARD, R. AND WEXLER, A. "Belaying the Leader," *Sierra Club Bulletin,* 1946.

MARCH, BILL. *Modern Rope Techniques in Mountaineering.* 2d ed. rev. Manchester, Eng.: Acerone Press, 1976.

MARCH, BILL. "The Running Belay," *Summit,* April-May 1979, pp. 12-30.

MAY, W.G. *Mountain Search and Rescue Techniques.* Boulder, Colo.: Rocky Mountain Rescue Group, 1973.

ROBBINS, ROYAL. *Advanced Rockcraft.* Glendale, Ca.: La Siesta Press, 1973.

ROBBINS, ROYAL. *Basic Rockcraft.* Glendale, Ca.: La Siesta Press, 1971.

SCOTT, DOUG. *Big Wall Climbing.* New York: Oxford University Press, 1974.

WEXLER, A. "The Theory of Belaying," *American Alpine Club Journal,* vol. VII, no. 4 (1950).

17 | Vehicles and Rigging for Transporting the Injured

THREE GENERAL CATEGORIES of aids are available to move someone who is injured or cannot help himself: improvised methods, soft or flexible vehicles, and rigid or hard vehicles.

Improvised methods are generally the quickest and easiest. A simple seat and chest harness, for example, can be used to lower an inexperienced hiker a short distance down a cliff. Improvised technique is usually considered last by rescue teams, which tend to concentrate on complicated harness, tragsitz, and litter systems that unnecessarily complicate the operation. Improvisation demands creativity and clear thinking, but solves a lot of problems (weather, nightfall, objective dangers, deteriorating condition of the patient) by instant action to avoid them. Such technique in climbing and rescue work is the subject of Bill March's excellent book, *Modern Rope Techniques in Mountaineering.* March outlines methods available to any climber with standard equipment — the tricks to get yourself out of sticky situations. And there's always the classic axiom of alpine climbing: speed answers most problems by climbing right on by them before they must be encountered. If the falling ice begins at 10 A.M., why not watch it from above?

Soft Vehicles

A *soft vehicle* for victim transport is a specialized piece of rescue gear without a hard spine, allowing it to be collapsed or folded for transport in a pack or in some other readily manageable manner. An example is an

Raising on El Cap's Salathé route. *Photo L. Lefkowitz*

extra seat or chest harness or piece of webbing carried down to the victim by a rescuer. There are a few other strictly rescue devices worthy of mention.

Fig. 17.1 Schematic of a Tragsitz.

Tragsitz First developed in Europe, this is basically a canvas or nylon backpack that allows the rescuer to carry the victim piggyback style (Fig. 17.1). It has been successfully used in Yosemite, but it has its limitations, like anything else. The rescuer who wears it must be strong enough to maneuver and endure the physical stress of the victim's weight during the lowering operation, especially on low angle rock. The two are independently attached to the rope such that the victim rides on the rescuer's back. It might be possible to separate them, but it would be extremely difficult unless they reached a ledge where they could untie and move around. Therefore it is almost impossible for the rescuer to perform first aid while he and the victim are both strapped in, if medical problems develop. Calm and competent victim evaluation is necessary beforehand, for the victim could easily die were he to pass out midway down a wall. The patient must have only minor injuries, and not be in danger of losing consciousness.

The tragsitz was designed for use on vertical or near-vertical walls. The less steep the wall, the more the victim's weight must be supported by the rescuer. Hence, getting started over the edge is often the crux of the lowering. The best wall on which to use a tragsitz is a vertical one, where all the weight is taken by the tragsitz and the lowering ropes, not by the rescuer. The rescuer can easily control his rotation with his feet, and guide both of them around obstacles. Usually two lowering ropes are used; knot passing and other maneuvers are accomplished at the top with fixed brakes. Occasionally the traveling brake arrangement is employed. Since the tragsitz is a soft vehicle, it is easy to transport, and

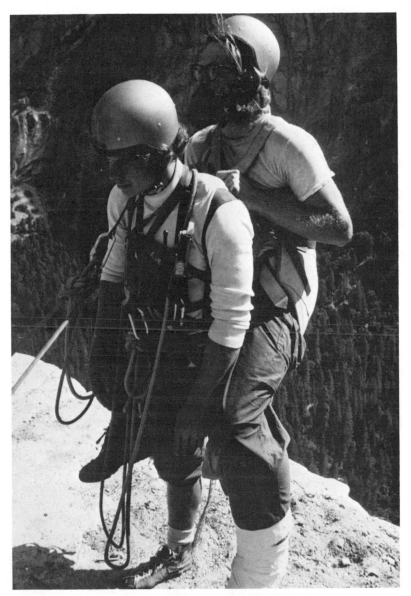

Tragsitz in use for raising. *Photo Tim Setnicka*

this is a major advantage. In cold conditions, though, the tragsitz tends
to restrict circulation and encourage cold injuries.

Fishnet or Screamer Suit When Yosemite entered into active
association with military SAR organizations, it acquired a new tool now
well proven in mountain SAR operations. The fishnet or "screamer
suit" was an outgrowth of the military's SAR program research. It is
basically a short, one-piece, coverall garment made of nylon fishnet.
You pull it on, snap closed a series of hooks, and you are in a suit from
which, no matter which way or how you turn, you cannot fall. In addition, there are two sets of straps sewn into the suit — one emanating
from the chest area and one from the seat — that clip together. These
straps can be adjusted so the occupant can maintain a sitting position or
can be raised in a horizontal one. The idea behind this design was combat SAR: before the helicopter arrived at the scene, a wounded person in
any state of consciousness could be suited up and readied for hoisting.
The suit has been used to great advantage in helicopter operations, but
off ledges rather than out of jungles.

Fishnet suit in use during El Cap raising. *Photo National Park Service*

Another possibility for this suit is a litter attendant wearing it strictly for comfort during the lowering or raising operation. The suit can be backed up by tying into a climbing harness worn underneath. Rational but injured climbers can be buckled into the suit and raised alone, unattended.

The disadvantage of the suit is that the fishnet material can stand little abrasion from scraping on rock. Furthermore, victims who require I.V.s or have spinal injuries are not supported well at all by this suit. For these sorts of injuries, use rigid transport vehicles.

Rigid Transport Vehicles

Rescue aids of this kind lend maximal support and protection to the victim through their inflexible designs. They are basically *noncollapsible*, although some disassemble into two or three pieces, like the breakdown Stokes litter. Complete victim protection is the major advantage. The major disadvantages include considerable weight and cumbersomeness. It is hard work propelling a rigid litter up a wall to a ledge or over a talus slope. The work is made easier by breaking down the litter into several loads. Rigid vehicles require that the victim be tied in, and that at least one attendant guide the litter around obstacles, as well as take care of the victim's medical needs, while the litter is being raised or lowered. The victim usually cannot help during these operations, or his assistance is rather limited, because he has been immobilized in the litter.

A further disadvantage of the rigid litter is its buxom dimensions, making it difficult to ease through a tight spot in a cave or in thick undergrowth. However, the disadvantages are far outweighed by the fact that the injured person is so well protected.

Stokes Litter   The so-called Stokes litter is the most popular litter in North American mountain rescue. Made of welded tubular steel, it is very robust (Fig. 17.2). It has the right mixture of weight, size, and portability for most rescue work, and yet is still extremely durable. Yosemite has about twenty cached in various sites around the Park, and these have certainly been the most often used litters.

One way to modify a Stokes in order for it to collapse into two parts for a packframe is to use stainless steel quick-release pins. These pins hold together a lot of equipment under stress, like hang gliders, and have proven their reliability. The Sierra Madre crew uses hydraulic screw couplings to hold their Stokes together. Large turnbuckles can also be welded onto the Stokes for the same purpose. There seem to be two types of Stokes: one made entirely of hollow main tubes, and a newer model with hollow main side tubes and flat, solid bottom supports. The second type can also be modified, though this may be a bit harder. Each litter weighs about 15.4 kilograms.

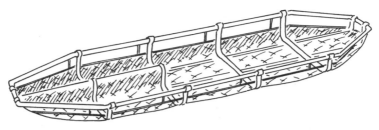

Fig. 17.2 Standard Stokes litter.

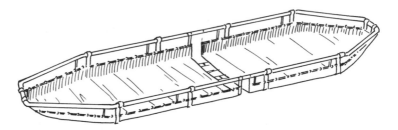

Fig. 17.3 Modified Stokes — nylon liner replaces wire, crotch divider is removed, and the litter is modified to break down.

Another modification eliminates the stock wire mesh of most models, and replaces it with a custom-fitted nylon cloth liner (Fig. 17.3). The liner is laced into the litter and fitted snugly, so that a person lying in the litter is suspended above the bottom. The nylon is the heaviest coated cordura cloth, very durable. The wire mesh tears easily and affords no real protection to the litter passenger. A skid plate of plate aluminum is bolted onto the bottom to prevent rocks and vegetation from poking the victim. Rocky Mountain Rescue Group installed a steel litter liner in their breakdown Stokes; it works well but increases the weight.

A final modification is the removal of the center crotch divider. This makes it possible to place a full backboard or orthopedic body splint into the litter without any problems. A one-piece or folding backboard can be cut from plywood with leg extensions to fit in a standard divided

Stokes. The victim should be secured in the litter with seat belt straps or with webbing or rope lacing him down to prevent movement in any direction.

Collapsible Stokes litter. *Photo Tim Setnicka*

The Stokes remains the type of litter most often used in technical rock raising and lowering and in helicopter operations, mainly because of its superior strength.

Jakes Litter The Jakes litter (Fig. 17.5) combines tough plastic and foam with an aluminum frame. The manufacturer designed this litter so that it can be broken down into three pieces without further modification. It weighs about 16.3 kilograms, carries nicely on a pack frame, and affords the victim maximum protection due to its basket-like design with high sides and smooth bottom. The Jakes slides easily over snow, ice, and rock, and has 9 to 14 kilograms of positive buoyancy, making it good for river rescues. It also has a canvas top with a transparent plastic

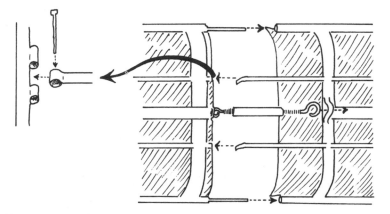

Fig. 17.4 Detail of one method of modifying a Stokes to break down.

window which stretches the length of the litter. This litter has been used quite successfully in Yosemite to transport victims in a prone position outside on the skids of a small helicopter without room inside the cockpit for someone to ride prone. A simple rack was designed and installed, and the injured person rode in comparative comfort. The Jakes litter has also been used in helicopter hoist operations without incident.

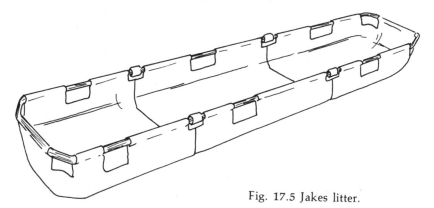

Fig. 17.5 Jakes litter.

Thompson Carrier The Thompson family of litters is another type of plastic litter that works well in mountain SAR (Fig. 17.6). These are constructed of durable polyethylene plastic and come in either breakdown or one-piece models. They do not corrode or rust. They have positive buoyancy, which adapts them for water use nicely. An optional circular, hard-plastic protective cover in two pieces goes over the entire length of the litter, a great advantage in areas of rockfall. Weatherproof, well insulated, and relatively frictionless, they are fine for winter conditions.

The Thompson Carrier family includes two models designed to be drawn by a snowmobile or skier, or carried on a pack frame. The litter weighs about 15 kilograms.

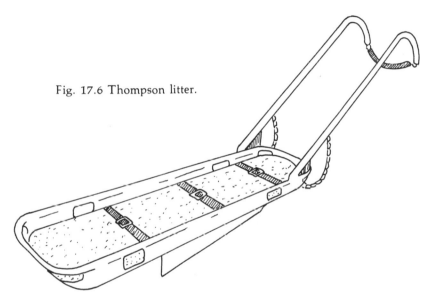

Fig. 17.6 Thompson litter.

Cascade The Cascade Toboggan and Rescue Equipment Company makes a fine heavy-duty rescue litter (Fig. 17.7) mainly designed for use on snow by ski patrol or rescue personnel. It is formed from fiberglass and has detachable handles for a skiing attendant. In at least one case, the handles have been modified to snap on behind a snowmobile. This is a very stable and durable litter, but it does not break down, and it weighs about 23 kilograms.

The Cascade Company also manufactures a lighter weight, two-piece fiberglass litter. This model weighs about 8.4 kilograms and is transported by packframe without any problems. In addition, a single wheel assembly like that of a bicycle or optional trail handles, may be purchased for the litter, making the unit quite versatile.

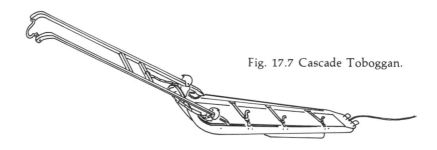

Fig. 17.7 Cascade Toboggan.

Akja The Akja (Fig. 17.8) is a specialized snow evacuation litter which comes in two pieces, fashioned in Austria from aluminum in a shape like a banana with a rounded, curving bottom. One attendant moves on skis in front of the litter, alone or with another skier behind, and he acts as its braking and steering mechanism; a chain is often dropped in front of the sled as an auxiliary brake. The Akja is not meant to be deployed over rocky terrain; a belay may be necessary at times. It should only be used by experienced skiers, lest it get away. Its round bottom makes it an excellent sled to evacuate someone from a steep mogul field, but it is unstable on flat or evenly sloping terrain. Immobilization of limb and spinal injuries in the Akja is complicated by its curved configuration. The sled weighs about 18 kilograms without its handles. Nonetheless, the Akja has its moments of invaluability, often on ski slopes in developed recreation areas.

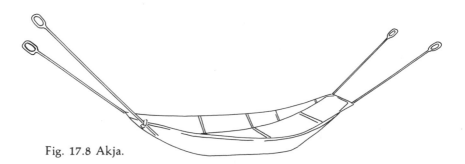

Fig. 17.8 Akja.

Neill Robertson Litter The U.S. military has come up with its own rescue devices for its particular needs, such as the fishnet suit already mentioned. An additional military rescue aid is the Neill Robertson litter, a semirigid poleless litter used for med-evac missions requiring vertical hoists. It has a central spine made out of wooden laths; around the spine runs a system of canvas buckles, completely immobilizing the victim from head to toe. The litter can be carried by flexible canvas handles sewn into it — but because of the soft construction, the victim is not as well protected as he is in other rigid litters. Rescue personnel need sufficient training to strap a victim into this litter correctly and quickly.

Forest Penetrator   U.S. military helicopters like the CH-46 have an internal hoist system, operating out the rear ramp or through a meter-square "hell hole" or near the front of the helicopter. A forest or jungle penetrator (Fig. 17.10) was developed for use in conjunction with this type of helicopter, so the penetrator is often used instead of a horse collar to hoist people.

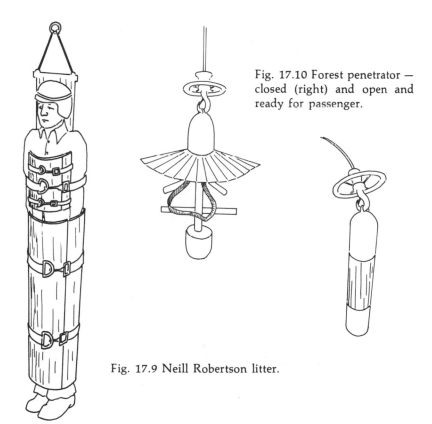

Fig. 17.10 Forest penetrator — closed (right) and open and ready for passenger.

Fig. 17.9 Neill Robertson litter.

Disassembled, the penetrator is a capsule a meter and a half long. It is lowered to the ground on the end of a long hoist cable. Personnel on the ground release side locks, and the spring-loaded capsule extends itself as an umbrella-like canopy opens. The penetrator has two safety belts and two seats folded down. Safety belts go around each person's back (two people may ride at once) and under the armpits. Each sits facing the other, straddling the capsule between his legs. A tug on the cable or a thumbs-up gesture signals for the hoisting to begin.

Besides being able to carry two people at a time, the penetrator has another advantage in that it is hard to fall out of — falling can be a big problem when inexperienced riders use a horse collar. The penetrator has worked well for rangers doing rescues on ice walls in areas like Mount Rainier National Park, due to its ease of movement through tangled terrain and its superb protection of the injured.

Collapsible Stokes on wheel. *Photo Tim Setnicka*

Wheel Litters

The question of a wheel carriage assembly for different types of litters, especially the Stokes, always comes up. The Thompson Company does market such a unit. Most of the other wheel assemblies seem to be made by specific groups for their own purposes.

Sierra Madre SAR has a fine system designed and built by Russ Anderson around a single, heavy-duty, knobby, all-terrain tire. The tire is mounted on an aluminum frame fastened to a breakdown Stokes by small clamps; these clamps hold machined parts in jigs called "distakoes." The system is very stable and lightweight, but has no braking system built into it, so a rope belay is necessary on steep trails.

Closeup of wheel unit for litters. *Photo Tim Setnicka*

Yosemite has some Stokes litters equipped with a litter carriage mounted on two heavy-duty bicycle wheels set about sixty centimeters apart for stability. The system uses regular center-pull bicycle brakes. This is more stable than a one-wheeled vehicle on wide trails, but if one wheel hits a bump, the litter may upset. The brakes work well but are still insufficient on steep hills; a belay is mandatory. Ross Rice has improved on this design for Sequoia National Park; his rig uses two lightweight motorcycle wheels with center brake drums common on any motorcycle. These work unusually well and require less maintenance than the Yosemite system.

The Southern Arizona Rescue Association also has a single-wheel litter featuring a brake system built into the wheel's hub.

In the following section the term "litter" is expanded to include any type of transport vehicle, regardless of whether it is an improvised, soft, or hard type. Litter rigging is the preparation of a victim in one of these vehicles for a technical evacuation. These methods serve well for cliff, rock, snow, ice, or crevasse rescue with a few minor modifications.

Standard Rigging for a Rigid Litter

For the classic method of rigging a litter, all one needs is two 11mm sling ropes about 15 meters long. Webbing suffices as an alternative. The standard knots are a bowline and a figure of eight. Yosemite's system (Fig. 17.11) uses the figure of eight because this is a stronger knot and is less likely to loosen when not under tension. The bowline on a coil remains the knot used to tie the sling rope to the litter rails, where it easily adjusts the position of the litter in relation to the rock.

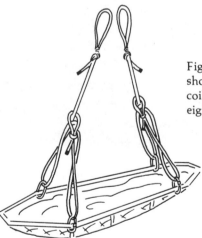

Fig. 17.11 Classic litter rigging using short sling ropes to tie bowline-on-a-coils on the litter rails and figure of eights to the lowering ropes.

Carabiners are essential for connecting the rail and the rope because otherwise the rope can be seriously abraded by the rock wall. Also, carabiners enable one to detach one set of the sling ropes from one side of the litter in order to load a victim. This is especially useful when the rescuers are hanging from Jumars or are on a small ledge. A variation is readily performed to prepare a litter for passage along a Tyrolean (horizontal) traverse (Fig. 17.12).

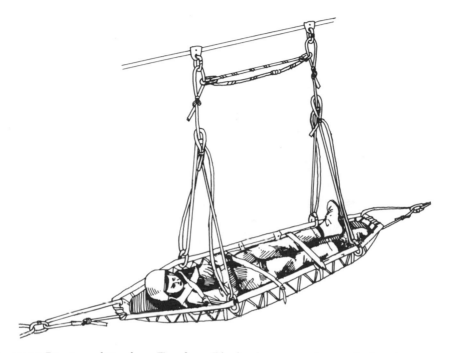

Fig. 17.12 Rigging a litter for a Tyrolean. The haul rope may be attached to the lead pulley, helpful when the main Tyrolean rope is very slack.

Prerig for a Litter

The basic rigging for a litter will get the job done in most cases. After a number of litter operations, we found that occasionally we needed more adjustment than we could get with the standard system. So Lloyd Price and Pete Thompson developed a prerigged system that facilitated litter adjustment between almost dead vertical and horizontal positions without having to reassemble anything (Fig. 17.13). The system utilizes prusik loops on 11mm rope. This makes it possible to keep a victim's head lower for shock, or higher, or in whatever position is needed (Fig. 17.14). We can, further, adjust the overall angle of the litter to the wall. Because each of the four supports is independent, one support can be detached for loading the victim while maintaining maximum stability. The prusiks are infinitely easier to adjust while under tension than a bowline on a coil.

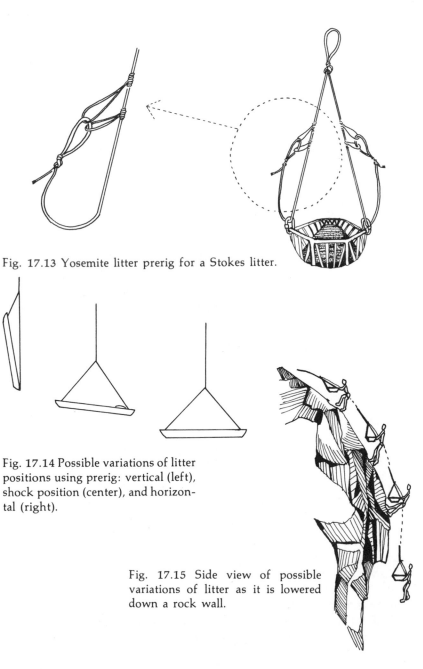

Fig. 17.13 Yosemite litter prerig for a Stokes litter.

Fig. 17.14 Possible variations of litter positions using prerig: vertical (left), shock position (center), and horizontal (right).

Fig. 17.15 Side view of possible variations of litter as it is lowered down a rock wall.

The Rocky Mountain Rescue Group uses six previously constructed Goldline litter ropes (collectively called a "spider") to rig litters (Fig. 17.16). This method is more stable during loading, because when one of the three members of the spider is detached, the other two stabilize the

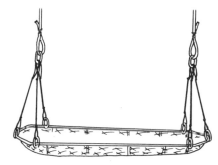

Fig. 17.16 Rocky Mountain Rescue Group's spider. Each end of the spider has an eye splice in it.

litter. However, the spider allows very little flexibility in adjusting the angle of the litter to the angle of the rock. Generally, the spider must be used with two independently controlled lowering ropes, as the two sets of three legs do not join at a common point.

Attaching prerig to litter. *Photo Kenneth Andrasko*

Prerig for Helicopter Hoist

Using the pattern of the prerig, one can design a special rig for helicopter hoists with the Huey type of helicopter (Fig. 17.17). For a useful range of adjustment and adequate access to the patient, the legs of the prerig we use for rock lowerings and raisings have to be about one to two meters long. This posed a special problem for our early helicopter evacuations: when the litter was raised by the winch as high as the hoist could take it, it was still below the door level of the hovering helicopter.

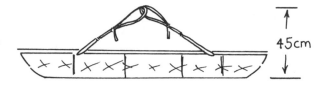

45cm

Fig. 17.17 Maximum allowable height for an efficient helicopter hoist by a Huey-type helicopter using an external winch.

A crewman then had to step out on the skids and tip the litter in order to drag it inside. So, a shorter version was constructed in order to let the litter swing inside the helicopter. More on helicopter operations later, in Chapter 21.

Helo prerig. Carrying sack and straps are labeled. *Photo Kenneth Andrasko*

Rigging the Litter Attendant for Vertical Work

Whenever an injured person is maneuvered up or down steep rock in a litter, he must be accompanied by one or perhaps two attendants. The attendant's job is to help the litter along, avoid obstacles, stay in communication with the belay site, and keep a constant vigil on the victim. To do these jobs, he has to be rigged for mobility; he must have his mind on his duties, yet feel comfortable enough in his surroundings to be able to use both hands freely. This is one reason why in Yosemite we never put the brake system on the litter, for that would give the attendant an additional duty. What is more, a fixed rope with a bouncing load on it will suffer more localized damage from rough rock than a moving rope will.

Attendants placing victim in litter while hanging free. *Photo Abbie Keith*

For high angle walls, one attendant is sufficient, but for lower angle rock or for intensive patient care, two may be necessary. In Rocky Mountain Rescue's scaffold technique, two are definitely needed to constantly control the angle of the litter.

One way to rig litter attendants is illustrated (Fig. 17.18). The attendant wears a seat harness or the equivalent. If an operation of long duration is anticipated, the screamer suit is usually worn as well, but a harness is still cinched under the suit as a backup. A long tail rope (10 to 20 meters) provides the basic tie-in. One end is clipped or tied into the two hauling or lowering ropes, not into the litter. About three meters from the tie-in, the tail rope is affixed to the attendant's harness. He may elect to pull in another 3 meters or so and tie in again to his harness. The free end of the tail rope is then tied into the harness, so that he ends up connected to the tail rope at the end and in one or two intermediate spots.

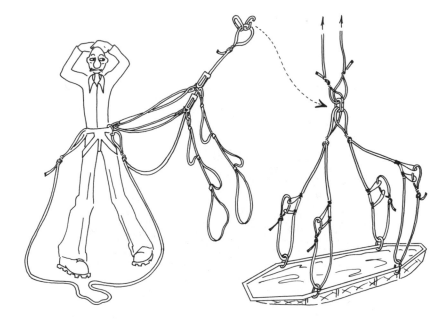

Fig. 17.18 Rigging the litter attendant.

Next, two Jumars (or Gibbs or prusiks) with aid slings are each tied off to his harness in the standard manner. The Jumars are attached to the hauling line just below the knot on the lowering rope. So now, along with being tied onto the tail rope, his Jumars are directly attached to the tail rope and his harness. By using one or both Jumars, he can easily control and adjust his position next to the litter. The purpose of the long tail rope is to encourage flexibility so that the attendant can stop the litter and jumar down to a ledge to knock rocks off; or he can jumar above the litter to free the lowering ropes if they get caught behind a flake; or he can climb or pendulum horizontally to set up an intermediate station or directional anchor to move the litter laterally. The attendant is independent and can easily adjust his position; he can concentrate on watching the victim and observing how well the rope is running.

Attendant and litter rigging. *Photo Kenneth Andrasko*

The attendant may decide to take along all sorts of additional equipment: a 50 meter rope, pitons, bolt kit, water, food, bivouac gear. At the least, he should be able to sustain himself and the victim in bivouac circumstances for half a day. A bivouac could unexpectedly occur if the lowering ropes jammed, a change in direction became necessary, an intermediate directional station was needed, and so on. All of these situations result in stopping the lowering or raising ropes for an indefinite period.

Rigging the litter for two attendants is accomplished in the same manner as described above, but each attendant has his own tie-in and tail rope. The result is a highly adaptable litter rigging system that gives the attendants free rein to respond to the plenitude of problems likely to arise.

AMC litter bearers in the Great Gulf of the White Mountains of New Hampshire, 1910. *Photo Appalachian Mountain Club*

BIBLIOGRAPHY

CHAPTER SEVENTEEN

ALSCO SPINKS INDUSTRIES, INC. *Product Information — Fishnet Suit.* P.O. Box 11099, Fort Worth, TX, n.d.

CASCADE TOBOGGAN AND RESCUE EQUIPMENT, INC. *Ski Rescue Equipment.* 1977-78 Product Catalog, 25802 W. Valley Highway, Kent, WA, 1977.

JUNKEN SAFETY APPLIANCE COMPANY. *Product Catalog.* 3121 Millers Lane, Louisville, KY 40216. n.d. (Supplier of Stokes type litters.)

KALMAR TRADING CORPORATION. *Product Catalog, 1978.* 43 Park Lane, Brisbane, CA 94005, 1978.

LIBERTY MOUNTAIN SPORTS. *Product Catalog, 1978-1979.* P.O. Box 306, Montrose, CA 91020.

MacINNES, HAMISH. *International Mountain Rescue Handbook.* New York: Charles Scribner's Sons, 1972.

MARCH, BILL. *Improvised Techniques in Mountain Rescue.* England: Jacobean Press, Ltd., n.d.

MARCH, BILL. *Modern Rope Techniques in Mountaineering.* 2d ed. rev. Manchester, Eng.: Acerone Press, 1976.

MARINER, WASTL. *Mountain Rescue Techniques.* 2d. Eng. lang. Innsbruck, Austria: Oesterreichischer Alpenverein, 1963. Distributed by The Mountaineers, 719 Pike Street, Seattle, WA 98111.

MAY, W.G. *Mountain Search and Rescue Techniques.* Boulder, Colo.: Rocky Mountain Rescue Group, 1973.

THOMPSON CARRIER Co. *Product Catalog.* 1742 Butler Ave., Los Angeles, CA 90025, n.d.

TRANS-AID CORPORATION. *Product Catalog.* (Manufacturer of Stokes litter.) 20314 S. Tajauta Ave., Carson, CA, 90716, n.d.

TYROMONT. *Product Catalog.* (Distributor of tragsitz, Akjas, and other European mountain rescue equipment.) Gebr. Kollensperger, Salinegelands, A-6060 Hall, Tyrol, Austria.

Part Four
Rescue
Systems

Descending the Pointe des Ecrins

From Whymper's *Scrambles Amongst the Alps*, 1871

18 | Lowering Systems

WHEN IT BECOMES evident that a rescuer must be lowered to a party in trouble, a basic system is called into play to carry out the descent. The simple arrangement employed in Yosemite is based on nothing more than carabiners and ropes, modifying the standard six carabiner rappel discussed earlier in the descending chapter. However, other friction devices can be substituted for the carabiners if desirable.

Because of this rappel system's local use by most climbers, there is an added advantage — safety — because everyone is able to inspect everyone else's work, making sure the carabiner gates in the brake system are in correct position, knots are tied accurately, and everything is clipped in properly. If only one or two people were familiar with the equipment, the safety margin would be greatly reduced. Experienced climbers recruited for the rescue adapt to this system right away, due to its incorporation of standard gear and technique. Specialized equipage like power winches can be handled only by practiced rescuers, a real problem during manpower shortages. The philosophy is simple: design a universal system that can be easily modified for any rescue situation, and is comprised primarily of technique already familiar to climbers, and then master it.

As a general rule in Yosemite, we always try to lower rather than raise, as then we can use gravity as the principal driving force in the system. In raising, a counterforce or pull must be exerted to overcome gravity. When lowering, we can make rock friction work for us, while in raising it works against us. So we will go out of our way to lower rather than raise a victim and his rescuer if at all possible.

Lowering a climber with a broken leg 700 meters down the Nose of El Capitan. *Photo National Park Service*

A schematic illustration (Fig. 18.1) shows the four independent anchor configurations. Each rope has its own braking arrangement and prusik (or equivalent) safety backup. Two ropes introduce an adequate safety margin to allow for rockfall damage, abrasion, bad anchors, or poor technique. Each belayer is clipped into an anchor. Neither rope is the official lowering rope or belay rope. There is no need to separate the system into main lowering and belay components, and there are distinct advantages in having both systems the same.

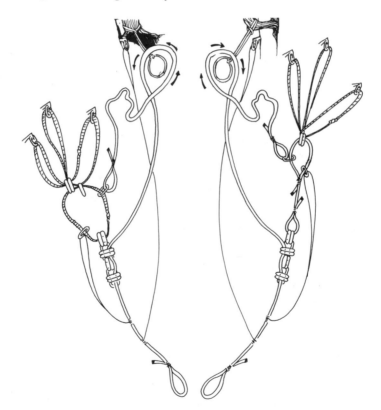

Fig. 18.1 Simplified schematic of Yosemite lowering system using carabiner brakes. Belayers represented by loops with arrows at top.

To *set up a lowering system,* four independent anchors are fabricated and rigged for equalized loading in the appropriate direction. An overall observer for the lowering site (either the rescue leader or someone else

Fig. 18.2 Detail of six-carabiner brake; note gates should be reversed.

appointed to this office at this particular station; each station has someone acting in this capacity) coordinates activity. The ropes are flaked out so that they run smoothly, the combined belaying and lowering friction systems are put in place, and edge rollers are positioned and anchored if necessary. The leader stays in communication with all other stations involved in this aspect of the rescue operation, usually via radio. In many cases, a spotter positioned right on the lip of the lowering station, or lower down the slope or cliff at a prime vantage point, greatly facilitates the whole show by diagnosing the most favorable routing. A separate, anchored rope for the spotter allows him to freely jumar up and down for better visibility. An additional belay is advisable but not essential, although you will find that he will do a lot more observing of the litter and less of his anchor when belayed.

Theoretically, the spotter's observation position allows him or her to recognize potential problems — pinnacles, loose flakes, narrow vertical cracks that might trap the lowering line, sharp edges or crystals that might damage the rope, ceilings that need to be avoided — ahead of time, and conjure up solutions. Directional anchors are often installed while the main system is being created above if the obstacles are forecast ahead of time. Forced realignment of the ropes during the lowering is common, and should be anticipated. Having three or four spare rescue pulleys available for instantaneous redirectioning and use as edge rollers speeds progress.

Edge manager and directional observer during raising. *Photo L. Lefkowitz*

Lowering stations and crews during the Nose rescue. *Photo National Park Service*

If the lowering is continuous, i.e., if it occurs from a series of anchor points a rope length apart due to the complexity of the terrain or the need to traverse a slope or because the ropes available are not long enough for a single lowering, then numerous lowering stations must be located down the length of the route. Ideally, at least the station immediately below is prepared while the station currently in use is double checked, and then the lowering begins anew. Thus, if sufficient trained personnel are on hand, two or three teams of rescuers leapfrog downward by rappel or downclimbing (or descending fixed ropes left in place on the way up), set up subsequent stations while other teams complete operations above, and eventually lower the patient and descend themselves to the next belay point, already in place and ready to go. In alpine topography, with its plethora of ridges, gendarmes, and gullies more variegated than the relatively smooth granite faces found in Yosemite, this leapfrog technique will be essential. Frequent directional anchors and lowering stations will have to be employed. The system remains the same on snow and ice, utilizing the requisite anchors.

If necessary, both ropes may be passed through one brake arrangement, although this increases chances that a single sharp edge or falling rock could cut or damage both ropes simultaneously. If both ropes do run through a common brake, it generally is harder to pass knots. A possible exception to this is the use of an open design friction device, such as the Rocky Mountain Rescue Group's brake plate, wherein knot passage is simplified regardless of the use of two ropes.

To *pass a knot* on one rope, the load is slowly transferred to the other rope. The knot in the now slack first rope can be passed through the brake. Both ropes still maintain the prusik safeties during the process.

The use of one or two prusik safeties on each rope is a subjective choice. Two prusiks were first used in Yosemite on lowerings during big wall rescue operations in the early 1970s. Since these lowerings of 300, 600, or 1000 meters demanded more than one rope, knots had to be passed. The second prusik acted as a safety when passing a knot through the first prusik. With the use of longer ropes, or lowerings not requiring knot passes, the second prusik became somewhat unnecessary (Figs. 18.3-5).

Another obvious reason for maintaining the use of a second prusik is that two prusiks in sequence are stronger than one if tied correctly.

While this needs to be quantified on a testing machine, it seems logical. Therefore, in straightforward lowerings with no knots to pass and no anticipated reasons to stop the lowering, say to bypass an obstacle on the way down, prusiks could be dispensed with, although this should be a very carefully chosen option.

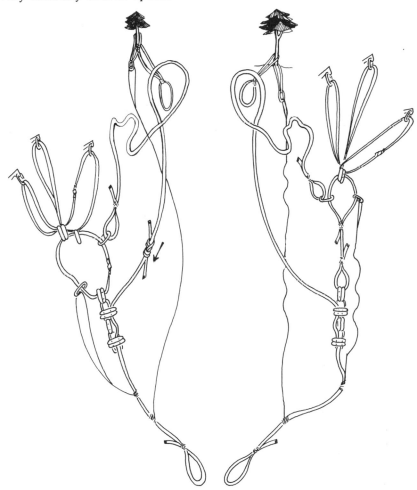

Fig. 18.3 Passing a knot during a lowering operation. As the knot on the left rope approaches the breaking system, the right rope takes the load.

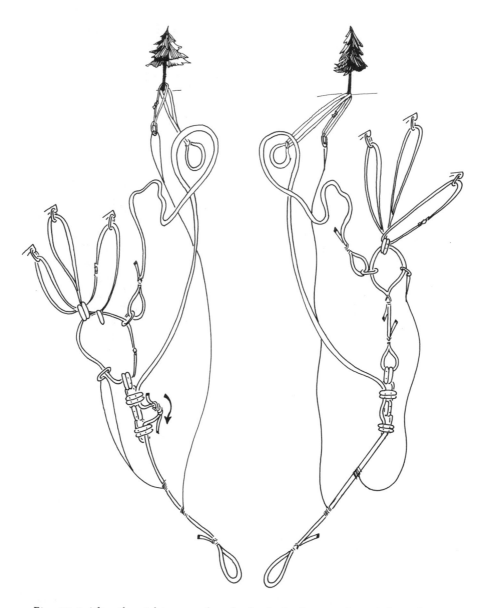

Fig. 18.4 After the right rope takes the load, the knot is clipped through one brake system at a time.

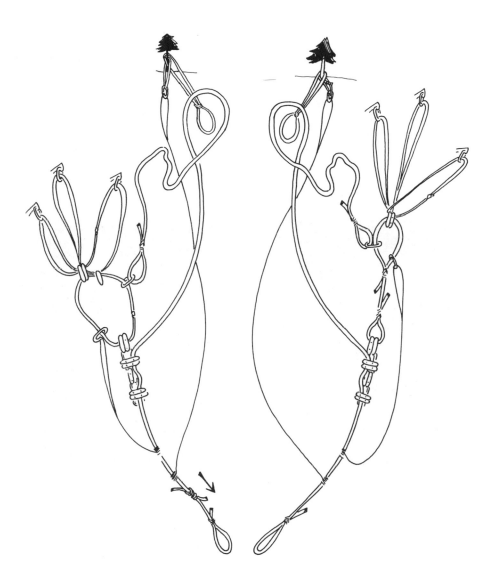

Fig. 18.5 The right rope continues to be lowered slowly and the knot is passed through the carabiner and the prusiks one at a time. This way the system is still belayed even if the right rope should suddenly break. During this process the prusiks are not set.

At times, the increase in safety that *prusiks* provide as backups is offset by the time consumed in their installation and management, by the increased complexity of design, and by the problems of monitoring the additional people needed to run them. The belayers should, however, have a half-meter prusik or similar ascending device available to immediately affix to the lowering ropes in the event of a delay, mechanical failure, or change in strategy. Gibbs ascenders and the new yellow Jumars work well for this function and are instantly installed. What's more, neither of these devices must be continuously managed by an attendant, unlike prusiks, so they tend to decrease overall confusion.

Setting up prusik backup for a six-carabiner brake. *Photo Kenneth Andrasko*

Prusiks must be tied and installed short enough, about half of a meter, to insure that they do not stretch and travel over the edge of the lowering ledge when the load is transferred to them during knot passage. It is very difficult to retrieve them at this point, and they definitely lose their reliability when tensioned and exposed to a sharp or crystalline edge, where they may be readily cut. Likewise, caution should be exercised when the knot that is being passed goes over the edge, as it can catch on nubbins or in the edge rollers.

Returning to the description of the lowering system, after the slack rope is clipped back into the brake system and the prusiks are retied above it, the second rope is slowly let out until the load is distributed again onto both ropes. It helps to stagger the knots on the ropes, although they will almost invariably be a meter or more apart. If one rope is rigged differently from the other, the system becomes more complicated. There is no reason why the ropes cannot be used to belay one another while distributing the load equally; this is much safer than having one rope carry the entire load.

Taping knots to protect the rope during lowering. *Photo National Park Service*

There are plenty of variations for lowering systems. One uses figure eight descending rings in lieu of six carabiner brakes for friction. Many mountain rescue groups in southern California have had good success with this system. Experience has shown that the ropes tend to twist more on the way through these rings than they would going through carabiners, especially if an extra turn of the ropes around the ring is added to increase friction. This twisting could cause problems on a long lowering, and is probably not very good for the rope, which tends to kink more readily thereafter.

Even more specialized friction devices for lowering have been developed by the Rocky Mountain Rescue Group in Colorado, among other groups. Their *brake plate* is much stronger than any climbing rope, and can easily withstand more than 2700 kg. The brake plate is similar to the whale's tail discussed in Chapter 14.

Figure eight ring as friction device for self-equalized lowering system. *Photo Kenneth Andrasko*

One may easily increase or decrease friction by altering the wraps of the lowering ropes around the arms of the plate. Both ropes of the lowering system can run simultaneously through the device, and the belayer can tend the pair. Remember that moving ropes should not run over each other, so rescue personnel should know what system of wrapping is suitable for specific situations. Rocky Mountain Rescue Group's Louis Dahm states that one pair of slots is about equal to one carabiner brake bar. If a great amount of kinking occurs in the lowering rope, it can twist or slip out of the slots in the plate when the system is not under tension.

Passing a knot when lowering with a brake plate often requires a secondary friction system — another brake plate, six carabiner brake, descending ring, or a brake bar and carabiner arrangement. The secondary lowering system is constructed and a third lowering rope is clipped in (and a fourth rope, if two knots are to be passed simultaneously) to do the job. These backups should be anticipated and implemented before the need to pass a knot arises. The load from the main lowering ropes is taken by the secondary ropes, and the knots in the main ropes are then allowed to pass through the brake plate. Once the knots are through, the secondary ropes lower the load until the force once again is translated to the main ropes (Fig. 18.6).

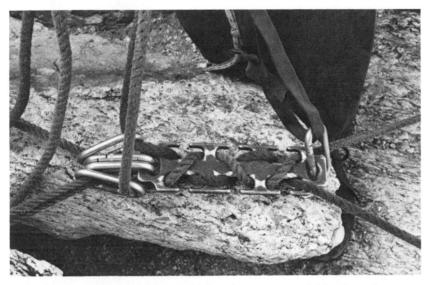

Rocky Mountain Rescue Group's brake plate in action during litter lowering. Note reversed carabiners to anchor rope on left. Both lowering ropes run through plate simultaneously. *Photo Tim Setnicka*

Depending on how the ropes are wrapped, you may be able to pass a knot by holding tension on the first rope and unwrapping and rewrapping the knot in the second past the plate. The load is transferred to the second rope, and then the same manipulation is used to pass the knot in the first rope, made slack for this purpose.

Another variation utilizes brake bars for the friction system in a manner similar to the six carabiner brake (Fig. 18.7). Since only one carabiner is used, one must take care that the weight of the litter, victim, and attendant does not overload the carabiners which are carrying the brake bars. Using two separate brake bar systems helps distribute the load and force, and seems prudent.

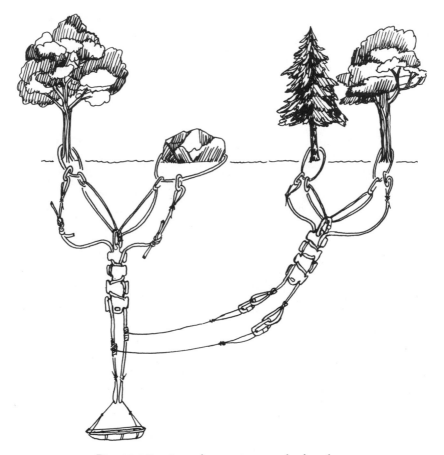

Fig. 18.6 Passing a knot using two brake plates.

An alternative and less efficient lowering system uses a main lowering rope with a second, *separate belay* rope. This system must be well designed, and one must be assured that the belayer could hold the entire system during any stage of the lowering in case a problem arose or a knot had to be passed. Usually a friction device has to be rigged for the belayer so that he or she can hold the weight of two or three people. It is probably just as easy to rig two identical systems, without discriminating between the functions of lowering and belaying. After all, this is an age of equality and androgyny, right?

Fig. 18.7 Brake bar lowering system using both ropes in one brake bar system (left) and single ropes in separate brake bar systems (right).

Occasionally it will be advantageous to have the lowering friction system travel along with the patient, rescuers, and tragsitz or litter. The rescuer is then able to directly control the rate of descent. It is more difficult to pass knots, perform intensive first aid, or maneuver extensively with this arrangement, compared to a fixed brake friction system.

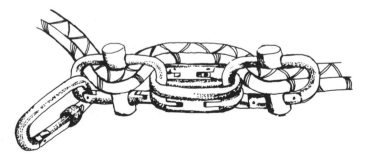

Fig. 18.8 Detail of double rope brake bar friction system.

However, fewer rescuers are needed, since the ropes are simply fixed to anchors at the top, and little adjustment of the top anchors, feeding of ropes, belaying, and general management of the system is necessary.

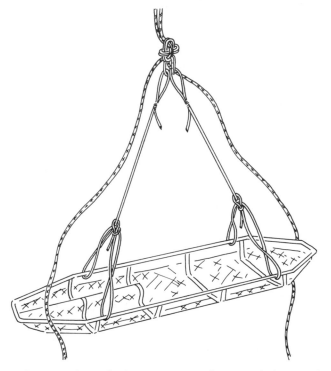

Fig. 18.9 A six-carabiner brake system rigged to travel along with a litter.

The result, however, is that *all* of these roles are shifted to the litter attendants. Not only must they adroitly guide the litter down the slope through obstacles and monitor the patient's condition, but they must also untangle the ropes below, pass knots while hanging *en rappel*, maintain communication with the rescuers above and below (usually by radio, out of necessity), and retrieve the ropes for the descent from the next belay and anchor station. All of this may be overtaxing even for an eight- or thousand-armed Indian deity with a host of lesser gods at his command. Few rescue groups regularly employ the traveling brake method as a result.

Body recovery. *Photo Butch Farabee*

Both lowering ropes are generally clipped into the same point of attachment to the litter or other transportation device. The Rocky Mountain Rescue Group, however, says they have good luck with using two separate, independent lowering ropes which give the litter stability similar to that of a scaffold. Communications must be maintained at all times (often via radio), and the belayers need to be constantly aware of commands from the litter attendants below. There is danger that the litter could suddenly realign itself into a vertical or aslant position because a rope shifted. Passing knots is also a lot trickier with this system. With both ropes clipped into a central point on the litter, though, the danger of sudden reorientation is largely eliminated.

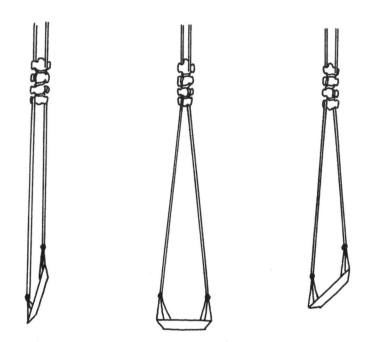

Fig. 18.10 Rocky Mountain Rescue Group's two-rope independent scaffold lowering system.

Occasionally a prusik will get jammed by mistake or intent, and will end up taking the load. You may be able to pop it free if it has retained the basic prusik knot symmetry (they do shift into other configurations). Popping a prusik involves a sudden pull back on the knot with both hands, or a sharp strike with the heel of one hand, whereupon the knot may slide free. More likely, you will have to release most of the tension on the rope by pulling up on the lowering (or raising) ropes below the jammed prusik. This can easily be accomplished by rigging a simple 2:1 or 3:1 mechanical advantage system. Once some of the tension is released (about 20 cm of slack), the prusik or mechanical safety (such as a Gibbs) or a knot that has jammed in the brake can be freed. If time is critical, a knife works wonders on a taut prusik or the sling holding the ascender. This is a good argument for always using nylon sling with a safety prusik or mechanical ascender instead of a chain of carabiners (Fig. 18.11).

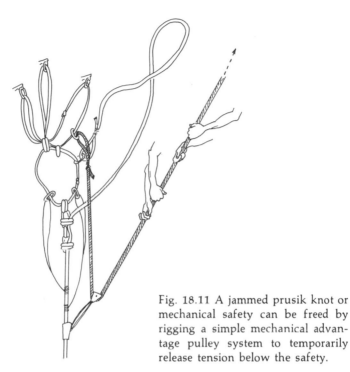

Fig. 18.11 A jammed prusik knot or mechanical safety can be freed by rigging a simple mechanical advantage pulley system to temporarily release tension below the safety.

Low Angle Litter Lowering and Evacuation

When the evacuation takes place on low angle rock or talus, a different type of litter and attendant rigging is necessary. *Low angle* can be loosely defined as any slope on which the lowering rope alone cannot support most of the combined weight of the litter, victim, and attendant, so that holding the litter away from the rock is too strenuous for one or two attendants.

Usually a single belay rope is used to help stabilize the litter. Each attendant is tied into the litter or belay rope in some manner. In some cases, it might be wise to still keep two in action, if the angle is steep enough that everyone would be endangered if the rope were cut on a sharp rock, or the belay or knots failed. There is often more loose rock on low angle slopes than on steeper ones, increasing the likelihood of rope damage by rock fall. By custom, six litter attendants, three on a side, share the burden, but four will do if the victim is small. The attendants are generally clipped into the litter rails by short slings, depending on the seriousness of the terrain.

The belay rope can be tied to the litter with a bowline or figure of eight knot. The rope is wound around the end of the litter before it is tied off, as shown in figure 18.12. This helps both stabilize the system and distribute the force away from a central weld found on some litters, a potential breaking point. If it is apparent that the litter will have to be belayed for awhile, then carried, then lowered on belay again, tie a meter-long loop with a short sling rope or piece of webbing as shown in figure 18.). This way carabiners can be used to clip into and unclip the litter from the belay rope. These methods are also used to rig a litter for snow and ice evacuation.

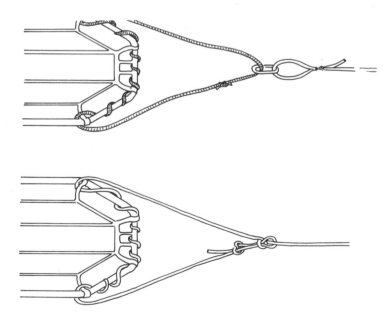

Fig. 18.12 Two simple ways of rigging a litter for a low angle evacuation: with a bowline, or with a short sling rope and figure of eight with a locking carabiner attaching the two.

Depending on the angle of the slope, different kinds of friction systems can be used to assist the belayer (as discussed in Chapter 14). Often, however, one or two wraps around a tree will create enough friction and eliminate the problems of setting up another system; but, it is important to note that the sheath of a kernmantle rope has been damaged more than once when too much friction was needed. If this is the case, a simple brake system can be set up to increase friction using brake bars, figure eight rings, or six carabiner brakes.

Lowering system set up for a short drop. *Photo Tim Setnicka*

To help the litter attendants maneuver the litter, *carrying slings* are indispensible. About six meters of 25mm (1″) webbing are folded in half and the loose ends tied together by a simple overhand knot, or, a piece of 50mm webbing half that length works fine. Usually six of these slings are attached to the litter rails by a simple girth hitch (or a sewn loop in the end of a single sling) and then run up along the carrying arm, over the shoulder and behind the neck, and then down along the other arm.

Talus evacuation with quick belay. Upper belay station is being dismantled and set up below. *Photo Kenneth Andrasko*

The knot can be adjusted to help the arm away from the litter rail grip the webbing. These slings help distribute the load more evenly, critical if you have to go any distance at all. One can also pass them over the shoulder and back under the rail, and raise or lower the litter at will by pulling up or down on the loose end like a pulley line.

To carry a litter over very large boulders or steep sections or through tight spots, where the attendants cannot walk more than a step or two, the caterpillar passing technique is introduced. A minimum number of attendants hold the litter in place, while the rest move ahead and below and line up in pairs facing each other. The litter is advanced to the next pair, and passed by hands shuffling along the rail as all of the attendants holding weight remain stationary; they do not move with the litter. Once the litter goes by a pair, they fall out and scramble around to the front of the line below. The litter can still be belayed if necessary, and the medical specialist in charge of the patient can remain at his or her head throughout. Any number of helpers over five can take part, until they begin rolling rocks on one another, stepping on each other's feet, and not clearing well to the outside in tight or steep terrain. The carrying slings render little assistance in passing, and should be tucked in the litter out of the way. Once down beyond the boulders or trail obstacles, the slings can be broken out and used accordingly.

Caterpillar technique with a climber critically injured in a 120-meter fall when rappel anchor failed. *Photo Tim Setnicka*

Carrying a litter on a scree evacuation or along a rough trail for multiple kilometers is very taxing. Try it, with an 80 kilogram patient suffering mock head and back injuries. Practice is essential for good teamwork. The key to smooth handling and avoiding compounding extant injuries is conscious movement and decision-making in the group. If the group is inexperienced and not used to working together, it may be best for a litter leader or commander to be in charge. Often this leader will be the same person who is in charge of the field operation. On larger rescues, he will not be.

The role of the litter chief is to promote complete communication within the group about all necessary considerations: the medical needs of the patient (as determined by the EMT in charge, who stays at his or her head at all times, unless consciously and verbally relieved), the demands of the terrain (when caterpillaring is required, or when only two or four bearers should take over in a tight spot), and the condition of each rescuer (who is tired or losing footing repeatedly or must adjust personal equipment). If the group is operating well, then little overt leadership need be exercised. Otherwise, the leader sees to it that all of the above factors are continuously considered. All raising and lowering movements made by the attendants are directed by someone to coordinate the action and prevent injurious jarring and tilting.

In rough country, it is helpful to send ahead one or more of the attendants who have just carried and are awaiting their turn again to clear the trail of hanging branches, loose rocks, and other impediments, and to scout out the most favorable route. This may be a good task for an attendant or friend of the subject who is having physical or psychological trouble with the evacuation, if he or she is accompanied by someone else in good spirits. Keep them busy, but keep them out of the way.

Remember that the fellow in the litter has no control over the proceedings. Jokes about this being your first time out in the mountains, or about that one poor soul you heard about who was dropped off of a slippery log bridge in a Thompson carrier and shot class IV rapids for two kilometers until they finally caught him at a hydro dam, are not exactly reassuring. At least feign professionalism, unless the patient is in good humor. Keep branches, carrying slings, hair, and all else out of his or her face; the fear of further injury or of being dropped is high.

All movement around the patient is conscious and verbal to avoid surprises to him and the others and to sidestep confusion. If the EMT — who is normally "married" to the patient until the ambulance is reached — or the leader leaves to call on the radio or scout or whatever, each should appoint a successor. Tell the victim what will happen next, and keep up a steady flow of soothing talk. Hearing is one of the last senses to go, so a semiconscious person may still benefit from encouragement and hear informal pessimistic comments. There are cases where the patient after recovery has asked rescuers why they gave him up for dead. On a long carry, the leader may decide to reduce his or her role in moving the litter, in order to remain fresh and clear for the decisions and problems yet to come. Group dynamics, however, may suggest that, even in extreme hardship, the leader carry with everyone else. It's pretty hard to give orders graciously if you've been strolling along in the rear drinking coffee all day.

Body recovery at base of El Cap. Carrying straps allow rapid adjustment of the load. *Photo Kenneth Andrasko*

The litter must become a secure unit that is easy to move around into any position. Standard 25mm webbing or wider stock, with buckles or not, is a permanent part of the litter and is crisscrossed over the patient once inside. If a backboard is in use, it helps to place a blanket underneath it to add padding against jarring and rocks and to aid in removal from the litter. The sleeping bag (a synthetic rectangular bag with a zipper all the way down one side and around the bottom is best), blankets, and plastic sheeting kept in the litter are put to best advantage to combat the elements and patient movement. Extra clothing and blankets are stuffed around the head, extremities, and waist of the subject to prevent shifting on steep sections.

The straps are fixed down low on the side tubing of a Stokes so that they hold the body firmly in place, and do not slip along the railing or abraid against the rock. Naturally, the straps must be taut, yet without inhibiting circulation or respiration, especially in cold weather when the threat of hypothermia is very real. Try to remove all hair barrettes, jewelry, and snaps or buckles, or whatever might be uncomfortable or affect breathing and circulation. It should be possible to turn the litter completely upside down with virtually no body movement inside. Especially if vomiting begins, or if the route narrows dramatically, it's common to have to tilt the stretcher on its side. Whether the head or feet of the occupant advance downhill or uphill first depends on the suspected injuries and is a medical decision; frequent changes of direction result.

A few more tips. Switch carrying sides regularly, so that one side of the body is not worn out by the effort and stooping. Tall attendants are most useful in front on downhill runs to encourage a level keel. Judicious use of the carrying slings all of the time, to slightly vary the distance between shoulder and litter rail and take fluctuations in terrain into account every few seconds makes for a fluid ride — and belayers can be sent ahead to prepare anchors and manage ropes in leapfrog fashion. The whole idea is to get the patient down to the roadhead and out of the litter as soon as possible, so that you can put the damn thing down and have a cold one!

BIBLIOGRAPHY

CHAPTER EIGHTEEN

See the sources listed for Chapter 19, Raising.

"CARREL LOWERED ME DOWN."

19 | Raising Systems

WHEN THE ONLY realistic choice in a rescue situation is a raising operation, new problems occur. Raising generally requires more people, time, and equipment, and it stresses all components of the system more than lowering. There are many means of raising a victim, including pulley systems, hand winches, and power winches, all dependent upon mechanical advantage to lift the load.

A powerful raising system facilitates the operation, but it also makes it easy to overstress and break haul ropes and anchors. The addition of mechanical advantage also reduces one's sensitivity to the size of the load. So it is de rigueur to monitor any raising system carefully, and prevent the forces from even briefly approaching this disaster point. A belay and back-up safeties are especially important for any raising operation.

In order to understand the following simple raising systems, it will be helpful to look at the theory of how mechanical advantage systems really work.

For this discussion, we will consider pulley systems in a state of equilibrium. Equilibrium is when a pulley system under a load is not moving; the forces trying to raise the load are equal to the weight of the load. The load is hanging under tension but is not going up or down. These *theoretical* pulley arrangements have no friction in the pulleys or elsewhere. In reality, however, there is a tremendous difference between trying to raise a load with a 3:1 Z system utilizing efficient pulleys and one using only carabiners.

Raising on El Cap. *Photo National Park Service*

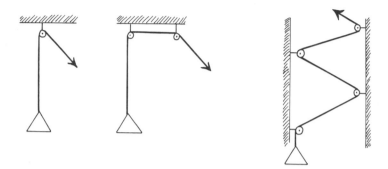

Fig. 19.1 No mechanical advantage. All the above are 1:1 systems.

If any load (for example, 100 kilograms) is fully supported by a rope, it represents a 1:1 system. It will take 100 kilograms of pull to keep the load in equilibrium. All of the examples in figure 19.1 illustrate 1:1 systems (remember, these are theoretical frictionless systems), that offer no mechanical advantage.

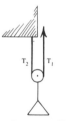

Fig. 19.2 A simple 2:1 pulley system. $T_1 + T_2$ = load at equilibrium.

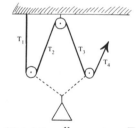

Fig. 19.3 4:1 pulley system. $T_1 + T_2 + T_3 + T_4$ = load.

Consider a load such as a pail of water held by Jack and Jill. Theoretically, each of the two arms is supporting half the weight of the pail. Now if we replace Jack and Jill's arms with a rope and pulley, we have a 2:1 system. Each portion of the rope on either side of the pulley is supporting half the weight of the load (Fig 19.2). It is the continuity of the rope around the pulley that equalizes forces T_1 and T_2. The reason Jack and Jill's arms each take half the load is because they coordinate movement. In any mechanical advantage system, it is the *continuity* of one rope going around all the pulleys that automatically coordinates the distribution of the load. This is the fundamental concept behind pulley use.

Since the system is at equilibrium, it is easy to see that if one more kilogram of force were added to T_1, the system would be out of equilibrium and the load would slowly begin to rise. At equilibrium, the rope tension always equals the load. A typical 4:1 system is illustrated in figure 19.3. Disregard the dotted Y shape; most likely these two pulley wheels would be side by side on the same axis, eliminating that Y.

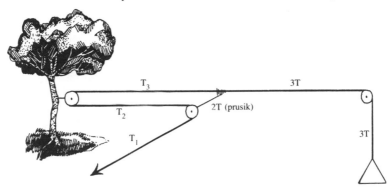

Fig. 19.4 3:1 pulley system. $T_1 + T_2 + T_3 = $ load (3T).

A 3:1 pulley system can be analyzed as follows (Fig. 19.4). At equilibrium for this example, the T value would have to equal 33.3 for a 100 kilogram load because the T force is enlarged three times by the mechanical advantage system. It is important to note that the connection between the main haul rope and the lead pulley (usually a prusik) has a $2T$ force on it, less than the $3T$ force of the load. Note how the prusik (or Gibbs or Jumar) breaks the continuity of the rope. In an actual raising system, this connection should be made intentionally from a slightly weaker material, so it will break before the main haul rope if the system is overstressed.

Rescue pulley in raising rig with Gibbs ascender. *Photo Tim Setnicka*

One may easily combine the basic 2:1 and 3:1 systems, multiplying their total theoretical lifting rating. A 3:1 system combined with a 2:1 forms a 6:1 system (Fig. 19.5). Again, using the example of a 100 kilogram load, we may assign values to the basic force T, entered into the system as T_1, approximately equal to 16.6 kg. The $6T_1$ force is the result of adding $2T_1$ and $4T_1$. $4T_1$ is the result of adding $2T_1$ plus $2T_1$, and so on.

The final example demonstrates how two 3:1 systems are combined to form a 9:1 system (Fig. 19.6).

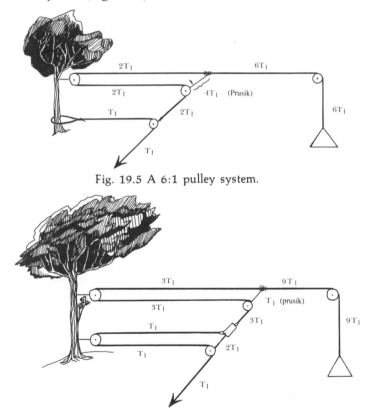

Fig. 19.5 A 6:1 pulley system.

Fig. 19.6 A 9:1 pulley system.

The Z rig (Fig. 19.11) is one most commonly used to raise litters, especially if six or eight rescuers or random beefy helpers are available to pull the raising rope. Prusiks serve as safeties, and support the raising

Raising rope and Z rig with belayer in foreground. *Photo Tim Setnicka*

and lowering ropes whenever they stop during the operation. In addition, during raising a separate belay rope is brought into play, with its own prusik or Gibbs safeties. The belay rope is often one of the two lowering ropes initially used to reach a victim. Passing knots is not a major problem, and is easily performed by transferring the load to the belay line prusiks, as in figures 19.7 to 19.10.

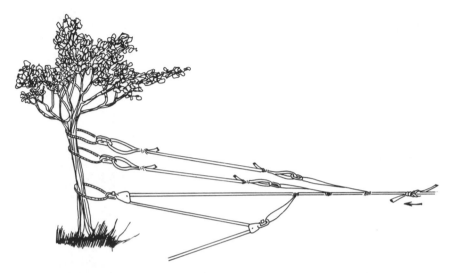

Fig. 19.7 Passing a knot while raising. The knot is passed through each obstacle as in passing a knot while lowering. Use a separate belay rope and friction device with this system.

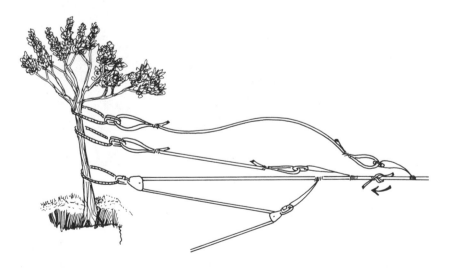

Fig. 19.8 Figure eight knot passes first prusik; with load on second.

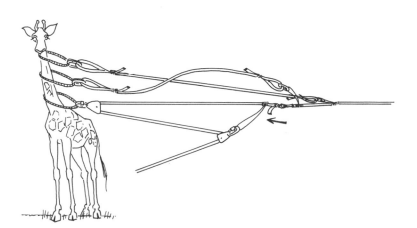

Fig. 19.9 Knot passes second prusik with load on first.

Fig. 19.10 Knot passes pulley prusik.

For rescue work, good pulleys are necessary, as carabiners or small, inefficient nylon pulleys designed for simple crevasse rescue or for hauling packs on wall climbs create too much friction and abrade the rope. An article in *Off Belay* magazine listed the efficiencies and advantages of some popular pulleys used in climbing and rescue. The authors set up a 3:1 Z system, and measured actual pulley factors for each pulley and the actual mechanical advantage offered by a Z rig incorporating each brand of pulley. *Pulley factor* is equal to $\frac{\text{output rope tension}}{\text{input rope tension}}$.

The pulley factor varies but is at the maximum when a full 180° change in the rope's direction occurs (Table 18).

Table 18

Comparison of Actual and Theoretical Friction Values
of Popular Rescue Pulleys

	Pulley Factor	Actual Mechanical Advantage	Theoretical Mechanical Advantage
No pulley (over a carabiner)	.66	1:98	3:1
Recreational Equipment, Inc.	.70	2:40	3:1
Mountain Safety Research	.81	2:44	3:1
Bellingham Mountain Rescue	.91	2:73	3:1
Russ Anderson, Inc.	.93	2:79	3:1
Frictionless pulley	1.00	3:1	3.1

SOURCE: "Notes on Equipment and Technique," *Off Belay* 39 (December 1977): 18-19.

Dynamometer rigged to anchor to register stress on it and raising rope. *Photo George Meyers*

With a few large pulleys, it is possible to modify the housings so knots will pass freely through the system, further easing the raising.

There are certain disadvantages to this raising system. A large, safe place is generally needed for an efficient hauling crew to set up and work. It usually takes at least seven or eight people to pull 120 or 160 kilograms on a 3:1 Z rig. The number of bodies required is determined by edge friction and length of haul. Bombproof anchors are essential for any raising operation. A dynamometer rigged into the hauling ropes helps eliminate guessing about stress on the ropes and anchors.

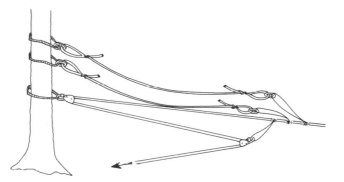

Fig. 19.11 A 3:1 Z pulley system. Note prusik safeties.

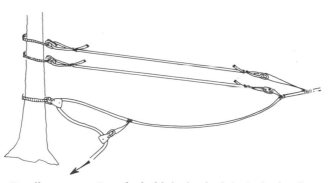

Fig. 19.12 Z pulley system. Prusiks hold the load while the lead pulley is reset, as well as acting as safeties.

In rigging pulley systems, it is necessary to master two or three basic configurations (Figs. 19.11 and 19.12, 19.13, and 19.14). If one system is not quite efficient enough to do the job, a different one can quickly replace it. A complete pulley raising arrangement similar to the one used in Yosemite to raise a litter 450 meters in sixty minutes is shown in figure 19.15.

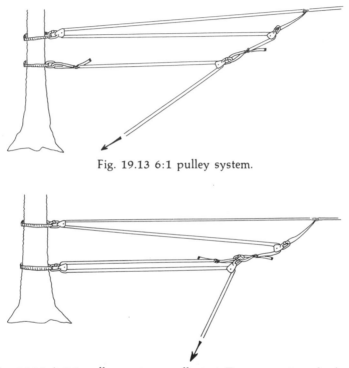

Fig. 19.13 6:1 pulley system.

Fig. 19.14 A 9:1 pulley system, really two Z-systems piggy-backed.

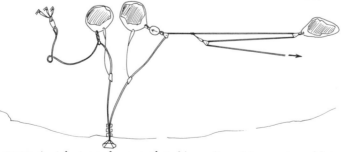

Fig. 19.15 Aerial view of a complete Yosemite raising system. Note the placement of the dynamometer and edge rollers.

Occasionally it is necessary to haul lighter loads (10 to 45 kilograms). This can be accomplished with prusik knots or whatever ascenders are available. The method commonly used in North America is the *Yosemite hauling system*, developed in the early sixties by Royal Robbins, schematized in figures 19.16 and 19.17. Small 25cm pulleys work well for light hauling. For heavier loads, the small pulleys in the configurations shown in figures 19.18 and 19.19 provide additional mechanical advantage. Larger pulleys (50 to 100cm) are generally used for major loads when hauling a litter or load with a Z set-up.

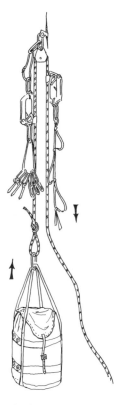

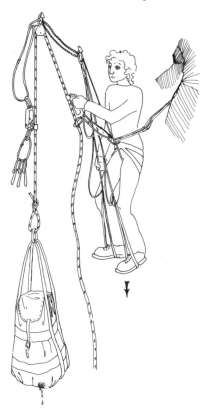

Fig. 19.16 The basic Yosemite hauling system.

Fig. 19.17 Yosemite hauling system. By doing deep knee bends, a person can use body weight to haul loads instead of using only his legs.

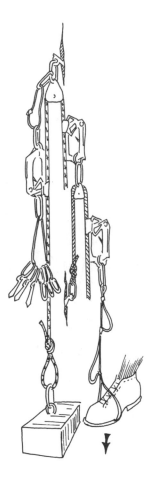

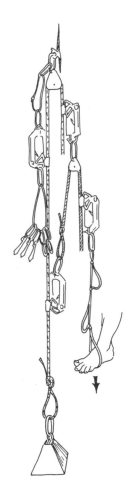

Fig. 19.18 Yosemite hauling system with greater mechanical advantage.

Fig. 19.19 Another way to increase mechanical advantage in the Yosemite hauling system.

Another more specialized type of raising system uses a *hand winch*. This is nothing more than a grooved drum with a ratchet handle. The haul rope is placed over a drum moved by the ratchet handle. One of the most popular hand winches is the Maasdam (Fig. 19.20), the standard winch in Grand Teton National Park for many years.

Yosemite hauling system on Half Dome. Deep knee bends pull up the haul bag while the left hand pulls on rope to ease edge friction. *Photo Kenneth Andrasko*

The park staff in the Tetons has found it necessary to modify the Maasdam winch slightly for 11mm (7/16'') climbing ropes in the following manner. The winch drums were originally designed to be used with 13mm (½'') rope, and the smaller, more flexible climbing ropes will slip. The grooved drum is built in two halves, and the inside of each half must be ground down about 8mm (1/32''). Spacer washers are placed along the outside once the drum is reassembled. The resulting narrower groove prevents the smaller rope from bottoming out and slipping. The stock hooks and swivel on each end are replaced with steel clevises or locking carabiners. The frame of the winch is stronger than the rope, so it can be used effectively as a tie-off point for a Gibbs or prusik safety.

The handle's arc of travel should be adjusted to prevent the face of the primary ratchet from hanging up on the cogs. This is easily accomplished by limiting the forward motion of the handle to a point consistent with proper meshing of the cog and ratchet. Do not try to force the handle one cog farther. At least one accident has occurred when someone has attempted to force the ratchet farther than the reachable cogs; the resultant hang-up created extreme torque on one cog, snapping it off. Enough force developed to shear off the remaining cogs, and the drum spun freely. There were no prusik or Gibbs safeties on the hauling rope, in case something like this happened — a *major* error.

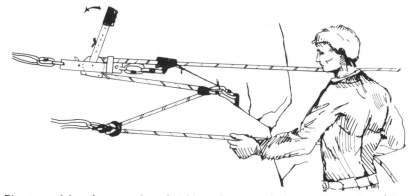

Fig. 19.20 Maasdam winch and Gibbs safeties used for raisings in Grand Teton National Park. Normal belay technique is applied.

The complete Teton raising system (Fig. 19.21) takes into account possible winch failure by separately belaying the object being raised. Furthermore, the haul rope is belayed from an anchor separate from the winch's anchor.

The manufacturer states that at a load of approximately 1180 kilograms, the handle of the ratchet begins to bend. The winch is definitely strong enough for SAR work. The ratio of lift is 10:1, and the weight of the unit is about 3.2 kilograms. The advantage of this system over a Z rig is that in a confined area it works well and requires fewer people to operate, as only one or two folks work the winch at a time, taking turns. A disadvantage is that only one rope can pass through the winch. Occasionally it is advisable to work two haul ropes at once in high friction situations or areas of constant rock fall; two ropes will fit through large pulleys.

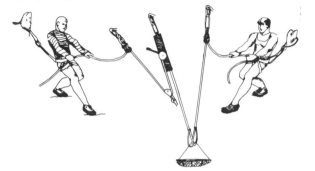

Fig. 19.21 Schematic of complete Teton raising system. Two separate belayers, in upper left and right.

The Wright Hoist Division of the American Chain and Cable Company makes a strong hand-operated load puller with a stress rating of 2050 kilograms, as given by the manufacturer (Fig. 19.22). This winch uses four-and-one-half meters of non-climbing nylon rope to hook to the load, which is then ratcheted back onto the drum. Or, the rope can be hooked to the frame and a pulley placed on the load for an added 2:1 mechanical advantage. Manufacturer's specifications state that the tensile strength of the single haul rope is 680 kilograms, or 1360 kilograms for the doubled 2:1 system. The entire unit weighs 3.3 kilograms and is called the Wright Pull-A-Way.

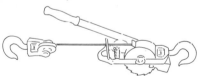

Fig. 19.22 Wright Pull-A-Way.

Any number of these come-alongs or rope pullers are manufactured around the country, and in an emergency they could all be used for rescue work. However, they should always be backed up by separate safeties and belays (Fig. 19.23).

The question of *power winches* always comes up. One which works well with rope is the one modified by the Sierra Madre Rescue Group in southern California. It uses a portable chain saw engine coupled to a

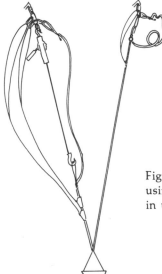

Fig. 19.23 Schematic raising system using a Wright Pull-A-Way. Belayer in upper right.

capstan winch made by Mini Winch, Inc. The rope that goes around the capstan is a braid-on-braid tight weave specially manufactured to meet Sierra Madre's requirements by Tubb Cordage Co. The winch works well, and its raising capacity is about six meters per minute. A dynamometer is hooked to the winch anchor to register stress on the system during the raising operation. A separate belay rope with a figure eight ring used as a friction device serves as an additional safety and belay. Gibbs ascenders act as safeties on the haul rope. A very fine safety set-up indeed. The entire system is organized the same as the Yosemite raising arrangement shown in figure 19.24.

The Mini Winch Co. (a division of Triway Manufacturing, Inc., Marysville, Washington) has recently developed a small, capstan-style, gasoline-powered portable winch. This may prove to be one of the best commercially made winches yet seen for search and rescue. Yosemite National Park just acquired one, and the initial tests have been favorable. Both 11mm kernmantle and ½" Goldlon (a domestic kernmantle) rope have worked exceptionally well in practices. The winch is powered by a compact, 80-cubic-centimeter (4.8-cubic-inch) Tecumseh two-cycle engine. The engine shaft goes directly to a centrifugal clutch and then into a gear box (100:1 reduction ratio), in turn transferred to a wide capstan.

The housing of the capstan unit is cast aluminum, and tests to 3800 kilograms in tensile strength. The manufacturer rates its single line pulling capacity for rolling weight, on a 20° incline, at 5500 kilograms. The single rope, deadweight, vertical lift capacity is quoted at 1360 kilograms. The entire unit is compact (51x26x24cm), and weighs about 12.4 kilograms. The only modification needed is a change in the method of anchoring. The winch comes with a two-meter, galvanized steel 0.5cm (3/16″) aircraft cable connected to the winch housing by a 1.3x-15cm bolt. The cable has been replaced by two pieces of 0.6x6x9 centimeter flat steel with locking carabiners clipped into them. In this way, any self-equalizing anchor can safeguard the winch.

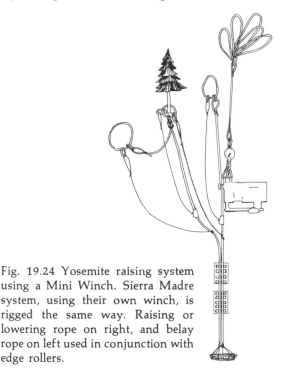

Fig. 19.24 Yosemite raising system using a Mini Winch. Sierra Madre system, using their own winch, is rigged the same way. Raising or lowering rope on right, and belay rope on left used in conjunction with edge rollers.

The rope's raising speed is controlled by a combination of engine rpm's and a few kilograms of tension applied to the free end of the rope after it is wrapped around the capstan drum. The maximum speed is given as 12 meters per minute. An important consideration in using this winch is the potential heat buildup if the capstan is running and only a slight amount of tension is placed on the free end of the rope. The winch has a built-in reverse lock, but the haul rope should have a prusik or Gibbs safety on it as well. The people or the litter being raised likewise need to be belayed separately (Fig. 19.24).

Sierra Madre power winch in raising rig with dynamometer on left. *Photo Tim Setnicka*

Hamish MacInnes and his Scottish search and rescue organization have developed a gasoline-powered rope winch that can lift two people vertically at approximately 3.2 kilometers per hour (2 mph) for hundreds of meters. The engine sports seven horsepower and there is a double rope-locking device both behind and in front of the capstan. Total weight on the unit is about 36 kilograms.

Assuming there are no mechanical difficulties, these power winches greatly reduce personnel and space requirements in a raising operation. There must be enough backups present to insure the whole system; in case of mechanical snafus, alternate raising components could then be rapidly substituted.

Miniwinch in action. *Photo Tim Setnicka*

Some Ways to Manage Ropes and Edges

Any time ropes are used on a SAR operation, the overriding safety concern is damage to the ropes brought about by abrasion, rockfall, or other traumatic injury. This is one major reason for setting up two-rope raisings and lowerings. In Yosemite rescues, we have only damaged ropes through abrasion and poor rope management. If one carefully manages and plans, the problem of overloading the system by a sudden shock can be virtually eliminated. The rescue leader in particular should identify and avoid the myriad dangers present by liberally applying the methods illustrated in figures 19.25 to 19.27.

One can smooth any sharp edges the rope must run over by adroitly blunting them with a hammer as a last resort, or preferably by padding them with canvas or leather straps held in place by short prusiks (Fig. 19.25). The latter method reduces friction as well as protects the rope. Old fire hose, a pack, or a haul sack works fine for this purpose and for static ascending or rappelling ropes.

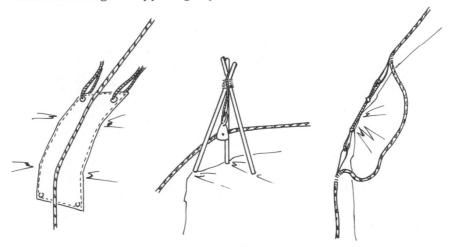

Fig. 19.25 Canvas rope padding.

Fig. 19.26 Tripod and pulley to protect against edge.

Fig. 19.27 Prusiks and slings looped together to take the load on a bad edge.

A much more elegant solution is the use of edge rollers, especially for moving ropes, as in raising or lowering maneuvers. The English use nylon rollers in an aluminum frame. Russ Anderson has developed a highly flexible design for the full spectrum of rock and terrain found in the U.S. Large pulleys also function admirably as edge rollers, or you can suspend a rope over an edge (Fig. 19.26) on a tripod or from an upper crack or tree branch.

If the ropes will be tied off for awhile and used as fixed ropes (for someone jumaring, for example), and padding like a haul sack is not available, use webbing and prusiks over particularly bad spots to take the tension and the weight of the loaded rope (Fig. 19.27). It is a lot cheaper to replace a few runners than an entire rope. At least one fatal accident has occurred recently in Yosemite from jumaring a rope hanging free over an unprotected sharp lip. Many of these solutions were unfortunately learned the hard way.

Anderson edge rollers. *Photo Tim Setnicka*

Pulleys as directional anchor and edge roller. *Photo Kenneth Andrasko*

Combining Lowering and Raising Systems

Frequently it is necessary to smoothly and instantly transfer the rigging from a lowering to a raising configuration. Few problems result if a two-rope lowering system (Fig. 19.28) is used. Once the litter and attendant reach the victim, and even as he is being treated and placed into the litter, one of the lowering ropes can be rerigged as a belay rope for the raising operation. During this switch, the other rope continues to belay the litter (19.29). As soon as the belay for the raising is established, the second lowering rope is rigged into a winch or pulley system and used as the hauling rope. The raising then proceeds as in any other operation, with the usual back-up prusiks and anchors (Fig. 19.30).

A 400-meter rope en route to helispot in haul bags. *Photo Tim Setnicka*

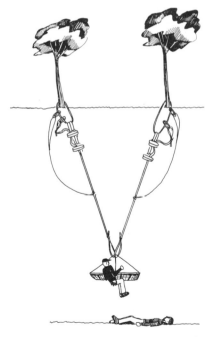

Fig. 19.28 Combining lowering and raising systems.

Fig. 19.29 Right rope becomes a belay rope.

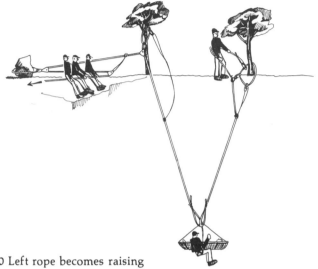

Fig. 19.30 Left rope becomes raising
rope.

As in lowerings, rescuers are sent ahead to prepare higher belay and
raising stations if the operation necessitates multiple raisings due to the
complexity of the terrain or ropes that are too short. Likewise, directional anchors with pulleys may have to be located below the belay station to avoid obstructions.

Managing a big rope on a spool. *Photo George Meyers*

Both of these tasks should be performed while the litter is being organized to prevent delays. In multiple pitch raisings, the next higher station is, ideally, completely set to commence raising when the litter arrives at the belay station below it. Coordination by radio is virtually essential.

Combining a lowering with a raising and aerial traverse. Close communication is essential. *Photo Kenneth Andrasko*

What About Cable?

The battle between cable and rope advocates is a never ending debate. The issue will probably never be fully resolved. It is a bit like comparing apples and oranges; they are similar, but each has special advantages and disadvantages. The majority of organized rescue teams in the U.S. use ropes and rope technology and thinking. This is in marked contrast to Canada, New Zealand, and most of Europe, where cable predominates.

No doubt part of the reason is that SAR organizations in other countries like Germany, France, and Switzerland are more highly organized, and cover the entire country with a network of equipment caches and coordinated local groups able to train and work closely together. In the U.S., there is no national field SAR organization, rather, each agency — federal, state, and county — has its own organization and affiliated groups and members. Very often the people associated with SAR teams are professionals in law enforcement or one of the various park or forest services with colateral duties. A large number of volunteer group members are fairly spread out in a bigger and less densely populated country than any in Europe, and so you may want to keep the technology simple. Most of these people practice infrequently, and are already familiar with standard ropes, climbing equipment, and methods of establishing belays, tying knots, and setting up anchors. As a natural result, many rescue and search systems are composed of locally popular recreational technique.

Using cable for SAR work employs a totally different and specialized technology. Cable demands additional training, tools, and a good measure of mechanical awareness and aptitude. SAR organizations that are well organized and have a great deal of personnel consistency can operate cable rescue systems with great success, say for the recurrent rescues off of the north face of the Eiger in the Bernese Oberland, where equipment is more or less left in place.

A few basic comparisons between cable and rope are in order. Cable has negligible elasticity when compared to climbing ropes, and this is considered an advantage for rescue work. Lately, however, low-stretch caving ropes have surfaced as a good compromise between the two. Handling cable is generally more difficult; the twisted, stiff nature of the cable makes kinking and snarling a significant management and safety problem. Cable must be carried on a spool to help prevent kinking. If a significant kink does occur, the cable is substantially weakened and most likely the kink will have to be cut out of it. Once a cable is cut, loops are formed in the ends and held in place by force-fitted swedges. Special couplings are used to reunite the two loops. The splicing of cables does not occur in cable rescue gear. Pulleys and edge rollers for the appropriate cable size are allocated and orchestrated in a fashion similar to any rope system to keep the cable from abrading on or cutting into the rock.

Cable clamps safeguard any operation, like prusiks or Jumars. They cannot, however, allow one to ascend a cable in the way a rope ascender works.

Rocky Mountain Rescue Group's cable winch. *Photo Tim Setnicka*

Only the highest quality cable is used; in the U.S., this is 3/16" (0.5cm) 7x19 military specification aircraft cable. Translated, this means that there are seven strands, one of which is a core strand, with each strand made out of nineteen twisted wires. The 3/16" is the diameter of the final product. Checking a cable for wear and knowing when to retire it are generally more straightforward than with rope. The number of broken wires and their location can be visually determined, unlike in kernmantle ropes, and industry standards and specifications are available to help calculate the relative strength of the cable.

The inelastic properties of cable (less than 1% stretch versus over 25% for an 11mm climbing rope with the same load) are at times a disadvantage. If a cable is shock-loaded — suddenly required to hold a strong force — the low-stretch characteristic has an equivalent low energy absorption capacity. A strong cable can be suddenly shock-loaded by dropping about a hundred kilograms only thirty centimeters; this may stress it very close to its breaking point. A climbing rope will easily absorb the same load with little, if any, damage. Cable management requires that extra care be taken to insure against shock-loading at any time.

Using cable for lowerings requires the use of a belay of some sort. The *brake block* is a large hardwood block that looks like a pulley but does not turn in its housing. The cable is wrapped around it and slowly fed through, allowing a controlled descent. The more wraps, the more friction. Care must be taken when passing cable couplers around the block. A short piece of rope between the person or people being raised and the cable acts as a shock absorber and prevents any sudden overloading of the cable which might otherwise occur.

A cable raising system generally uses a capstan-style winch powered by hand or engine. The most popular cable winches are made in Europe and are available from distributors like Tyromont Inc. in Austria. These winches use either two hand cranks or a large ratchet lever. The cable is wrapped around a drum that is turned slowly, thereby raising the load. While highly portable, winches must be set up in a stable area with enough room to work.

Power winches always seem a panacea to any rescue situation, and there are a number of them in use. Most are commercial models modified for SAR work. One of the best is owned by Rocky Mountain Rescue Group in Colorado, and was developed and built by Lewis Dahm. It is a hydraulic winch, and uses an open, 100cm, V-shaped metal capstan. The winch is fairly complex to operate without a reasonable amount of training. But, it performs extremely well, and has successfully lowered

Leaving the accident site for a trip up to the top of the Salathé wall on El Cap.
Photo L. Lefkowitz

six litter attendants and a victim in a Stokes litter 1580 meters down an immense scree slope. The cable is slowly let out by means of the winch instead of a brake block. Once down, one need simply reverse the direction of the capstan and raise the load. A safe maximum speed for a 450 kilogram load is about 37 meters per minute in either direction, although the winch is capable of operating at a crawl.

The hydraulic model is very compatible with cable because of the smooth starting, slowing, and stopping capabilities versus a power-driven, geared, mechanical winch that might shock-load the anchors, cable, and attendants. The possibility of using an electrical winch has been studied, but the dynamic downbraking proved problematic, on top of the absence of a portable and readily available power supply.

Cable technology is for the most part unknown in the U.S., largely due to dispersed and diverse SAR organizations and the composition of the American rescue problems and situations. A distinct lack of availability and widespread use tend to discourage groups from working with cable technology. Several of the references listed for this chapter in the bibliography, especially MacInnes and May, treat cable rescue in considerable detail. Cable rescue is just as valid as any other search or rescue method, and should not be discounted or downplayed. Apples and oranges will just never be the same.

BIBLIOGRAPHY

CHAPTER NINETEEN

ANDERSON, RUSS. *Product Catalog.* 324 Foothill Ave., Sierra Madre, CA 91024, n.d.

GRAND TETON NATURAL HISTORY ASSOCIATION, *Mountain Search and Rescue Operations.* Moose, WY, 1969.

MAASDAM POWER PULL, INC. *Product Catalog.* 3130 North Hollywood Way, Burbank, CA., n.d.

MACINNES, HAMISH. *International Mountain Rescue Handbook.* New York: Charles Scribner's Sons, 1977.

MAY, W.G. *Mountain Search and Rescue Techniques.* Boulder, Colo.: Rocky Mountain Rescue Group, 1973.

MINI WINCH. *Product Brochure Model T 3000.* Triway Manufacturing, Inc., 4117 78th Place N.E., Marysville, WA 98720, n.d.

"Notes on Equipment and Technique," *Off Belay* 39 (December 1977): 18-19.

OLSEN, JAMES. "Use of the Maasdam Power Pull Rope Winch for Technical Rescue Operations," National Park Service Memorandum, Grand Teton National Park, dated Oct. 2, 1973.

WENZEL, DON. "Efficiency of Rescue Pulleys," *Off Belay* 34 (August 1977): 14.
WRIGHT HOIST DIVISION. *Product Catalog — Wright Type "R" Pull-a-Way.* 890
Tennessee St., San Francisco, CA 94107, n.d.

20 | Tyrolean and Rope Tensioning Systems

OCCASIONALLY, ONE FINDS that traversing in a more or less lateral direction avoids a hazardous or long and complicated operation. Once in a great while, such as when crossing a river or deep canyon, this will be the only reasonable choice. These lateral belays and transfer systems are collectively called Tyroleans, after the region in Austria. They take a bit of time to set up, but are fairly simple in design.

The basic system is illustrated in figure 20.1. The rope leading directly to the connecting knot can be pulled like a rappel line from one side to retrieve the ropes when you are through. Just make sure the knots will be on the correct side, and that the rope will not hang up if it slips down around the base of the anchor. Prusik loops (at least two) are used to hold tension on the rope once it is pulled tight, but *not* overly tight, by one person. It is better to put very little tension on the rope, and place its ends high enough on the anchors so the rope visibly sags. This means the first person across will have to pull himself uphill to get to the other side, a *much* better and safer course than overstressing or breaking the rope or, more likely, an anchor. Aid slings (étriers) clipped onto the anchors serve as a ladder to climb up and down on and ease the struggle to set up the system.

By using a Z rig to introduce mechanical advantage, and by tying it off to the anchor or itself, one can devise an adjustable variation on the standard Tyrolean system. This configuration (Fig. 20.2) uses a belay rope kept fixed under tension and a second rope with a Z system, so that a traveler on the rope can be raised or lowered as necessary. This is the

Photo Tim Setnicka

basic system used for river rescue. If a lot of people or gear must be moved across, the first person can use Jumars attached to his waist harness; once he reaches the center sag point, he can jumar horizontally uphill (Fig. 20.3). And, he can pull the second person across on the line if he trailed a rope behind him (Fig. 20.4).

Fig. 20.1 Basic Tyrolean, retrievable when rope is pulled on the knotted side.

Fig. 20.2 Adjustable Tyrolean.

Fig. 20.3 Jumars can help on crossing a Tyrolean. A chest harness is even better.

Fig. 20.4 Second person across or The Chicago Clothesline system.

High anchor points and lots of slack in the raising and lowering rope insure that no rope damage occurs due to overstressing, and that there is vertical adjustability. The sling used to attach the harness to the fixed belay rope should be slack enough to allow for necessary adjustments. A chest harness is quite helpful for comfort as well as safety. In rare cases, as when a litter has to cross the void, a large load may be readily rigged with sling ropes or a prerig as discussed in Chapter 17.

River rescue. *Photo George Durkee*

The possibility of severe rope tension and anchor strain are major considerations. Any Tyrolean should be set up with as slack a rope as possible. Pulleys should be used instead of carabiners to minimize the friction generated on the main suspension ropes by the passage of objects or people. The safest way to accomplish a Tyrolean with minimum rope stress is to rappel down one side to the low point, with your ascender rigged and ready for the pull uphill to the other shore. The rope must be extremely slack or else you will not be able to take tension off your rappel rig once you are hanging in the middle of the rope. A friend of mine spent over an hour hanging in the middle of a Tyrolean trying to solve this problem, finally accomplished with a heroic effort. If you are uncertain about the traverse, you can jumar down the rope instead of rapelling.

Fishnet and pull lines in river Tyrolean. *Photo George Durkee*

Rappelling to low point and jumaring up other side. *Photo Tim Setnicka*

In designing and using any Tyrolean system, beyond properly pretensioning the suspension rope, it is important to consider the actual force or tension T on the suspension ropes when loaded. The actual force dramatically increases as the loaded rope approaches the horizontal.

Tyrolean harness rigging, with safety tie-in carabiner on left. *Photo Tim Setnicka*

Consider the following example, using one climbing rope strung across the canyon, river, stream of lava, whatever. Angle A (Fig. 20.5) is determined by both the load placed on the rope and how tightly the unloaded rope was initially pulled and tied off. If a very taut Tyrolean is necessary, the rope must be pretensioned considerably in order to minimize angle A.

It is possible to calculate the tension T in the rope and the force placed on the anchors by, say, a 90kg climber as follows. The downward force vectors equal the upward force; both F_1 and F_2 are equal to the climber's weight, in this case 90kg. To calculate the resulting tension T, it is necessary to diagram the relationship between F_2 and T. T is the result of two vectors that form a right triangle, and as T is half the supporting force, this reduces F_2 by half, or $\dfrac{F}{2}$.

Angle A is also reduced in half, $\dfrac{< A}{2}$. If we move vector y up to form

the right angle of the triangle (Fig. 20.6), then we have cosine$\dfrac{< A}{2} = \dfrac{\frac{F}{2}}{T}$.

Solving for T we derive $T = \dfrac{\frac{F}{2}}{\cos \frac{A}{2}}$. So if a rope loaded with a 90kg

person forms an angle A of 30°, T is calculated as $T = \dfrac{\frac{90}{2}}{\cos \frac{30°}{2}}$, then T

$= \dfrac{45}{\cos 15°}$, which becomes $T = \dfrac{45}{.966}$, and $T = 46.5$kg. The tension

of the rope allows an abundant safety margin.

As Angle A increases toward 180° (horizontal) with the same 90kg person on the rope (Table 19), the results are quite different.

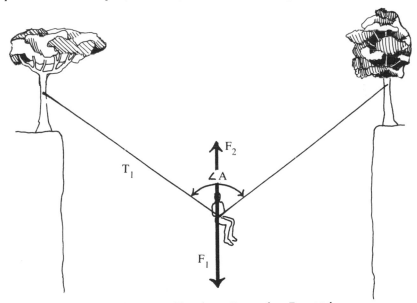

Fig. 20.5 Stress on Tyrolean. $F_1 = 90$kg, $F_2 = 90$ kg.

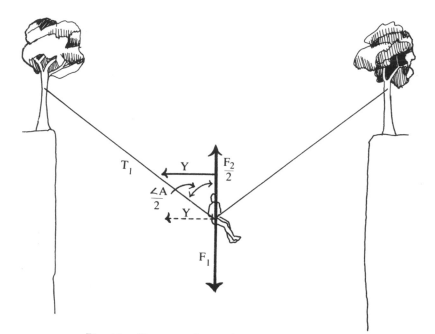

Fig. 20.6 Vector analysis of Tyrolean system.

Table 19

Relationship Between Rope
Tension and Loading

If angle A is:	The resulting tension T for a 90 kg load is:	The general relationship between T and L:	
15	46.6 kg	T	½L
30	46.5 kg	T	½L
45	49.1 kg	T	½L
60	51.9 kg	T	½L
75	57.2 kg	T	½L
90	63.6 kg	T	¾L
120	90.0 kg	T	L
150	174.6 kg	T	2L
175	1035.0 kg	T	11.5 L

There is an important field consideration to be gained from this discussion: it is hard to pretension a rope to a predictable angle *A* because of rope stretch and variable loading. If you do attempt to increase angle *A*, recognize the consequences. Keep as much slack in the system as possible to prevent a high *T* value. Ergo, knowing how to descend and ascend a slack Tyrolean system forestalls the need to depend on a tight one and test your mathematics.

Simple diaper sling and swami tie-in for river crossing. *Photo Mead Hargis*

Often a rope has to be tightened. There are a number of ways to do this, depending on the equipment at hand. One must prevent the problems of nylon running over nylon and study the angles formed by the rope as it bends back on itself (over a carabiner or pulley or another rope), greatly reducing its strength. Prusiks serve as good weak links, and will slip or break at about 550kg before overstressing begins.

Mead Hargis suggests that one should never tighten a rope with more force than one person can pull with no mechanical advantage, i.e., 1:1. The mechanical advantage systems shown are handy at times, though. They are 3:1 theoretically, but provide much less advantage in practice because of primary tree friction and secondary carabiner friction. The actual mechanical advantage is approximately 2:1 or less.

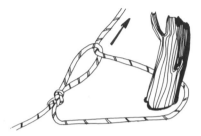

Fig. 20.7 Rope tensioning methods. Simple but potentially dangerous because of the knot and nylon against nylon friction.

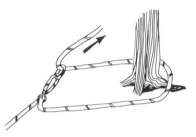

Fig. 20.8 A safer variation than the previous one.

Fig. 20.9 Much better method; no knot in rope and no nylon against nylon.

Fig. 20.10 In this way the prusiks act as a ratchet as tension is pulled.

Fig. 20.11 Better system than before; no knots and the prusiks act as safeties.

If the technique shown in figure 20.12 is employed, the advantage will be less than 2.1. This is sufficient to tighten the rope and yet low enough to prevent overstressing the system. If the prusik breaks, the system provides its own back-up safety. If the prusiks in figures 20.7 through 20.10 break, you will be left holding the bag! As in figure 20.12, these systems can also be rigged with their own safeties. Figure 20.14 illustrates a more efficient tightening technique, while figure 20.15 shows a fancy and pretty bombproof final version. Happy tightening!

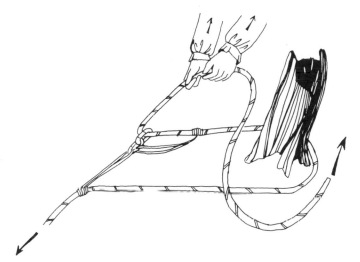

Fig. 20.12 When pulling tension a simple belay can be made by passing the rope around the anchor so if a prusiks breaks . . .

Fig. 20.13 . . . a disaster is averted.

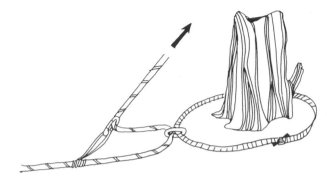

Fig. 20.14 A low friction variation of figure 20.9.

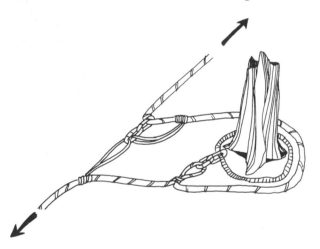

Fig. 20.15 Variation of 20.11 with a safety in case of prusik failures.

BIBLIOGRAPHY

CHAPTER **T**WENTY

M**ac**I**nnes**, H**amish**. *International Mountain Rescue Handbook*. New York: Charles Scribner's Sons, 1972.

Adjustable height Tyrolean and raising system. Similar to three-rope river rescue method in Chapter 22. *Photo Tim Setnicka*

21 | Helicopter Technique

"Like all novices, we began with the helicopter . . . but soon saw that it had no future and dropped it. . . . If its engine stops, it must fall with deadly violence for it can neither float like a balloon nor glide like the aeroplane. The helicopter is much easier to design than the aeroplane but it is worthless when done."

—Wilbur Wright,
inventor of the airplane

Helicopters in Action — The Power and the Glory

In May, 1978, two climbers were climbing the 600-meter standard route on Quarter Dome in Yosemite, a Grade VI, i.e., a route taking over two days.

At about 1 P.M. on the first day, the leader was looking around for a place to rest some 20 meters above his belayer when he suddenly fell. He pendulumed into the rock, critically injuring himself and finally coming to rest hanging free on the rope, three meters above his partner. The belayer slowly lowered his friend to a small one-by-two meter sloping ledge. He knew immediately that the leader was severely injured because his face was covered with blood and he was not fully conscious, only moaning in pain. Eventually, mouth-to-mouth resuscitation was necessary and the injured climber started breathing again.

His partner went for help by rappelling seven pitches and running five kilometers to a telephone. He reported the incident at 5 P.M. It was

Photo Kenneth Andrasko

immediately decided to ask for military assistance from Naval Air Station LeMoore, which has performed extensive search and rescue work in Yosemite and Sequoia-Kings Canyon National Parks.

From the Park Service contract helicopter, SAR rangers witnessed a dramatic scene. The injured climber was waving his arms sporadically, hanging virtually upside down on a sheer rock wall, his face covered with blood. He was about 300 meters down from the top of Quarter Dome; it was obvious that he would not live long without immediate help.

Plans for a major rescue operation took shape, including flying twelve climbers to the top of Quarter Dome and lowering one or two down the wall to the victim. At best, this would take hours, and it was 5:45 P.M. and getting dark. There was little choice, so the contract helo began to shuttle equipment and rescuers to the top of Quarter Dome.

At 6:25 P.M., "Angel-1," a twin-engine Huey-type helicopter arrived in Yosemite Valley and immediately embarked on a reconnaissance of the scene. Aircraft Commander John Sullivan and copilot Don Swain hovered near the injured climber and blood-splattered rock, devised a plan, and sped back to the Valley floor.

"He's still alive, Butch," Sullivan told Ranger Butch Farabee, "but he won't live long."

"Yeah, we know. What is your plan?", Butch inquired.

"I think we can get him off by doing a cliff evolution. I think we can swing Benny [the crew chief] into him if we hover high enough," Sullivan answered.

"Okay, go for it," Butch said. "We'll tell the rangers on top." Sullivan's crew then emptied the helicopter of all excess gear to lighten it.

A cliff evolution is a type of helicopter rescue developed by the search and rescue personnel at LeMoore, similar to fixed-rope helicopter technique common in Canada and Europe. One or two crewmen rappel down fixed ropes from a hovering helicopter, stabilize an injured person, attach him to the ropes, and then hang tight while all personnel are flown away, still suspended underneath the helicopter, to a landing zone where they are eased down. In this case, the victim would be unable to help himself, and the distance beneath the helicopter would be extreme — 65 to 100 meters.

As Angel-1 lifted off again toward Quarter Dome, Lt. Sullivan and his crew rebriefed this plan over the helicopter intercom system. Crew Chief Revels would rappel out of the helicopter, assuming Sullivan and Swain could ease the helicopter in close enough to the face to get over the injured climber. Crewman Decicco would watch the main and tail rotor clearances as the helicopter hovered near the wall, and monitor Crew Chief Revels while he was out of the helicopter. Crewman Delgado would belay Revels on a separate line, in case of a problem with the main rope.

After four to five minutes of experimenting, Sullivan and Swain found a spot where they could hover above the victim, but it was much higher than optimal due to the steepness of the face.

Sullivan began to ease his helicopter toward the wall. During this process, the pilot concentrates on the helicopter's controls and watches a single reference point outside. The copilot watches the hundred or so gauges and lights and reports engine, fuel, torque, and temperature information to the pilot every 20 to 30 seconds. When hovering, there is no forward air speed to help lift the aircraft; only engine speed and rpm's keep it in the air. The engines and gearbox may overheat during prolonged hovering, causing a mechanical failure or a hastily aborted hover. Anyone suspended below the helicopter would be killed or seriously injured.

As Sullivan continued to ease next to the wall, Dicicco stuck his head out the side door, and called out the main and tail rotor clearances to the pilot over the intercom system. Once over the injured climber, Sullivan held his hover.

"Okay Benny, anytime," Sullivan told the crew over the helicopter's intercom system (ICS). A hundred-meter rope was dropped out of the right side door. Revels knelt there while Decicco gave him a last-minute safety check. Decicco looked at Delgado, Revels's belayer, and when the thumbs up was given, Revels backed out of the doorway and began his spiraling descent. Sullivan continued to hold Angel-1 close to the rock; the main rotary blade was less than three meters from the cliff.

"He's about 50 feet down, Sir," Decicco called over the ICS, "75, 100, about halfway . . . 175 . . . 250. He's even with the climber now, but we'll have to move him in closer to the wall." Still one meter away from the struggling victim, Revels radioed, "Move in, I can't reach him!"

Sullivan told his crew, "Get ready! Decicco, watch that damn wall!"

"Yes sir," said Decicco, lying flat on his stomach, helmeted head sticking out of the door watching both Revels and the rock. "Easy right, sir; easy, sir; right six feet, sir; tail is clear; hold your hover, sir; HOLD your hover."

The main rotary blades of the helicopter were now less than two meters from the wall. The only possible escape in the event of an engine failure would be to drop to the left without turning the tail rotor into the rock. Enough control might possibly be reestablished for an autorotation — into 30 to 40 foot trees — but it would be certain death for both Revels and the victim.

Revels rerigged the climber's harness so it could be clipped onto his own harness. Revels was twisting around, unable to stand on anything; the victim was barely conscious and kept sporadically fighting him. Continuous bleeding all over Revels's hands made it difficult to determine what his injuries were.

After fifteen minutes of hovering, Sullivan could feel the sweat running down the inside of his flight suit. After twenty minutes of hovering, he felt his arms and back tense up from the tension of constantly working the controls.

Finally after twenty-two minutes of hovering, Revels radioed that he was ready for lift-off. Sullivan prepared to take the extra 90 kilogram load on one side of the helicopter. Revels was still restraining the barely conscious victim and keeping his airway open, while making three attempts to cut him free from his ropes. At last, the two of them swung out beneath the helicopter.

Decicco helped Sullivan ease Angel-1 away from the rock. "Easy; left, sir; the tail is clear . . . easy left . . . okay to start a turn to the left . . . Benny's looking good down below — minimum swing . . .", and so forth until touchdown in Ahwahnee Meadow, a five-minute flight away. Some 70 meters below the moving helicopter, Revels was still trying to keep the climber from hurting himself or Revels, or, worse yet, unknowingly disrupting a piece of equipment.

Once on the ground, Revels swiftly unbuckled himself and the injured climber while rangers supported him, still miraculously alive. He was rushed to the local medical clinic where doctors stabilized his condition. Angel-1 waited to transport the injured climber to a hospital outside the Valley for immediate surgery to relieve the pressure on his brain. The entire rescue took less than one hour from the time Angel-1 first landed in Yosemite Valley.

Fixed-line flyaway. *Photo Kenneth Andrasko*

General Considerations for Helicopter Use

Over the past fifteen years or so, perhaps nothing has changed SAR work more dramatically than the development and refinement of helicopters, especially those with turbine engines. Their widespread use in the Vietnam war helped rapidly introduce them to all aspects of American life, from firefighting to shuttle service to medical evacuation. The new helicopters allow quick and easy access to, and extrication from, almost any remote area. The speed and efficiency of many recent SAR operations has been primarily a function of the availability of these versatile workships.

Some of the more powerful ships have even provided an aerial operations platform to work from while hovering ten meters from a big wall or steep slope.

Many of the traditional limitations of aircraft in SAR use have been minimized or overcome entirely. High intensity lighting, infrared goggles, close range radar systems, and special navigation techniques have increased capabilities for night operations. Rescue sites are now more accessible because highly trained crews in the new ships employ techniques like one-skid landings or hovers above ground, with rescuers rappelling down or being hoisted out. Some of the military ships carry crewmen whose sole duty during takeoff, landing, and bad weather is to observe and continuously report to the pilot main and tail rotor blade clearances and other obstruction information. This vastly increases the work capacity and precision of the helicopter by allowing safe operations in very confined spaces with constantly changing factors, like updrafts in tight canyons. Also, larger engines make it possible to do things like high altitude hovering, or landing on the summit of Mt. McKinley (6194 m/20,320 feet).

Along with these newer helicopters have come some modern heli-rescue techniques which, combined with older techniques now made safer by the newer machines, give the rescuer a full bag of tools to solve SAR problems.

Helicopters are great SAR tools and have significantly decreased the time an injured person must remain in the field. Helicopters have saved time, effort, and lives. But one must maintain an alternate SAR plan, a "Plan B," and always evaluate the total effectiveness of using a helicopter in each phase of a given operation.

Tight helispot used to rescue lost camper. *Photo Tim Setnicka*

In many parts of the country, such as national parks and wilderness areas, the use of helicopters is illegal unless there exists a critical situation. One must always contend with the problems of fuel, wind, air density, altitude, temperature, and torque. Mechanical breakdowns tend to be infrequent but they do occur, with very serious consequences, and pilot error is not unknown. Weather and darkness have made flying hazardous ever since the Wright brothers first got the whole idea off the ground. SAR personnel must always consider the negative impact of any one of these factors: bad weather, malfunction, darkness. We therefore want to stay *helicopter independent* in SAR planning and thinking, in spite of the seductiveness of constant reliance on helo support.

There are innumerable military and government manuals on helicopter safety. The National Park Service and National Forest Service both have excellent publications on hand signals, wind direction, landing zones, clearances, and selections. Study these if you will be involved in ground support work. The following comments summarize some of the important points contained in these publications. The best SAR preplan for helo support is founded on personal familiarity with the particular helicopter and crew you will be working with, and training in the procedures they prefer. On-the-job training is much better than reading books (like this one).

When evaluating the option of helicopter use in a particular operation, one must consider several questions.

1) How serious is this SAR? Does it warrant the cost and complexity of helo support?
2) Given the type of helicopter available, what are its limitations under optimum conditions?
3) What is the pilot's experience and willingness? Has he flown already today?
4) What are the current weather conditions, and how many hours before dark?
5) Where is the helicopter now, and how soon can it be where it is needed?
6) Is there a faster (but perhaps more strenuous) way of doing the operation?
7) Is there a safer way to do the operation, especially considering the dangers introduced by and the safety of the helicopter and crew?
8) Should a fuel truck be ordered to stand by during the operation, with "professional" helitac, heliport personnel available to assist?

The decision between use of the helicopter and alternative strategies is based on what functions one needs performed, within certain safety and time frame constants. Likely tasks include:

1) Reconnaissance of a situation and victim location
2) Simple victim pickup from a landing zone
3) Transportation of rescue personnel to and from the scene
4) Equipment transport via sling loading
5) A hover jump operation
6) A one-skid landing operation
7) Rescuer rappels from the helicopter onto the scene
8) Hoist maneuvers involving rescuers or the evacuation of victims by hoist
9) Pendulum techniques introducing a rope, hoist cable, or load onto the scene for a variety of purposes
10) Fly aways, with the victim and rescuers underneath the helo on fixed ropes.

Helicopter Search and Reconnaissance

A helicopter can be used not only as an aerial observation platform to search for a victim, but also for reconnaissance of an area or situation. Precise information on terrain, natural barriers, trail routes, and hazards can be gathered immediately, facilitating the planning of an operation. Direct contact can be made with the victims by hovering away from them and asking questions through a P.A. system or with hand signals. In a few instances, a helicopter has dropped a radio to the people involved and avoided a major operation by allowing SAR personnel to talk them to safety. The idea of using a large board on which messages could be printed and displayed from the air has been discussed.

Glacier rescue at altitude. *Photo Dick Martin*

Specific search patterns for aerial search have been developed by the military; they usually involve some form of grid search. Helicopters are especially useful for hasty and Type II and Type III grid searches if sufficient money and fuel are available.

The practical considerations of where and how to land a helicopter in the field accompany all reconnaissance and search tactics, and virtually all field use. Wilderness landing zones not listed with the FAA or on any aeronautical chart fall into two categories. The *helispot* is any designated landing area that does not have road access. A *heliport* is a designated landing area that is accessible by road.

Helicopter Design

It is important to understand a few basic principles of how a helicopter flies and why it can land or hover only in certain areas and under certain conditions. The physics of helo flight determine landing zones.

For this discussion we'll use the type of helicopter with a large main rotor and a smaller, vertical tail rotor. There are also some helicopters with two rotor blade systems of the same size, where the rotors turn in opposite directions.

The larger, horizontal rotor is referred to as the main rotor, and the smaller, vertical rotor is called a tail rotor. The main rotor may have many blades, but all helicopters have at least two. The Huey type helicopters are examples of helos with a two-blade main rotor as well as a two-blade small rotor.

In cross section, the rotor blades are a classic airfoil, shaped like an airplane wing. The air flows faster over the top of the airfoil than the bottom, creating lift. The angle of the blade to the air flow is called the angle of attack; this angle and the speed of the blades creates and controls lift.

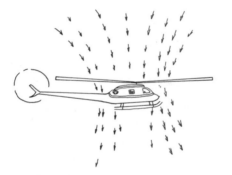

Fig. 21.1 Pattern of air flow through helicopter rotors when no surrounding obstructions.

The pilot has three major control systems for the helicopter. The *collective* varies the main rotor's angle of attack and commands vertical movement of the ship, in conjunction with engine rpm controlled via a hand throttle. The plane in which the rotor blades spin is controlled by the *cyclic*, which tilts the spinning rotors in any direction and produces forward, backward, and sideward movement. Two *foot pedals* alter the pitch of the tail rotor, effectively a rudder. The tail rotor counters the torque effect of the main rotor, preventing the helicopter body from spinning in a direction counter to that of the main rotor as power is increased. Manipulation of the foot pedals enables a hovering helicopter to pivot around its vertical axis at zero airspeed.

The next time you watch a helicopter take off, try to follow the sequence of events. After sufficient engine and main rotor rpm are attained, the pilot uses the collective to increase the angle of attack of the rotor blades. This begins to lift the helicopter off the ground, and takes a great deal of engine power and torque. As soon as he has assessed the power margin, the pilot will move the cyclic forward to begin a transition from vertical lifting to forward flight. As the helo builds up airspeed, additional translational lift is generated by the flow over the rotors. After effective translational lift speed has been reached, the engine power required to continue to turn the main rotor at its constant rpm is reduced, and the pilot can lower the collective and fly straight ahead at higher airspeeds without climbing. Or, he can climb by maintaining the collective at a relatively high setting.

Consider a situation in which a helicopter hovers, a maneuver similar to the first part of takeoff. Only engine rpm and the collective create the lift necessary to keep the helo in the air. On a warm day at high altitude, hovering next to obstructions, a helicopter's engine and transmission are operating close to redline. This rapidly produces heat and wear on the mechanical system. The pilot is under stress too, because he must maintain altitude and correct position, check blade clearances, and monitor instruments. The increased mechanical stress on the machine, the physical and mental stress on the pilot and crew— all this affects safety margins.

The general rule is to absolutely minimize hover time. Rescuers might, for instance, walk to a landing area rather than being hoisted or one-skidded out of a tight spot. The probability of a downdraft, power settling, or recirculation effect occurring is high during a hover. Downdrafts can occur at any time and are a constant danger, especially in canyons or against walls. Power settling is usually associated with a condition of high gross weight and a descending flight at or near hover power. When a helicopter descends into its own disturbed air mass created by rotor wash, this type of lift loss results. Recirculation is a similar phenomenon, except that the helicopter is commonly operating in a confined area, say a tight canyon. Confinement increases the instability of the air mass by the action of the rotors, and lift is lost (Fig. 21.2). The only way to recover in these situations, after maximum power is used, is to partially lower the collective and move the helicopter into forward or sideward flight in order to escape the disturbed air mass. Overall, the importance of minimizing hover time cannot be overemphasized.

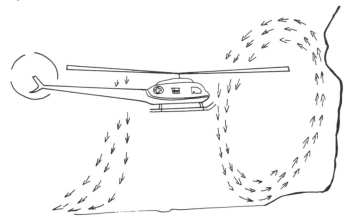

Fig. 21.2 Pattern of air flow when hovering next to a large obstruction.

Landing Zones

The selection of a good landing area is based on a number of factors (Fig. 21.3). Try to establish a landing area that gives maximum advantage to the helicopter in taking off into the wind and making the transition to forward flight. A run-out is prudent for hovering tactics, in case there is a loss of lift due to recirculation of air flow, downdrafting, or loss of engine power. The helicopter may be able to immediately drop into forward flight, gain airspeed, and recover maneuverability.

Fig. 21.3 General types of helicopter landing sites. Ridge top — generally the best.

If possible, locate a spot on an exposed knob with a 360° range of approach and take-off options. A 20 meter minimum width (in the case of a Huey) approach and departure path, as long as possible, should be cleared, to avoid the safety compromises of vertical take-offs.

Helos should be able to land and take off into the wind to increase lift, especially at higher elevations. Avoid sloped landing zones. If the only possible spot is in a canyon or on bottom land, remember that a vertical takeoff is considered dangerous at any elevation, and that a small helicopter must be at least 100 meters above the ground in order to safely autorotate or glide back to the ground in case of power failure. Avoid dead air spots on the lee sides of ridges or canyon bottoms. The best path for take-off on level ground should be at least 100 meters long and slightly downhill. In glacial cirques and canyon bottoms, make sure there is not a downdraft from a neighboring ridge. If the canyon is deep, the helicopter will need a long forward run to gain enough altitude to pull out over the rim.

Fig. 21.4 Landing on canyon bottoms.

A last resort is a "hover hole" helispot, where the pilot must slow to a hover above the landing area and then descend. When taking off, he must gun the engines to power straight up until clear enough to begin forward flight. The dangers are obvious (Fig. 21.5).

Mark the landing zone in some manner. An *H* pattern or *T* pattern is considered standard. Colored or reflectorized material may also be used. Wind direction should always be indicated with smoke, streamers, hand signal, or by radio contact. Packs and rescue gear should be weighted down and loose natural debris removed to prevent rotor or engine damage.

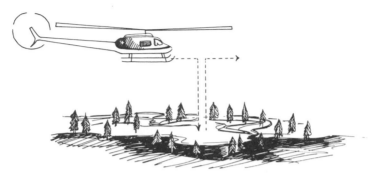

Fig. 21.5 Landing in hover hole.

General Helicopter Safety

Before approaching a helicopter, make sure the pilot has got the ship down on the landing area the way he wants it. Often he will need to jockey the helo around a bit before he feels comfortable enough to ease the power off, a noticeable change in engine pitch. The almost universal "thumbs up" sign can be given by either you or the pilot. If the pilot is not ready for you to approach, he will let you know in a hurry.

You should approach or leave a helicopter only at an angle visible to the pilot. As you approach the ship, squat in low profile to maximize head and rotor clearance. Don't look at the ground, though — keep watching the pilot. Depending on the landing zone and other flight factors, he may have to hold a bit of power on. If so, the helo may pull off suddenly due to precarious positioning, or if it goes into ground resonance (the helicopter begins to vibrate due to harmonic imbalance between landing gear and rotor blades). In either of these cases the helo must become airborne. The same cautions about sudden lift-off are particularly pertinent to landings on snow and ice.

For one-skid or hover boarding and exiting operations, extra caution should be used, and a few signals and procedures discussed beforehand with the pilot. Stepping in or out of a helo balancing on one skid should be done very e-a-s-i-l-y to avoid a radical weight change on one side of the ship.

Helijumping is more serious yet, and before attempting it one should have a helmet and solid boots at the very least. Jumping is much faster and less complicated than rappelling or hoisting, and is a reasonable technique if you work with an adequate safety margin and within the limitations of the particular helicopter.

One-skid landing, signaler, and departure technique. *Photo Kenneth Andrasko*

A general rule of thumb is to try to find or make a place to land, rather than performing one-skid or hover flying circus routines. Any helicopter work is hazardous, so if you can decrease the uncertainty by moving an injured victim to a proper landing area instead of picking him up with a hoist, it is advisable to do so. A routine evacuation for a broken leg can transform into tragedy in an instant if the helicopter goes down for any reason. Landing zones are a given in helicopter work. Master their use. If the victim is critically injured, it may be decided that touching down or hovering for only a split second is the answer. Think it through.

Picking a landing spot (or helispot, as it is sometimes called) can be tricky in flat terrain with intermittently thick forest. The width of the landing zone is gauged by pacing off the length of the rotors plus an additional half-length. However, if obstructions surround the area, the helo may still be unable to land because of its power limitations. Indicate wind direction with smoke, dirt kicked or thrown in the air, a small smoky fire, or streamers; or, put your back to the wind and extend both arms parallel (Fig. 21.6). If the landing zone slopes, be sure to approach or leave the helicopter from as crouched a position as possible. When the pilot is idling or shutting down, the rotors lose their momentum; just before they stop they often dip very close to the ground, or the wind forces them down. Approaching on the uphill side is therefore life-threatening.

Fig. 21.6 A few simple ways to indicate wind direction: smoke flare, back to wind, streamer, dirt kicked.

Once around the helicopter, remember the danger zone of main rotor clearance and that of the tail rotor (Fig. 21.7) There is no reason, ever, to go back past the skids or the side doors. If you must change sides, be sure to walk around the front of the helicopter, where you and the pilot can always see each other. While loading or unloading, try not to step or stand inside the skids. If the pilot has to suddenly pull on power and lift off, you probably won't want to be between the skids or back by the tail rotor.

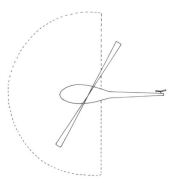

Fig. 21.7 Safe zone in which to approach the helicopter.

Wear goggles and a hard hat with a chin strap that fastens. Always buckle in when in the ship.

On any SAR, a safety or helispot coordinator should be officially designated. This person has a hard hat, goggles, and radio. He focuses his attention strictly on loading and unloading people and equipment safely, keeping in mind the helicopter's safety as well. This person can weigh loads, schedule flights within the weight limits the pilot has given him, load people, brief them on how to open doors and on emergency procedures, keep the helispot secure, and in general be responsible for a safe operation. The same goes for landings at the other end of the operation if necessary. On big operations, everyone tends to be preoccupied with what he or she is going to do upon arrival at the rescue site, and safety is often forgotten. Hence, one safety officer whose main job is to help the helicopter and its passengers think about safety is advisable.

Sling Loads

If your helicopter is equipped with a sling loading hook, all the better. Sling loading people underneath a helicopter on a mechanical hook is, to say the very least, extremely unsafe, but you can still fly a large amount of equipment into a site efficiently. For example, on a technical rescue on a cliff face with no landing site nearby, rescuers could rappel to the brink or they could be flown into a landing spot some distance from the scene with only basic bivouac gear. Meanwhile, most of the rescue equipment could be sling loaded directly into the rescue site at the lip, thus saving all the time and effort necessary to carry it.

Pilots tend to look at sling loading as consisting of two basic problems: the weight of the load, and the aerodynamic properties of the load. Weight limitations are determined by the helicopter type and related flying factors of altitude, temperature, and winds. Aerodynamic considerations question whether the load will fly evenly or begin to swing, rise, or become involved in some violent mongrel motion. The length of the sling rope varies, but is usually over 70 meters. The pilot's experience dictates many specifics the rescue leader needs to know.

A load of myriad bits and pieces like packs, ropes, and litters is fine if each piece is weighed separately and the whole is secured together by a cargo net, parachute canopy, or similar catch-all. A swivel is necessary and is hooked directly into the cargo hook below the helicopter (Fig. 21.8). The sling rope is attached between the swivel and the load. The load, sling rope, and swivel are neatly laid out in front of the helicopter, in the pilot's view. The swivel is attached while the helicopter is sitting on the ground, and is brought to the cargo hook directly from the front, not over the skids or from the rear of the ship.

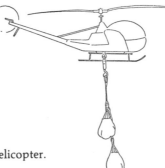

Fig. 21.8 Sling loading by helicopter.

Once the signal is given, the pilot slowly raises the helicopter until the sling rope is taut, and then he gradually compensates for the load's weight. Usually he will not want to fly passengers while carrying sling loads. On the ground at the drop site, someone wearing a helmet and goggles assists the pilot in positioning the load and giving the drop signal (Fig. 21.9). If possible, avoid having someone working with the load under the helicopter. If someone must secure the load once it is dropped, he must have a helmet and goggles, as the swivel and sling rope are dropped along with the load.

Fig. 21.9 Hand signals used in sling loading work. "Steady" (left), and "release the load" (right).

More than one sling load can be carried at the same time, in tandem. The heaviest load should be placed at the bottom and a short sling rope (one meter) is used to attach each succeeding load to the heaviest.

Sling loading has been a standard way to move objects and equipment for many years in firefighting and commercial enterprises. It is a proven method and one which the SAR team should actively cultivate. Equipment is also easily air dropped if fragile items are packed properly.

One-Skid Landings

One-skid landings occur when one skid (or a part of it) or wheel of a helicopter is placed on the ground and the helicopter retains high rotor rpm's to keep it level in the air. During the loading or unloading process everyone should move efficiently, be mindful of their tasks, and change position slowly and smoothly. The pilot needs time to adjust his controls for the increased or decreased load coming onto or off of one side of his helicopter. The last thing a pilot wants is a clumsy 110 kg rescuer pumped full of adrenalin and suffering from mountain sickness or fleas.

Close all doors securely, and make sure nothing will fall out or inhibit the pilot's control. This is especially critical in small helicopters without extra crew members to double check for mistakes. Remember, *you* are riding in the ship! Extreme care must be taken when there are dual controls and a non-pilot is sitting in the copilot's seat. Any slight bump of the controls as someone gets in or out can result in disaster.

One-skid landing on pinnacle. *Photo Dick Sale*

Frequently, the tightness of the landing area where a one-skid takes place is steep or complicated terrain. Do not run uphill onto the rotor blades, or scramble out of the way along a rock arête where one slip will mean a long fall. Often it is impossible to move away from the helicopter. Hold your position and wait for the ship to complete its task and take off. Protect yourself however possible from the usual hazards, which would normally be noted but are not always readily apparent when a helicopter's engine is screaming full-throttle one meter away from your head on the top of a pinnacle.

Helijumping

Helijumping officially began in 1947 in conjunction with firefighting activities. Like any new program, it had its difficulties and was prohibited for a few years. In 1957, the program was reinstated under United States Forest Service regulations with standardized techniques. Helijumping is still infrequent, due to increased hazards to the firefighter, but the techniques are sometimes used by SAR personnel and should not be wholly discounted.

Under the Forest Service guidelines, the jumper wears a thick, padded, two-piece suit with breakaway zippers. The suit includes heavy gloves and a motorcycle style helmet with a caged face mask. Sturdy high-topped boots are also required. All this paraphernalia provides safety to the jumper, who often launches into brush and small trees. Most SAR units do not have this gear available but under some conditions, when a victim's life is in danger, rescuers will jump anyway.

The critical factors are a helicopter that can safely come to a complete hover and an adequate jump spot. If possible, select a flat area which is open and bare of stumps, logs, and rocks. The maximum height of jumps into open ground should be under two meters. Jumping into brush and trees should only be done with approved gear. If a flat area cannot be located, choose a slope which is under 45° at a place where the helicopter can continue across the slope.

The jumper goes out of the helicopter on the uphill side. Check the area's run out, especially if it is a rock slab. If one must jump on a slab, it should not slope more than 20° or 25°. If the slab is close to a cliff or broken area, it has to be avoided. Never jump onto icy rock or any appreciably sloping snow or ice, no matter what. Jumping onto a glacier is possible, but remember the possibility of breaking through into a hidden crevasse. Now you see him; now you don't.

After the spot has been selected, let the pilot hover to check the area, pull into an approximate position as a test run, pull off, and go around for the jump pass. If there is some question about the jump site, use a pack as a test. It is much better to lose a pack than to injure a partner. Before anyone exits, the pilot and jumpers must agree on the jump location, tail and main rotor clearance, stability of the helicopter, minimum risk posed by ground hazards and vegetation, jump height, and general overall safety.

The individual helicopter will determine which side is used and how many jumpers can go at once. The pilot's experience is law. Some helicopters need a jump step with a hand grip installed before any jump could be considered safe. Others, like the Bell Jet Ranger (206A), can be jumped from with standard skid gear. The doors must be either pinned open or removed prior to any jump.

The general procedure for executing the jump is as follows. At the pilot's signal, the jumper prepares to jump. He unfastens his seat belt, refastens it behind his back, and prepares to step out to the skid step or onto the skid itself. The jumper constantly watches the pilot. At the pilot's signal, the jumper swings one leg out at a time onto the step or skid, keeping his shoulders well back toward the body of the helicopter. The closer the jumper's weight is to the helicopter's center of gravity, the easier and safer the jump becomes. When he is in position, he acts on the pilot's final signal and he *steps* (*not* jumps) off the skid gently, avoiding unnecessary forward momentum.

After leaving the skid, the jumper keeps his legs together and arms folded against his lower chest, with elbows snug against the body and chin tucked into the chest. Upon contact with the ground, the feet and knees absorb the shock and he remains in a prone position, trying not to roll until the helicopter has passed the jump spot. One should never jump with a pack, climbing hammer, hardware sling, ropes, knife, or other survival gear on his person. Everything else can be dropped before or after the jump has been safely completed.

After the helicopter is clear from the area, the jumper uses a "thumbs up" or similar signal to tell the pilot he is all right.

Helicopter Rappelling

Rappelling from a helicopter on a static rope is another tool which increases SAR operation efficiency. Helicopter rappelling can be performed, and should be considered, regardless of whether or not a helicopter is equipped with a hoist. Rappelling has certain advantages over hoisting: it is faster, safer (rope vs. cable), requires no mechanical winch systems, and is more accurate, as the rappeller can control his own rate of descent and landing point.

An overview of a few standard systems illustrates some of the possibilities.

The anchor point of the rappel rope should be bombproof, needless to say, and its use in accordance with the aircraft manufacturer's specifications and recommendations. Whenever possible, use existing

Helo rappel to victim during practice. *Photo Kenneth Andrasko*

deck rings or structural members, as any addition or modification requires FAA approval that the change is in concert with the manufacturer's use stipulations. Deck rings rigged properly and linked together into a self-equalizing unit form a simple and safe anchor which is readily set up. The hoist arm has also been used to anchor the rappel ropes. The U.S. Forest Service has developed a simple anchor bracket that attaches to the roof of a Bell 212 which has worked well. If there are doubts about a potential anchor point or system, check with the manufacturer before using it.

Once an anchor has been established, there are a number of rappel systems to choose from. The Sky Genie is a strong elongated metal spool that the rappel rope is wrapped around. Increasing the number of turns decreases the speed of descent; however, the rappeller can stop or control his speed as he wishes. The Sky Genie should be attached to a rappel seat or harness with a locking carabiner.

Sky Genie attached to airman's harness; rope on right goes to helo. *Photo Kenneth Andrasko*

One significant disadvantage, however, is that the rope must be a special braided nylon, not the kernmantle rope generally used in mountaineering. Laid rope such as Goldline also will not work well in the system. The rope used is 13mm (½″) diameter and very strong, with a tensile strength of 2600 kilograms. It is kept loosely stacked in a drop bag, which is jettisoned from the helicopter to deploy the rope.

In the military procedure for a Sky Genie rappel, one end of the rope is secured to the anchor point. The rappeller puts on his or her harness and attaches the Sky Genie to the rope, while still tied into the helicopter in some manner. The helicopter comes to a safe hover. At the aircraft commander's signal, the drop bag containing the rappel rope (usually 30 or 80 meter lengths) is, in the case of a Huey helicopter, tossed out the side door over the skid. Once the bag is on the ground, the rope is checked for any kinks or knots. If everything is in order, the rappeller unbuckles his helo safety belt, steps slowly out onto the skid, receives a final safety check, and upon an "o.k." from the pilot via the crew chief, begins a reasonably fast rappel, although not fast enough to cause heat damage to the rope.

As he descends, he watches for kinks or snarls. If the system were to get jammed and he could not free it, he would have to be promptly flown to a landing area and set down. Once he has reached the ground, he quickly unclips and the rappel rope is dropped down to him. It usually takes less than one minute for the full cycle of hover, rappel, and return to forward flight. Rappels are routinely made up to 75 meters with this device.

The U.S. Forest Service uses the Sky Genie for rappelling both firefighters and equipment into remote fire sites. So far over 5000 rappels have been accomplished with no major injuries.

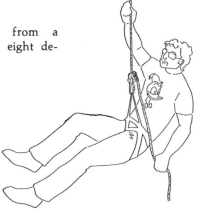

Fig. 21.10 Rappelling from a helicopter with a figure eight descending ring.

Another system uses a rappel seat, a figure eight descending ring, and standard kernmantle or Goldline rope (Fig. 21.10). The Los Angeles Sheriff's Department and the Montrose Search and Rescue Team use this system as a matter of course. The 13mm (½") Tubbs braided nylon rappel rope, either 30 or 60 meters long, is hooked onto a special swivel hook on the Sikorsky CH-34's hoist system and then dropped. The figure eight descending ring is placed on the rope by the crew chief and then handed back to the rappeller, who attaches it to his rappel seat. On signal, the rappeller steps out the door and descends quickly.

Standard six carabiner brake systems have also been used on mountain lay or kernmantle ropes in a manner similar to that described above. The six biner brake system is not as fast or as easy to place and remove as the Sky Genie and the descending ring.

Helicopter Hoist Operations

Most military SAR unit helicopters have cable hoists (or winches). Occasionally a commercial helicopter, such as an Alouette Llama, is equipped with a hoist. An SAR organization with access to such a helicopter has increased capabilities, for the hoist makes it possible to extract a victim from or lower personnel to an area where the helicopter could not possibly land.

Huey electric hoist and stacking rope in bag. *Photo Kenneth Andrasko*

Helicopter hoists are either electric or hydraulic; the aircraft model determines the type of hoist system. For example, a Huey UH-1N has an electric hoist, while a CH-47 and an H-3 have hydraulic systems.

The hoist on the UH-1N is fastened to a vertical column and has an arm or boom that swings out during the operation so that the hoist cable clears the aircraft's skid. One set of controls for the hoist is on the pilot's cyclic control and a second set is mounted on a moveable hand switch, which enables a crewman to maneuver and watch the hoist operation through the side door. The system also has a guillotine-like cable cutter which is activated by an explosive charge fired electrically in case of an emergency. The hoist has about 75 meters of useable cable and a maximum load capacity rating of 270 kg. The electric motor must have time to cool down if used beyond a certain duration; this is an important limiting factor. The SAR team should know the basics of the hoist system which will be in use, so that logistics plans take its limitations into account and allow a wide margin of safety.

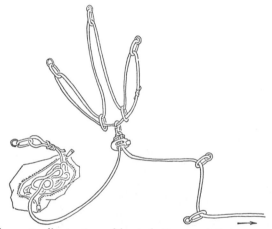

Fig. 21.11 Schematic illustration of basic helicopter belay system for use with hoist. The 11mm perlon rope is stored in a bag, goes through a friction device attached to a self-equalized anchor, and onto the cable hook.

Because helicopter hoisting involves cable and related mechanical devices, certain drawbacks are evident. The aircraft-quality cable used has all the properties of any cable — high tensile strength, almost no dynamic shock loading capacity, immediate weakening when kinked or crimped. Therefore, a belay should always be employed during any hoisting operation as a backup system. The idea of using ropes from a helicopter may seem anachronistic, but so far a simple belay system has saved two lives when a cable broke in California. Investigation after the accident revealed that the cable had become kinked, ironically, during a safety inspection. In these required inspections, the cable is carefully run out and checked, centimeter by centimeter, for any damage. Somehow during this process, the cable became kinked and later, when two crewmen were being hoisted up, it broke about three meters from the hook. The 11mm belay line caught the fall in flight and saved their lives. This system has been regularly used by LeMoore Naval Air Station, which is responsible for most hoisting operations in Yosemite and Sequoia/Kings Canyon National Parks.

The basic system uses a 90 meter 11mm kernmantle climbing rope attached by carabiner to the deck rings (Fig. 21.11). The hoist system (not the cable, which has a much higher rating) has a rating of 270kg, and the rope one of well over 1800 kg, allowing a more than adequate safety margin. The rope is secured as far back from the hoist cable as possible in order to help reduce the amount of spin of the hook, especially when the load comes close to the skids. (A tail rope to someone on the ground can also help.) The rope is then attached to a belay plate anchored in a self-equalizing fashion to three deck rings, each with a minimum rating of 450 kg. Sometimes the rope is just clipped into carabiners in the deck, and the system uses this friction for the belay system (Fig. 21.12). The majority of the rope is kept stacked in a bag, from which it feeds during the operation. One end of the rope is attached to the "D" rings of the rescue device, and the other to a separate deck ring. A person belays as if he were belaying a climbing leader, and is tied into the helicopter. If the hoist or cable fails, the people now held by the rope are flown to the nearest landing area. This system demands practice and coordination between SAR personnel and crewmen.

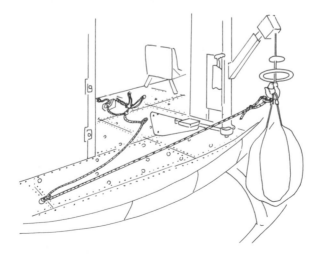

Fig. 21.12 Schematic of belay system in place in a Huey-type helicopter.

It is highly recommended that, if a group has not worked or practiced with a particular helicopter crew or organization, a briefing be held before any operation, no matter how simple. This need not be a long or involved session. Those on the ground and in the air must understand a few hand signals, hook-up procedures, hoist capabilities, wave-off and other emergency procedures. The obvious must be made more obvious. Training and communication are the keys to success.

There are a number of operations which can be performed with the hoist. For hoisting trained personnel, the *horse collar* is the fastest and simplest (Fig. 21.13). The collar is a padded, horseshoe-shaped arrangement which is placed over a person's head and shoulders. It can be put on quickly, but is not safe for an unconscious or semi-conscious victim. Only those familiar with the collar should use one, since it is possible to come out of it.

Los Angeles Sheriff's Sikorsky helo raising a trained rescuer with a horse collar. Holding a pack in this manner prevents falling out of the collar. *Photo Tim Setnicka*

The fishnet, or "screamer suit," is another soft vehicle for transporting injured, young, scared, semi-conscious, or unconscious people with no spinal or other major injuries apparent. The main advantage of the suit is that one needs little training to ride in it and cannot possibly fall out of it under normal use. It is also more comfortable than a horse collar, can be adjusted to both vertical and horizontal positions, and is easily carried in a pack or haul sack.

Fig. 21.13 Horse collar in use.

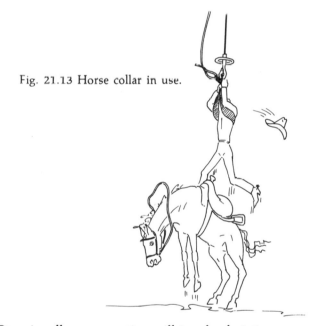

Occasionally an operation will involve hoisting someone in a Stokes litter or Neill Robertson stretcher. This is a bit more tricky, because the victim usually cannot assist himself during the hoisting, and it can be a problem to stabilize the litter while it is entering the helicopter. It is extremely important to know what type of hoisting system is to be used, and where the hoist is located on the helicopter. For example, a CH-47 has a square "hell hole" which will accommodate a litter in the vertical position nicely, but which is inadequate for a horizontal litter unless a crewman reaches down, tips the litter, and works it inside the ship. A UH-1N Huey helicopter has a hoist mounted by the pilot's side door which swings out past the skid. In this case it is much easier to get a horizontally raised litter in the ship. Know the limitations beforehand in order to insure speed, safety, and efficiency. And, prepare the victim completely before the helicopter begins its hover pickup.

Screamer suit. *Photo Tim Setnicka*

Most of the hoisting operations in the Yosemite area are performed with a UH-1N Huey helicopter (Fig. 21.14). Its side-mounted hoist system has about 80 meters of usable cable. Stokes litters, either the solid or the breakdown type, are commonly used. A helicopter pre-rig is taken along on the rescue if there is any possibility that a helicopter hoist will be needed. The pre-rig insures that the correct distance between litter and hoist hook attachment (45cm in this case) will result, so that the litter can be moved quickly into the helicopter without hitting the floor of the ship.

A 90 meter 6mm tail rope is also carried along and attached to the foot of the litter to eliminate spinning and instability during raising. The tail rope is fastened with an oval carabiner; the ship crewman simply drops the rope down once the litter is aboard. The rotor wash keeps the rope from being sucked upward when dropped, especially if a weight such as a carabiner and knot is added to the end. One must be careful, however, if the helicopter is next to a wall or on the ground, because the air (and possibly the rope) will be recirculated as it bounces off of solid obstructions. Check the biner carefully for damage or mark it.

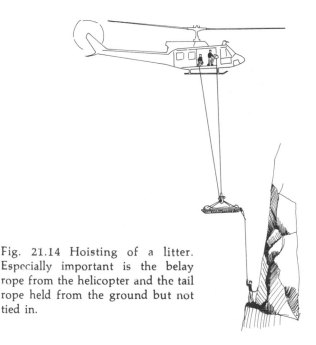

Fig. 21.14 Hoisting of a litter. Especially important is the belay rope from the helicopter and the tail rope held from the ground but not tied in.

The victim is tied into the litter securely and has a swami waist belt, a climbing harness, or the screamer suit as a backup belay clipped directly into the hoist hook. In addition, straps or long pieces of webbing criss-cross the victim from head to toe to inhibit movement and insure that the litter will be stable. Hands are tied in, in most cases, so they will not be injured on the helicopter as the litter is hoisted in.

When all is ready, the helicopter is called in and the hoist hook is lowered. If possible, the hook should be grounded to discharge any static electricity which may have built up. For speed, one person holds the hoist hook and its cable weight, while a second opens the hook and attaches it to the pre-rig on the litter. A third person stands by and guides the tail rope. The tail rope is never attached to anything on the ground, but simply fed directly out of the bag it is carried in to reduce the probability of snagging. The tail rope tender is safe from being pulled off the ground or ledge by the helo's sudden movement or an emergency; he or she is never connected to the helicopter or tied into the tail rope, and the helicopter is never anchored to the ground in any way at any time during the operation.

Hoisting a climber out of the backcountry; note screamer suit and belay rope. *Photo Tim Setnicka*

Once the hookup has been completed, the litter is simply raised while the tail rope stabilizes it. To accomplish this, the helo must move away from the area to decrease the angle between the tail rope and the ground. The crewman quickly pulls the victim inside and releases the tail rope.

It is essential to have clear communications between ground and air during the operation via hand signals or radio. Voice communication under the hovering helicopter is made possible by an effective noise cancelling device such as a covered earphone and a lip microphone. A radio system adapted from a standard military or other noise cancelling flight helmet system has been used with small handie-talkie 5 watt radios with good success. Nicknamed a "Snoopy" helmet, it is easily plugged into a local radio net and provides excellent communications for those working under a hovering helicopter. It is usually worn by the person coordinating the ground operation, who acts as a foreman.

A helicopter evacuation from a steep talus slope or a ledge or a wall is more complicated. The first consideration is the security of everyone involved by some sort of back-up belay system. No one should ever be unclipped, for all must be able to attend to a variety of tasks as the operation progresses without having to worry about falling. With safety as the primary concern, the second consideration is that the helicopter should never be tied directly to the ground, and the third, that the victim should be secured or always belayed.

Hoisting a Stokes litter while hovering. *Photo Kenneth Andrasko*

There are many ways to belay a litter while still not tying it firmly to an anchor point or using a belaying device (which would make quick emergency release impossible). One way is to have two people who are both clipped in or belayed hold and secure the litter (Fig. 21.15). This is their only job; other rescuers are responsible for catching the hoist hook and attaching it to the litter. Again, it is best to allow the hook to ground itself by touching the rock to discharge any static electricity which may have built up in the cable. This method works well in terrain which is steep but not so precarious that one small slip might cause the litter to fall or slide free.

Fig. 21.15 One method of belaying litter for a helicopter hoist. The two people on the ends of the litter are simply steadying it while a third hooks the litter to hoist hook.

If the terrain is steeper, or the victim is on a ledge or ridge crest where there is little working space, one or two people can belay the litter with short slings, the tail rope, or webbing. One end of the sling is secured to the anchor point. The other end is run through the litter — usually through a carabiner on the side rail — and passed back to the belayer, who holds it taut but does not tie it in, and can let go immediately.

The litter must be supported in some manner, often by the belayer's holding onto the sling or webbing, which can be readily released after the hookup or in case of an emergency. Make sure that there is less than one meter of sling between the belayer's hands and the carabiner on the litter. This prevents a knot from forming as the litter is lifted (in the same way that the end of a rappel rope can make an overhand knot if pulled too quickly).

Litter being pulled into ship. *Photo Butch Farabee.*

A final sobering procedure is standard for most military operations. During a hoisting, a cable cutter or guillotine is within close reach of the crew. If anything goes wrong and a wave-off situation develops, the cable and any belay ropes will be cut without second thought in order to save the helicopter. The litter and attendants will be sacrificed, a possibility that one must acknowledge during the size-up and planning stages of the SAR.

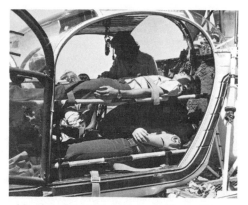

Helo rigged to accept multiple litters. *Photo Tim Setnicka*

Pendulum Maneuvers

The helicopter may not be able to hover directly above the target (ledge or buttress) on a vertical or overhanging wall. A pendulum motion can swing a haul sack or rescuer into the people on the wall. The bag is lowered on a rope or hoist cable and swung inwards (Fig. 21.16); either by a crewman simply pushing and pulling on the rope, or by rocking the helicopter by moving the stick (cyclic). Rope is better than cable alone, because cable may scrap on the skids, causing wear, or may rub against the swedges on the hook. The load must be clipped into the ledge and unclipped from the rope swiftly. This method has been used to successfully swing a haul sack 12 meters horizontally to some climbers on El Cap Spire and Camp V ledge on El Capitan. Practice ahead.

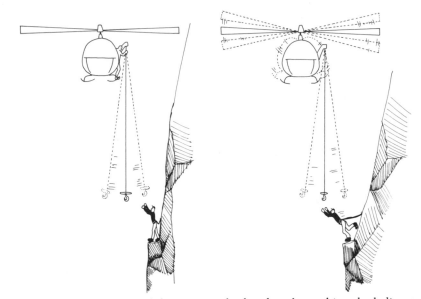

Fig. 21.16 Creating a pendulum motion by hand, or by rocking the helicopter.

Fixed Line Fly-Aways

Occasionally, a helicopter with a hoist is not available or the load would stress the hoist system. In these circumstances, a static line fly-away using standard mountain ropes may provide the solution. In fact,

using climbing ropes can greatly increase the safety margin. An example
of such a system is the one currently employed by the U.S. Naval SAR
crews at LeMoore, California (Fig. 21.17). They use the Sky Genie
military descending system.

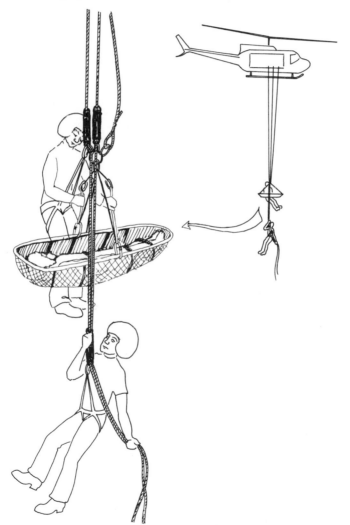

Fig. 21.17 The Sky Genie system for the fixed line fly-away hook up.

Penduluming survival gear to climbers trapped on El Cap Spires, El Capitan.
Photo Butch Farabee

The procedure is as follows. The first rescuer rappels out of the helicopter on a single rope in the standard manner. He takes the Stokes litter with him (assuming it's needed) by letting it dangle between his legs about three feet below. The second rescuer rappels out of the helicopter on a different anchor from the first, most likely self-equalized deck rings. The second rescuer also takes a belay line rigged on a third, separate anchor and a third Genie to be hooked onto the litter.

Fixed-line flyaway. *Photo Kenneth Andrasko*

Once on the ground, the two rescuers usually stay clipped into their rappel systems for safety. As soon as possible, they secure the victim into the litter or a screamer suit. The first rescuer now removes his rappel device from his harness, but leaves it attached to the rope and clips it into the litter. The same rescuer then takes the third Sky Genie and attaches it to the rappel rope of the second rescuer and also to his own harness. Meanwhile, the second rescuer has attached the first rescuer's rappel rope to his double Sky Genie so both rappel ropes run to his system. Lastly, the second rescuer ties the belay rope he brought into the litter and first rescuer.

Naval airman and critically injured climber flown off of Middle Cathedral Rock being lowered by helo to field after flyaway. *Photo Tim Setnicka*

At the signal, both the rescuers and the litter are lifted and flown beneath the helicopter to a safe landing area, where all three are gently deposited. The rescuer on the bottom is set down first. He controls the descent of the other rescuer and the victim by holding or releasing tension on the ropes.

This system is extremely safe, with the maximum allowable force estimated at 1100 kg, compared to 270 kg for the hoist system on the UH-1N. The odds of breaking three ropes are slight. The system utilized equipment and procedures normal for the U.S. Navy. In less complicated circumstances, one rescuer could do the same job if he were familiar with the system by rappelling down to the victim with a belay attached, outfitting the victim in a fishnet, and attaching himself to the victim by carabiners. The rescuer than signals for lift-off, and the two are flown to a nearby landing zone. This modified cliff evolution has been used on several actual SARs in Yosemite. In one, the crewman and victim were suspended over 100 meters below the helicopter.

Unclipping injured climber. *Photo Tim Setnicka*

Fixed and static line operations occur in the context of other SAR skills. Adaptation and practice are the keys to success. Another system has been used in Europe and Parks Canada for many years, with considerable acclaim and few accidents. It features two 46 meter climbing ropes knotted together at intervals and permanently clipped into a swivel fitting on the underside of the helicopter designed for this purpose. The ropes are tied into a special buckleless harness that the rescuer wears. He stands in front of the helo as it gently picks him up like a sling load. Once airborne, the rescuer flies backwards due to air flow until he sticks one arm out horizontally and lets the air turn him around frontward. The pilot can place the rescuer on a ledge where he can unclip, or the pilot can hover while the rescuer clips the victim into his harness. The two are then flown off.

All of these helicopter techniques, especially the last few, are as dramatic as they are dangerous. But helicopter use is not the panacea for SAR problems. We must guard against becoming "helicopter junkies," always depending on a helicopter to perform and support our operations. One final story to drive this point home.

One spring, two experienced rock climbers were carrying loads up to the East Buttress of El Capitan, planning to return and start the climb the next day. On the way down, they walked out on a slab to avoid some brush. The lead climber grabbed a manzanita branch and it promptly broke, sending him flying down the steep slab to the talus below. His partner scrambled down to him, found him unconscious, and went for help. When the SAR crew arrived, he was dead — probably killed upon impact.

Getting to the scene required a fifty-minute run up steep talus and a two or three pitch climb up loose fourth class rock. A military helicopter with hoist capability was requested to start toward the area. When we found that the victim was dead, we radioed the helicopter that there was no hurry.

We decided to load the body into the litter and have the helicopter hoist it rather than spend the rest of the day lowering it down dangerous talus and carrying it out. The weather was fine, with little wind and azure skies. We briefed the details of the operation with the pilot and crew over the radio, and Paul Henry, a ranger who knew the precise location, rode along to direct the helo.

When ready, we moved the litter onto a large ledge which dropped off five or six hundred feet and placed it near the edge. Dan Sholly and I positioned ourselves to do the hookup and manage the tail rope.

The helicopter's rotor blades began to turn down in the meadow before the sound of the engine made its way to us. Once airborne, the helo spiraled upward, made a pass, and did a routine power check before it came in. The pilot gently eased the helo into a solid hover about eight meters above us, as there were no obstructions. The pilot was grinning at us, and we could see Henry preparing to pull the litter into the ship as it rapidly rose on the hoist cable.

The crew chief started to reach out and grab the litter when suddenly the helicopter rocked once to the left. We both thought that odd. An instant later, the engines suddenly altered pitch and the helo dropped without warning and banked hard to the left, narrowly missing us on the ledge. I saw the surprise in the crew chief's face as he braced himself and shot a glance at the pilots before the helo fell from view. We watched in horror as the helicopter described a complete descending spiral toward the stout pine and talus below.

Body recovery, El Cap. Note tail rope. *Photo Kenneth Andrasko*

"The damn thing's crashing! I CAN'T FRIGGING BELIEVE IT!", I yelled, pounding the ground with both hands. Sholly was yelling something equally rational into the radio.

Transfixed, we stared as the helicopter, now sliding rather than turning, glided another half circle and slipped sideways into the trees out of sight. The sounds of a tremendous crash followed hard on the roar of cracking, decapitated trees.

An instant later everyone was running madly down the fixed ropes and broken rock, rolling stones down on ourselves and burning our hands in haste. All we could think of was getting to the helicopter before it exploded, in case someone was still alive.

Suddenly a voice came over the radio. Henry's voice — "Stay clear! We're all clear of the ship, which looks like it's going to explode any moment . . . we're all OK except for a few minor injuries."

A miracle. Later, when we reached the group, I kissed both the pilot and Henry. They didn't complain.

That night, after many especially delicious beers, the pilot said that he suddenly lost power for as yet undetermined reasons. He adroitly banked left to avoid us and the ledge, and began autorotation procedures, only partially successful because of the confined space. Just before they piled into the trees, the corpsman aboard slammed the left side door when he saw the trees coming. The other crewman would have been thrown out the door. The crew chief was able to keep the fire down temporarily with a fire extinguisher while everyone evacuated and helped the pilots out through their small access door just before the entire cabin burst into flames.

To this day no one knows exactly why the helicopter suddenly lost power. I'm not sure what Harry Reasoner, the noted television news commentator, had in mind when he spoke the following on February 16, 1971, but let it stand as a warning to those involved with helicopters in search and rescue:

> "The thing is, helicopters are different from planes. An airplane by its nature wants to fly, and if not interfered with too strongly by unusual events or by a deliberately incompetent pilot, it will fly. A helicopter does not want to fly. It is maintained in the air by a variety of forces and controls working in opposition to each other, and if there is any disturbance in this delicate balance, the helicopter stops flying, immediately and disastrously. There is no such thing as a gliding helicopter."

Helo rescue operation in Yosemite, 1949. *Photo National Park Service*

BIBLIOGRAPHY

CHAPTER TWENTY-ONE

ALSCO SPINKS INDUSTRIES, INC. *Product Information — Fishnet Suit.* P.O. Box 11099, Fort Worth, Tx, n.d.

BILL HELICOPTER COMPANY. *Natops Flight Manual. Navy Model. UH-1N Aircraft.* Bell Helicopter Company, 1976.

SKY GENIE DESCENT CENTRAL, INC. *Product Catalog.* P.O. Box 6405, Fort Smith, AR, n.d.

SULLIVAN, JOHN A. *NAS LeMoore Search and Rescue Standard Operating Procedures.* U.S. Navy, LeMoore Naval Air Station, Ca., n.d.

U.S. DEPARTMENT OF AGRICULTURE. *Inter-Agency Helicopter Management Training Guide.* Washington, D.C.: U.S. Printing Office, 1973.

U.S. FOREST SERVICE, REGION SIX. "Rappeller's Training Guide." Unpublished lesson plans for training source, U.S. Forest Service, 1976.

22 | Whitewater SAR

RICK SMITH AND I were working together one night and talking about the major issue of the evening, where to go for a dinner break. Your-turn-to-buy Smith had unfortunately suggested one rather expensive place with mediocre food. Luckily, the dispatcher called just then and said she had just received a report of a person stranded in the Merced River at a place known as Steamboat Falls. After alerting some of the rescue crew to don their wet suits, we grabbed basic equipment from the rescue cache and roared off. Steamboat Falls was about fifteen kilometers down the Valley.

As we approached the area, we were flagged down by two park visitors, who quickly showed us a man out in the river. He was their brother, and was bracing his feet against an underwater rock right at the lip of a short waterfall that was the opening volley of a several kilometer stretch of nasty rapids. The brothers said he had been hopping from rock to rock while fishing when he slipped and fell. Somehow he had desperately managed to stop himself precisely at the brink of the falls. All we could see was his head; the rest of his body was underwater.

"Hurry up, man . . . I'm getting cold and can't stand here much longer," he yelled above the river's roar.

With little choice in the matter, Rick uncoiled the rope while I took off my hat and defensive equipment. With a bowline on a coil around my waist and a sitting belay provided by Smith, who somehow — by trickery, or by immediately grabbing the rope — had become the land half of our impromptu amphibious operation, I gallantly waded into the

Body recovery at base of 120-meter Vernal Falls in Yosemite.   *441*
Photo Tim Setnicka

foam. It was possible to cautiously work my way out close to the rock, but I could only reach about halfway to him through the waves.

"Give me your hand!" I yelled to him. "O.K.," he murmured. Soon I had a tight grip on it. "Move across in front of me!" The current threatened to drag us downstream toward Modesto, but with a little help from the rope, we both safely beached on shore. He was shaking uncontrollably from hypothermia, after being immersed in the mountain waters for over twenty minutes.

Just as we reached shore, the wet suit crew drove up, raring to go.

"We had to go for it. Didn't have time to wait for you guys," Rick told them, a little apologetically. They looked equipped for an underwater demolition raid on Gilbraltar, all decked out in black rubber and orange foam.

"Yeah, but there's got to be a better way," I added as I squeezed out my soaked uniform and regulation boots. "Shucks, we could have easily drowned. Or rather *I* could have . . . ," I corrected, looking over at Smith in his properly pleated dry pants. We ended up going to that expensive place he suggested after all, but he bought.

There *are* much better ways of performing whitewater search and rescue operations than grabbing a rope and jumping into the froth. *Whitewater*, in this chapter, is any stream, river, creek, waterfall, or other rapidly flowing body of water which creates turbulence as it flows over, around, and through natural or man-made obstacles. Whitewater rescue comprises the safe recovery of someone or something from the water, *not* in the manner of the previous story. Because of these obstacles, heavy flow, and unusual patterns of force, special problems are encountered by anyone involved in search and rescue in this environment.

Whitewater SAR methods contrast with standard technique for slow moving bodies of water like flatwater rivers, lakes, reservoirs, and the oceans. SAR activities in these environments are just as difficult, but often involve teams of fully outfitted SCUBA divers, lifeguards, and power craft, utilizing surf rescue boats, buoys, and other paraphernalia. While whitewater activities occasionally demand SCUBA divers, more frequently wet-suited searchers equipped with masks and snorkels suffice, supported by some type of boat or raft, ropes, and shore personnel. If ropes are used incorrectly, as in the incident above, a rescuer can drown almost instantly. There is safer technique for whitewater SAR that keeps the personal boots and duds budget down, too.

River Features

Anyone involved in whitewater SAR should have a basic knowledge of whitewater features. The term "river" for our purposes is broadly defined as any rapidly flowing body of water moving through a channel characterized by numerous rapids or waterfalls and obstacles. A river does not have to be "wild" in the wilderness sense of the word to necessitate whitewater techniques (e.g., a series of man-made dams and weirs), nor does an officially designated wild river have to be a fast flowing, dangerous one.

Rapids are any area of rough, turbulent water flow. The sizes and types of rapids are infinite in number. They are formed by the interrelationship of river gradient (slope); the number, size, and type of obstacles; the narrowness of the channel; and the rate of water flow and volume.

The pattern of water velocity in a whitewater course varies with the location along the route, as well as with river depth. In general, water in a channel flows faster in the center and on the surface than along the river's shores and bottom, due to friction with the relatively corrugated riverbed. The speed and depth of a river is also affected by the channel's undulations for the same reason. Water does, though, flow faster on the outside of a turn, resulting in greater erosion, a locally deeper channel, and the likelihood of snags and undercut banks. The inside of a bend has slower moving, shallower water in comparison to that in the middle or outside of the channel.

A swift current in shallows may produce small waves called *riffles*, often symmetrical in appearance. As a river's gradient, obstacles, narrowness, volume, and rate of flow increase, the resultant features become spectacular as well as potentially dangerous.

At the beginning of most rapids, a number of V-shaped, smooth waves appear, called *tongues* (Fig. 22.1). Wave wakes formed by water flowing over obstacles (like underwater rocks) meet to form a V that is relatively free of obstructions. The largest of these tongues generally identifies for the paddler the safest point of entry into a set of rapids.

As water surges into a rapid, large waves which seem to be fixed in place are frequently formed. These stationary *standing waves* or *haystacks* are generated by water continuously coursing over fixed obstructions, unlike the progressive motion of ocean waves. They normally are arrayed in rows perpendicular to the current, and usually mark the river's deepest and fastest pitches. The largest of these (up to three meters in the U.S.) are called haystacks.

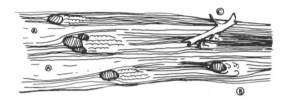

Fig. 22.1 River features: A) tongues, B) eddy, and C) strainer.

Probably the most potentially dangerous features that form in whitewater are *reversals*, also known as *holes* or *hydraulics* (Fig. 22.2). When water flows over an object beneath the surface, it curls upward and back upon itself. The largest holes, usually behind large, steep rocks, can hold a swimmer or boat in suspension. Holes are readily identified by floating debris circling in one spot instead of moving downstream in an area of strong currents and rapids. The most serious occur wherever water falls the quickest over a barrier — at dams and waterfalls. Holes can easily trap a body, and very often are too dangerous to search.

Fig. 22.2 Reversals

At any place along a river's course, a *strainer* may develop. Anything that combs the water passing through it and can block the passage of an object in the current, such as a swimmer or boat, is a strainer: trees, bridge abutments or pillars, pipes or cables. In the early seventies, several rafters were killed in a much publicized accident while floating the Snake River in Wyoming with professional guides when their raft was pinned against a bridge piling.

Eddies are pockets of calm water, often moving in a circle or even upstream, located on the downstream side of obstructions like rocks. For kayakers and rafters, they provide ideal resting spots in the middle of rapids, and allow time to recover from one set of problems and to chart the route through the next. A vacuum is created by fast moving water flowing around an obstacle, much like the dead spot behind a large trailer truck that encourages slipstreaming by small cars. This low pressure area is a haven of calm water in the midst of the flow.

Waterfalls of any size pose obvious hazards by greatly increasing the probability of upset craft, traumatic injuries, and entrapment in large hydraulics.

Survival in Whitewater

Anyone suddenly thrown into a turbulent, cold, and uncontrollable environment faces imminent injury. The best single source of protection and comfort for the upset paddler is a good *personal flotation device* (PFD) which comes up high around the chest and neck to help keep the head out of the water. One study[1] showed that almost 90% of those drowned in whitewater had not been wearing PFDs.

If suddenly dumped into rocky rapids, one should float face upward and look downstream, keep feet extended out in front to ward off rocks, and use a backstroke to change position when necessary. The PFD will protect the torso. The idea is to move as soon as possible toward shore at a spot where one can safely land. If this is impossible, look for a rock that can be mounted, and get completely out of the water. Be certain to stay upstream of a boat caught on a rock or strainer, to avoid being trapped between the boat and object. The last thing one should do is desperately hang onto a branch or rock while struggling against the current. The cold and current quickly sap strength.

This all sounds good in theory. But like being caught in an avalanche, surviving whitewater involves striving for a lot of objectives all at once, with the proper presence of mind. These rules and tricks should be recited to oneself every time a hazardous situation is encountered. Slowly go over them at the beginning of a SAR water event or a recreational river trip. Keep in mind that the *basic rule* is you and your partners FIRST; boats, rafts, canoes, second; and paddles and cameras

---

[1] Waddell, Ted and Judy, eds. "Summary of Significant Visitor Protection Statistics," unpublished National Park Service document, 1976.

last. When dumped, 1) get feet downstream to fend off rocks if thrown into the water; 2) head for shore quickly, via what seems like the safest route toward the shore that is, ideally, both closest and the easiest from which to reunite paddlers and boats; 3) jettison or secure anything that might catch on a strainer or rock, like a camera, long straps on a PFD, a loose spray skirt; 4) hang onto the boat if possible, and stay upstream from it; 5) get out of cold water as quickly as possible — this is more important than trying to make it all the way to shore; 6) keep an eye on equipment (especially paddles) that might have broken free; 7) watch your companions in the water or in other craft, to instantly ascertain that they are conscious and swimming, to help yourself and to retrieve others, and to have some idea where someone might be caught in a hole if he is not visible; 8) look downstream, if possible, to plan a route to a point of safety — eddy, rock, shore — if it is difficult to reach shore right away, to avoid any major obstacles ahead like a large drop or a walled canyon.

Well-dressed whitewater searcher, including fishnet suit. *Photo Tim Setnicka*

Each person should be constantly concerned about the welfare and location of his partners at all times. There are two general categories of ways that people die in cold whitewater: immersion hypothermia, and entrapment in some manner and drowning. Certainly direct trauma, say a head concussion causing unconsciousness and death by drowning, does produce fatalities, but not as frequently as one might expect. Other factors leading to death by drowning include poor physical condition, exhaustion, inaccessibility and improper use of PFDs, inability to swim, and water conditions.

A person suddenly immersed in cold water, especially that colder than 10°C (50°F), even if unhurt, immediately begins to suffer life threatening problems. These are summarized by the term *immersion hypothermia*. Gasping, especially while swimming in rapids, begins right away. The likelihood of swallowing water increases greatly, aggravated by panic. The rapid deterioration of a swimmer's mobility in cold water was documented[2] by A.F. Davidson, and is summarized in the accompanying chart.

Table 20

Effect of Water Temperature on Body

Water Temperature	Useful Work	Unconscious
0.3°C (32.5°F)	less than 5 minutes	less than 15 minutes
4.5°C (40°F)	7.5 minutes	30 minutes
10°C (50°F)	15 minutes	60 minutes
15°C (60°F)	30 minutes	2 hours
20°C (70°F)	45 minutes	3 hours

Immediate response is required to help anyone caught in a cold water environment.

Entrapment is the pinning of someone in or under the water. Even if the victim can keep his head elevated, he can quickly come under the influence of immersion hypothermia and eventually drown. If trapped underwater, the results are obvious. Unlike large rocks, which deflect the current and swimmers, strainers allow water to pass directly through them. The force of the current will press a person against them. So

[2]Davidson, A.F., "Survival — The Will to Live," *American Whitewater* 12, no. 1, Summer 1966, adapted.

beware of grasping a tree branch right at the surface in swift water and trying to climb onto it. If your boat collides with an obstacle, lean *downstream* toward it to avoid swamping, and then try to maneuver around the obstruction.

The other type of entrapment entails the pinning of a boater between a raft or canoe and a rock or bridge abutment. Not infrequently, extremities wedged between rocks lead to drowning. By keeping legs high, either in front or in back, depending on whether one is protecting himself while going through rapids or swimming for shore in the standard fashion, a swimmer can usually avoid this problem. Caution is mandatory, however, whenever a rescuer or paddler wades into whitewater to render assistance.

First and second aid for the immersion hypothermia victim is the same as for any other type of hypothermic patient. The body's heat is wicked off by a cold environment, in this case water, until unconsciousness commences and the heart begins to fibrillate (beat in a rapid, erratic way), leading to death. Stop heat loss by getting the victim ashore, warming him internally with fluids, and insulating and warming him externally (a sleeping bag with warm rocks or a friend helps the process). Further discussion of hypothermia is the province of the chapter on Field Medical Considerations.

Mouth-to-mouth resuscitation in the water. *Photo Craig Patterson*

Immersion hypothermia from cold water often combines with *near drowning*. Plain old drowning is a term reserved to label expiration; near drowning describes a person who has been underwater, unconscious, and is not breathing. Near drowning and its effects have been studied extensively by Dr. Martin J. Nemiroff of the University of Michigan Hospital. Dr. Nemiroff's studies have proven that there is an exception to the general rule that after four minutes of not breathing (hence a lack of oxygen to the brain), irreversible, permanent brain damage takes place. In fact, Nemiroff's studies have documented the survival of a number of persons who were submerged in cold water (below 20°C (70°F)) from four to thirty-eight minutes. All recovered without any brain damage.

The reason is the mammalian driving reflex that occurs when a mammal submerges into cold water. It reduces the oxygen needs of the tissues, decreases blood supply to the skin, muscles, and organs, and reserves the remaining oxygen carried in the blood for the brain. This same mechanism allows a moose to immerse its head in a frigid pond all day while feeding. What all this means is do *not* give up mouth-to-mouth and CPR in four minutes; Keep Going! How long? Remember that after thirty-eight minutes a victim suddenly responded.

One spring, two rafters overturned in knee-deep water in the Sierras and panicked. Each stood up and held onto a small tree in the river, screaming for help. The "rescue" involved a wet-suited swimmer walking out to them with a rope belay fixed to his quick release harness, and more or less escorting them back to shore. One man was shivering uncontrollably and gasping for breath. At the hospital it was learned that his temperature had been lowered by 1.5°C (3°F) just by standing in the 7°C (45°F) water for about ten minutes. So be prepared to act immediately in whitewater SAR situations, as the hypothermia, pinning, and near drowning combination may rapidly immobilize and kill the folks in trouble.

The Whitewater Preplan

For areas where whitewater search and rescue efforts are likely, the organizations who respond should prepare a detailed preplan specifically addressing river SAR. Some of the preplan recommendations below have been adopted from "White Water River Rescue Techniques," by Ted and Judy Waddell (available from NASAR).

1. All groups involved should have up-to-date standardized river maps. Duplicate names must be eliminated and alternate descriptions agreed upon to avoid confusion.

2. Aerial photographs of a river and its shorelines provide invaluable references for planning purposes. Photographs and notations at low, medium, high, and flood levels will help identify differences in river hazards and accessibility.

3. The river's pattern of impoundment, if any, must be known. If a river is dam-controlled, ascertain the water release schedules, and the procedures for different seasons and days of the week. Find out who has the authority to order dam shut-down or release, and where he can be reached by telephone during odd hours.

4. A map illustrating access to various locations during different seasons and water levels ought to be drawn. This is obviously a lengthy task, but one definitely worth undertaking.

5. Helicopter overflights allow some feeling for the river as a whole, especially during searches. Photographs can be taken during one event that will aid in future emergencies.

6. Potential or known river hazards should be indicated on the above access and water level maps.

7. Flood patterns of the river and its tributaries should be documented and studied.

8. The sequence of ice development, if any, and the pattern of winter use by different groups (skaters, ice boaters, trappers) should be watched.

9. Local river rescue resources — local experts who know the river, helicopters, boats and rafts, trained personnel who know about boat recovery, drivers in summer and winter, Emergency Medical Technicians, ambulance service, so on — need to be monitored.

10. The SAR history of an area, both from the files and while under the influence of a few beers with locals, can be researched. Find out about past rescue technique and evaluate its effectiveness in comparison to a unit's proposed rescue and search plans.

11. Equipment should be identified and modified to suit your needs — make sure gear has positive buoyancy, is watertight, and is compatible with other equipment. Locate and prearrange use of equipment (like helicopters) not stored in your rescue cache. Some recommended items for whitewater operations are listed.

Rescue and Evacuation

Gear for rope-assisted rescues and evacuations

ropes — climbing, and floating types (polypropylene and non-stretch ropes are best)
ascending devices
braking and friction devices
carabiners, pulleys
anchoring devices (chocks, nuts, bolts)
climbing seats and harnesses
webbing and slings for anchoring
helmets for staff and victim
Stokes litter
Thompson litter with positive buoyancy
helicopter hoisting equipment, i.e., fishnet, prerigs
line gun and supplies
extra dry clothing for wet rescuers or victims

Water related gear

dry bag
boat and paddles
extra paddles
craft security and transportation devices (locks!!, vehicle racks)
wetsuits
personal flotation devices for rescue staff and all victims
dry, buoyant storage for all sensitive gear, equipment and personal possessions
whitewater raft
kayaks
dry wool or synthetic pile sweater and pants or underwear

Miscellaneous Items

binoculars
lighting systems
public address/loudhailer system
boat-to-shore, boat-to-boat communications systems
standardized maps
winch
vehicle modified for transport and storage of all equipment

Whitewater Search

At the *first notification* of an incident, a firehouse response similar to reaction to an avalanche incident is required. The theory and strategy of the effort is similar to that outlined in Part II: Search Management. Hasty search teams, usually pairs of rescuers, immediately should be placed along the river on both sides, and at the same time if at all possible (Fig. 22.3).

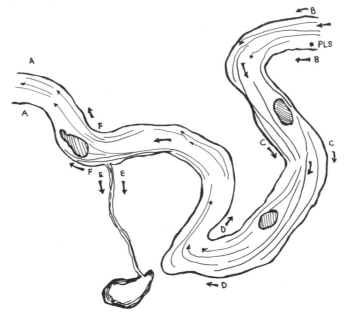

Fig. 22.3 River search methodology. Adapted from Jon Wartes.

Deployment in this fashion allows rescuers to reconnoiter areas inaccessible to a team on the side closest to the obstacle. Two teams immediately work their way downstream from the point last seen, but other teams need to be leapfrogged ahead to begin from points farther downstream. Searchers along the shore can detect an injured person who was able to get out of the water but who may be hidden from view from the air.

If not too much time has elapsed, confinement lookouts should be dispatched to a stretch of slower water downstream that is relatively open and easy to observe, in case the victim extricates himself and leaves the search area. Do not underestimate the distance the river could have carried the victim in the elapsed time since immersion. If no obvious slack water is evident, then quickly determine where roads intersect the river, or where a bridge offers clear observation, and get a confinement pair with minimal rescue gear to that location. Confinement boundaries can be calculated by multiplying the time that has elapsed since the accident times the river's velocity.

Searching a hole with a pike from a belayed Tyrolean. *Photo Tim Setnicka*

As a general rule, searchers should stay out of the water unless properly equipped (PFD, belay, wetsuit). If they must enter the water, they should do so only up to their knees, in places where they can see the bottom. In water above the knees, one can become buoyant and susceptible to the force of a strong current. Remember that the hasty search is a quick survey for someone in immediate danger, hanging on a rock or branch. Searchers ought to be clue-oriented and watch for equipment and clothing along the shore and in eddies or strainers. By searching the banks as well as the shore, the odds of detecting clues or the victim are greatly increased. The Type II and Type III grid searches adapted to whitewater are for recovery of bodies, and involve probers, wet-suited swimmers, and divers.

The use of a helicopter, preferably one capable of prolonged hovering, is highly advantageous for a fast and complete hasty search. The helicopter is an aerial observation platform which can fly low and slowly. If the light is right, usually around noon, when shadows are minimized and sunlight penetrates instead of reflects, an airborne observer can see down into pools and on top of surface features much more readily than shore teams, which have their own problems climbing along bouldered and steep-banked channels with poor visibility. Depending on the river, the helicopter may be able to one-skid or hoist the victim out of danger, completing the rescue more efficiently and much faster than a conventional team with wet suits and ropes. The safety of the rescue party needs to be continually considered, alongside the more obvious requirement of speed.

A basic understanding of the features and hazards of whitewater is crucial for personnel involved in water events. This enables them to recognize areas of high probability of victim location, and attunes them to the dangers to the rescue team. One of the best ways to gain this knowledge is simply to go out on river trips a couple of times a year, preferably right at the beginning of the whitewater season when accidents start to become frequent. SAR teams can facilitate informal "training" trips by arranging to borrow rafts and kayaks, and otherwise making it easy for members to get out on the water. Unit members with water safety, SCUBA, canoeing, and other specialized experience can be identified, included in the whitewater preplan, and trained together.

Frequently a hasty search crew launches canoes, kayaks, or whitewater rafts for use with ground and air searchers. Especially in areas where the river travels a gorge or an extremely overgrown area and is hard to check by air, this is common. Three boats are the minimum necessary for a run of a section of any difficulty. Rescue and first aid equipment, radios, and related gear should be split up among the boats; better yet is doubling up on some equipment, so the main radio will have a backup when it gets soaked accidentally.

Some basic rules should be followed: 1)the lead boat is never passed, 2)the sweep (the last boat) never passes any boat, and 3)each boat keeps the one behind it in sight, waiting if necessary. Naturally the operators of these boats should be experienced, as a rescue is not a training trip. They must be free to concentrate on checking features for clues, rather than worrying about swamping.

All boaters need to keep a few rules in mind as they search the river. On difficult stretches, the lead boat might consider having some support from the bank in case of swamping or pinning. In tight channels, each boat should wait for the one ahead of it to clear before starting down, lest a collision or multiple capsizing transpire. Once through a difficult stretch, each boat usually waits and watches in case the next boat has a problem. Lastly, the buddy system prevails. Each boat constantly checks its partners, like a belayer monitoring a leader or second, immediately prepared to assist in any way. No set rules cover all situations, but the idea of continuous responsibility of the members of a SAR group for one another cannot be overemphasized.

SCUBA diver recovering body. *Photo Tim Setnicka*

If a hasty search and repeated sweeps of the helicopter and boat crews reveal nothing, then a painstaking, wet-suited Type II and III search may be warranted. Swimmers protected by belays and armed with probe poles with hooks on the end are most effective. Safety of the searchers is the first consideration, as it is assumed at this point that the victim is dead. Anyone entering the water must wear a PFD and wet suit. Standard 9mm (⅜") full-length wet suits favored by kayakers work fine. The heavier 12mm (½") suits used by divers are restrictive, and necessary only in very cold waters. Using long probe poles, such as the pikes used in firefighting, helps extend the search area. Diving masks and snorkels are handy for work under rocks and in pools. Weight belts are generally not worn, unless full SCUBA gear is required to comb significant areas of calm but deep water.

Searching deep pools or a very slow moving river is performed with the same simple technique and patterns that a SCUBA team uses to search a lake. Keep it simple. Poor visibility and the irregular bottom contour offer enough challenge without the worry of negotiating difficult or complicated patterns.

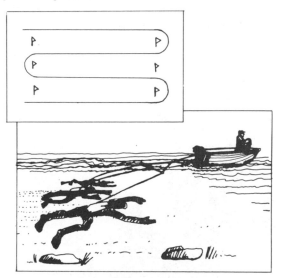

Fig. 22.4 Towed diver search pattern.

As in other types of search, except avalanche search, begin at the point last seen (PLS). Each sweep should overlap slightly. The specific search pattern is based on visibility, bottom contours, a number of divers, and size of victim or object — in other words, experience. If the search area is large, start with the deeper water first to eliminate decompression problems, if any. Maintain what little visibility you have by starting downstream and working upstream against the current, so muck and sediment will be carried away from the area being investigated. Do not tread water or strike the bottom in shallows if at all possible, as this stirs the sediment.

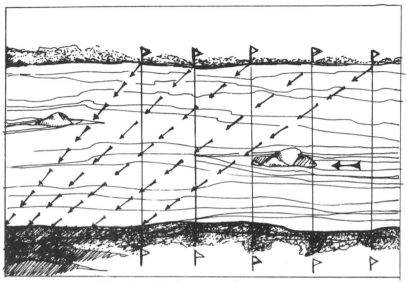

Fig. 22.5 Single arc search pattern.

Underwater grid and sweep searches use string lines like a land
search, though with some interesting variations. A search pattern weight
of some sort helps keep things neat and orderly during the search. One
type of weight with a swivel on it is placed in the center of a grid. The
divers hold a reel of line, usually fifteen meters long, and simply let it
out from the reel to increase the radius after they swim each circle.
Another method incorporates a line tender on a boat or rock on the surface, who feeds cord when the divers tug on the line, gradually increasing the diameter of the circle. In both of these methods the line
must remain taut. This circular search pattern is fundamental, and can
be used both on open water or from shore. The tender briefs the divers
on the pattern and procedures, establishes some means of communication between boat and divers, and coordinates shore support and safety
divers. Other search patterns include a straight line pattern involving actual lines or compass bearings, and the standard checkerboard grid
pattern for recovering small valuable objects or bodies in an area without
current. For large areas with good visibility, divers can be towed (Fig.
22.4) behind a boat driven at less than eight kilometers per hour. The
two line must be at least three times the water's depth in order to maintain the optimal search angle. The divers simply scan the area; the width

and length of the sweeps are determined by the boat driver, who studies the divers' bubbles to readjust the pattern. Marker buoys should be mused to mark progress. If there is significant current, the single arc pattern is best. Normally, a combination of patterns is necessary (Fig. 22.6).

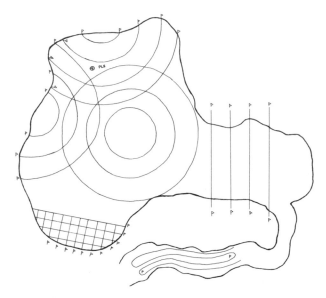

Fig. 22.6 Combination of different patterns to fully search a water body.

Underwater search technique utilizing divers is generally a Type III tactic, although towing divers behind the boat, depending upon conditions, can serve as a Type II method if divers and time are limited.

Often there are areas along and in a river that can only be searched at great risk to those involved. These sections should be avoided even at the cost of an incomplete search. Recovery is never worth the risk of additional lives. Most unregulated rivers will decrease in flow and volume at some later point, after a rainy season or winter run-off, when they can be more thoroughly studied. Regulated rivers can often be checked temporarily in an effort to assist the search effort and reduce danger.

Ropes in River Rescue

The use of ropes for throwing has, of course, been a standard technique for water rescue ever since doughnut-shaped life preservers were hung on bridges and ships. This simple technique should not be overlooked, especially during emergency circumstances. Anytime someone is tossed a rope, two things which sound ridiculously obvious must be kept in mind. One is to secure the end of the rope in some way, either by tying a loop and holding it loosely in the non-throwing arm, and the other is to make sure that once someone has caught the toss that you can provide a secure belay and not have to let go of the rope under the force of the current.

Belayed body recovery from deep pool. *Photo Tim Setnicka*

Everyone has his or her own style of throwing a rope. A basic technique is to secure one end, flake it out on the ground (rather than working from a coil), and hold three to six coils in one hand and three to six in the other. Throw with an underhanded motion with both hands, one following slightly behind the major throwing arm. Some SAR folk prefer a monkey's fist at the thrown end of the rope, while others feel that any knot there is likely to snag.

The use of ropes in whitewater SAR when attached to or held in some manner by a rescuer in the water is both dangerous and controversial. It requires that the swimmer has whitewater experience and is strong in heavy water. The rope is attached to the searcher by a quick-release mechanism; a chest harness is generally preferred to a waist harness, as it keeps the head above water. Do not tie in with a bowline around the waist. With a release harness, if a swimmer tangles his rope around an object or himself, or is dangling on the end of it like a brook trout, he can release himself and not be forced under by the force of the water. A variation is to tie in to a chest harness at the *back* between the shoulders, and have the swimmer face downstream on his back; the head stays out of the water, and swimming is easier. If released in a series of rapids, the swimmer still must be able to negotiate it feet-first or by swimming faster than the current to steer effectively. The added flotation provided by the PFD and wet suit protects against hypothermia and injury from collisions with miscellaneous impediments. It is possible to swim with a coil loosely hung over a shoulder or held in one hand, but this method tends to restrict the swimmer and the swimming motion, and often tangles the line. What's more, the rope might be dropped or pulled off accidentally at the wrong time. Still, in an emergency this may be all you have. Just don't tie in with a bowline on a coil . . . !

Whitewater Rescue

Hopefully the hasty search has located the missing person safe and unhurt on a rock poking out of the water. Still, he or she must be rescued right away, especially if partially in the water, as immersion hypothermia will already be at work. A bullhorn or portable P.A. system helps reassure him while the rescuers rig their systems. Depending upon the circumstances, there are a number of ways to get out to them and bring him. These setups work well as regular river crossing tricks, too, for general backcountry travel or for positioning rescue personnel during a SAR event.

Exactly what method you use to rescue someone depends on a number of factors. Speed is the critical element, balanced by safety. The rescue mentioned in the opening of this chapter illustrates a poor, or at the very most, marginal performance. If someone is in the water, the strong swimmer method is one of the fastest to set up if conditions are favorable along that particular stretch of the river. If there is more time, and he or she is on a rock and not in immediate danger, or if the current is particularly strong, a Tyrolean is preferable, although it requires swift access to both sides of the river. If lots of time and a boat or raft of some sort is available, then the belayed boat method is best. Hence, the choice of method depends on 1) condition of victim (immersion hypothermia, traumatic injury, panicky); 2) personnel (strong swimmer and wet suit available? possible to get people to the other side or to work from one side?), 3) equipment available (no boat nearby or too wide for Tyrolean ropes), and 4) time (water level rising, darkness approaching, bad weather).

Strong swimmer method — belayed swimmer (not tied into rope) begins river crossing. *Photo Kenneth Andrasko*

Crossing a stream or a river during a search or rescue may be immediately necessary, so it should be attempted first by the simplest possible means. This includes using dry logs or boulders to hop across. If this is not possible and wading is necessary, choose the widest possible point, generally indicative of the shallowest and slowest moving water. This often runs counter to inclinations to cross where it seems narrowest and quickest. During wading in most mountain streams, some type of footwear should be worn to protect the feet and aid in traction. Minimize the load carried if at all possible, and release the waist band, if any, from around your waist in case of a spill. Ever try swimming with a pack on?

An ice axe, pike pole, or strong green branch adds a third leg if one leans upstream onto it and forms a tripod. Move one point at a time, theoretically maintaining balance. One technique involves facing upstream with legs spread, torso broadside to the current. Another has the wader face across the stream, with the pole or ice axe downstream. This places the smaller surface of one's side towards the current, but balance is more difficult. In both methods, once the water gets up to around the hips, watch out, because swimming is the next step.

Group crossings are always mentioned in accounts like this, but unless someone is extremely scared or unsure of himself, most people seem to prefer the solo crossing technique. It's a bit like hiking together in a group — easy to describe, but difficult to do. The facts, however, indicate that crossing is easier with arms linked and hands hanging onto a sapling or one's own wrists, in a line parallel to the current and facing the opposite shore. The person at the head of the line, who should be the largest, breaks the current for the rest. The people downstream help stabilize the upstream point man. If conditions are really nasty, the fellow upstream can assume a three-point stance while the person behind him holds onto his belt. This sounds a little like turn-of-the-century football, but it works.

Strong swimmer has reached subject and is preparing for his belayed swim to shore. *Photo Tim Setnicka*

If a hand line can be rigged, so much the better. Anyone crossing should not be tied into the line, but instead only use it for support in case his footing is lost. The best material for a hand line is non-stretch rope, if available.

Belaying one another across is a risky business. One spring two climbers finished climbing the Leaning Tower in Yosemite, and tried to cross Bridalveil Creek about two kilometers above the edge of Bridalveil Falls. The creek was roaring, so one climber tied in in standard fashion around the waist, while his partner attempted to belay him. The current instantly swept him downstream to the end of the belay rope, which was anchored and securely tied off. He was held under the water, and drowned.

A final method to cross a raging river is to call a helicopter. It sounds absurd, but if there is one available, use it.

The first actual rescue technique is the *strong swimmer method*, an in-water maneuver that depends upon a skilled water rat who is comfortable in heavy current. The first time people hear this method explained, they raise their eyebrows and say, "But you will drown yourself and probably the victim too." Keep that in mind as we examine this method more closely. The method makes a number of assumptions.

1. The victim is not injured, is mobile, seems to have a cool head, and is not likely to panic.

2. Rope ends are tied in a hand loop and hand-held, or are fastened with a quick release mechanism.

3. A safe run-out downstream exists, so if the rescuers must cut loose, they can make their way to shore.

4. All rescuers wear wet suits and flotation devices which cannot be pulled off.

5. The victim is given a flotation device before he enters the water.

Fig. 22.7 Strong swimmer rescue method. Swimmer is belayed out to victim, who is then belayed back to shore by shore personnel and swimmer.

The strong swimmer technique (Fig. 22.7) proceeds as follows. The rescuer swims out above the victim with two belay ropes and one or two tender ropes. He must do this from far upstream, to give himself time to line up properly. He either carries the rope in a loose coil or on a quick-release harness. It can take two or three tries to reach the victim, if the river is high and swift. He can use eddies to rest, fighting up behind a tree or grabbing a big rock, then proceeding the rest of the way. Once he reaches the victim, he immediately secures the flotation device to her. The rescuer explains the procedure, then securely attaches one of the two upstream belay ropes to the victim, along with a tender line (now a belay rope). The victim then enters the water and swims for shore on signal. The upstream belay line is held taut and the haul line is pulled in very quickly while being belayed simultaneously. The flotation device insures buoyancy. Prior to the signal, all lines have been pulled tight to see if they might snag under water. Alternatively, the victim and rescuer can come across together, which helps reassure the victim.

The second technique is an adjustable *Tyrolean* (Fig. 22.8) system. It can be utilized for an injured or distraught victim, or when there is not a safe run-out downstream (so that rescuers cannot enter the water purposely, as in the previous method).

Fig. 22.8 Tyrolean rescue method.

There must be a rescuer on the far side of the river to anchor the Tyrolean ropes. He gets there by hiking or by crossing at a safe spot using this or another method. A line gun or bow and arrow can be used to shoot a light line across a river in order to enable the main ropes to be drawn afterward. We started out using a bow and arrow in this Robin Hood method, but we didn't own the bow and arrows. So each time a rescue developed, we had to run over to the owner's garage and dig through it until we found the gear. One time we had to break in when he wasn't home, and the SAR account had to pay for the repairs. Another time we forgot the arrows and ended up doing one of those classic TV dialogues: "I thought *you* were supposed to bring the arrows . . . !" "*Me?*, I thought YOU were supposed to get them . . ." and so on. Not too professional. When we managed to bring the arrows, someone would invariably stand on the line and the arrow would be fired on a solo flight across the river. The final straw was when someone who was not too well versed in archery let go with a tremendous shot and almost skewered a bystander! Enough was enough.

Tyrolean crossing. *Photo George Durkee*

A line gun was purchased, and the bow and arrows were honorably retired back to their garage forever. This particular line gun is manufactured by the Hall Ski Lift Company, which uses them as part of their rescue system designed to get skiers off chairlifts in the event of sudden breakdowns. The Hall gun uses a blank .22 caliber cartridge to fire two types of projectiles. One is a blunt styrofoam plug about nine centimeters in diameter and twenty centimeters long. The other is an all-metal projectile that looks like a large antipersonnel military round about three centimeters in diameter and is twelve centimeters long. The Hall line gun uses two types of braided nylon line, the heavier about the same diameter, appearance, and strength of standard parachute cord. It is wound in a spool that uncoils when pulled from the inside. The spool is inserted into a hollow plastic holder below the barrel that accepts the projectile. The end of the line is tied onto the projectile. With the larger, styrofoam projectile we have had no problem spanning seventy or a hundred meters using the lighter line. It usually takes two attempts, as there is a tendency to aim high in an effort to correct for the arc, but the gun is so powerful that you only have to hold it a meter or so above the target at seventy meters for the projectile to score a direct hit.

Hall line gun. *Photo Kenneth Andrasko*

Avoiding trees and power lines is occasionally a problem, but again the accuracy of the gun is such that they can usually be circumvented on the second try. A potential hitch is running out of projectiles or spools of line, but prior planning should take care of this worry.

Catch the projectile and thin line the instant it hits. The thin line will be instantly swept downstream and can easily snag. If loosely held up over someone's head, it should clear the water. We have had no difficulty with tying one 11mm rope directly to this thin line and pulling it across. During this process, keep tension on it so the larger line does not hit the water, get swept downstream, and snag. Once the end of the 11mm is completely across, second and third ropes can be pulled across.

Establishing a Tyrolean. *Photo Kenneth Andrasko*

A standard Tyrolean (Chapter 20) is then set up, usually with one rope as the safety belay, and the second on a Z-system for lowering or raising. Plan to put as much sag as possible in the raising and lowering rope to minimize the chances of failure in the rope or anchors. This means anchoring this rope sufficiently high above the water level, say by climbing a tree trunk. The rescuer is belayed across to the victim by being tied securely into suspended Tyrolean ropes. He is also tied into a third rope that belays him from shore as he moves across. Once above the victim, the rescuer can be lowered to him by adjusting tension with the Z-rig. First aid is administered if necessary. A flotation device and a harness are fastened on the victim, or a Stokes litter is rigged and pulled across to the site. The rescuer ties the middle of the haul rope to the victim so he can have one end for a belay when he returns to shore after the victim is safely across. Then the victim is pulled to shore, while the rescuer remains tied in and waits his turn.

If the river is very wide or without suitable anchors for establishing a standard Tyrolean, a horizontal Tyrolean may be set up incorporating a small boat. Boats and rafts devoid of a pronounced bow may be used if care is taken to keep the bow from diving into the current instead of planing above it.

Tyrolean river rescue. *Photo Tim Setnicka*

One way of setting up this *belayed boat method* (Fig. 22.9) uses one long rope as the main Tyrolean rope, with a Z-system on one end if its mechanical advantage is thought to be necessary to bring the raft upstream. The stronger the current and the larger the boat, the more advantage will be required. The raft is attached, with the bow pointing upstream, to a pulley placed on the main rope stretched upstream from the target. A separate rope is fixed to the side of the pulley closest to each bank. The ropes act as safeties, and assist in positioning the boat in the river for correct alignment with the downstream target. The main rope is gradually slackened, allowing the boat to float downstream, while the belay lines are continually adjusted to keep it directly above the target.

The rescuer in the boat should be wearing a wet suit and PFD, as well as carrying a PFD for the victim. It is critical that the rescuer sit in the

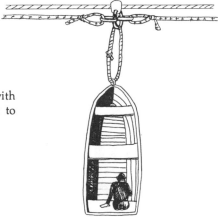

Fig. 22.9 Belayed boat rescue, with Tyrolean adjusted to allow boat to move up and downstream.

boat toward the stern, or else, especially in the case of a blunt-bowed craft, the force of the current will cause it to nosedive and swamp. Once the boat has its passenger aboard, the belay and main ropes can be pulled in and the craft maneuvered back to shore.

Another rigging, the *three rope Tyrolean*, was demonstrated by Tuolumne County Search and Rescue in Northern California (Fig. 22.10). The first, main rope is simply a fixed line placed across the river at a convenient working spot. To this fixed line is attached one pulley. One or two carabiners are fastened to the pulley, tied to a length of rope that will roughly equal the width of the river. Also attached to the carabiners is a second pulley. A long rope is run through this second pulley, with one end tied to the boat or raft. The other end is secured to an anchor on shore. The second rope helps position the raft by its ability to pull the raft toward the opposite bank. The long third rope pulls the pulley and the raft back toward shore if necessary, and by gently allowing slack lets the raft be carried downstream toward the target.

Both of these systems work well. Radio communication between the parties on both banks is almost a necessity, to coordinate and speed the process.

Frequently the victims are rescued or are able to get out of trouble on their own, but their boat or raft remains jammed on some rock or other obstacle in the river where the force of the current holds it in place. The term "river rescue" for paddlers refers to recovery of swamped craft and crew. In slow current the damage to the boat can be light, but stronger current, eight or more kilometers per hour, can break or bend a canoe or kayak around the obstacle and severely warp and damage it. A swamped canoe in an eight kilometer current is withstanding about 950 kilograms of force (kiloponds).

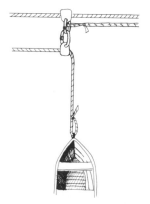

Fig. 22.10 Closeup of three-rope Tyrolean method, with rope used to position boat up and downstream.

Slalom racer trapped in boat during race in Maryland. Another competitor has jumped in and is holding his head above water, as the throw ropes proved of little use. *Photo American Whitewater*

Retrieving a boat, even if severely damaged, is usually recommended not only for ecological reasons but also to remove an attractive nuisance that encourages others to attempt salvage. Traditional tactics for rescue of boats and crew by other paddlers — the tired swimmer, helpless victim, and canoe-over-canoe rescues — are explained in many of the books listed in this chapter's bibliography.

One spring we had a minor river rescue involving two ill-equipped and inexperienced paddlers in a flimsy rubber raft designed to look like a $2,000 Avon product. They dumped on a stretch of rapids, but were rescued unhurt with a minimum of problems. The biggest headache was disposing of the raft, which managed to lodge itself against some hefty boulders in a very nasty, wide section of the river. At the time we had not discovered the belayed boat method, and the area was much too broad for a reasonable Tyrolean to be set up. Efforts to use the strong swimmer method proved too dangerous due to the extended series of rapids. Fortunately somebody thought of a new technique, the *John Wayne method*. This involved ranger Paul Henry's pulling out his service revolver, taking close aim, and shooting a hole in the raft. It immediately deflated and sunk out of sight until three months later, when it was picked up as trash along a dry portion of the river bed. While effective, this method is not recommended as a standard rescue technique. It generally fails to meet favor with the raft's owner.

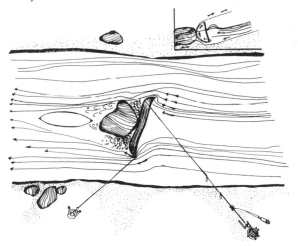

Fig. 22.11 Boat recovery with tow lines and winch. Adapted from the AMC *White Water Handbook.*

Some practical suggestions on boat recovery (Fig. 22.11) are given below.

1. Work with the current; in most cases the current will favor swinging one end rather than the other downstream.
2. Attach your line to pull on the entire hull rather than on weaker thwarts, seats, or cargo loops.
3. Raise one end of a solid boat to lighten it and cut down on the pressure applied by the current.
4. Lift a boat in shallow water with several persons, or lever it free with heavy poles.
5. Attach a hand winch or power winch from a vehicle to the high side of the boat by making one turn around the hull. This distributes the load evenly, instead of concentrating it on one point of attachment. The boat should also roll off the rock when it begins to come free, reducing the requisite force to less than that required to fight the current directly. In lieu of a winch, a mechanical advantage system using pulleys and safety prusiks may be successfully substituted, depending on the size of the boat, force of the current, and how badly the boat is wedged in place.
6. Use non-stretch rope to avoid the elongation of nylon. This is a job for manila, Dacron, polypropylene, or caving rope.
7. Tie a second line to the stern or bow along with the main winch or pulling line, as it is usually not placed in the best position for pulling the boat ashore once the craft is set free.

Searching along a *waterfall* provides unique problems and hazards. In 1977, during a period of extreme drought, a tourist climbed over a railing past two signs warning of danger and out into the middle of a flailing water course. He decided to wade to the lip of 130-meter-high Vernal Fall to look over and take a photograph. As he approached the lip of the falls, he realized it might be impossible to return and madly attempted to leap to shore. The raging current swept him off balance and over the precipice. Eyewitnesses said that he never hit the large pool at the bottom, because of the relatively low volume of water at that time. Apparently the body had hung up on some feature along the waterfall's vertical gradient.

A search commenced. Expansion bolts were placed high along the lip and off to one side by climbers in wet suits. These were used as a high directional anchor, with a rope run up to them, through a pulley, and down again. The rescuers would be traversing horizontally from the side, and would otherwise be subjected to long pendulum falls. A searcher in a wet suit then tied in through this top belay so that he could walk out through the waterfall on a ledge system. A second, horizontal belay was also used, so he could be pulled back at a moment's notice. Hardhats were worn but probably would have been of little value if a large log came over. Lookouts with radios were placed above the falls to keep things from being tossed in, and to warn if something large like a tree was on its way.

Belayed body recovery. *Photo Tim Setnicka*

The system worked well, and a large area was covered by a searcher with a pike pole and tight belay. After about thirty-five minutes, the victim's body was hooked and recovered. It had become wedged between a large flake and the main rock wall.

In another bizarre example of searching around waterfalls, a married couple committed suicide by jumping off of Upper Yosemite Falls, 440 meters high, during the winter. A large cone of ice always forms at the bottom of the fall, as the water droplets freeze on their way down. In order to search the area, SAR personnel had to wear wet suits and mountaineering boots with crampons, and carry ice axes in order to negotiate safely on the frozen cone. Standard climbing belays and orange helmets were brought into play. The sight of the black, orange-tipped figures darting around and through the fog and water and ice was highly surreal.

There will be occasions when an experienced kayaker can help in a rescue attempt. It is common practice among kayakers to help one another after a capsize by backing a kayak up to the paddler in the water so he can hang onto the rear grab loop. The swimmer continues to kick while the kayaker paddles directly upstream, moving over to the nearest shore with an upstream ferry maneuver. Kayakers have also taken equipment and lines across the river for rescuers in lieu of the line gun or bow and arrow method.

Lastly, there will be occasions when power and jet boats are available to rescue someone. It is better to make the final approach facing upstream against the current, rather than attempt to pluck someone off of an obstacle while floating rapidly downstream.

Whitewater search and rescue often poses new and different problems which, like any other type of SAR, may require the creative use of fairly abstract technique (ice axes or bows and arrows) in their solution. Keep an open mind, but just don't tie in with a bowline on a coil for a belay!

BIBLIOGRAPHY

CHAPTER TWENTY-TWO

LEWIS, TOM, *Organization Training, Search, and Recovery Procedures for the Underwater Unit.* Littleton, Colo. 1974.

LINTON, STEVEN J. AND RUPERT, EDWARD A. *Dive Rescue Handbook.* Ft. Collins, Colo.: Concept Systems, Inc., 1978.

McGINNIS, WILLIAM. *Whitewater Rafting.* New York: Quandrangle/The New York Times Book Co., 1975.

TEJADA-FLORES, LITO. *Wildwater: The Sierra Club Guide to Kayaking and Whitewater Boating.* San Francisco: Sierra Club Books, 1978.

URBAN, JOHN T. *White Water Handbook for Canoe and Kayak.* Boston: Appalachian Mountain Club, 1976.

WADDELL, TED, AND WADDELL, JUDY. *Whitewater River Rescue Techniques.* La Jolla, Ca.: NASAR paper 77-1020, 1977.

From Ethan Allen Reynold's account of Cataract Canyon in *Cosmopolitan*, November 1889.

23 | Snow and Ice SAR

SEARCH AND RESCUE EVENTS amidst the deep snow and hard ice of winter or big mountains pose their own special problems. The technique, tools, and skills of traveling and living in the rigors of winter are all summoned at once during the prolonged exposure to the elements that characterizes a winter accident or search. While the surge of interest in the backcountry sports of winter mountaineering and camping, cross-country skiing, and ice climbing has heightened the awareness of SAR teams to cold weather operations in technical terrain, the attendant growth of alpine climbing in summer has resulted in many cases in more frequent rescues of less experienced climbers.

Perhaps the single most fundamental element of snow and ice SAR activity is a broad-based foundation of personal and team skills in all facets of skiing, climbing, and winter survival. The first step in managing any SAR situation is to enlist the participation of trained, competent sportsmen in the medium in question: ice cliff, cave, or coconut grove. The substantial objective hazards of high alpine topography — rockfall, crevasses, avalanches, and weather — produce an atmosphere of danger and uncertainty for novices. Mastery of basic skills enables personnel to turn their full attention to the technical rescue details at hand rather than concentrating on the mechanics of movement and the suppression of uncertainty.

Snow and ice, even more so than rock, occur in infinite variations on a basic theme. All are phases or manifestations of the hydrologic cycle of mountain environments, but like fine pastries in a highly creative

Photo Kenneth Andrasko

Viennese bakery, all sorts of beguiling and bedevilish combinations are possible from the same few ingredients according to the whim and fancy of the pastry chef. In short, unlike rock formations, snow and ice rapidly change consistency on a minute-to-minute, day-to-day, and seasonal basis.

This capricious capacity for change was graphically demonstrated one recent winter to two climbers anxious to attempt the ascent of a frozen waterfall fairly low down in the Sierra. Winter climbing conditions are generally marginal there because of temperature fluctuation. After studying the cycle of sunlight and melting and the technical difficulties of the climb for several days, they decided the ice was safe and composed a strategy. The pair successfully negotiated the technically very demanding climb of well over a hundred meters the next day. After a brief respite in the bright sun on top, they packed up and were starting down when they heard a tremendous crash — the entire frozen waterfall let go and descended to the ground en masse!

Nothing was left but a giant cone of ice blocks in the talus. The temperature had risen two degrees higher than on the preceeding few days and it was enough to melt the ice bonding the climb to the rock in a few hours. A story like this provides the ultimate argument for always artfully evaluating ice and snow conditions and traveling at the time of day or night offering the most favorable circumstances and stability. Unfortunately this is especially awkward during a rescue, given the medical and safety prerequisites of the victim. A fickle environment of this sort merits a closer look at its origins.

The overall process of *snow formation* is well understood at this point, though many of its intricate steps remain an enigma. Snow formation is derived from the uplift of a warm air mass in the atmosphere via one of three general phenomena: uplifting due to topography, such as over mountain ranges; uplifting from counterclockwise circulation around a low pressure area; and the raising resulting from the collision of a warm air mass forced up and over heavier, colder air.

As the uplifted air rises, it cools and expands. As this occurs the air mass loses its capacity to support the water vapor produced by the cooling action. The mass is considered saturated when it can no longer hold any additional water vapor. If the conditions are right, frozen water vapor condenses around impurities in the air like dust. These ice nuclei nurture the formation of ice crystals that eventually fall as snow.

Snow on the ground, especially new snow, is constantly modified by a plethora of factors including gravity, wind, temperature, slope aspect, load, avalanches, and heat exchange with the atmosphere and the earth's surface. All these continuously metamorphose snow and alter its character and type over time. The snowpack on a mountainside continues to develop from fresh powder to granular snow or hard ice via the influence of temperature and pressure gradients. The snow crystals, called *grains* when they are in a snowpack, become rounder and connected by necks when pressure is the primary metamorphosing force. The air spaces between necks in a snowpack are called pores. If these degenerating snow crystals continue to melt together and the pores seal off and are isolated, first *firn snow* and then glacier ice (or eventually water ice in some circumstances of intense pressure and cold) form. If temperature is the primary force, the snow grains remain large and poorly bonded. Unstable layers of such snow are usually referred to as depth hoar and are highly unstable. Depth hoar plays a significant role in the generation of snow slope instabilities culminating in avalanches, and is further treated in the chapter on that subject that follows.

Ice forms in another way of interest to climbers and rescue personnel. *Water ice* is generated directly by temperature drops that freeze rain, mist, fog, or ground water, producing what is on occasion known as live ice. Water ice is the sort commonly found in steep gullies and waterfalls frozen in winter, the scene of much recent technical climbing activity. A whitish opaque color indicating significant amounts of trapped air characterizes water ice, while a blue or blue-green hue signals the presence of large ice crystals under pressure in glacier ice or very solid water ice. *Black ice* normally contains a high percentage of dirt and debris congealed into a kind of alpine cement often uncovered on north faces and in gullies. Protection placement and step chopping in black ice are truly laborious.

SAR events in winter or cold environments demand tactics and equipage at variance with that standard for summer operations. A search or technical action in winter is generally longer in duration, as travel becomes at times more taxing and usually more technical and complex than in summer conditions (although in some places snow covers scrub brush and hardens to virtual highways over the top of otherwise impenetrable tracts). Shorter winter days with a higher potential for bad weather mean less likelihood of helicopter maneuvers or rapid solutions.

SAR personnel must carry more personal gear to insure comfort and survival, and must be skilled in movement over snow. Closer attention to all details of personal and technical equipment for the victim as well as the rescuers is essential. Attenuating every cold-weather exercise is the threat of hypothermia and frostbite, all too frequent complications for active snowshoers and skiers let alone victims strapped into litters or sleds. Before the technical aspects of SAR on snow and ice are discussed, some further emphasis on the rigorous requirements of undertakings in the snowy ranges is in order, in the form of a discourse on appropriate winter gear.

Equipment and Clothing

Any commentary on equipment and clothing has to be accompanied by a preface disclaiming ultimate knowledge and judgment. As good friend, experienced winter mountaineer, and SAR master Bob Howard once quipped, "One of the truly great things in this world is the ability of any two people to get into arguments about equipment. Equipment discussions rank with debates about politics, religion, and sex for their ability to create dissent and counterarguments." Massive amounts of research and development by manufacturers are woven into the design of much new gear these days. This almost insures that any firm recommendations on equipment will be outmoded by the time they are published. Local customs are often the best guidelines for proper outfitting for a particular geographic area and activity. With these caveats in mind, some recommended personal equipment for winter SAR workers is discussed briefly below.

A winter *backpack* needs larger-volume compartments than a summer one because of the additional clothing and unique items (snow shovel, larger pots to melt snow, so on) dragged around on winter ventures. Removable sidepockets vastly increase capacity and are readily made or purchased. Carry several buckled straps or short lengths of cord to fasten snowshoes, foam pads and the like to the outside of the pack.

The tubular aluminum frame packs popular for three-season backpacking also suffice for snow camping, but skiers and snowshoers find the external frame restricts the complete poling motion of the arms and hampers balance. Soft or frameless packs have surfaced in the last decade and proven excellent for skiers as they transfer weight close to the body along the spinal cord. Unfortunately they require careful arrangement of items during loading, and many models are a bit small for winter camping. Any number of new models with adequate capacity and sophisticated suspension systems have emerged on the market however. Internal frame packs enhance rapid packing but are slightly more unwieldy for the skier. Experiment . . . before the alarm bell rings.

A winter *sleeping bag* should have a minimum of eight centimeters of dead air insulation on top of the bag's user, depending on the severity of the conditions to be encountered. Bags filled with synthetic materials like Polarguard and Fiberfill II weigh about 30 percent more than goose or duck down bags, but cost less and offer advantages in wet tents or weather. For short or weekend trips, down bags are the most practical, due to their low weight and high compressibility. For longer winter excursions, where morning frost accumulates in the filling and the probability of wet tent floors or plunges into streams is higher, a synthetic-fill outer bag over a light down bag or an all-synthetic one is preferable. The combination or substitution is heavier but more reliable than a down sack, which loses most of its insulating value when wet. The double bag concept is unsurpassed for conditions of extreme cold. Choose a bag long enough to accept boots and a plastic bottle full of hot water nestled down by the feet, and any clothes that need to be dried. A bivouac sack, a small bag or sleeping bag cover of breathable Gore-tex or cotton-polyester cloth combined with waterproof nylon, keeps off frost accumulation and blowing spindrift, adds some 10 degrees C of warmth, and is light and compact.

Carrying a solid winter *tent* is far more practical than building snow shelters or returning to base camp each night. Snow caves and igloos do provide security in foul conditions and are warm though somewhat unpleasant emergency hostels. An overwhelming array of solid, spacious (preferably dome-design) winterized tents is available. Choose one with snowflaps and a completely enveloping and tight waterproof fly, and treat all fly and floor seams with seam sealer. A zippered cookhole is ofttimes a source of leaks but in winter it expedites cooking and cleaning inside the tent; a sponge and wisk broom ease these chores. Lightweight tents are a pleasure to carry, but usually are not large enough to house a victim and rescuers for a bivouac. Make sure at least one tent will fulfill this hospital tent function.

A thicker *foam pad* than that used in summer is necessary for camping on snow. A 13mm closed cell or 40mm open cell foam pad sheathed in waterproof material helps neutralize the coldest nights. Select foam designated as suitable for real cold, as some brands crack. A full-length pad is optimal, but a half-pad with software goods under the legs and head saves weight and bulk in moderate temperatures.

Melting snow into water to quench the group's thirst demands a *stove* with high heat output, stability, ease of use, and a high-volume fuel tank. The smaller SVEA and Primus stoves popular for lightweight trips measure up poorly in these respects. The larger Primus (Optimus) 8R and 111B, Coleman Peak 1, Phoebus 625, and MSR stoves all perform well in winter. The Phoebus and Coleman are the quietest — a boon when cooking and conversing inside a tent. A small foam pad cut to the size of the stove insulates it from the cold ground and keeps it from melting through the tent floor or into the snow. Fuel requirements are roughly doubled in winter. Aluminum containers with fresh gaskets are best; some polyethylene bottles are not dissolved by white gas but may be brittle in extreme cold. A nesting set of cook pots is most practical, but consider adding one large pot in case it is necessary to thaw frozen extremities. Wide-mouthed plastic water bottles accept chunks of snow and electrolyte and sugar-drink powder. Soft plastic cups and bowls do not break in packs, burn mouths and hands, or lose heat as fast as metal ones.

The simplicity of preparing instant and freeze-dried *foods* makes them valuable for the fatigue and time constraints of rescue work, despite their lack of appeal to cultivated palates. Emphasize high-energy trail snacks and fats (to burn in cold weather), and bring at least an extra day's rations just in case.

In terms of *clothing*, it is actually easier to stay warm dragging sledges across Arctic ice floes than skiing in more temperate mountains. Arctic temperatures are so consistently low that snow almost never melts on clothing. Conversely, relatively warm winter temperatures allow clothing to absorb moisture from snow constantly, reducing its value as insulation. Do not let mild temperatures fool everyone into laxness about proper dressing and extra gear. Remember the *layer principle* — many layers of light wool or synthetics are warmer and more versatile for heat regulation than one heavy garment. Wool items are warmer when wet than any other wet garments. Some of the newer synthetics like Polarguard and polyester pile are lighter than wool and dry faster. Down is lightest in weight but useless when wet and slow to dry. At night, place damp clothing between the inner and outer sleeping bags or right inside if it will be possible to dry the bag in the morning. Another option is to store wet clothes in a plastic bag inside your bag to keep them from freezing overnight.

For *storm clothing*, rely on coated (waterproof) nylon, or Gore-tex in a cagoule or rainpants and jacket (more protective and flexible). Traditional cotton-nylon blends do not stop rain or wet snow, but are fine for wind protection and warmth when active. Hoods are crucial in wind and cold, and deflect snow from a warm balaclava (a knit wool cap with pull-down face and neck protection). Snow goggles are essential for cold, windy, or bright conditions and sling work under helicopters. The double-lens models designed for downhill skiing are superb but still benefit from an occasional pass with an anti-fog stick or cloth. Glacier glasses are fine in reasonable times.

Proper clothing and Hegg sled during Ellesmere Island traverse. *Photo Allan Bard.*

Wet cotton *underwear* saps heat from the body, and wool irritates sensitive skins and does not wick perspiration away from the skin well. Try a cotton-polyester blend and bring a spare, or the fishnet pattern for active days, or the new polypropylene underwear. Cover with layers of wool and polyester pile shirts and sweaters. Leather *glove* shells are rugged for dry, warm days, and warmer with wool gloves inside them. Heavy, dense wool or pile mittens underneath Gore-tex or cotton-polyester overmitts and thin contact gloves of nylon to insure against frostnip from direct contact with metal take care of severe cold. Extra handwear is essential.

Nylon ski *knickers* shed snow nicely, but wear wool knickers or heavy wool pants in colder weather. Add breathable synthetic powder or snowmobile pants or wind pants for the most severe days; the ones with zippered sides that can be put on over boots offer better ventilation. Breathable *gaiters* keep calves warm and snow out of boots, but allow body moisture to escape. For wet snow or rain, waterproof gaiters are superior.

Wool-synthetic blend *socks* combine warmth when wet with durability. A thin pair of light silk or wool or synthetic socks next to the skin circumvents the wool itchies. Do not wear extra socks in summer boots for cold weather, or circulation will be impaired. Instead, a combination of heavy wool socks inside of, and insulated *overboots* over, a light boot can be just as effective as a mountaineering double boot (although the latter, with a Supergaiter or overboot, constitutes the best possible amalgamation). Fit any winter boot with a felt or synthetic pile insole to decrease heat loss to the snow (the source of most loss), and insert a dry pair whenever possible (in extreme cold, change at midday). Change socks often. Climbers in Alaska and in other cold places have adapted neoprene skin diver's socks worn inside double boots covered with Supergaiters (insulated overboots without soles that cling to the welt of the boot by means of a cable yet do not hinder step-kicking or rock climbing). Full overboots can be converted to mukluks once in camp by adding an insole and stocking feet, great for stomping around. A ragg-wool sock or neoprene or nylon bootie pulled over ski touring boots prevents cold feet when the action is slow or the temperature low.

For sun protection, take two pairs of glacier glasses or goggles, sun creams with Paba, and Glacier Cream or zinc oxide and Labiosan for the lips and nose.

Tennis visors save noses on spring excursions.

A whole host of miscellaneous items almost make winter SAR exercises fun: plastic trash bags, candle lanterns and headlamps, ski waxes and climbers and other paraphernalia, 30 meters of light nylon line and avalanche cords, toiletries, and a wrist or pocket watch with alarm to gauge daylight and coordinate air support.

Team equipment, depending on conditions and terrain, normally includes pocket radio transceivers (reliable but expensive), snow shovel and snow saw, folding saw, smoke flares and flare gun, camera, and radio. An altimeter assists in navigation and serves as a barometer to monitor weather changes. Carry basic survival, repair, and first aid supplies in addition to personal gear. Inevitably a snowmobile breaks down or six rescuers have to stuff into one tent, and the event transforms into a real test of survival skills. At the risk of generating yet another incomplete list of Essential Goodies everyone should have at all times, the following items are presented as worthy of consideration.

Survival

Matches in waterproof case, lighter
Firestarter or candle
Compass, maps
Space blanket
Sunglasses and cream
One dime for emergency phone
    call (25¢ in Fairbanks . . .)
Signal mirror
Whistle
Candy bars
Bacon bars or pemmican
Tea and bouillon cubes
Can or pot for melting snow
Extra socks and mittens
Large garbage bags
Flashlight

Repair

Sewing awl
Parachute cord
Pocket knife with awl
Repair parts for stoves, tents, packs,
    if not improvisable
Extra basket for ski poles, spare
    ski tip
Extra bale or cable for binding or
    snowshoe binding parts
Screwdriver (possibly on pocket
    knife), screws, pliers

Steel wool to tighten loose screws
in binding
Fiber tape, wire, extra nylon straps
with buckles

First Aid

Band-Aids and gauze rolls
Sterile gauze pads, 7 or 10cm size
Small first aid book
Aspirin, Tylenol
Triangular bandages
Antibiotic ointment
Adhesive tape for blisters, major
wounds, and broken equipment
Medication for diarrhea (Lomotil)
Medication for intense pain (Co-
deine, Demerol, injectable mor-
phine)
Other medications (antibiotics,
decongestants, sleeping pills,
cough suppressants) as dictated
by personal experience
Scissors, tweezers
Pencil and paper to record vital
signs and symptoms and times
Vaseline, moleskin
Safety pins
Elastic bandage
Salt tablets or soda and salt mix

Over-Snow Rescue Technique

SAR events in terrain covered with ice and snow or in winter of
course follow the same steps of mobilization and organization as other
rescues. When first notification of a situation is received, an immediate
response by a hasty team is imperative. This advance guard should be
fast and yet carry enough equipment to locate, reach, and stabilize the
victim and provide needed shelter, warmth and medicine, especially if
unfavorable weather threatens. The complications of safe and efficient
team transport and victim evacuation can be considered once the blitz

teams are deployed. In some cases there are no choices to be made. It may be mandatory to instantly move the subject if avalanche danger is extreme, an intense blizzard white-out engulfs the summit, or pulmonary edema symptoms have occurred.

For the purposes of this chapter and book, snow and ice or winter rescues can be divided into two broad categories. *Over-snow, non-technical rescues* require snowshoes, skis, sleds, and snowmobiles or other vehicles as the most efficient means of travel. If the victim's location is known, the main problems are ones of transportation. The other class is *technical rescues* involving maneuvers over steep snow and ice that necessitate mountaineering equipment — ice axe, crampons, ropes, and anchors — and the skills of the alpinist to negotiate safe passage. In circumstances of this sort, the problems are often technical in nature, and include reaching the party in trouble, arranging an evacuation over hazardous ground, and avoiding objective dangers like falling ice, cornices, and avalanches.

Movement over snow and ice has always been a challenge to ambitious journeyers. Man responded far back in the darkness of prehistory by developing a number of travel aids that have changed relatively little to this day. Primitive snowshoes have been found and carbon dated to at least 4000 B.C. by archeologists working in Asia. Cave paintings in Scandinavia dating back over 4000 years depict a human figure on skis. Mechanical over-the-snow contraptions of various and sundry designs have been around since the 19th century.

Each of these three major snow travel methods has certain advantages and drawbacks for rescue work. Skis, for instance, enable swift progress when encumbered with only relatively light loads and provide a slight rest during downhill runs. On the other hand, skiing is definitely more a function of skill and training than snowshoeing, and skis are inconvenient when pulling litters, climbing steep or broken country, or traversing through woods with them strapped to the rucksack.

Snowshoes are versatile and can be fitted to most any winter boot. The basics of their use, while a bit tricky on windslab or deep powder, can be learned on the spot without extensive practice. Snowshoes work beautifully for towing sleds and hiking through scrub brush and heavily timbered slopes. Edging is problematic on steep inclines, but newer lightweight models have cleats built into the binding under the ball of the foot to improve traction. Alternatively snowshoe crampons can be affixed to virtually any model.

Tying rope climbers. *Photo Tim Setnicka.*

For SAR activities, the significant point is *versatility*. Every field crew member should be competent on each travel aid, not only to promote efficient planning and logistics but also for safety, as one method often depends on another as a backup. Skis or snowshoes go along on snowmobile rescues and are not infrequently called into service by the operator to walk out thirty kilometers to the road when the machine sputters to a halt. Likewise cross-country skiers must know how to operate and gauge the limitations of snowmobiles.

In nontechnical terrain a rescue is not as simple as transiting from here to there. At worst — in deep powder, during a blizzard, at night — the task is dangerous, time-consuming, and seemingly impossible.

If an injured or sick hiker can be coerced into helping himself, so much the better. An exemplary evacuation technique often overlooked is nothing more than removing the exhausted or injured party's pack and skis and having him or her walk out without these encumbrances, using ski poles for balance if desired. This method works especially well in spring and in ranges where the long hours of sunlight and relatively high winter temperatures cause the snowpack to solidify to a hard crust. Early morning and evening are the proper times to enlist this method, as postholing in the soft, deep snow of midday is certain to prove more exhausting than skiing.

Likewise a tired or injured skier may be relieved of his pack and supplied with *rope climbers* rigged on his skis by a rescuer. Rope wrapped around the bottoms of the skis introduces enough friction to ease ascending and descending sharp-angled gullies and forest, eliminating the concentration and energy sapped by traverses, kick turns or Telemarks. These climbers are improvised by securing any coarse, small-diameter rope to the tip of each ski and wrapping the cord around the ski down past the binding, adding a few knots if the occasion calls for extra traction. Fasten the rope to the tail via an old sock slipped over and tied or with a clip fashioned from available wire or a piece of coat hanger. These climbers are great in impossible waxing conditions and for pulling sleds. Spare conventional climbing skins can be brought along for victim use if handy.

Improvised sled. *Photo Tim Setnicka*

In an emergency, an *improvised toboggan* or litter fashioned out of available parts and equipment, including aluminum pack frames and skis and poles or branches, offers adequate transport to the roadhead. One of the innumerable possible sled designs requires two or four skis and poles. The skis are laid down parallel to each other and crossed ski poles, sticks, tent poles or ice axes are lashed together with nylon cord to add rigidity. Pad the toboggan with foam mats and clothing and sleeping bags for some meager comfort. Short lengths of rope or ski poles are attached to the binding of the outside skis to serve as tow lines. A variation on this theme is the snowplow sled, in which the skis are tied together at the tips and separated at the bindings with a rigid branch or pole about 50 centimeters long. Ski pole baskets hooked over both tips, with the poles running along the skis to the binding and branch intersection, hold the snowplow position intact. Fill the space between the skis with a soft pack, ropes, boughs, whatever. Sheets of tough, rollable plastic and children's boats work too.

While sleds of this sort have been used successfully to move victims across rough backcountry, they are decidedly inefficient and demand a strong and preferably large party of rescuers working on skis with climbing skins or on foot to propel them. Other options and equipment need full consideration if they are cached elsewhere and the victim's condition will tolerate some delay. Any serious injury must be carefully considered to weigh the advantages of rapid evacuation in a makeshift sled versus the possibility of complications from the rough trip.

The more efficient ways of moving someone over snow by hand generally utilize specialized commercially manufactured sleds of a variety of designs. One ingenious model manufactured by K/F Precision Products is a foldable heavy-fabric sled that weighs about two kilograms and is capable of supporting around 180 kilograms (although one rider and gear seems like the maximum). This straightforward unit is basically a bed of fabric stretched above a pair of skis and held in place by ski poles and two short vertical risers affixed on each ski. No modification to the ski equipment is necessary. The whole unit rolls up into a cylindrical stuffbag about 12 by 60 centimeters that can be conveniently portaged on any pack.

The sled is short for some adults though, and the cloth bottom of the sled sags under body weight, somewhat limiting its efficacy for some injuries. Padding is essential to prevent further injury to the victim's back or stomach (the riding position in sleds is dependent on the malady) from surficial irregularities. As the full weight of the load is transferred to two skis acting as runners, the sled tends to settle and plow in fresh or soft snow, making it hard to pull. For a lightweight, highly portable snow litter though it is superior to the improvised sled detailed above as a result of its greater subject comfort and diminished drag. It travels over hardpack and through flat country somewhat more readily than the makeshift version.

Another suitable vehicle for victim transport over snow was developed by the NPS climbing rangers in Grand Teton National Park. A canvas cover was fitted snugly over the bottom and sides of a Stokes litter, found in most mountain areas throughout North America. With this compact and light cover a standard Stokes is instantly converted into a snow evacuation toboggan. Adaptation of this kind is especially convenient for operations in mixed alpine terrain, where snowfields and glaciers have to be crossed during a predominately rock and talus rescue evacuation. In the summer months when climbing and rescue activity is greatest, this rapid versatility is highly desirable, at little cost of additional weight. Bottom covers lend themselves to manufacture by local rescue teams in light of their simplicity. Attention must be given to the method of securing the cover on the litter, as it can fill with snow or peel back as the Stokes slides down a slope. Naturally traverses over rock shorten the cover's lifespan.

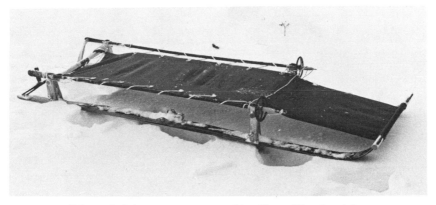

Fabric sled for cross-country skis. *Photo Tim Setnicka*

The most favorable design for winter toboggans is one which features a solid bottom and sides for optimal glide over snow and protection of the occupant. The materials are generally lightweight alloys (as in the Akja) or strong and light fiberglass or soft plastic (as in the Thompson and Cascade products discussed in detail in Chapter 17). Virtually all solid litters of this sort incorporate the use of metal handles that enable a skier to snowplow in front of the sled and control its speed and direction with the handles as he descends a slope.

Backcountry deployment of these sleds is hampered by the problems encountered in uphill climbs and movement across flat expanses. Most of these sleds were conceived with the requirements of skier evacuation from established alpine ski areas in mind, not with consideration for the trials of pulling a victim through broken country. However these commercial toboggans are well-constructed, roomy, and comfortable vehicles that move facilely through most snow conditions due to weight distribution across the breadth of their ample bottoms. All have good stability and most have some sort of runner or bottom finish to minimize sideslip on hardpack or ice. All of these factors make them particularly advantageous when operated in conjunction with snowmobiles. As many of these toboggans are owned by professional ski patrols in developed ski areas, they may be readily accessible for backcountry emergencies even though they are awkward to pull without modification.

Hegg sled on Ellesmere Island. *Photo Allan Bard*

What is clearly one of the best systems for towing a loaded toboggan or sled behind a nordic skier for both uphill and downhill pitches has been designed and manufactured by Erling Hegg of Nord-Hus, Inc. Hegg has experimented with a number of sled and skier configurations over the past decade. The final product is the *Hegg sled* and harness Ned Gilette, Wayne Merry, and others choose to pull a hundred kilograms of equipment on multiweek cross-country ski trips into extremely remote tracts like the St. Elias range in southeastern Alaska and the ice floes of Ellesmere Island in Arctic Canada.

Hegg's solution to the discomfort and immobility of the solid, metal-handled sleds features a combination shoulder and waist harness incorporating spring-loaded shock absorbers on each side of the skier. Fiberglass poles run from the shock absorbers back to the toboggan, an elegant one-piece fiberglass shell that Hegg calls a "pulk." This arrangement allows the skier complete arm and leg freedom so he may ski in his usual diagonal stride uninterrupted by the presence of the sled. The rigid poles (as in the other designs) keep the sled from overtaking the skier on downhill runs and facilitate control by transferring its weight to the skier's hips. While the skier is pulling uphill or across on level ground, the shock absorbers ameliorate the jarring effect of his stride. Both the concept and the product's performance are excellent. The Hegg sled was the model chosen for backcountry evacuation during the 1980 Winter Olympics in Lake Placid.

Pulling anything while maneuvering on skis is inherently fraught with balance, slippage, and entanglement problems, especially if three or four average, tired skiers are toiling at once. The best harness rigging for heavy, long pulls is a fan array similar to one method of hooking a dog team to a sled. This fan pattern, however, is not suited to glacier travel, lest the wider skier distribution only increase the probability of a fall into a crevasse. Each skier is connected with the sled or toboggan via a separate rope or pole running to his waist. The other traditional pattern for harnessing sled dogs is the single or tandem file, with each canine (or skier in this case) clipped into either one or two lines emanating from the front of the sled. The latter configuration requires considerable discipline and coordination in comparison to the relatively anarchistic fan pattern, which helps separate everyone's skis or snowshoes.

Skis worn for sled pulling benefit from a heavy wax treatment for extra traction, but rope climbers or climbing skins fare much better in borderline conditions. Snowshoes seem to work the best, especially the tailless bearpaw or Green Mountain varieties suited to agile turns in dense undergrowth and kicking steps up steep inclines.

Occasionally it is necessary to belay or pull a toboggan down or up a dizzying slope by means of a safety rope. A few simple points are mentioned at this stage in the narrative rather than in the following technical section of this chapter, for the terrain in question does not really demand the use of full winter technical equipment and technique.

Fan pattern of sled harness rigging. *Photo Bob Hoffman*

Only rudimentary belays need be arranged in most instances. A simple *tree belay* will suffice — one or more wraps of the rope around a tree or large bush generally provide adequate friction to absorb the energy of a sudden slip by the sled attendants. A pair of skis held together and jammed into solid snow as far as possible constitute an informal *snow picket* of sorts, and may also serve as an adequate though marginal artificial anchor around which to belay directly or to tie in the belayer. Care must be taken to protect the rope where it runs over the edge of the ski by liberally applying padding. Another option is to tie off the skis with a sling. Deadman anchors (described more fully later) consist of skis or stout branches tied off similarly and buried in a deep trench, and are fashioned in a moment in most snow conditions. A simple six carabiner brake can be introduced once a sling has been girth hitched around a tree or one or another of these artificial anchor points, and relied upon to protect the descent of a loaded sled in the same way that system is used in a lowering.

The defiance of gravity required to raise a loaded toboggan up an outright hill is achieved in a number of ways, none of them magical. The *counterweight method* (Fig. 23.1) centers around a rope hooked to a carabiner on a directional anchor or a pulley. One end is tied to the sled; the other is given to two rescuers who simply walk downhill using the force of gravity on them to overcome its influence on the sled, moving it upward. This rigging does not feature any mechanical advantage but under good conditions (i.e., packed snow offering a favorable coefficient of friction) the force needed to raise a sled is quite low compared to that demanded for a raising system on steep rock. As the snowslope angle is most likely less than half that of vertical rock, the pull of gravity is dissipated into the slope in the form of friction, in turn diminished by the smooth snow cover.

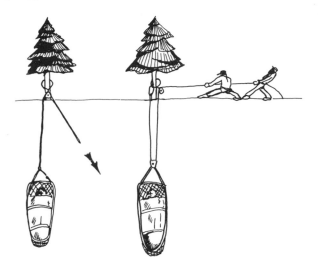

Fig. 23.1 Two methods of raising toboggans — via the counterweight of two rescuers walking downhill (left), and through the use of a simple 2:1 pulley system.

A simple *2:1 raising rig* can be installed by placing a pulley on the sled. The raising rope is tied into the anchor on top of the slope, run through the pulley on the toboggan below, and then back up to the anchor. A directional sling allows two or three workers to pull in tandem, raising the sled. This same technique has been used to raise injured climbers able to assist in self-rescue from cliffs by their own small parties. In some situations (when the trapped climber is capable of cooperating with the rescuers and the lip configuration of the crevasse is conducive to this rope arrangement) a 2:1 raising rig with a pulley or carabiner on the climber is feasible for crevasse rescue. (More on this subject later.) These are two of an assortment of means of hoisting a loaded sled up a steep incline. The terrain, distance to be traveled, and number of rescuers on hand determine which tactic is most suitable. With adequate manpower and ropes, for example, the team could leapfrog pairs ahead to fix raising rigs on impending obstacles so that the sled could be hauled up immediately upon arrival.

Over-Snow Vehicles

All of the preceding manual methods become only gruesome possibilities hopefully never called into play if some type of over-snow vehicle can be commandeered to evacuate the victim. Vehicles of this sort fall into two broad groups. One is characterized by smaller machines for one or two riders with open or nonexistent cabs, single or double tracks powered by a two-cycle engine, and skis on the front for steering. These *snowmobiles* are numerous, readily obtained on short notice, and transported without major complication in a pickup or on a trailer. The operation and repair of snowmobiles is far less involved than for larger vehicles.

Many of the snowmobile designs currently popular in the U.S. feature high speed, heavy suspension, and wide skis, all of which may limit their use in some terrain and snow conditions. The single-track, lighter machines are best for mountain search and rescue purposes, although lightweight and agile machines do take talent and practice to operate.

Loading injured children onto Thiokel from Akja sled on Mt. Rainier. *Photo Pete Hart*

In contrast, the second category of larger, heavier over-snow machines like *Thiokols* features vehicles with two or four tracks and (usually) enclosed cabs that are harder to locate and operate. They provide excellent shelter for the riders and can haul many personnel at once. However, they are expensive to buy or rent and are hard to suddenly transport from one area to another even with their own trailers. Often local power and utility companies, telephone companies, ski areas, and state and federal conservation agencies offer their machines for SAR functions. Prior arrangements are generally necessary, and should be included in the preplan. These machines must be operated by a trained, experienced driver who normally doubles as mobile mechanic as well. The large size and weight of Thiokols and other models limits their field application but when they work well, they potentially eliminate the complex logistics of a major project rescue involving a large number of field personnel.

Fresh, deep snow presents serious problems for over-snow vehicles, as do precipitous snowfields, for both make climbing, braking, and traversing more challenging. The operator's skill in many instances means the difference between success and failure.

Besides hauling crew members and supplies, over-snow vehicles can tow cross-country skiers, a practice known as ski-jouring. Rig two ropes in a fan configuration with one skier per rope, or for short runs just drag one long knotted rope that everyone can grasp at appropriate intervals. The first method is more luxurious if the tow rope is tied around the middle of a pair of ski poles to improvise a convenient handle. Snowmobiles are marvelous beasts of burden for support logistics, and rush in supplies and equipment and evacuate victims on sleds in a fraction of the time and effort consumed by a party on skis. Thompson manufactures a hitch and pulling bar compatible with most stock snowmobiles. Modification of a Cascade toboggan for snowmobile coupling is uncomplicated. Especially in broad-ranging searches in cold or stormy weather or rescues requiring movement of vast quantities of gear, the snowmobile speeds the operation and heightens the probability of success. Dress for the ride though — those one-piece snowmobile suits of heavy nylon and insulation are constructed that way for a reason.

Contingency plans for the operators and passengers of over-snow machines are essential. Carry skis or snowshoes and survival gear in case of breakdown, an all-too-common occurrence. Alternate victim evacuation plans must be formulated in the event the machines cannot reach him or complete the operation due to unforeseen circumstances.

In short, over-snow vehicles are felicitous tools of profound significance to some field maneuvers but are dependent on the operator's skill and the machine's mechanical and terrain limitations, tempered by good judgment. Find the best local machines, mechanics, and drivers and work them into the SAR winter preplan.

Technical Snow and Ice Rescue

A rope might have been unstrapped from someone's rucksack and uncoiled at some point to lower a toboggan down an unappealing slope with a simple tree belay. True snow and ice rescue, however, commences when snow conditions and terrain make it necessary to don ice axes, crampons, and possibly ropes to replace snowshoes or skis. SAR situations of this sort involve rescue of climbers or the inexperienced from glacial icefalls, frozen waterfalls, or high-angle snowfields.

Participation in and management of these problems presumes personal experience and expertise in travel and survival in all facets of alpine topography. The dangers to oneself and others are substantial due to the unpredictability of anchors and snow and the preponderance of sharp axes and crampons, as beginners learn with startling regularity. Discussion of selection and manipulation of ice tools and technical climbing technique constitutes a tome in itself, and a task best delegated to works scribed by experts in the field. The bibliography of this chapter provides a number of sources; see especially *Climbing Ice* by Yvon Chouinard, *The Ice Experience* by Jeff Lowe, and *Freedom of the Hills* by a committee of The Mountaineers.

Anchors on Snow and Ice

As in rock climbing, first considerations for technical snow and ice work include placement of anchor points and fabrication of stout anchor systems. Establishing adequate anchors in alpine terrain (mixed snow, ice, and rock, sometimes including glaciers) involves equal parts art and science uniquely blended with a dose of experience. While the basics of placing rock protection can be grasped relatively quickly, most climbers find that an understanding of the subtleties of security on snow and ice evades them longer. The rock encountered in alpine settings is more likely to vary capriciously from solid pegmatite or dolerite or granite to loose volcanic intrusions or sediment strata than in frequently climbed crags. Ice, on the other hand, is a product of the hydrologic cycle and is temperature-dependent — what is a slushy gulley today may be rock-hard black ice an hour or a day later in the aftermath of an avalanche. Ice and snow, like the water from which they descend, are fickle and forever in flux. They need to be studied carefully and watched constantly in order to be cognizant of the dangers but able to profit from the speed and fun they allow.

With the exception of ice gullies and frozen waterfalls, most alpine ice is variegated — a frozen broth of hard snow, aerated cauliflower clumps or hollow chandelier ice over crevasses and rock bulges, and armorplate black ice in dark corners. Thus the protection technique described here applies to the microenvironment rather than to general topographic features — a hundred-meter couloir (gully) may offer four or five types of ice and snow within its length. In the same way, a glacier could be "wet" (covered with snow above the firn line of snow accumulation) for one pitch and protectable by snow anchors, and "dry" (bare ice below the firn line or exposed for other reasons) a short distance below or just off to the side where glacier ice is exposed in a serac block or tower, necessitating ice-screw belays. The consistency or density of the medium at hand dictates both climbing and protection technique.

Off-snow anchor and lowering station in moat. *Photo Kenneth Andrasko*

Very often, especially in couloirs or mixed climbing over snow, ice, and rock, one can establish *off-snow anchors* on rocks poking through, outcroppings on the edges of a snowfield, or trees or huge blocks instantly tied off. Rely heavily on rock protection if available, as the time saved and security gained are considerable. Snow and to some extent ice protection is inherently less strong and predictable — as the temperature rises, screws and flukes (portable aluminum-plate deadmen) and pickets tend to melt or pull out and ice blocks warm and break their bond. In many rescue situations belay anchors can be set off the route and ice screws or flukes placed as directional anchors to guide the rope and litter up or down the best route on the ice.

Stout belay stances are almost unavoidable in moats, the crevasse-like holes along the edges of snowfields or gullies where the snow has melted away from the warmer rock. Solid hip belays are possible from these protected crevices. Small crevasses in which a belayer can brace himself standing or sitting are also excellent belay spots, though best backed up with snow or rock anchors. Even in poor or marginal snow conditions (e.g., deep powder, an avalanche slope, wet snow) off-snow anchors can insure bombproof lowering and belay stances.

Ice Protection If rock anchors are scarce for an ice climb or descent, *ice screws* and *ice pitons* work admirably. The premier ice pins were elementary metal spikes with barbs and rings. Prototype ice screws were large, threaded lag screws with rings first used in the 1950s by the Swiss. Over the intervening two decades both species have been immeasurably improved by redesign, largely in the decade beginning in the late 1960s. Two basic designs exist: tubular threaded screws and the solid drive-in Wart Hog pitons. The most popular brands in the U.S. currently in production include the Chouinard and Salewa screws (20-25cm for glacier and water ice and longer ones for soft ice and hard snow); the Lowe Snarg, a new tubular piton with threads that is driven in and screwed out; and the Chouinard and Salewa Wart Hog-design pitons, also driven in and unscrewed.

Like rock pitons, ice pitons and screws derive the major portion of their holding power from the quality of the individual placement and the holding power of the surrounding ice (rather than the materials used). Unlike rock pitons, however, ice pins slightly melt the surrounding medium during placement. If the air temperature is below freezing, the ice generally refreezes, solidifying the anchor. In above-freezing conditions, however, the refreezing process is slowed down and high water temperatures and the sun combine to warm metal pitons enough to melt out screws originally secure. Screws and especially pitons tend to fracture cold, brittle ice as they dislodge ice during insertion. Sometimes one type of anchor works better than another, so both should be carried and used liberally. It is worth noting that under ideal conditions some screws have tested to over 2000 kilograms before failure while ice pitons tested to about 1000 kilograms.

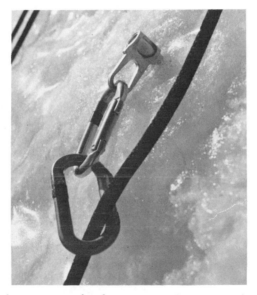

Chouinard ice screw in hard water ice. *Photo Kenneth Andrasko*

Ice pitons of any design should be placed in the ice at about a 45-60 degree angle to the slope. The correct sheer-load angle maximizes holding power. Before *placement* scrutinize the microterrain to assess the quality (density and brittleness and thickness) of the ice in small pockets, steps, pillars, and bulges. Select from one of these scoops the most plastic and the thickest ice with the least amount of white hue and bubbles (indicating air). Clear away any loose, brittle surface ice to guarantee insertion into solid layers. Often one must excavate down as much as a half-meter to reach sturdy ice. Small shelves or pockets combat fracturing in the upper layers and bending or extraction, and protect the screw from direct sunlight (snow packed over the screw serves the

same purpose). Extremely brittle ice from intense cold or lots of air fractures or "dinner plates" off large circular chunks of ice shaped like delft
china pieces as the screw or piton is forced into the ice.

Start a screw or piton by making a small hole about the diameter of
the tube with an axe or hammer pick. Then pound in the screw until the
threads catch. In soft ice a tube screw can usually be screwed in with
another screw or an axe pick for leverage. In hard ice, pound the head
regularly with a hammer as the tube is turned to encourage it to cut
deeper. Tubular Forrest or Lowe hammer picks work beautifully for setting screws, as the tube removes a core of ice slightly smaller than a
screw, which then eases in nicely. A screw or especially a piton should
never be tied off halfway like rock pitons if at all possible. If necessary
one can tie off two screws, one above the other, with a tight sling to distribute the load. Place the screw all the way until the eye is forced flush
with the ice and pointed downhill or in the direction of pull.

Hammering in Hummingbird hammer for self-belay on ice in order to place ice
screw anchor. *Photo Kenneth Andrasko*

Removing screws and most pitons is a matter of screwing them out
using a hammer or an ice axe like a brace and bit. In cold weather chop
away the first three or four centimeters of ice around the head and any
bumps that might hinder its rapid rotation by the axe. Never hit an ice
screw or piton back and forth in the way one removes a rock piton.
Sometimes stubborn placements benefit from a firm tap or two on the
anvil to break the frozen bond. To clean the core of a tubular piece for

further use, warm it in a parka pocket for awhile if necessary and then remove the core with an axe or tool carried for this purpose if a piton will not fit.

A typical belay in soft alpine or hard water ice for two climbers consists of a minimum of two pitons or screws placed vertically or horizontally one to two meters apart. Substantial ice pillars normally provide simple but effective tie-off anchors as well. Rescue work requires greater anchor strength and safety margins. Hence it is standard practice to *self-equalize* all anchor points into a system that readjusts itself under loading and the failure of one or more points. The technique is the same as for rock anchors as delineated in Chapter 16.

Self-belay on ice is an informal security method that consists of aggressively whacking in one or more ice tools as solidly as possible and clipping into them with a sling to the waist harness. Tools with hammer heads can be pounded in with another hammer to relieve any doubt. Naturally the tie sling to the tool should not be too long or too weak. Once secured in this manner, the climber goes about his business of cutting a fast step to stand in and constructing a full belay, working with the litter, or whatever. The tools can be left in place or replaced as backups once the proper stance is ready. As managing frozen rope on ice can be a problem if it is in the way of a raising or lowering, drape it in huge five or ten-meter loops over an axe placed conveniently to the side. Self-belay is just that, not a means of protecting the movement of others.

Snow Anchors Anchor points in snow also vary in type and number necessary depending on snow conditions and steepness of slope. The simplest protection or rappel point is a *bollard,* a tapering horseshoe or teardrop trench dug, cut, or stomped into the snow, depending on consistency (Fig. 23.2). The softer the snow or the steeper a slope, the larger and deeper the bollard must be to comprise an adequate snowmass. An end of the rope or liberal sling is laid in the trench and tied off in a loop. The top of the horseshoe should be incut downhill to keep the rope from jumping out of it. In soft or questionable snow, many wraps of the rope or a pack, tent, or tarp is drafted for padding inside the trench to reinforce it against the slicing action of the rope. Bollards in hard snow and ice are tremendously strong and swiftly constructed.

Another genus of snow anchor with superior holding power in soft snow is the *deadman.* The deadman is any object (preferably flat and long or broad) tied off, placed in a cut trench with a groove for the rope, and buried. An ice axe, large chunk of ice or rock, pack filled with snow, or several solid branches are all serviceable. The larger, heavier, and deeper the anchor, the stronger the deadman; requirements vary with the density of the snow, with deep powder providing the ultimate test. As the name suggests, bodies work wonderfully; it is, however, rather difficult to find recruits.

Fig. 23.2 Ice bollard anchor. Size of bollard depends on solidity of snow or ice.

One popular species of deadman is the *snow fluke* (Fig. 23.3). The fluke is a square of aluminum 15 to 30 centimeters wide fixed with a cable tie-in and hammered into the snow at about 45 degrees to the slope. The newer flukes are rigged like kites to maintain a proper angle of attack and to dig themselves deeper into the snow as the pull on them increases. Some feature a roof bend to increase strength and stability.

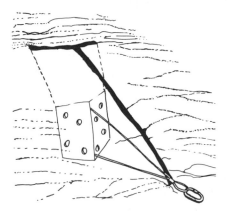

Fig. 23.3 Snow fluke, showing proper placement with self-equalized sling.

Large flukes often have holes drilled in them for lightening (as do the long aluminum snow pitons called pickets). An incorrectly set fluke is liable to pull out. Digging a T-shaped slit with the cable laid perpendicular to the plate encourages the cable to cut down and become taut under a load; otherwise the arcing cable exerts an upward force, extracting the plate. Piling snow on top of a well-hammered fluke with a deep cable channel is the final touch to avoid surprise belays.

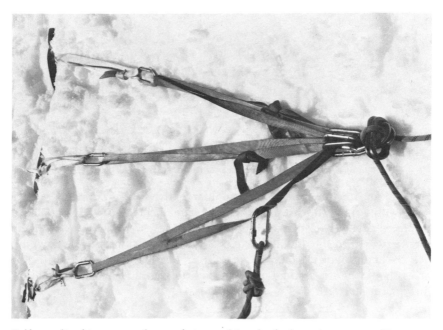

Self-equalized ice axe anchor and six-carabiner brake lowering system. Top rope goes to litter. *Photo Kenneth Andrasko*

If snow conditions permit, several ice axes sunk into the snow about a meter apart (in firm snow) offer a fast self-equalizing anchor. Always stomp the snow firmly before placing the axe, and choose the densest snow available. A loop of rope or a sling is girth-hitched or looped around the shaft of each axe and all are united into a self-equalized anchor (Fig. 23.4). Wooden or weak axes should be positioned with the elliptical shaft-shape (and hence the pick) pointed in the direction of pull; aluminum or strong-shafted axes are better placed with the broad side of the shaft (pick perpendicular to the pull) facing the direction of loading, offering greater surface area and resistance. Cut or shovel away unconsolidated surface layers until firm snowpack is reached for good purchase.

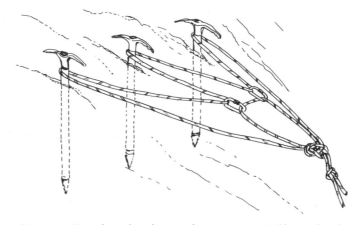

Fig. 23.4 Two-loop bowline anchor in snow. Self-equalized.

Another quick ice axe anchor popular in the Tetons connects two ice axes with a tight short runner. While this method is not truly equalized, if placed correctly both axes support the load. A second runner fixes the brake system to the downhill axe. Have someone stand on the downhill ice axe to dissuade it from popping out. In both of these methods the ice axes should be inserted at an angle slightly uphill from the vertical for maximum strength.

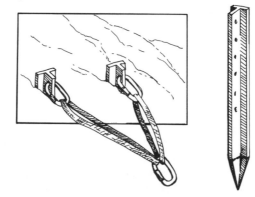

Fig. 23.5 Snow pickets placed in snow for self-equalized anchor.

Because these two methods are instantly set up, especially the second Teton anchor, two teams can leapfrog down a slope with a litter virtually non-stop. The lower of the two teams establishes an anchor and brake so that the lowering rope is clipped in immediately when the upper belay team comes to the end of the rope and the litter arrives at the anchors.

A *snow picket* (Fig. 23.5) is a specialized anchor that can be interchanged with an ice axe as a belay (or protection) anchor. Pickets are cut from high-grade aluminum T- or angle-stock with a point cut on one end. The length varies but is close to a meter. Commercial pickets are available from SMC and other distributers, but homemade ones of quality stock work fine. Holes drilled every ten centimeters in the top half accept tie-in carabiners or webbing for any snow depth, and lessen the torque on a picket otherwise girth-hitched. Pickets have the auxiliary function of mammoth pitons, just the right thing to bash into a big crack in poor rock or into a small moat between ice and rock.

Teton double-axe anchor with lowering system. Right rope goes to litter. *Photo Kenneth Andrasko*

Belaying and Lowerings

Belaying on snow and ice necessitates one of the above anchors or a sitting hip belay, boot-axe belay, or a hip-axe belay with a strong-shafted axe. The first is a variation of the traditional hip belay of rock climbing, with the belayer braced in a socket or small crevasse in the snow with heels dug in well. The *boot-axe* and *hip-axe belays* rely on the planted axe for support for the rope, with the axe buttressed by a boot (or the thigh and hip) stamped in the snow and up against the shaft in the direction of pull.

In some cases one of these hasty belays is all that is necessary to safeguard or lower a sick climber. If any doubt exists, combine a hip belay with a picket or fluke anchor. The most time-consuming anchor is a multi-point, self-equalized one incorporating a frictional device for a lowering or a pulley system raising on technical terrain. Solid belay and lowering stations must be achieved at any cost of time, reemphasizing the need for adequate anchor backups and the ability to mix different sorts of technique creatively.

Boot axe belay. Note left hand pressing on axe to keep it in place. The least reliable belay. *Photo Kenneth Andrasko*

Once the anchors are in place, a *lowering* on snow and ice proceeds the same way as in any rock rescue. A friction device slows the descent of the toboggan or litter, although in soft or rough snow it may have to be dragged down. One lowering rope suffices unless a second belay is warranted due to rockfall, the possibility of rope injury over sharp edges, or a questionable but unimprovable anchor. Depending upon conditions, a litter attendant may be able to hold or stop or temporarily belay the litter in the event of complications.

Lowering over a lip with ice axe as edge protector. *Photo Kenneth Andrasko*

Unlike most rock rescues, a snow lowering features a toboggan lowered feet-first in a vertical position to prevent tipping and to optimalize steering and tracking. Tie the attendant directly into the foot of the litter on an adjustable sling, to allow mobility to belay or move to the subject's head or side for medical or maneuvering reasons. Or he can be on a separate belay from above in order to minimize the load on each anchor. On rare occasions a lowering occurs where it is desirable to keep the litter horizontal. If the angle of the slope is low, only the uphill sides need be attached to the lowering rope. If the slope is too steep for this or the litter must be held level for medical or maneuvering purposes, use a regular litter prerig or the equivalent. Again, the attendant clips into the litter or is belayed on a separate rope.

Lowering on Mt. Rainier toward helo on glacier. The next belay station is being set up below. *Photo Dick Martin*

Raising a litter up a steep couloir or a vertical ice face (say up the side of a crevasse) generally requires a mechanical advantage system of some sort. A common 3:1 rig and a Maasdam hand winch have both been operated in rescues on Mt. Rainier. The basic system (Fig. 23.6) relies on a multipoint anchor for the main anchor, Gibbs or Jumar ascenders for mechanical rope grips, and one rope for hauling along with a separate belay if possible. The Maasdam winch is rigged for a raising in the same manner protrayed in Chapter 19, with the exception of snow and ice anchors instead of rock tie-ins.

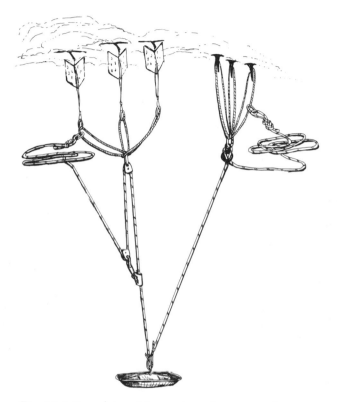

Fig. 23.6 Complete raising or lowering system for snow.

Crevasse Rescue

Mountaineers very often display a rather cavalier approach to glacier travel. They are more intent on the technical difficulties ahead or behind them, and see glaciers as obstacle-filled highways to and fro. But glaciers are beautiful, alive, intricate bodies of ice full of deep, cold suprises called *crevasses*. Glaciers behave much like rivers, flowing, twisting, turning, and scouring their way down from the heights. Cracks appear in the brittle ice from the stress and the deformities caused by the rock outcrops or drops the ice must avoid or surmount.

These crevasses range from hairline fractures to impassable canyons capable of devouring whole caravans of Airstream trailers and Greyhound buses, and constantly change form. On the "wet" stretches of glaciers covered with snow even the most gargantuan crevasses may be hidden by accumulated snowfall. Glacier travel is the art of deciphering the physics of the ice's movement, predicting dangerous zones, and threading a safe route through the labyrinth.

Whenever a glacier bypasses or overrides a deterrent to its progress, jumbled *icefalls* are produced, collections of rough lines of ice-block *serac* towers and deep, ruptured crevasses, all highly unstable. Virtually always a giant crevasse known as a *bergschrund* forms where the head of the moving glacier breaks off from the steep, comparatively fixed slopes of its upper reaches on a face of a peak, or where the glacier's snowfield meets rock buttresses.

Ice fall on Gillam glacier, Mt. Deborah. *Photo Kenneth Andrasko*

Route finding on a glacier is similar to scouting a safe course through avalanche zones. A few guidelines exist but little is absolute and much based on experience. Probing with an ice axe for hidden crevasses as one climbs and weaves calls on all of the senses — sound, changes in texture and snow color, intuition — and solid interpretation of the data they collect. Careful examination of a lot of incongruities and a number of falls into holes fosters keen understanding. Watch for broad patterns of crevasse formation, and continually look off to the sides to detect evidence of fissures there to extrapolate their possible presence in your route through the middle of the glacier or snowfield (which may also sport crevasses in some places). Listen carefully to the sounds underfoot for hollows, and look for localized alterations in hue.

Everyone must rope up on glaciers covered with snow (*wet glaciers*). Jump small slits energetically and with ample margin, and belay larger ones. Rely on forward motion to carry you over weaknesses and onto solid snow. Avoid moving among seracs or through icefalls by traveling along rock moraines or circumnavigating tangled areas. In icefalls that must be traversed, climb with all due haste and preferably when the temperature is lowest and the ice stablest — after dusk or early in the morning. The ice blocks and crevasses can be used to advantage for protection by throwing the rope around serac blocks and irregularities at corners and belaying from small bare crevasses, the glacier equivalent of moderate, continuous alpine ridge climbing where one protects progress by weaving the rope on alternate sides of flakes and blocks.

Belaying crevasse crossing on dry glacier in Wind Rivers. *Photo Craig Patterson*

Choose a route along a glacier that detours around large, intersecting crevasses (the most dangerous, as several members of the party could fall in at once, and there is no clear route) by studying the glacier from atop the terminal or lateral moraine or a hillock or serac. Plan the whole route if possible by observation of spots where crevasses are widest, most regular in pattern, and hence relatively predictable, and most threatened by seracs or avalanche from above. Definitely rope up on all wet glaciers and belay at questionable sections. Crossing crevasses involves end runs, jumping (beware of soft snow collapsing on the lip on either side), or braving *snowbridges*. All snowbridges are uncertain and must be carefully belayed. The belayer moves up to within a few meters of the lip and fashions a solid belay with flukes or whatever is necessary. Often someone can be belayed down along the suspected hole to a vantage point offering a cross-sectional view, elucidating the bridge's thickness and length or a better route. Tradition dictates that the lightest person go first, without her pack if desired and on her stomach in truly marginal circumstances. If she feels herself going in, she should lurch forward with axe in hand outstretched, laying in the snow to distribute weight and thrusting the axe in for support in firm snow.

Make sure the bridge will still be safe at noon if the return route is the same. Memorize the route, in case the descent takes place at night or in deteriorating weather. Wands (bamboo or other stakes with flags) are popular for marking crevasses and turns along the track. Obviously it is essential that the entire party not fall into the same crevasse. To this end consideration should be given to walking in an echelon formation when moving parallel to the general direction of fractures instead of following in one another's footsteps.

In his book *Climbing Ice* Yvon Chouinard lists five basic rules for safe glacier travel: 1) the team must always use a rope on wet glaciers, 2) the belayer must be able to anchor the rope in any conditions after a fall, 3) the fallen climber must be prepared to extricate himself, 4) the belayer must be able to send down either the end of the rope or another rope to the fallen climber, and 5) the belayer must know how to haul out an unconscious victim. One might add a few more guidelines. Dress in warm clothing even on torrid days, as exposure is a major cause of death or incapacitation in crevasse accidents; leave a parka near the top of the pack; and evenly distribute the anchors for the belay and rescue rigs among the party so that the bearer of all the ice screws and flukes does not dramatically drop out of sight. A sling or loop or the end of the rope tied to one's pack serves as a way to unstrap it for prusiking out of a hole without losing it. Naturally glacier travel is a complex aspect of mountaineering that can be only briefly touched on here; consult the authorities.

Self-Rescue from Crevasses

Two methods of crevasse *self-rescue* prevail, though in a number of incarnations. Traditionally these riggings employ prusik or other soft ascending knots (like the Penberthy knot). Mechanical ascenders like the Jumar or Gibbs models have gained prominence in the last decade, although some of the toothed designs (e.g., Jumars) slip when icy, unlike the Gibbs; their use is discussed in Chapter 13. While these two methods are described with prusik loops since they are inexpensive and universally available, for SAR work the mechanical descenders are indispensable in crevasse or alpine rescue despite their weight and expense, and may save a life.

Prusiking out of crevasse. *Photo Pete Hart*

Two or three climbers tied into one rope or two rope teams journeying close enough to support one another is the convention. The idea is to artfully manage the rope such that it stays off the snow, and to have about fifteen meters coiled around the leader's and tail person's shoulders to act as a second rope thrown down to a dangling climber in the aftermath of an unfortunate misstep. A bowline on a coil is tied around the coils and the swami belt or harness, to transfer the load of a fall to the tie-in and to prevent strangulation.

Each climber installs two (or three, if a chest loop is added) foot loops on the climbing rope above the bowline by tying them on with prusik knots. A middleman on the rope fixes prusiks on both ropes in front and back, as either might arrest his fall. The loops are tucked through the harness down toward the feet, and stuffed into pockets out of the way.

When any member disappears through the surface, the other climbers instantly become belayers, falling into self-arrest position or thrusting in axes. Hopefully the rope will cut into the edge of the crevasse, adding friction and slowing the descent. Once the belayers have stopped the fall, the one closest to the crevasse places a robust anchor and eases the load onto it with his prusiks, in much the same way one ties off a fallen climber on rock (Fig. 16.13). Several types of anchors (screws, flukes, pickets) ought to be carried by seconds and leaders as glacier cover varies in density. Axe anchors are often insufficient for the strains of a hauling system. A bombproof anchor allows the belayer to move about freely and untie (if necessary) in order to throw an end of the rope or his coil down to the fallen climber.

The unlucky soul who suddenly finds himself hanging from his rope, spinning around, unable to touch the sides of the crevasse, and pulled over by the weight of his expedition pack realizes in a flash why all the rope and prusik precautions have been taken. The first step of extrication, assuming no or only minor injuries, calls for the climber to remove his pack (after assuring it is indeed clipped into the harness or rope). This relieves much of the pressure dragging the climber over backwards. If a harness is not worn a waist loop alone constricts breathing, so a *baboon sit* must be performed to transfer weight to the thighs with a sling or an ice axe passed over the feet between the back of the thighs and the rope (refer to Chapter 14).

Next he would do well to relax for a moment, communicate with those above if possible, and look around to fully consider all the self-rescue options. Can he be lowered to walk out a side ramp? What about climbing out with his ice tools or by chimneying with the assistance of a little tension once the pack has been hauled? Communication is customarily difficult, though helped if someone above is belayed to the edge or down the length of the crevasse to an opening. If the extraction appears at all involved, the climber digs into the top of his pack for extra clothing; parkas are easiest to get on in these circumstances.

Assuming ascending his rope is the only realistic choice, the climber can prusik in numerous ways. The following are widely taught. The first means is the *Bilgeri method* (Fig. 23.7) utilizing two ropes alternately raised from above and stood in by the climber. A free end of a rope is tossed down to the victim. The crevasse edge it passes over is cut away or padded with closed cell foam pads, rucksacks, or ice axes (in that order of preference) before weight is transferred onto the second rope so it will not bury itself. All are tied off to prevent shifting or loss.

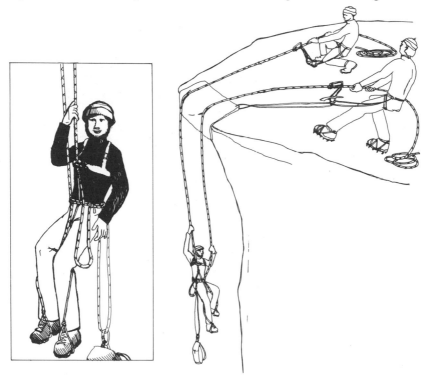

Fig. 23.7 Bilgeri method of crevasse rescue through alternate raising of two ropes.

The climber ties a prusik loop or étrier and ascender to the second rope and the rope from which he is hanging, or he ties foot loops in the ends of two ropes thrown down. Both ropes are run through a carabiner on a chest harness or sling to inhibit falling over backwards; a third and possibly fourth prusik serve the same purpose. Both ropes are tied into solid anchors on top with prusiks or ascenders since they will be raised frequently. The object is to alternately haul up one unweighted rope less than a meter, anchor it with the ascender, have the climber step up onto that rope's foot loop and move up his chest prusik. The other rope is unweighted now and can be raised a half-meter and stood in, in turn un-weighting the other rope for raising. A real fight is usually obligatory to master the snowy lip, as both ropes will be cut into the snow somewhat, even with padding. If possible have a belayed partner at the lip of the crevasse ready to help with those last few meters.

Raising victim in Jakes litter with two attendants and spotter, and belaying and hauling ropes. *Photo Dan Horner*

All free-standing rope technique must be practiced in favorable conditions. A few tricks help. One is to anchor the two ropes well apart to combat the insufferable twisting and spiraling that slows progress and calmness (likewise the climber can push the two ropes apart to steady them and him). Another is to position a spotter at the lip or in a narrow spot in the hole to communicate with the victim and relay his commands of left and right or red and purple or whatever to distinguish which rope is to be raised. Thirdly one can tie into the climbing rope two meters from the end for any glacier travel so that a footloop will always be on hand.

The *Texas prusik* or Texas high-step is a second method of self-rescue. Cavers are the main proponents of this technique, though it has caught on in big wall climbing somewhat. Two prusiks are required: one running from the rope to the waist harness, the other from the rope to both feet. If tied at the correct length, the harness prusik gives the arms a rest. To proceed up the rope one stands up in the lower prusik foot sling and advances the upper (harness) prusik in common three-prusik fashion. After sitting on the upper prusik and relaxing, the climber moves the foot prusik. Getting past the lip of the overhang is generally problematic and a second employed there in the way described in the first method helps. Practice any prusik technique on local crags so that the exact lengths and manipulation of the prusiks is well understood. Of course the standard three-prusik ascending method illustrated in the chapter on ascending does work for self-rescue from crevasses, but it is a bit slower when speed is essential.

Rescuing the Injured

Rescue is a true conundrum when the fall injures or renders unconscious the victim, especially if assistance is limited to only one or two others. Of most immediate concern is suffocation of a victim hanging on the end of the rope from his swami belt or harness. It may be necessary for someone to urgently climb, rappel, or traverse from the end into the crevasse while on belay. Make sure this does not result in *two* climbers trapped in a hole with only one on top! The in-crevasse assistant relieves the weight on the victim's abdomen and lower chest by *rigging a more supportive harness* and chest sling, placing a prusik or mechanical ascender on his rope above him, and running a sling clipped to his harness up through it and back down to the rescuer's foot (Fig. 23.8). He then stands in the sling, using body weight to pulley the victim up and relieve the tension on the swami, and transfer it to the new harness and chest sling. A baboon sit is another temporary solution. Alternatively the belayer can lower the climber until a prusik fixed to his harness and the second rope comes taut. Lastly, in some instances where the crevasse tapers down or is filled with a block below, the victim can be lowered until he rests on the ice. Medical care commences as soon as the victim is on a stable block or in an improvised harness.

Fig. 23.8 Rigging a supportive harness on a free-hanging unconscious victim. Adapted from Bill March.

Occasionally a rescuer can rely on the double jumar technique to augment the efforts of a conscious climber to ascend the rope. The rescuer jumars next to the victim on a separate rope and raises one of his Jumars for him (see Chapter 13). Managing the crevasse lip is only slightly easier with this method.

Raising an unconscious or seriously injured subject is difficult at best. A 2:1 or 3:1 pulley system is popular; infrequently a hand winch is necessary. These systems, except for the anchors and edge problems, are devised in the same manner described in Chapter 19. The 2:1 pulley rig discussed in reference to litter raisings on snow is readily adapted for crevasse work (Fig. 23.9) but only if the lip is not too obtrusive and the victim is able to cooperate.

Fig. 23.9 Use of 2:1 pulley system to assist slightly injured climber out of crevasse. Edge friction may prove to be too great.

One trick is to place anchors on the far side of the crevasse and suspend the raising rope over its middle by means of a sling and carabiner (Fig. 23.10). With little manpower and equipment, a rescuer could attempt to piggyback an injured climber out in a Tragsitz improvised by cutting leg holes in a rucksack, though significant lips or overhanging sides would make the success of this desperate effort unlikely. At times it is necessary to pull the victim over to the side of the crevasse to rescuers below. One way of doing this is to invert a Jumar on the rope to the victim, hang a loaded rucksack or hardware rack on a sling from the rope of the Jumar (now pointing down), and fix a free rope or loop to its bottom (now facing upward). Drop the rucksack into the crevasse until it slides down to the victim, and then pull on the rope as desired — the Jumar will grip the rope right by the victim. Small parties involved in rescues on steep rock or ice should keep this clever tactic in mind.

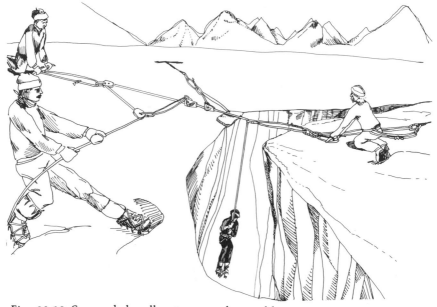

Fig. 23.10 Suspended pulley to ease edge problems.

One story of crevasse rescue argues many points cogently. In late June one year, two experienced climbers left Camp Muir on Mt. Rainier early one morning, attempting the summit by the Fuhrer's Finger route. As they neared the saddle and were closing on the summit at an elevation of about 4200 meters, the lead climber crossed a snowbridge in an effort to gingerly span a major crevasse. He was attempting circumnavigation of the end of the crevasse, tracing a route a previous party had walked successfully.

In order to follow in the leader's path the second had to move to within two or three meters of the lip to establish a boot-axe belay. Unexpectedly the leader disappeared out of sight. Since he was about twenty meters away he fell in a penduluming motion back toward the belayer. The belayer partially caught the fall but the force was so strong that he too was pulled into the crevasse, leaving his ice axe stuck in the snow near the lip.

The leader was lucky. He landed 25 meters down with equal force on both feet and was not hurt. The belayer fell over 35 meters and landed on his side, breaking his pelvis. In spite of this the belayer slowly climbed up to the leader, who was in a better spot for a bivouac. Only the stove was lost during the debacle. They spent the rest of the day chopping a tent platform out of the ice and easing the injured belayer into the tent and his sleeping bag.

Surmounting crevasse lip with one attendant, Mt. Rainier. *Photo Pete Hart*

The next day, their third on the mountain, the lead climber struggled to climb out of the crevasse. He ascended to within five meters of the top but could not negotiate the overhang. The pair scratched a message on a tin can and tossed it out, and even tried burning their rubber crampon protectors to create smoke and attract attention, but to no avail. A great deal of time was spent trying to collect meltwater since the stove was gone. A desperate plan was hatched to tunnel vertically through the overhang if they were not discovered soon.

By midday on the fourth day they were considered overdue and a search began. Fortunately the lone ice axe had been spotted by two local climbers who had investigated; they could not see the bottom of the crevasse nor did they hear answers to their shouts. As the weather was favorable an aerial reconnaissance was requested. On the first pass at 5 P.M. the two were noticed in the hole.

Six rescuers were shuttled up to the crevasse by air and two immediately rappelled into it with an EMT kit and a Stokes litter. The other four set up two self-equalized anchors, each consisting of two snow flukes and one ice axe. A Maasdam hand winch was fixed to one anchor for raising and a friction device to the other for the belay rope. The injured climber was strapped to a backboard and then lifted into the Stokes, in turn moved back in the deeper section of the crevasse better suited for a raising. The winch raised the litter and one rescuer 35 meters in about 45 minutes. The edge was managed with a closed cell foam pad and an ice axe handle or two. Although the raising began well after dark, no special lighting other than individual headlamps was utilized. Getting the litter over the lip required the assistance of one or two additional rescuers but was not a setback.

By 2 A.M. everyone was out of the crevasse and the litter had been evacuated to a helispot at 4270 meters. The weather appeared stable, but alternative plans for a lowering operation were formulated which called for a long, involved mission, especially in bad weather. Shortly before 6 A.M. a MAST helicopter from Ft. Lewis landed and extricated the injured climber.

All aspects of the operation went extremely smoothly, a function of the competence and training of the rescuers and the good weather that allowed helicopters to participate. Yet the account hints at the potential for mishap and tedium inherent in the complicated nature of crevasse rescue. What if the axe had not been seen, or the helicopters unable to fly, or a storm materialized?

BIBLIOGRAPHY

CHAPTER TWENTY-THREE

BRIDGE, RAYMOND. *The Complete Snow Camper's Guide.* New York: Charles Scribner's Sons, 1973.

BROWER, DAVID. *Manual of Ski Mountaineering,* New York: Ballantine Books, 1967.

CASCADE TOBOGGAN AND RESCUE EQUIPMENT, INC. *Ski Rescue Equipment.* 1977-78 Product Catalog. 25802 W. Valley Highway, Kent, WA, 1977.

DESCENT OF THE AIGUILLE DU MIDI.

CHOUINARD, YVON. *Climbing Ice.* San Francisco: Sierra Club Books, 1978.

DUNLEVY, DAN. *Winter Ground Search for Lost Skiers.* La Jolla, Ca.: NASAR paper 77-1010, 1977.

FERBER, PEGGY ED. *Mountaineering, the Freedom of the Hills.* 3d ed. Seattle: The Mountaineers, 1969.

GILLETTE, NED. *Cross Country Skiing.* Seattle: The Mountaineers, 1979.

GRAND TETON NATURAL HISTORY ASSOCIATION. *Mountain Search and Rescue Operations.* Moose, WY, 1969.

K/F PRECISION PRODUCTS. *Product Catalog.* 826 North Winchester Blvd., San Jose, CA 95128, n.d.

MARINER, WASTL. *Mountain Rescue Techniques.* 2d Eng. lang. Innsbruck, Austria: Oesterreichischer Alpenverein, 1963. Distributed by The Mountaineers, 719 Pike Street, Seattle, WA 98111.

MAY, W.G. *Mountain Search and Rescue Techniques.* Boulder, Colo.: Rocky Mountain Rescue Group, 1973.

OSGOOD, WILLIAM AND HURLEY, LESLIE. *The Snowshoe Book.* Brattleboro, Vt.: The Stephen Greene Press, 1971.

PATTERSON, CRAIG. *Mountain Wilderness Survival.* Berkeley, Ca.: And/Or Press, Inc. 1979.

SMUTEK, RAY, "Crevasse Self-Rescue," *Off Belay* 40 (August 1978): 2-7.

TEJADA-FLORES, LITO, AND STECK, ALLEN. *Wilderness Skiing.* San Francisco: Sierra Club Books, 1976.

THOMPSON CARRIER CO. *Product Catalog.* 1742 Butler Ave., Los Angeles, CA.: 90025.

TYROMONT. *Product Catalog.* (Distributor of tragsitz, Akjas, and other European mountain rescue equipment.) Gebr. Kollensperger, Salinegelande, A-6060 Hall, Tirol, Austria.

24 | Avalanche Search and Rescue

AVALANCHES AND GLACIERS posed the earliest mountain search and rescue problems known to history. Strabo, a Greek geographer, first wrote of massive avalanches and the "horrors of falling into chasms abysmal" (crevasses) during his travels from 64 to 36 B.C. The evidence indicates that avalanches caused many deaths and injuries to the armies of Hannibal on his epic crossing of the Alps in 218 B.C. He lost not less than 18,000 men, 2,000 horses, and several elephants to cold and avalanches.

By the Middle Ages several peoples had populated mountain valleys in the Alps. To a large degree life in these remote villages was ordered and controlled by avalanche danger. From the 15th century on there are numerous records of terror and disaster in the Alps. Although the historical record of avalanches in the U.S. is less than a hundred years old it contains equally amazing accounts.

In 1569 an avalanche roared down a slope near Davos, Switzerland and smashed through the ice of a lake with such force that it killed a large number of fish by concussion and threw them out onto land! In 1720 an avalanche descended and killed 237 head of cattle and over 100 people while burying some 60 houses in the village of Rueras in Switzerland. Napoleon's armies lost hundreds of men during their campaigns in the early 1800s, suffering the same fate as Hannibal's armies centuries earlier.

An amazing avalanche hit the village of Trun in Switzerland in 1808. A blizzard lasting three days deposited five meters of snow on the sur-

Cornices, hanging glaciers, and ice fall on the north face of Mt. Deborah, Alaska Range. *Photo Kenneth Andrasko*

rounding mountains. After it cleared the sun came out, precipitating an enormous avalanche. It roared down in a westward direction and destroyed a number of houses, then swept up the opposite side of the valley and devastated a large forest. It then recoiled back east down through the valley and destroyed more forest. It rebounded again to the west doing little damage, but returned *again* to the east where it flattened a half-dozen cowsheds. Back to the west it hustled after that, this time burying a barn full of cattle. Incredibly enough it rebounded once again to the east and flowed over some low hills with enough force to mass again and turn for a fourth and final run to the west to bury houses of the main village to their rooftops as an encore.

Some of the most monumental killer avalanches occurred in South America. On January 10th 1962 in the Santa Valley of Peru an avalanche killed more than 4,000 people. The saddest statistic was compiled by the 1970 earthquake that shook Peru and released a monstrous avalanche that buried the city of Yungay and killed over 20,000 people.

The worst avalanche disaster in the U.S., in terms of the number of people killed, occurred on March 1st 1910, when a passenger train snowbound in Washington state was swept off its track and into a canyon. Ninety-six people died.

Historically a startling variety of methods have been employed to search for and rescue lost souls buried in avalanches. From at least medieval times onward, clairvoyants, magicians, and soothsayers were summoned to locate avalanche victims, although their records of success were never carefully audited. One popular technique of the 17th century involved placing bowls of water along the sides of an avalanche. Pieces of bread were thrown into the bowls, and the manner and position in which the bread oriented itself was somehow interpreted to indicate the whereabouts of the victim. Unfortunately the type of bread required — whole wheat, raisin and oatmeal, a heavy pumpernickel with carraway — is a bit of intelligence lost to the ages.

The origin of the avalanche probe is unclear. It is known, however, that over 2,000 years ago Strabo wrote of seeing wooden staffs carried by the inhabitants of the Caucasus mountains near the Black Sea. Strabo reported that if a person were buried in an avalanche he could push the staff up through the snow and indicate where he was. When the method was reversed is unknown, but clergyman Nikola Sererhard, who lived in the Alps, wrote in 1742 of probing for a victim from the snow's surface. Today there are numerous types of avalanche probes made of metal or fiberglass rods that collapse into pieces to simplify carrying. In case Jean Dixon is unavailable, or the team is all out of French sourdough bread, it is worth studying more pedestrian methods of locating avalanche survivors.

In December of 1886, a young Swiss man set out to deliver a load of flour to a nearby village. It was snowing heavily so he decided to turn back shortly after he and his horse had started, but they found the road blocked by an avalanche. As he shoved his way through a second one raged down, swept him 300 meters, and buried him. A policeman found his horse and sounded the alarm. After the storm cleared 40 workmen began probing for his body. They knew he was dead as they had been unable to search the night before on account of the high avalanche danger, and victims simply did not survive more than a few hours.

Meanwhile below the snow, the young delivery man heard the sounds of the probing but was worried. He knew they were working with heavy, two-person probes used to locate roads and houses. He listened intently to the sounds of the probing growing louder. Suddenly he heard a rod come down close to him. The next time it came down it grazed his shoulder so he hung onto it. The workers at the surface could not pull up the probe despite their best efforts until they suddenly realized why. Franz-Joseph was immediately dug out after his 29-hour ordeal.

Modern research has investigated devices to pick up heart beats, breathing sounds, and body heat. Attempts have been made to make the most of different densities of snow, gravitational fields, X-rays, radar scanning from helicopters, and metal detectors, but with only limited success. Standard avalanche tactics and strategy are still based on probe lines and trained dogs.

The basic principles of search management apply directly to solving avalanche search puzzles. It is the author's personal opinion that many of the principles incorporated into other types of SAR originated in our responses to avalanches.

Thinking About Avalanche Potential

In the 20th century it is rare for a delivery boy to get caught in an avalanche. Unlike many small European countries with huge mountain ranges running through them, the U.S. does not harbor large populations in the mountains. Instead people travel to them for recreational pursuits, although exceptions like Aspen and Vail do exist. Who then gets caught in avalanches?

The best records of significant avalanche activity were collected into a fascinating historical perspective forming the two volumes of *The Snowy Torrents*, (the first volume edited by Dale Gallagher, and the second by Knox Williams). One surprising fact about avalanches becomes apparent after some investigation. Of the 140 documented case studies in *The Snowy Torrents*, a full 44 percent of total avalanche fatalities were winter climbers, mountaineers, or ski tourers according to an analysis by Ray Smutek of *Off Belay* magazine (see the December 1977 issue, page 9). This is a very high percentage for these groups compared to the huge number of other winter recreationalists on downhill and cross-country skis. In recent years the average number of avalanche deaths is about fifteen. Between 20 and 25 per cent of each climbing season's fatalities are brought about by avalanches.

This lop-sided percentage dramatically illustrates the need to develop an awareness of avalanches and related phenomenon. Wilderness avalanche search and rescue presents different problems from SAR in developed downhill ski areas. Instant mobilization and transport to the accident site are absolutely essential due to the short time of victim survival compared to other search and rescue situations (Fig. 24.1). Franz-Joseph was just plain lucky! Immediate, efficient action after notification is the key. Responses to an avalanche report are always of an emergency nature; there is no measured or evaluative initial response.

Avalanche and crevasse SAR are both heavily dependent on the surviving party members — they must take fast and effective measures, unlike in other rescue situations where the injured can be tied off while someone goes for help. Energetic initial search action is paramount in wilderness avalanches, as the search technique for party members is the same as that for an organized SAR group. An organized team has strength in numbers, perhaps better equipment, and can cover a larger area, but the accident survivors have time on their side. It is time that kills avalanche victims even if they are uninjured.

Awareness of avalanche dangers is not enough, though a critical step. Conditions differ constantly with time of day and year. Prevention is by far the best SAR tactic. Mead Hargis suggests what might be called the *chicken technique* — if there is any serious doubt about the safety of a slope or glacier, maybe you should not be there!

These potential hazards appear subtle to the uninitiated mountaineer while a seasoned veteran sees danger signs all around him. Because of the continually changing conditions potential dangers must be checked and eyed constantly. One expert on avalanche forecasting gave his rule of thumb for judging slope stability thus: "There is no one rule of thumb." While this axiom is not useful as a field guide, it is sound advice.

Basically avalanche prediction is all a question of gaining solid decision-making experience in the mountains. Often the problem is the safest route to travel. If there is only one choice, should the group stay where they are and bivouac? What if they have climbed too high too fast and are experiencing altitude symptoms or have an injured member along? Or consider the general rule of never skiing in areas of avalanche danger after a storm — how soon will they be safe? An hour? A day? After it slides once?

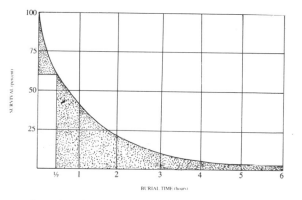

Fig. 24.1 Survival probabilities for buried victims decrease rapidly with time. After half an hour, the victim's chances drop to less than 50%. Courtesy Knox Williams and *Off Belay*.

As mentioned in the Hargis chicken method sometimes one has no business being in an area at all. One May two local Teton climbers decided to climb the east ridge of Grand Teton. No one else was in the mountains as virtually none of the slopes had really slid yet despite the arrival of spring. When they failed to return they were spotted from a small plane, both dead from an avalanche that swept them over 300 meters down a couloir. The warning signs were there.

More frequently a fine trip with a couple of friends deteriorates into survival as a result of the weather or an accident. A friend tells the story of being seven or eight days into an expedition on Mt. McKinley in Alaska. Their base camp was situated on a large glacier not too high on the mountain when a tremendous spring storm hit, dumping almost two meters of snow virtually overnight. Huge avalanches started coming down the steep slopes that rose above the glacier on either side; some ran all the way across the glacier and up the other side of the valley. This became a bit disconcerting. They hastily moved their camp to a position protected by a small rock outcropping, said a full set of Hail Marys, and were fortunate that no avalanches engulfed them. The course of action was clear — dig in and stay put in the safest possible spot until the storm and slides stopped. Alternatively they could have opted for a hasty retreat but might have been exposed to objective dangers on the way out in poor conditions, including the possibility of losing the route. It all came down to a matter of experience and hard-nosed calculation of the odds. Retreat does not always prove the most prudent course.

Avalanche Signs and Symptoms

In the previous chapter on snow and ice SAR the changes and metamorphosis of crystals in a snowpack were briefly discussed, including depth hoar formation. These processes are not as simple as portrayed here. Required reading for anyone traveling into avalanche country is the U.S. Forest Service's superb *Avalanche Handbook* by Perla and Martinelli, which exhaustively details these events. Get a copy and study it.

When a snow-covered slope fails — this is called *an avalanche* — it does so in one of two general ways. One is a loose snow avalanche, and the other is a slab avalanche. Slab avalanches are further classified into soft or hard slap types.

Loose snow avalanches occur on snow slopes lacking internal cohesion, i.e., there are weak bonds among the snow grains. They are most often observed in freshly fallen cold snow, or in very wet snow. The loose snow avalanche begins at or near the snow surface when a small amount of snow is displaced and starts down the slope. This initial mass sets an increasing amount of snow into motion and an avalanche is formed, usually fan-shaped. Loose snow avalanches occur frequently throughout the snow season, and vary in size. Small ones are called *sluffs*, and are symptomatic of slope instability. Watch for them, especially during a snowstorm. The term also refers to continual slides of new snow off of steep terrain during or soon after a storm.

Loose snow avalanches pose a hazard to unsuspecting skiers or climbers because they can easily flow into stands of timber that seem otherwise safe, unless the trees are growing very close together. Finally, a loose snow avalanche generally has a small single point of origin which widens downslope as more and more snow is displaced, in a classic tear-drop pattern. For ski tourers on an open slope, a small loose snow avalanche may not be a direct danger but for a party in a gulley or couloir a loose snow avalanche snowballs into trouble.

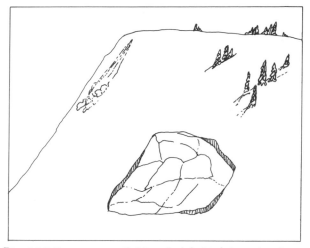

Fig. 24.2 Loose snow (left) and slab (right) avalanches.

On the other hand the *slab avalanche* occurs when relatively large layers or slabs of snow are suddenly released en masse. Slabs form in cohesive snowpacks, thus the slab's ability to propagate a crack upon failure. Slab avalanches are far more dangerous than the loose snow variety and more difficult to predict. A fracture must encompass a significant area in order for it to release. The construction of the snow-pack is one of relatively solid and stiff layers of snow resting over one relatively weak layer, regardless of the solidity of the underlying strata. The overlying stiff layers are stressed mainly because gravity is trying to pull them downhill. If the force of gravity prevails on the stiff layers, the weakest layer fails and the slab breaks free. Or the weak layer may fail, placing sudden stress on the upper layers.

In a *soft slab avalanche* stress comes from new snow deposited with the help of wind, slope angle, temperature, and slope aspect (the direction it faces) in areas of high accumulation. The wetter, denser, and deeper the snow (a function of temperature), the more weight added to areas of high accumulation, stressing the underlying snowpack. Eventually the loading of the slope is so great that the underlying layers rupture, creating a soft slab avalanche.

These release during and just after snowstorms. Watch for sluffs and avalanche tracks on adjacent slopes. Study what happens underneath your feet since your weight on the snowpack replicates, in microcosm, the forces brought to bear on the slope. By listening very carefully, like at a chamber music concert in black tie and tux, you can discern sudden changes in the structure of the music your feet make on the snow. A particularly hollow sound can be investigated at once by a quickly belayed jump or three on the slope, in an effort to crack off a slab or start a sluff.

Slab avalanche in Northern Selkirks, British Columbia. Starting zone, track, and runout are obvious. *Photo Reed Markley*

The ice axe can be used as a lever in whatever nascent cracks exist, to try and push off a small section of slab. Also, the axe can act as a probe to test the resistance of various layers, much the way a blind woman feels for potholes and grass with her cane. Much of the time suspicion about a slope on a climb is first aroused when, in the middle of fleet cramponing or laborious postholing in soft snow, something feels a bit different, and the investigative senses take over from automatic pilot. What is it that has changed? Why? What does it mean both now and on the way back? Usually the best answer is obtained by digging a snowpit and studying the composition of the snowpack.

If the storm has been over for a day or two and the weather is good, be alert for *hard slab avalanches,* often the most difficult to detect. The architect of the hard slab avalanche is strong wind, which forms a hard, dense snowpack. Although you might be able to walk on it, this slab is under stress on steep slopes and can fracture just like the soft slab avalanche. The difference between a safe wind-packed slope and one ready to avalanche may be just one weak but very significant layer.

The best method of evaluating whether a particular snowpack is prone to slide is to dig a *hasty pit.* Use the shovel carried for digging emergency shelters and for recovering your partner in case of an avalanche to dig a trench large enough to let you closely examine the snow layers in comfort without constructing a grave. Someone should have a small 15 or 20 power magnifying glass.

Dig the pit as close as is reasonably safe to the probable fracture line and down to the ground (if possible) or at least to the permanent snow. Examine the differences between the snow layers. Observe the grains of snow through the magnifying glass, especially those layers that appear the largest and loosest. Look for thin strata of ice covered by new snow.

Any snow grains that resemble granulated sugar are probably *depth hoar,* which forms as a result of the great temperature difference between the relatively warm earth compared to the sub-zero air temperatures experienced in the Rockies. The temperature gradient allows snow crystals to grow into larger, rounder shapes through sub-limation. These crystals are like ball bearings and lack cohesiveness and can release under the stress of a meter of new snow. Layers of graupel or hail that never had a chance to consolidate from an early fall storm act like marbles on a slanted playground, capable of sudden release.

Especially after an unusually warm spell and during spring conditions beware of water running through the snowpack. Depth hoar strata in particular relinquish what little cohesiveness they had, propagating large wet slab avalanches.

The value of digging a hasty pit was unsurpassedly set forth by Ron Newcomb of the American Avalanche Institute of Jackson Hole, Wyoming, complete with the slides to prove the story. One winter he was teaching the field technique of safe winter travel and route finding to a group of students. They were touring in the backcountry around Jackson Hole after a new snowstorm had deposited about a meter of powder over the previous twenty-four hours. The class surmounted a ridge that afforded a wistful view into a vast amphitheater of perfect powder snow in crisp, sunny weather. A few sets of ski tracks gracefully descended in linked turns, and one skier was just finishing his rhythmic performance. Spellbound, the class prevailed on Ron to include the bowl on their route. They immediately skied over to the top of it, full of delight in their find.

Just to make doubly sure the alluring run was safe, Ron had them dig a hasty pit; he felt the slope had not completely consolidated yet. The students enthusiastically set to the chore. A major layer of instability was discovered less than a meter below the surface. As they were discussing what this meant — that it could release at almost any time — as an educational exercise, a huge tension crack suddenly appeared, yawned, and ran directly through the middle of the hasty pit while two students were still examining layers! A massive slab avalanche took the bottom half of the pit's wall with it in a grand roar down the potential ski run. All, especially the students in the pit, were duly impressed. There was talk of Ron having psychic powers, and of his using them as a teaching device, but his ordinary humanness in subsequent days quickly put that somewhat frightening idea to rest.

Route Finding

Adroit, knowledgeable decision-making in avalanche country can be more beneficial than instinctual route finding. Most of the judgment required involves specific options of timing with regard to terrain, weather, and slope stability evaluation.

Most avalanches release on slopes between 30 and 45 degrees in steepness. The total avenue of an avalanche consists of three separate elements collectively known as the *avalanche path*. The *avalanche starting zone* or the *fracture zone* ranges at most between 25 to 53 degrees in steepness. The starting zone releases snow down what becomes known as the *avalanche track*, which culminates in the *runout zone*. The slope of the avalanche track varies from the horizontal up to 90 degrees down a rock or ice cliff.

Along with slope angle the slope profile is important — is it concave or convex? A concave slope acts as a good catch basin for snow and is a prime candidate for a starting zone.

Signs of previous avalanches like treeless slopes, a trimline of broken or scarred trees along the edges of a track, or "flag" trees (with branches torn off on all but one side) are warning signs. Do not miss them. One of the best indicators of current danger is the presence of recent or ongoing avalanches on adjacent or similar slopes.

Seasonal weather patterns affect avalanche potential in different ways depending on the massif or range. The Cascades, for example, generally do not develop depth hoar because of the relatively warm, wet winters in comparison to the cold of the Rockies. But normally during the early and midwinter months rapid temperature changes transpire in the early morning and late afternoon, increasing avalanche hazard. Rapid warming increases the water content and viscosity of the upper layers and can melt a weak bond between lower layers, or create enough running water to undermine even very solid top layers of snow or ice. Many north-facing slopes are most dangerous in midwinter as they are prone to the formation of weak layers in their snowpacks, for they remain cold and are slow to stabilize after a storm.

In late winter, midday and afternoon melting on south-facing slopes provides lubrication that increases instability. During summer months sudden snowstorms result in avalanches which are totally unexpected.

A full 85 percent of avalanche accidents occur during a storm or within 24 hours of its end. The storms need not be large; several centimeters of heavy, wet spring snow can trigger major avalanche activity in the right conditions. Persistent cold temperatures hinder settling. If a storm does set in, travel during the first few hours is generally safe except in narrow couloirs, where sluffs can cause problems. After several hours have elapsed a bivouac in a safe place is probably in order.

Along with watching the weather and terrain while traveling *always* monitor the snow's stability. Even if a few days have gone by since a storm, check for settling and cracking snow, graphic illustrations of tension in the snowpack. If no one is about, toss a hefty rock off a ledge onto the suspect slope, or roll down some rotund snowballs.

Hollow-sounding snow is a danger sign. Stamp each new patch of snow with boots and ice axe, listening intently for any change in snow density. The feel of the snow underfoot is another clue. Develop an acute awareness of the subtlest alterations in your environment when in dangerous circumstances. By recognizing that the wind now hits your left cheek instead of your right one in a small cirque, you might realize that the wind circulates unusually there and drops snow in a pattern different from just around the buttress. Take that into account when choosing a route. And above all know how to dig and use hasty pits.

The safest routes are along ridge crests and slightly on the windward side but away from where *cornices* form. Cornices are mushrooms of accumulated snow on the leeward side that grow in successive layers added by each snowstorm and slowly deformed by gravity. If the load of new snow is too heavy the cornice disappears, usually under the strain of a climber walking on its top or during sharp temperature fluctuations.

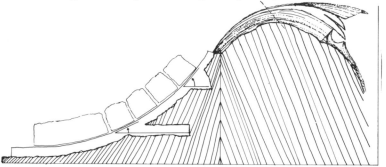

Fig. 24.3 Cornices and snowpack development on windward side of ridge. As slope angle increases and constructive metamorphism occurs in snowpack, stress increases and may produce fracture lines and angular blocks in windslab. Cornice grows on lee side; location of probable fracture line is marked. Adapted from *Avalanche Handbook.*

Cornices tend to sever about 20 degrees toward the ridge from the line one assumes they will break along. Give them plenty of room when climbing along or beneath them (to be avoided at all costs). Frequently cornices form at the tops of couloirs leading up the leeward side of ridges or bowls. Study the route before committing the party to a half-day under cornices. Cornice fracture cracks do make great rapid belay stances just like small crevasses if the conditions are right. Remember that it may be necessary to tunnel up through a cornice up against the solid rock or ice supporting it to exit from a gulley; everyone else except for the kamikaze conscript should be tied in out of the descent path. Far too many superb mountaineers — Hermann Buhl in the Karakorum and Bugs McKeith in the Canadian Rockies, to name but two — have walked off of cornices to their death.

If travel on ridge tops is not feasible, stay out in the bottom of a broad valley far enough from the potential runout zone. Avoid slopes with new or old fracture lines. If one has recently slid, check to make certain it will not slide again. Remember where certain changes in snow density, depth, and formation took place and which slopes slid in what conditions, so that this intelligence can be applied on the way back or the next time you or a friend ventures that way again. Talk to people who have been in the area recently at ranger stations, climbing shops, and ski areas, and pass along information about the conditions you found there.

SUMMIT OF THE MOMING PASS IN 1864.

Be wary of any cliffs, crevasses, or bergschrunds below toward which a small avalanche could sweep the party. Constantly look up above the party, to isolate in advance the dangers that threaten the path ahead. And try not to tell that long story — about how you were all pretty loaded in the High Sierra one snowy night and locked the hutkeeper out of his hut during an all-night storm or whatever — while eating lunch 300 meters below a huge cornice on a warm day.

Remember that leeward slopes, while comfortable to walk in during a storm, accumulate snow from the windward side. Travel from one dense stand of trees and rock outcropping to another, using them as safe zones. Cross each questionable stretch as quickly as possible. When ropes are indicated the belayer should not tie into the rope in case the entire slope goes. Otherwise it is a little like having an aircraft carrier tied to one piling during a hurricane.

If circumstances dictate travel in an avalanche path, think ahead to the possible consequences of a slide. Could you ski out of it? What is the immediate plan of rescue? What will you probe with? How close is help? Review all the possible scenarios, as in entering whitewater rapids on a river trip.

One person should cross an avalanche path at a time while the others watch. Do not assume after the first person is across that the slope is stable, or because there are tracks from a previous party all is well. Likewise, do not decide after crossing it that the slope is stable and will not slide later. Stay as high as possible on the slope to avoid concave starting zones and potential fracture lines — with a little luck you might be able to ride down on top of the slide if it goes, a little like Pecos Bill riding out that plains tornado. If the starting zone must be climbed or descended, do so as quickly as possible, off to one side near rocks and trees that anchor the snow, and straight up or down — not in a traverse that increases exposure and sketches fracture lines.

Everyone should put on his or her *avalanche cord*, a ten- to twenty-meter length of brightly colored nylon cord with markings indicating distance to the victim trailed behind, especially when skiing. If the group has avalanche transceivers, make sure they are turned on and set to the "transmit" setting. Go over how to find someone who is buried with a transceiver. More on these later.

Lastly, pick an escape route to one side of the potential fracture area before entering it. Run, pant, jump — anything goes in crossing a dangerous chute; just get across.

Avalanche Victims

What are the odds of being caught in an avalanche and killed? Of the 140 avalanche cases reported in the two volumes of *Snowy Torrents*, 120 were fatal slides that claimed a total of 173 lives. The ages of the victims ranged between 7 and 66 years, with the average at 27 years old. The majority of the fatal accidents happened in the backcountry, which Knox defined as "any area in which an organized group of rescue personnel lies more than thirty minutes away." Any delay in getting a good search and rescue operation initiated at the scene no doubt significantly decreases the chances of discovering a victim alive (Table 20).

In spite of the relatively small number of climbers, ski mountaineers, and ski tourers (this only includes data through 1971, before the ski touring boom) when compared to the total number of backcountry users in a broad spectrum of winter activities, fully 44 percent of the fatalities were in these three groups. Climbers comprised a sobering 30 percent of the total. One minor consolation is that most killer avalanches are triggered by the victim. The avalanches which do kill people are classified as small to medium in size. An amazing 68 out of 69 killer avalanches were slab avalanches.

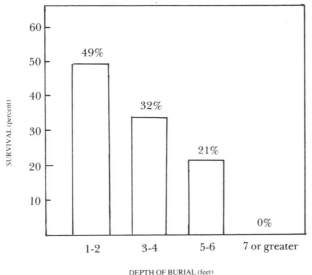

Fig. 24.4 Depth of burial and survival. Used by permission of Knox Williams.

One out of every 10 persons caught by an avalanche is killed, and a completely buried person only has a one-in-three chance of survival. The buried victim (disregarding depth of burial) has only a 50 percent chance of survival if he is not rescued in the first thirty minutes. When considering depth of burial, the odds of survival are significantly decreased (Fig. 24.4). Since it is hard to tell exactly what the victim's probability of survival is in the field, and the extreme cases mentioned in *Torrents* include a burial of over nine hours, rescue efforts must continue unabated.

Table 21

Time Lapse for Avalanche Victim Recovery

	Hours After Accident Before:		
Location	Sounding of Alarm	Arrival of Rescuers At Accident	Discovery of Victim
Developed areas	0.75	1.25	2.5
Backcountry	5.25	10	38
All rescues	3.5	6.25	20.5

SOURCE: Adapted with author's permission from "Portrait of an Avalanche Victim," *Off Belay* 36, December 1977, by Knox Williams.

Most of the people who die in avalanches perish from suffocation, either from snow directly clogging their breathing passages, or from an ice mask freezing around the warm face and curtailing the oxygen supply. Over 66 percent die in one of these two ways, the rest from various traumatic injuries, with head and neck injuries leading the pack.

Surviving an Avalanche

Ray Smutek reviewed both volumes of *Torrents* and noted specific *self-rescue* actions by avalanche survivors that may have meant the difference between life and death for them. Most of the information in *Torrents* was obtained from professional ski patrolers and snow rangers employed in developed recreation areas and charged with daily avalanche control work. Unfortunately the statistics show that a large percentage of backcountry avalanche victims were killed, so the information on survival technique used by these folks was almost nonexistent. What is more, because avalanches in developed areas are generally smaller and the chance of rescue greater than in the backcountry, it stands to reason there should be more survivors there.

Smutek summarized his findings in an article in *Off Belay* magazine (December 1977). He counted twelve cases where using a *swimming motion* was specifically credited with helping a victim survive an avalanche, and only four cases where it was tried without success. In these four cases the victim's skis or poles were cited as the major hindrance to attempting swimming motions. Avalanche swimming seems similar to the axiom that states that the leader should yell "Falling!" before doing so, in order to arouse the belayer from fantasies and slumbers. Sometimes the leader has the presence of mind to consciously

remember this, but other times — luckily — everything happens instinc-
tually. In any event, swimming works.

The value of discarding or *loosening equipment* was not conclusively
demonstrated. In some cases ski poles and skis still attached to the victim
protruded above the surface and led to rapid excavation by friends.
Other times equipment hindered swimming motions and helped pin the
buried victim down. Surviving an avalanche in the backcountry without
skis may still mean trouble, however, if the distance from the road is
great. No firm decision for or against loosening equipment emerged
from the case studies. It would seem that if avalanche cords or the like
were worn to promote visibility in the debris, that removal of encumbrances like skis or heavy packs would allow swimming efforts without
sacrificing their advantages.

Dragging out victim of climbing fall and gulley avalanche on Mt. Washington,
New Hampshire. *Photo Mountain Rescue Service*

One survival rule that did prove valuable was the *construction of an
airspace* in front of the face in some manner. Throwing an arm or hand
up at the last instant to keep snow from packing around the face was the
most common method. In the cases of some of the longest burial times —
one, two, and even an amazing nine hours — all the survivors either consciously or unconsciously created an air space in front of their faces.
One victim was completely buried and could only move his head, which

he simply battered back and forth until a cavern was formed. Another survivor actually ate all of the snow surrounding his face to carve an air space. So, anything goes — just create that breathing pocket. Realize that once the snow sets it will be impossible to move the arms or head to create an airspace.

As in diplomacy, in the underworld, and in going to the ballet, *keeping your mouth shut* is helpful. In many cases the breathing passages fill with snow and are plugged. A survivor who lived to tell of this phenomenon ended up on the surface after the ride, and was able to clear out the snow compressed into hard lumps in his nose and mouth.

Lastly, the technique of *raising a hand*, hopefully to pop through to the surface just before you come to rest, has been credited with saving a number of lives. But do not compromise the ability to build an air space in order to do this.

These basic notions require awareness and presence of mind to perform. The experience of one survivor is revealing.

> To prevent myself sinking again, I made use of my arms in much the same way as when swimming . . . Then I saw the pieces of snow in front of me stop at some yards distance . . . I instantly threw up both arms to protect my head in case I should be covered up. My first impulse was to try and uncover my head — but this I could not do for the avalanche had frozen by pressure the moment it stopped and I was frozen in.[1]

The survivor was soon found and freed by another member of his party, who had to chop him out with an ice axe. The interesting point is that this event transpired in February of 1864 in the Alps. Not much has changed.

As Smutek notes in his review article, "The amount that can be learned from the case histories in the two volumes of the *Snowy Torrents* is almost limitless . . . No snow mountaineer should venture out without the benefit of the knowledge they contain."

Avalanche SAR

You are now crossing a potential avalanche slope, because there are no other feasible route options. You have your pack straps loosened and avalanche cord on, or electronic transceiver turned on and in the "transmit" mode. Suddenly you hear a shout from one of the party and a deep, dull thump. What to do?

[1]Fraser, Colin *The Avalanche Enigma*, London: John Murray, 1966, page 30.

You can try to ski off on a rapid traverse to one side, or if in the center of the slope attempt to place both ski poles uphill and hold them together with both hands close to the ground in self-arrest position, or drop the poles and prepare to start swimming. Good reactions and presence of mind are essential. One's natural reaction is often to stay upright and oriented. If you do get bowled over, try to keep your mouth shut and suppress the desire to yell for help. Protect your head and prepare to create an airspace when you feel yourself slowing down. Once stopped, try to get up or struggle free. In an instant it will be clear whether or not you can extricate yourself; make an airspace then. Consider thrusting a hand through the snow. To find out which way is up, let saliva run from your lips to help orient yourself. Save your energy, and do not struggle after an effort has been made to stand up.

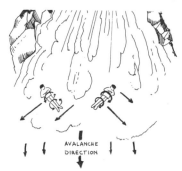

Fig. 24.5 Sideways rolling out of an avalanche. Adapted from Martin Epp and Karrimor.

A second technique for self-rescue from an avalanche and one similar to the swimming method is *sideways rolling.*[2] Some observers and avalanche survivors feel that the swimming motion is difficult to perform and unlikely to produce enough speed to keep the swimmer above the flow's surface. The rolling method maintains the body's original orientation to the slope, encouraging proper orientation both during and after the movement toward the sides of the slope through the flow. Vigorous rolling accelerates the body to a speed faster than the flow of the snow, somewhat facilitating control and steering, and keeping it above or near the surface.

Rolling out of an avalanche is not easy, but is straightforward in

[2]Probably the best description of this technique is contained in a short article entitled "Avalanches" written by Alpine guide Martin Epp expressly for the 1979 product catalog of Karrimor International Ltd., makers of fine alpine sports equipment.

terms of technique. First, as when entering any potential avalanche slope, unbuckle the safety straps on skis, take hands out of the wrist loops on poles, and loosen pack shoulder straps and remove the waist strap, if planning to jettison this equipment. Ski bindings should be set fairly loosely, so they can be instantly released. At all times while on the suspect slope know which side is closest and hence the direction of roll in the event the slope is triggered. When it goes, release the bindings (if on skis) with a quick twist and throw yourself down on the slope, *head uphill and toward the side* of the slope that is the goal of this maneuver. Using the arms and legs liberally to get started, roll rapidly and energetically off to the side and down like a barrel, the way you used to roll down grassy hills as a child. Try to accelerate and definitely keep moving, with the head still pointed uphill. Be sure to persevere — the last few rolls as the snow slows to a halt are the most important ones, and may help you gain the surface with a bit of luck.

As mentioned earlier, avalanche SAR is probably the earliest form of mountain rescue, with the ideas, philosophy, and technique dating back centuries. The basic evolution and order of events in avalanche SAR follows the framework outlined in the first nine chapters of this book.

Preplanning for recreational parties climbing or skiing through in avalanche country is comprised of recognizing and planning for the basic considerations listed below.

Terrain

1. Most avalanche starting zones are on slopes with an angle of 25-45 degrees.
2. Convex slopes are more dangerous than concave slopes.
3. South-facing slopes slide more often in spring and on sunny days.
4. North-facing slopes slide more often during midwinter, when they are not allowed to consolidate.
5. Leeward slopes catch wind-deposited snow and can produce conditions favoring hard slab avalanches.

Weather

1. Consider when the last storm took place and delay traveling at least 24 hours after a storm.
2. Snowfall of 2 centimeters or more per hour creates instability very quickly.
3. Sustained winds of 16 kilometers per hour or more can increase avalanche activity.
4. A temperature increase of 3-5 or more degrees Celsius can make the snowpack very unstable.
5. Rain or meltwater penetrates the snowpack and creates instability.

6. The warmer the temperature during a snowfall, the quicker the snow settles; colder snow settles slowly.

Stability of the Snowpack

1. Sluffs or small, loose avalanches indicate instability.
2. Large snowballs rolling down the slope are a danger sign indicating instability.
3. Tracks made by earlier travelers, including those of your own group moving just ahead, do not mean the area is stable and safe.
4. Cracks or fracture lines in snow slopes indicate instability.
5. Hollow-sounding snow beneath your feet is a danger sign.
6. A probing with ski pole or ice axe helps locate hollow or weak layers.
7. Avalanche activity and recent signs of movement on slopes facing the same direction as a suspect slope suggest unstable conditions on it.
8. Hasty pits help study the layer profile of a questionable slope.

Route Selection and Travel Considerations

1. Stay high and on the top of a dangerous slope and cross quickly.
2. Do not crisscross back and forth on a dangerous slope; instead go directly up or down the fall line, staying to one side or the other as much as possible, and moving hastily.
3. Travel between safe spots like rock outcroppings and dense timber stands as much as possible.
4. Stay off and out from underneath of cornices.
5. Remember that gullies and couloirs are natural avalanche paths.
6. Keep in mind that ridges offer the safest travel routes, on the windward side away from where cornices build.
7. Watch for changes of vegetation that indicate an avalanche track: broken trees, no trees, flag trees, different species of trees, so on.
8. Avoid avalanche starting zones if at all possible.
9. Avoid traveling after the first few hours of a storm. Bivouac if necessary.
10. If reasonable, use a rope and belay across dangerous stretches.
11. Use an avalanche cord or an electronic avalanche transceiver.
12. Carry at least two shovels per party, probe poles, a magnifying glass, and a couple of thermometers.
13. DIG THOSE HASTY PITS!

For organized or professional search and *rescue teams* responsible for avalanche SAR, preplanning involves heavy emphasis on instantaneous mobilization of personnel and necessary equipment into the field. The SAR preplan should be a practical, up-to-date operational guide that identifies members and rapid means of transporting them to any search within the team's area of coverage. The necessity for a quick response is illustrated in table 21, which shows the vast difference of time between the arrival of rescuers at accidents in developed areas (1¼ hours is average) versus in wilderness tracts (10 hours is average).

Because response time to an accident is so critical, it is doubly important that avalanche SAR equipment be well-maintained; stored at a convenient location, preferably close to sources of transportation (helicopter or at least near a winter landing zone, at the top of a developed ski hill, so on); and its use familiar to many SAR personnel. The following items are standard equipment for any avalanche hasty team:

One avalanche probe pole (collapsible or single-piece) per party member plus
    two or three extras
Two aluminum grain-scoop shovels
One electronic avalanche transceiver for each party member
Surveyor's plastic flagging
Willow wands
About a hundred meters of nylon parachute cord
Two-way portable radios with extra batteries
Minimal amounts of personal gear to allow a bivouac
Small EMT kit
Headlamps with extra batteries.

The avalanche preplan should also specifically delineate the search organization, especially field organization at the accident site. The overall structure of authority is much like any forest search, and again one person should coordinate the field activities and serve as the overall SAR leader to allow fast decision-making. Back at base camp or civilization an appointed operations leader handles all requests and questions as they come in from the field via the SAR leader. Direct communication between the two is preferable. The operations leader recruits whatever help is necessary to handle press and media relations, support activities, air and other transport problems, medical concerns and facilities, and so on.

Team leaders assist the rescue leader if the operation demands decentralization of authority because of size or terrain. Two teams can probe two different areas simultaneously or a dog team can work with a probe team if carefully coordinated, for example. The rescue leader is in charge of the field operation, including safety considerations such as posting lookouts, establishing radio repeater stations if necessary, securing and managing a helispot, insuring that the correct support materials are brought in, and so forth.

Notification for a climbing or skiing group involved in an avalanche is simply having a witness or survivor. Anyone in one of these roles, especially in a wilderness or remote setting, is the only chance the others have to survive. Seconds loom large so a survivor or witness *must* take *immediate* action in the correct order. More on this shortly.

First notification of an avalanche accident to an organized SAR team usually leaves them little choice of relative urgency in most circumstances. If the accident has been reported within a few hours or half a day, a *firehouse response* is standard. However notification of an avalanche incident five or six days earlier is a different matter. Regardless, some kind of response by a hasty team is usually merited until it can be substantiated that weather, snow conditions, and location may make a search impossible or seriously limit it.

Fig. 24.6 Overview of avalanche search area management. From *Avalanche Handbook.*

Assuming there is a chance of saving a life, rapid initial *callout* is essential. Ski areas with avalanche danger have preplans that mobilize not only ski patrol and maintenance people, but also other employees trained in avalanche search technique who can get to the scene rapidly. In wilderness SAR this luxury is not possible, but the team must plan an appropriately fast response. This means starting the hasty team into the field before it is completely assembled. If back-up personnel will be arriving soon and are in good communication, this staggered start helps get things moving. During extremely hazardous conditions or when there is a meter of new snow and only two people to break trail, this may not be expedient. At least consider it as a possible strategy.

A *secondary callout* should be initiated after a good-sized hasty team is underway. This secondary callout is for manpower and equipment to serve not only in the field but also in base camp and support positions. Support groups should also have avalanche search paraphernalia, but they carry full bivouac gear as well. Some recommended equipment for support teams includes:

Mountain tents, at least one large enough for victims and two attendants in case
  of bivouac
Litter and evacuation bags
Extra food, stoves, fuel, and related equipment for the entire party
Flares, radio batteries, extra headlamps or large lighting if needed
Complete EMT kit and additional oxygen, drugs, I.V. fluids, whatever.

Avalanche SAR *strategy* has some basic attributes that help establish a contained probability of area. Unlike most other types of search, confinement is not a problem and the boundaries of the search area are usually evident, established by the avalanche. The only bastard search that is feasible is the off-chance that the victim freed himself and staggered to the edge of the avalanche or no one was caught in it in the first place, both unlikely.

Deciding exactly where to search in the avalanche debris is not trivial in the case of a voluminous or deep slide. The theoretical method of doing so (see Chapter 6) is largely inapplicable as there is no victim mobility, and the statistical method of search area determination is only just beginning to see application as more data are aggregated. Most avalanche statistics as yet have no bearing on determining where to dig, but rather are quantified information about victim profile, survival rates, and orientation of body. The subjective system is the one used most often, with the democracy of the Mattson method brought in to help split the odds. Inspection of the accident site, location of clues and natural barriers, and avalanche danger all contribute to the process of deciding where first to look for an engulfed climber.

The *tactics* of avalanche search fall into three broad categories: probing, avalanche dogs, and avalanche electronic transceivers. The first two have been around for centuries, while the last has been a development of the past thirty years. For first arrivals or survivors at the scene of an avalanche accident, there are several initial field tactics which must take place immediately. The first action is determining and marking the point last seen (PLS) of the victim. Look at the surrounding countryside above the work area and quickly determine if another slide is imminent. If reasonable, post an *avalanche guard* to warn those below if another avalanche starts.

Next make a Type I *hasty search* of the avalanche debris for any signs of the victim. This includes probing carefully and thoroughly around any pieces of equipment. During this initial hasty search do not remove equipment or other clues unless necessary. Check uphill from the equipment because surface snow slides faster than the deeper snow that contains the victim. Use whatever is available to probe with — a ski pole, ski, shovel handle, or ice axe — if regular probe poles are not handy.

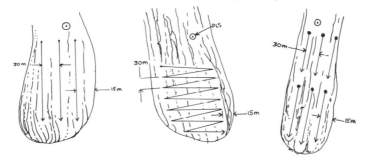

Fig. 24.7 Type I hasty search patterns for one team (left and center) and two teams (right). From *Avalanche Handbook*.

After trying around these visible clues, work over areas with the highest probability of containing the buried victim. Establish a line of travel of the victim, using the PLS and any equipment locations or other observations to project a trajectory of movement. Moving snow has the characteristics of a fluid like water. The avalanche path is similar to that of a wild river, and contains sections of deceleration like the outside of curves, and obstacles that can catch and hold a victim. These areas should be subjected to a quick Type I search and later, if necessary, systematically searched by other Type II and III methods.

In wilderness situations a critical decision must be made after the first few minutes of hasty searching. Should some of the party members (or just one) go for help? Is it more prudent for the search to continue with all personnel, or should one or more searchers be sent for assistance? Along with party size the time that it takes to notify the authorities and for them to return to the scene must also be evaluated. Because the first thirty minutes after a slide are so critical to victim survival, it is probably best to concentrate on an exhaustive, full-tilt search on the spot with all members of the group unless help is very nearby. Avalanches and cold water accidents demand the most immediate, all-out firehouse responses of all SAR situations.

Assuming the victim has not been found and help can be summoned without drastically reducing the effectiveness of the search, or that a hasty search by an organized SAR group has not yielded results, a Type II tactic is in order. Again, the tactics employed are probing, handling dogs, or scanning with electronic avalanche transceivers, or a combination of the three. One big difference in avalanche search strategy that sets it apart from other types is that the effort does *not* start at the PLS and work down, but rather begins at the avalanche debris at the bottom of the slope and works back toward the PLS. Most probably the victim was buried in the spots of heaviest deposition on the flatter portions of the avalanche path and in the runout zone.

In an age of technology, it is amazing that probing is still the most widespread method of searching for avalanche victims. This is especially surprising in the U.S., where trained avalanche dogs are not as readily available as they are in Europe. Numerous areas with high avalanche problems there rely upon on-call trained dogs, while in North America and Britain probing holds sway.

In wilderness search situations, Type II searching proceeds as if the survivors and helpers were working as members of a large, organized group. There are fewer workers less well-equipped, but the basic technique is the same.

Probing is divided into coarse (Type II) and fine (Type III) types, with the ultimate in avalanche searching — trenching — exemplifying an extreme Type III search tactic. A probe line involves twenty or so searchers armed with probes, usually 9 or 12 millimeters in diameter and about three meters long. The probe line advances steadily uphill, the direction that best keeps the spacing and pace even. The flanks of the probe line are marked by flags, surveyor's tape, or string to show what has been searched. Willow wands, once cut from willows but now usually one-meter bamboo garden stakes, solve many marking problems. Sometimes a string is stretched across the toes of the searchers to keep the line neat and orderly and the search as systematic and even as possible. If a strike occurs (a victim strike, not a labor strike against unfair working conditions), a shovel crew following the probe line digs down to investigate while the probe line moves on. The shovel crew also zig-zags around behind the probe line to study and exhume any clues that surface in the foot tracks. Speed is essential. If the search continues over many days or over a large area, a search map should be drawn, detailing which areas have been searched and how.

Coarse probe line. *Photo Sandy Bryson*

In the coarse probing technique, the searchers line up in an elbow-to-elbow spacing with hands on hips. If the number of searchers is limited, space the probers fingertip to fingertip, with the arms extended straight out from the shoulders. Each searcher spreads his feet about 50 centimeters apart. The probe is inserted only once, in between his feet approximately in line with his toes. The probes should penetrate at least two meters or through the avalanche debris to the surface of the snowpack.

The probe-line leader advances in front of the line like a British infantry officer of the 18th century, and gives the commands to the probers. He or she faces the line and watches the tops of the probes as they go in, to notice if one or more is higher than the rest. On his command the line steps forward about 70 centimeters as one unit, and probes once. In fingertip-to-fingertip spacing each searcher probes twice, once to the left side of his body and once to the right. If performed correctly, this method gives the same probability of detection as the first coarse spacing (between the legs). One signal is usually given for each sequence. The probe line leader should keep the line moving as rapidly as possible, to maximize coverage in the first hour.

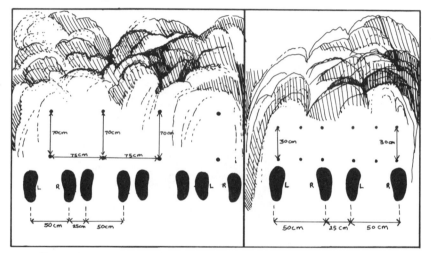

Fig. 24.8 Two fine probing patterns. From *Avalanche Handbook*.

Coarse probing is a Type II search tactic. Some probabilities of detection are listed in the *Avalanche Handbook*, based upon victim detectability, determined by position of burial.

Table 22

Victim Detectability by Position of Burial

Person lying on back or stomach 95%
Person on side 75%
Person in a vertical position 20%
Person in an average position 70%

SOURCE: *Avalanche Handbook*, Perla and Martinelli, page 192.

If coarse probing fails to find the victim, the area can either be reprobed via a coarse probe method, or a fine probe can be started.

Fine probing is a Type III search tactic and is roughly equivalent to a closed grid ground search; the coarse probe approximates open grid search tactics. The spacing is the same as in the coarse probe, elbow-to-elbow while hands are on hips. On command, however, each prober moves forward only 30 centimeters and probes three times instead of once, once in front of his left foot, once in the middle of his feet, and once in front of his right foot. The theoretical probability of detection of a fine probe, assuming one can probe deep enough, is 100 percent.

Fine probe. *Photo Sandy Bryson*

As in the difference between any Type II and Type III search method, the degree of probable detection versus the time required is the major consideration. The *Avalanche Handbook* gives the following statistics. To search an area 100 meters by 100 meters necessitates 20 searchers working a coarse probe line for about 4 hours. The same area can be searched by 20 searchers doing a fine probe in about 16 to 20 hours, four to five times as long. A trained avalanche dog can cover that tract in 25 minutes.

If the victim is still not located after fine probing, the ultimate in Type

III search tactics can occur: *trenching.* This tactic is utilized to locate vic- tims buried under huge amounts of snow who either could not be probed for or have yet to be found. Trenching takes days as it produces rows of trenches wide enough for a person to dig comfortably in, with the distance between trenches usually about one or two meters. The deep slits themselves are dug down to bare ground or to the surface of un- disturbed snow. The trench walls are probed in a systematic manner akin to fine probing. When trenching commences it is assumed that the chances of locating the victim alive are near zero. Lastly, the trenches are dug along the contours of the slope, not across them. Trenching takes days, and generally fosters a large-scale operation. Often the wait-until- spring option should be seriously considered.

This became the solution to a search through an avalanche that killed five climbers in Glacier National Park in 1969. On December 26th five young climbers left the St. Mary's, Montana area to climb Mt. Cleveland, the highest peak in Glacier at an elevation of 3200 meters. The five had been contacted by a local ranger, an experienced moun- taineer, who had warned them of the unpredictable weather and the ex- treme avalanche hazard. He failed to dissuade the five. The last time they were seen alive was when a Canadian resident hired by the group to take them across Waterton Lake (back to the United States) deposited them about five kilometers from Mt. Cleveland.

On December 31st a brother of one of the climbers flew over the Mt. Cleveland area to check on them but saw only fresh tracks interrupted by a new avalanche about half way up the mountain. Other tracks appeared to leave the avalanche but he was not certain of this observa- tion.

On January 2nd 1970 the brother and a Parks Canada warden journeyed to the south end of Waterton Lake but saw no sign of the climbers, who were not thought to be seriously overdue. Later in the afternoon an aerial reconnaissance was flown and two wardens began hiking in, following the climbers' tracks. The air search revealed no visi- ble sign of the climbers but the pilot did see the avalanche on the west face and reported tracks, either animal or human, leading in and out of it.

Early on January 3rd two ground parties headed toward Mt. Cleveland after the two wardens reported finding the group's skis and snowshoes some two kilometers from the lake. One group was to search the northwest ridge route while the other moved up from where the skis and snowshoes were found the previous day. The second group found a camp complete with tents, climbing gear, and a food cache just below the north face of Mt. Cleveland. The tracks continued from the camp into a cirque below the face.

It was apparent that the climbers had run into trouble but still undetermined whether they were alive and on the north or west face of the mountain. A full-scale SAR operation began on January 4th, with technical climbers brought in from Bozeman and Butte in Montana, Grand Teton National Park in Wyoming, and Jasper National Park in Canada.

On January 5th, after a day of briefing, planning, and transportation to the park, five groups were sent into the field to search the north face, the northwest ridge, the upper west face, and the lower west face, and to establish an observation post on Goat Haunt Mountain to scan the entire north face of Mt. Cleveland. The weather had deteriorated. The air search, ineffective over the past few days, was continued although a close inspection of the north face revealed no trace of the climbers. No evidence or clues were found after the first day, but the lower west face and the avalanche debris had not been searched due to the possibility of a higher group starting a slide on top of the searchers.

On January 6th probe lines were established across the north face avalanche debris and a visual search begun on the west face avalanche run out, which now could be safely searched.

In the early afternoon a pack that had been covered by a block of snow was found in the west side avalanche debris. Other groups were introduced to help with the search of this debris. Probing revealed a buried parka containing a camera loaded with film. The film was flown out and processed within the hour but did not reveal new clues.

On January 7th about 80 percent of the west side avalanche had been searched with probes and with a magnetometer (a magnetic avalanche searching device used by Parks Canada) but nothing new was found. The remaining search area was probed the next day, again without results.

On January 9th a major storm struck the area, making further search efforts impossible. By then it was clear there was no hope of finding any of the five alive. A decision was made among the participants, the authorities, and the parents of the climbers to suspend the search until spring. It was a tough but very realistic decision.

The Mt. Cleveland area was closed to the public. Foot patrols were sent into the area every few days in the spring to search for new evidence. On May 23rd a camera was recovered containing film that placed the group on the west face. Over the next few weeks additional pieces of climbing gear and equipment appeared above the icefall and at the toe of the avalanche. In late June it was decided to make a summit climb to see if one or more of the bodies were hung up on the west face, now free of snow. On June 29th five climbers began their ascent. Upon reaching the top of the icefall, the men noted a strong odor that seemed to accompany the melting water flowing from beneath the snow through a tunnel. They looked up the stream course with a flashlight and saw a body about ten meters upstream. The body was reached by digging down through two meters of snow. It was identified as one of the climbers, and had a red climbing rope tied to him. Trenching and probing revealed a second body under four meters of snow.

The final search and recovery efforts began on July 1st. A unique method was devised to search through the deep snowpack: water hydration. A large canvas funnel called a gravity sock (designed for wilderness fire fighting) was placed in a small waterfall with 70 meters of 25-centimeter hose attached to it. Sufficient pressure was generated to spray away the snow and ice, still more than five meters deep.

On July 3rd the three remaining bodies were recovered and the operation was finally over after more than seven months. This incident marked the greatest number of avalanche deaths that have occurred in one mountaineering accident in North America. It appeared that the party either had stimulated the avalanche that killed them or were hit from above when a slope released itself. They were young, talented, ambitious, and unlucky.

Avalanche Dogs

In early March of 1969 a lone car was noticed parked in the lot near the Paradise Visitors Center in Mt. Rainier National Park. A check of the license plate and a few telephone calls revealed that it belonged to a skier who had decided not to sign out for a solo trip to Camp Muir, high on Mt. Rainier. The skier was overdue, and an avalanche had been reported by other skiers along his probable route. A search was started and the route was swept for any signs or tracks, but nothing was found. Avalanche dogs were called in and arrived during the last few hours of daylight. They searched as much of the debris as possible before nightfall.

The next morning the dogs were sent out early. The weather was clear and calm. Within ten minutes, one of the dogs found the victim's body.

In the analysis of this operation in *Snowy Torrents*, case number 69-15, the three dogs were able to cover an area 100 meters by 400 meters in about four hour's time. It was estimated that it would have taken 40 probe searchers approximately eight hours to cover the same area. The value of a team of trained avalanche dogs cannot be overemphasized.

The forerunners of modern avalanche canines have been traced back to the 17th century dogs kept at the St. Bernard Hospice in the Alps. The St. Bernard breed extends back even further to 500 B.C., to animals imported from Tibet by the Greeks. These early dogs were "multi-trained" in a sense, because they were first recruited to guard the hospice from highwaymen and other riffraff. Mountain guides took them along on their outings as companions, and for their uncanny ability to find their way in adverse conditions. The dogs naturally became involved in search and rescue activities. One famous St. Bernard dog who lived in the St. Bernard Hospice in the 19th century, Barry I, is credited with saving more than forty lives, including that of a young child he found lying in the snow. As the story goes, Barry I licked the boy's face until he regained consciousness and was then able to cling to the dog, which half-carried, half-dragged him back to safety!

Trained dogs hasty searching runout area. *Photo Pete Hart*

560 Wilderness Search & Rescue

Surprisingly, legend has it that it was not a St. Bernard but a terrier that first pointed out the value of a dog for deciphering the whereabouts of avalanche victims. In 1937 a Swiss rescue team was called upon to help search for avalanche survivors. One of the rescuers took his small terrier named Moritizli along, probably for the same reasons the early guides took theirs. All the victims had been discovered except one. It was then noticed that the terrier kept sniffing around and returning to one spot already probed. When the dog began to bark and whine, the rescuers reprobed the area and disinterred the last skier — alive.

Spurred by this episode the Swiss Army, with the urging of dog expert Ferdinand Schmutz, sponsored a program to investigate the possibilities of training avalanche search dogs. Currently there are over 500 certified avalanche dogs in Europe, most of them German shepherds.

In the United States avalanche search dogs are not as numerous or as easily obtainable because American avalanche problems are not as serious as those faced by the Europeans. There are, however, many good dogs available, and their location should be known and noted in the SAR preplan, along with how to instantly notify the unit and get them transported to the scene. Prior arrangements and contacts take care of the details and make friends.

Some principles and concepts for incorporating trained search dogs into avalanche work listed in the paper *Search and Rescue Dog Training* by Sandy Bryson, a trainer and dog handler in California. A search dog team (one dog and one handler) can perform both a hasty search and a Type II grid search at the discretion of the operations leader. Avalanche dogs, if available, should go in with the first team. If not, they should be called for immediately after notification. Under conditions of extreme cold or high-wind, the dogs must be worked more slowly and in a much closer pattern, due to the difficulty of detecting a scent. Search dogs and probe lines can work an area simultaneously, maximizing coverage. If a dog has been trained correctly, he can detect the transmissions from an electronic transceiver and will follow them to the source.

Unlike other types of dog-assisted search, scent articles are not used to help find the victim. Rather, the dog is attracted to whatever scent he receives through the snow's surface. Dogs have detected people buried up to five meters deep under ideal conditions. Naturally the wetter and denser the snow, the less likely dogs will be able to pinpoint a victim at such a depth.

How strong a scent is diffused through the snow depends upon several factors, including the depth of burial, snow porosity, and the individual's emotional and physical state before inundation. Time of burial is another element of scent diffusion. Sandy Bryson gives a general guideline of 15 minutes for a scent to travel through one meter of snow but this can vary greatly, especially if the victim is frozen and dead.

When using dogs on a search, transport them to the site by helicopter, snow cat, chairlift, or some other mechanical means rather than having the dogs walk in, if at all feasible. This saves the dog's energy, for a dog needs 15 minutes to recover and get settled down to the business at hand if he has to walk. The work area should be cleared of searchers and equipment as soon as possible and allowed to cool down from all unrelated scents and distractions.

Digging for a find. *Photo Pete Hart*

The dog and handler usually start on the lee side of the search area and work into the wind. Initial tactics surround a quick hasty search during which the dog will hopefully pick up a scent and begin to follow it. When a dog indicates a find he will usually begin digging frantically. A shovel team should join him to speed the extrication process. Unlike in a probe line the dog will not be called off and expected to continue the search. Rather he joins in and is allowed to sniff whatever it was that interested him. Once the object is uncovered, the dog is settled down and started back on his search pattern looking for another scent.

Both multiple dog teams and probe lines can work at the same time, unless an avalanche is very small. It does take good management to maximize efficiency, attending to details like insuring that the probe searcher's scents do not cover the scent of a victim. An avalanche dog is a sensitive animal and tool, but he cannot work miracles. If a mistake has been made, though, it is usually the fault of the handler or the search manager, not the dog. Remember this.

One question always arises: how good is a particular dog? In Europe and Great Britain there is a three-level classification system used to rate or certify each animal. The ratings are simply "A," "B," and "C," with C the highest and most difficult to obtain. It takes a minimum of two years, for example, for a dog to gain an A rating. Some countries additionally give the handler a rating of "M" for mountaineer, which means that not only is the dog skilled but also the handler, identifying a trained, competent mountaineer who can take care of himself in the wilderness. A C rating denotes a remarkable dog, and is awarded by a panel assessing both skills demonstrated during practice and the dog's record of SAR in the field.

Dogs in the U.S. tend to be multipurpose trained, for police work, disaster search, wilderness search, whatever, as there is little need for avalanche specialists. Dog teams are geographically more widespread throughout our vast country than they are in Europe, in part due to the relatively light demand in any one region. This multipurpose training is of great benefit for one dog group can provide a multitude of different services on a year-round basis, promoting good working relations. A disadvantage of this U.S. approach is that there is no single rating system which certifies dogs and handlers. There are excellent teams available; they just have to be recognized before they are needed.

Trained dogs should be used whenever possible in avalanche work, and in regular searches in all terrain. They can eliminate right away the labor-intensive quality of hasty searches as well as Type II and Type III grid searches. Aspects of training dogs are covered in detail in several sources. See in particular the *International Mountain Rescue Handbook* by Hamish MacInnes, *Search and Rescue Dog Training* by Sandy

Bryson, *Avalanche Handbook* by Ron Perla and M. Martinelli, and *The Avalanche Enigma* by Colin Fraser.

Avalanche Transceivers

Professional ski patrolers, ski guides, and backcountry nordic skiers frequently carry a personal electronic avalanche transceiver. If someone is buried in an avalanche, the unit sends out a local signal that can be detected by switching other units onto "receive" and homing them in on the covered transceiver. Any SAR groups anticipating avalanche work should have these electronic units in the rescue cache. A smothered skier can be found within a surprisingly short time if the searchers are skilled, almost artful, with their transceivers.

These small electronic boxes both transmit and receive one radio signal. During a trip each participant carries one and leaves it turned on and in the "transmit" mode when on questionable slopes. In the event of an avalanche the survivors change their units to "receive" and use them to home in on the one lost transmitter. The two most popular models in the United States are the Pieps and Skadi, both on the same 2275 Hz frequency, making them compatible. This signal frequency, however, is not universal, and is not compatible with some of the other transceivers manufactured in Britain, Switzerland, and Yugoslavia.

The Pieps comes from Austria but is available through a number of distributors in the U.S. The older model weighs little, about 200 grams, while the newer Pieps 2 weighs only half that and is 10x7x3 centimeters in size. The manufacturer lists its signal range at about 23 meters; it will transmit up to 20 days with fresh batteries.

The Skadi avalanche transceiver was the first one made. It is designed and manufactured by Lawtronics of Buffalo, New York, and is the choice of the majority of professional ski patrols, snow rangers, and other avalanche managers. Approximately the same size as the Pieps, the Skadi also transmits on 2275 Hz but a little farther (about 32 meters) and is more ruggedly constructed than the competition. A rechargeable battery that need not be removed from the unit operates it. The use of one Skadi for a search has been shown to replace the equivalent of 490 probe searchers! Electronic transceivers also search beyond the normal limits of a probe line. The Skadi has been used from the surface to track people below ground in caves and tunnels and may have some application in caving SAR.

The technique for searching with a transceiver can be summarized as follows. The specific information provided by each manufacturer should be read before the practice sessions begin. Like any piece of equipment familiarity with the transceiver is the key to success, not merely purchasing one and having it along.

When someone is buried, all survivors immediately switch their transceivers to the "receive" mode and put in the earpiece. The point last seen is marked, and depending upon party size and clues, the electronic search commences while a hasty search is made of the sites where equipment was found and of obvious obstacles. Mark the PLS with some equipment or a willow wand and then begin a Type II, open grid search pattern to scour the slope below the PLS. The pattern of the search varies according to the number of searchers and the size of the area (Fig. 24.9).

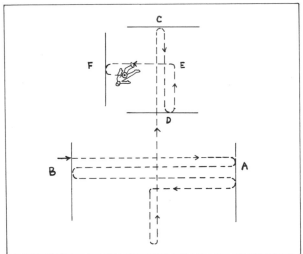

Fig. 24.9 Avalanche transceiver search pattern. From *Avalanche Handbook.*

A signal should be picked up fairly soon. The searcher lets others know he has a signal, but they continue their search in the case of multiple burials. As the signal gets louder, the searcher keeps turning the volume down until the signal fades out. This point (*A*) is marked. He then backs up along the same line until the signal disappears, again turning the volume down as the signal gets louder. He marks this point *B*. He goes to the midpoint of line *AB*, and turns one way or the other 90 degrees, and proceeds along a line perpendicular to *AB*, monitoring the signal as it gets louder, and turning the volume down until it fades.

Point *C* is established. Backing up, the searcher determines point *D*. Again he goes to the midpoint of line *CD*, turns 90 degrees, and starts a new line, *EF*. Each of these lines should be getting smaller and smaller until one is diminished enough that the searcher can hold the transceiver close to the snow and move it back and forth, obtaining an accurate fix. If a person wearing a transmitter is down two meters, one should be capable of pinpointing to within half a meter his exact position. The key to successful performance is field practice, practice, and practice. Don't let this invaluable electronic tool sit on the cache shelf.

Unless the search ends as one of the bastard variety (highly doubtful), some medical considerations are in order. Frostbite and hypothermia set in rapidly in this cold, wet environment. Suffocation rapidly causes death and is far more important a concern than the slower effects of frostbite and hypothermia. Traumatic injuries also cause death but the main considerations are locating and excavating the victim fast. Minutes count; the old rule of 4 to 6 minutes of little or no oxygen to the brain causing permanent brain damage holds true in snow.

Field treatment consists of monitoring and treating all injuries present plus shock. Initial patient assessment must insure that the patient has an adequate airway, is breathing, and is circulating blood *without* forgetting to treat and handle the victim for spinal and internal injuries, not always readily apparent.

Location of a dead victim triggers certain actions in the field regardless of weather conditions. Notification of local law enforcement authorities, the presence of a deputy coroner, and notification of next of kin must all take place in the proper order, as outlined in Chapter 9.

Failure to locate a victim means either he must be left where he lies to be found years later or perhaps never, in the case of remote accidents, or the operation waits until conditions improve later in the week, month, or year to continue searching.

A number of *avalanche schools* throughout the U.S. and Canada conduct intensive technical courses for ski and management professionals. Most combine training in the classroom with extensive field work, and make the otherwise obtuse *Avalanche Handbook* comprehensible. Some of these programs include the National Avalanche School sponsored by the U.S. Forest Service and the National Ski Patrol; the American Avalanche Institute in the Rocky Mountain states and Alaska, P.O. Box

308, Wilson, Wyoming 83014, phone (307) 733-3315; The Mountain School, P.O. Box 728, Renton, Washington 98055, phone (206) 226-2613; and the Sierra Avalanche Seminars, P.O. Box 8, Norden, California 95724, phone (916) 426-3037.

In summary, the cycles of snow and ice formation and movement determine the comings and goings of mountain travelers. In Alaska, for example, it is common practice to climb at night during the long summer days, when the colder temperatures stabilize the snowpack and somewhat diminish the extreme dangers of massive and localized avalanches, rockfall, and shifting seracs and crevasses in glaciers. In many ranges there is a fairly predictable cycle of weather, say storm clouds building in the late morning and snowfall in early afternoon on most days. Persistent attention to the dictates of the local conditions results in the creation of a climbing schedule that circumvents the periods of greatest instability.

Rescue teams in alpine terrain must follow the same logic. Camps must be situated in safe zones behind or on top of towering ice or rock bastions able to withstand the onslaught of major slides. Cornices are avoided, and ropes fixed in gullies to assist in ascent must be rechecked for removal of anchors or rope by periodic slides, and traveled during safe times of day. Timing in snow country very often depends on counting back from the time necessary to pass through a significant barrier or bottleneck on the route ahead or behind: an hourglass of ice or sloppy snow, a gully exposed to cornice debris from far above during the late afternoon, an icefall that splinters off seracs at an alarming rate at just about dinner time. Learn the limitation on passage through these cruxes and then plan the climbing and work schedule around these constraints. The key to managing avalanche travel and SAR work is the recognition that snow and ice are hugely flexible media that fluctuate hourly at the whim of the elements and the sun. One must learn precisely what their condition is at any given time, and accept the changes in schedule and logistics that they demand.

One final tale. In February of 1965 a young carpenter was working in a mining camp high in the mountains around Juneau, Alaska. An avalanche literally snuck up and engulfed him; he never heard or saw it. Fortunately he had a small airspace but he lapsed into periods of unconsciousness. There were over two dozen other workers buried by the avalanche and the search continued for well over 24 hours. Eventually a bulldozer was used to blade away the debris.

At one point the operator stopped when he uncovered something he thought to be clothes. As he bent down to pick it up someone yelled "Hey, watch my legs!" It was the carpenter, and he had been buried for more than 79 hours! He lived with some amputation of his left foot and the fingers of one hand due to frostbite, but the odds said that he should have died long before. While a few lucky ones have the gods on their side, most of us mortals do not. Be careful.

The existence of an avalanche slope does not necessarily mean the route or area is impassable. It does, however, dictate that certain precautions be followed. In this way one minimizes, if not almost eliminates, the problems of avalanche SAR. What avalanche search and rescue really means is to *search* for the safest route and most prudent course of action, and thereby *save* the party from the consequences of poor judgment. Most other rescues are body recoveries.

BIBLIOGRAPHY

CHAPTER TWENTY-FOUR

BRYSON, SANDY. *SAR Dog Strategy.* Published by author, 1978.

BRYSON, SANDY. *Search and Rescue Dog Training.* Pacific Grove, Ca.: The Boxwood Press, 1976.

DARTANNER, W.L., AND GORDON, B.E. "ELT Search," *Search and Rescue Magazine,* Fall 1976, pp. 13-16.

DILTZ-SILER, Barbara. *Understanding Avalanches.* Lynnwood, Signpost Publications, 1977.

FRASER, COLIN. *The Avalanche Enigma.* London: John Murry, 1966.

GALLAGHER, DALE. *The Snowy Torrents: Avalanche Accidents in the United States 1910-1966.* Washington, D.C.: U.S. Department of Agriculture, U.S. Government Printing Office, 1967.

GORDON, BRUCE. "Air and Ground E.L.T. Direction Finding," L-Tronics, 1976.

KIRK, RUTH. *Snow.* New York: William Morrow and Co., 1977.

Avalanche on the peak of Morteratsch.

LA CHAPELLE, EDWARD. *The ABC of Avalanche Safety*. Denver: Highlander Publications, 1961.

LAVALLA, R., FEAR, G., FREEMAN, M., AND McCOY, L. *Stormy Weather Search for ELTs*. La Jolla, Ca.: NASAR paper 76-107, 1976.

LAWTON, PETER. "Experience with Rescue Transceivers," *Summit*, June 1974.

LAWTRONICS. *Product Information*. (On Skadis). Buffalo, N.Y.: Lawtronics, Inc., 1978.

MARINER, WASTL. *Mountain Rescue Techniques*. 2d Eng. lang. Innsbruck, Austria: Oesterreichischer Alpenverein, 1963. Distributed by The Mountaineers, 719 Pike Street, Seattle, WA 98111.

MARTINELLI, M., AND PERLA, RONALD I. *Avalanche Handbook*. Washington, D.C.: Handbook 489, U.S. Government Printing Office, 1976.

PAULCKE, WILHELM, AND DUMLER, HELMUT. Hazards in Mountaineering. New York: Oxford University Press, 1973.

SMUTEK, RAY. "Portrait of an Avalanche Survivor," *Off Belay* 36 (December 1977): 8-12.

WILLIAMS, KNOX. "Portrait of an Avalanche Victim," *Off Belay* 36 December 1977, pp. 5-7.

WILLIAMS, KNOX. *Snowy Torrents: Avalanche Accidents in the United States, 1967-1971*. Washington D.C.: U.S. Department of Agriculture, U.S. Government Printing Office, 1975.

25 | Cave SAR

AS TOM VINES writes in *The Handbook of Cave Rescue Operations*, "Possibly no sport has as intense experience with an environment as does caving. On the surface, one is *on* a trail or *on* a climb. One is very much *in* a cave with a tactile stimuli . . . dampness . . . odor . . . and the vast presence of the earth pressing in as one navigates a tight crawl. Mysticism is a strong part of the caving experience, and in the selection of those who slide from daylight into darkness to explore."[1]

Caves have fascinated Americans for a long time. The Floyd Collins rescue effort in Kentucky mesmerized the entire country in 1925 on account of exhaustive day-to-day coverage by newspapers and radio of Floyd's unsuccessful two-week fight against death while trapped underground. That episode generated a landslide of articles and books and curiosity, and debate over the excesses of yellow journalism. His struggle for survival is perhaps the most classic expression of the rescue experience in any terrain for the lay public in this country.

Much of the rigging, raising, and tactical technique used in cave SAR is the same as that employed in rock or snow and ice rescue as detailed throughout this book; consult the appropriate chapters. Other caving technique and equipment has evolved specifically for life and movement in the unique cave environment.[2]

[1]Smith, Daniel I., ed. *Handbook of Cave Rescue Operations*, Huntsville: National Cave Rescue Commission, n.d., p. 9.

[2]I am indebted to Tom Vines and Robert Barlow for helping me introduce caves and cave problems through adaptation of some of their material, specifically, "Hazards and Rescue Problems in the Cave Environment," NASAR paper # 77-1019.

Caves and caverns can be divided into three broad types dependent upon *speleogenesis* — the way in which they were formed. There are solution, lava, and talus caves, and a few minor kinds like glacier caves.

Solution caves are the most common and extensive all over the planet, and are produced by ground water when it dissolves carbonate rock like limestone. Caves of this sort are very stable for they often run parallel to the rock strata and are not artificially cut across natural bedding planes like man-made mine shafts. The vast majority of solution caves are found in areas of *karst topography* characterized by sink holes, sinking streams, and multiple layers of limestone. The area around the Flint-Mammoth Cave System in Kentucky exemplifies classic karst solution topography.

A common misconception holds that all caves run parallel to the rock strata. In actuality, caves often form along joints resulting from localized tectonic activity that may have no relation to the planes of stratification. Whether or not rock strata are crossed depends upon factors like the density of the rock, the tilt of the layers, local hydrology, and the relationship of the various layers of rock. Vertical caves, for example, often develop when falling water breaks through a resistant stratum of rock and erodes a more permeable layer below. Caves are more stable than mines because caves are formed gradually over millions of years through natural action. The disruptive geological activity — the raising of the region above the water table or earth tremors and faulting — ceased, hopefully, long before the cave is entered. Mines are usually incisions along intrusive veins of a particular mineral composition cut by drilling and explosives that can shatter unsupported bedding, leaving many unstable zones.

A *lava cave* is formed when molten magma cools on the surface but continues to flow underneath, creating a tube. The caves run in the direction of the original flow, and appear similar to a carefully engineered subway tube in their fairly flat and even floors. Lava caves are unstable due to their relative shallowness and are subject to wind and water erosion that loosens debris.

A *talus cave* results from the accumulation of rock debris piled at the base of steep cliffs or deposited by glacial action. Spaces between boulders form passageways and caves occasionally large and interesting enough to be entered.

Caves are total darkness. Total and absolute. Perhaps deep sea divers also experience the sense of being completely surrounded and swallowed by an environment. Along with darkness, caves have a unique temperature and wind environment. Most caves maintain a fairly constant temperature, about equal to the mean annual temperature of the region. For example, a cave temperature around 10°C (50°F) would be an appropriate mean in the middle Appalachians, though too high for New England and too low for the Southwest. Air flow through a cave may be constant, intermittent, seemingly nonexistent, or oscillating. Some caves have "bad" air caused by carbon dioxide or monoxide or local geothermal activity, but most caves in the U.S. breathe adequately and hazardous atmospheres are very rare.

Speleothems in Big Room in Hidden Cave. *Photo James Steinberg*

Since the majority of caves in the U.S. are of the solution type, most are *wet caves*, that is, still in the developmental phase. The moisture level can range from occasional drips to underground rivers complete with waterfalls. As a result, caves are not so much simple passageways as complex labyrinths of incipient, three-dimensional waterways of all shapes and sizes. This wetness combines with steady cool temperatures to produce a high-humidity environment that is a natural arena for hypothermia problems. Therefore, wetsuits are often required on rescues in wet caves. In some caves the water level changes so drastically during a rainfall outside that there is the danger of being trapped and drowned by flash floods. Careful study of the cave map beforehand will reveal spots safe to retreat to during high water. Underground *siphons* occur where the only passage between two areas is through a constricted tunnel of water. Few specialists in cave diving have developed methods to cope with these situations. When someone becomes stuck in a normal cave passage, he simply slips off his gear and pulls it after him. In a water-filled passage this may be impossible. Cave diving rescues are often body recoveries because of the obvious low probability of victim survivability.

After considering that caving occurs in a perpetual state of cool, damp darkness, it becomes evident that cave search and rescue is not simply rock rescue in reverse. Certainly, a large body of technique is shared by both endeavors. Cavers, however, have more gadgets and technique for descending and ascending a standing rope than climbers, and are ahead of them in many aspects of research and development of technical innovations. If a climbing harness and shoes form the basic equipment of a rock climber, then the headlamp is the basic personal tool of the caver. While in controlled circumstances the absence of light may be an exciting experience, in a search or rescue event a mechanical or electric failure may mean extended terror. Hence cavers are experts in certain areas of technique and equipage of less concern to the climbing community.

Underground rock climbing must be done with great care; limestone, dolomite, sandstone, and slate are all relatively weak and unstable. A cave's surface is often wet and covered in mud, and hence does not provide good hand and foot placements. Pitons, nuts, handholds, and entire outcroppings which would normally seem secure can fail under little stress. Luckily caving requires relatively little actual climbing since one initially rappels *down* steep drops from above.

Route finding underground is a challenge. One can normally see only a few feet above or behind, as opposed to a surface climb with its constant reference to landmarks. Orientation is difficult, as passages twist, branch, divide and redivide, and perplex the careless or inexperienced traveler.

One of the most common cave emergencies is, not surprisingly, lost or "temporarily disoriented" cavers. When notification comes in, the situation calls for immediate attention. An appropriate response generally follows the order of events outlined for various types of search and rescue in the other chapters of this book.

First and foremost is the necessity for a cave SAR preplan — one which is current, useable, and realistic. Resources like local caving experts with first-hand knowledge of grotto intricacies should be identified well in advance. At first notification of an accident, these cavers should be contacted and asked to serve as advisors and planners to assist the search boss from the very beginning. Often fairly accurate cave maps unavailable to the public are held by various local organizations or active cavers. Determine if this is the case and incorporate several copies into the preplan along with a listing of phone numbers and locations of other resources, a full set of cave photographs and so on. With a bit of legwork the SAR team can identify local professional or otherwise skilled cavers or those with a working knowledge of particular caves. Meet, greet, and train with these local talents to coordinate basic operational and SAR field procedures. Find out what special equipment may be needed and where it can be located in an emergency. The single best source of information on all aspects of a cave is the local or regional chapter or grotto of the National Speleological Society (NSS). This truly national group is highly organized and circulates maps, information, and slide shows about caves all over the country, and is the focal point of the continuing diplomatic effort necessary to secure and retain access to the many caves found on private or government land. Local grottos meet monthly for the most part, and hence concentrate knowledge about regional caving far more than their relatively anarchistic counterparts in the climbing world. The NSS maintains a National Cave Rescue Commission as well, a source of slideshows and occasional publications about the subject and central clearing house for technique and expertise. More on it later.

The determination of mission urgency and action and resource priority, interview procedures, and appropriate initial response and callout are managed much the same way in cave SAR as in regular searches (as outlined in Part II). However special consideration is given to the uniqueness and dangers of cave environments in general and the specific hazards of the cave in question. Intensive and complete interviewing of a lost caver's friends, associates, and relatives should take place immediately to discover hints in lost person's comments before departure about where in the cave he or she was headed.

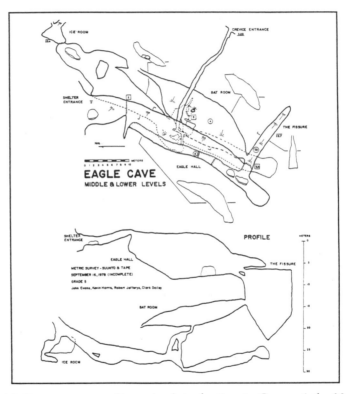

Fig. 25.1 Cave topo map. From An *Introduction to Caves of the Northeast,* National Speleological Society.

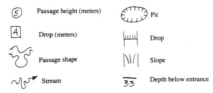

Fig. 25.2 Cave map symbols.

Planning data is compiled and organized in the same manner as any other search and the search organization likewise is comprised of the five basic functions. The establishment of a search area and generation of a search plan are not as easy as they seem on first glance. While it appears that the subject is contained within the cave and that this fact simplifies the search, the extent, diversity, and complexity of most cave systems is baffling to the uninitiated. The difficulty of searching each meander of a cavern in darkness (helicopters and aircraft are out!) with teams of searchers coordinated via poor and complicated communications systems requires that planners be astute cavers. This need for a competent cave SAR overhead team becomes immediately apparent to non-cavers when they enter a cave for the first time. For all of these reasons, the establishment of an accurate point last seen for the victim inside the cave (if possible) is extremely important. All the other search and planning data are critical to the conduction of an efficient and safe cave SAR effort too.

The subjective method of establishing a search area (detailed in Chapter 6) is perhaps the preeminent means of determining where to look for someone in a cave and what tactics to employ. Therefore knowledge of the geography of a particular cave and its history of use and accidents is invaluable. Hidden entrances to certain sections of the cavern may be known only to oldtimers or ardent explorers. The exact nature of each passageway in the cave system even remotely pertinent to the rescue must be well known. Otherwise the cave will have to be studied and explored as the operation evolves, hindering the planning process and increasing the reaction time. Certain stretches of the cave may well be track traps likely to show obvious signs of movement through a constricted spot — a low crawlway or narrow passage. Because many caves preserve signs for years without end due to the absence of weather, the question then becomes whether these are marks made by early cave explorers or other parties, or by the victim.

Certain known hazards like pits, waterfalls, siphons, and canyons should be checked as quickly as possible in case the lost person is trapped, stuck, or injured or will encounter these hazards shortly. The presence of hazards must be made known to the search boss right away by cavers familiar with the topography if the SAR preplan does not identify and locate these features.

The Mattson method of search area determination is also an important tool for cave search if a number of individuals have a solid knowledge of the cave's layout and understand search. Routes and passageways are selected by means of the Mattson method in the same manner as trails or segments of a search area. The possibility of a bastard search (one in which the victim has left the search area) is also considered.

Climbing up waterfall. *Photo Kevin Harris*

If the cave system is one with a well-known history, the statistical approach may be especially useful for predicting victim behavior. For example, most likely novices will be found along well-traveled routes; these should be considered high probability areas when organizing search strategy. On the other hand, experienced cavers may have wandered to more remote and unknown sections of a cave. It may be helpful to learn which parts have been the scene of recent exploratory activity. The behavior of any one victim is often closely related to the history of incidents in and use of a particular cave. The application of the statistical approach to cave SAR is still in its infancy and has not yet begun to even approximate the magnitude and detail of Syrotuck's research studies.

The theoretical method of establishing a probable search area is useful when considering victim mobility and potential travel distances. In caving applications, both are not conceived of as concentric circles from a point last seen (their normal search conceptualization), but rather as distances one might travel in certain passages, allowing for obstacles and terrain. This concept is automatically brought into play during a search in a large cave system or when a subject appears headed for a known hazard. More specifically, is he moving toward Mortimer's Hose and can he be reached before he runs into trouble?

Regardless of which method or combination is used to choose a search area, the underlying concept of binary search theory is still valid and a powerful tool for eliminating parts of a complex whole.

As in avalanche and technical climbing SAR, confinement is not generally a problem except in the case of multiple entrances to a cave. Confinement is possible in this type of cave by checking entrances and posting guards until qualified cavers can be ushered into the cave either as hasty teams or as search teams. Attraction technique like blowing whistles or shouting can be used but often is confusing and does not carry very far in caves, especially if waterfalls abound.

Search dogs, human trackers, trained cave searchers, and electronic and mechanical methods of searching all have been used with varying degrees of success in cave search. Helicopters and aircraft have an indirect role in cave SAR as means of transporting personnel and equipment to and from the scene. Therefore, the idea of cave SAR teams seeking training in air operations is not as absurd as it may first appear.

The most widely used cave search tactic is the open grid, Type II sweep search in which searchers walk or crawl in a configuration that assures an optimal chance of finding clues or the victim. Flagging the edges of the sweep is generally unnecessary due to the natural confinement of passageways, but may be useful in large rooms. More likely flagging and tagging will be used to label passages that have been entered, including details of team, time, and date in order to avoid searching some stretches twice and missing others completely.

All personnel engaged in a cave SAR event must be experienced and well-equipped. A group of searchers, so the story goes, entered a cave in one of the southeastern states a few years back with a large ball of string to trace their journey through the labyrinth. The searchers followed what they felt was the likely route of the lost party and unraveled the string, like Theseus in search of the Minotaur, to facilitate their return. After many confusing route options and hours, *two* lost groups plied the passageways, one of them absurdly dragging a tangled, broken, muddy line behind it. Rescues are not good times to learn skills — there is too much confusion, danger, and inattention to what other rescuers are doing.

Many caving skills involve vertical rope technique: ascending, rappelling, belaying, and generally feeling at ease while hanging free on a rope. The equipment used in raising and lowering systems must be simple, lightweight, and relatively small for transit through narrow passages. Simplicity is the key — moving parts and appendages clog with mud or break. The theory and practice of constructing bombproof anchors must be mastered due to the relatively weak limestone and other rock in which caves form, and the relative absence of flakes and cracks. Every skill must be rehearsed to the point where it can be performed in cold, wet darkness.

Bolts are as important in caving as in mountaineering and are potentially more dangerous. Limestone and other soft rock is difficult enough to secure anchors and protection in without the often humid underground environment which furthers rust and corrosion. Because of darkness, corrosion, moisture, soft rock, and secondary deposition (it is difficult to tell what is solid), the potential for disaster is high. Larger diameter and longer bolts than those used in granite help (two 9mm (⅜″) bolts for belays instead of the standard 6mm (¼″) bolts). Regular 6mm (¼″) Rawl-Drive and larger Rawl self-driving bolts are very common though. Take a hammer with a heavy head if anticipating placing more than an occasional bolt. Due to rapid rusting most bolts are found without hangers, and each party carries its own hangers, nuts, and a wrench or two — take plenty of a wide variety. Homemade hangers cut from angle iron were once popular. (See the section on bolts in Chapter 15.)

Drilling large holes with the appropriate bit and banging baby-angle pitons into them is another protection technique. Soft iron pitons (Cassin, Stubai, Simond, Charlet), the predecessors to modern chromemoly pins, work better in cracks in soft rock (especially limestone) than chromemoly pitons because their softness allows them to deform and fit the crack's irregularities and resist outward pull. Leaving them fixed in place is generally better than banging them out, doing more damage to the rock, and preventing later placements. Because of their plating they resist rusting. However, it is usually far easier and faster to take a lot of chunks of rope for anchors and to simply run a piece 20 or 30 meters back to a huge formation and tie it off than to use any of the above ironmongery. Practice conservation of these formations — called speleothems — though. They take thousands or millions of years to grow back.

After individual skills are developed, team practices should be held on the surface as well as underground, to learn the applications and limitations of personnel, technique, and equipment, and where to go for additional cave SAR support for actual operations. SAR exercises should force participants to wallow in mud, suffocate in tight squeezes, soak in waterfalls, load dirt in the eyes, and knock off and extinguish headlamps at inconvenient times. Beware of hypothermia during practices as well as operations.

The team must learn how to care for the victim. Moving him comfortably and rapidly is difficult above ground and virtually impossible, without practice, below ground. Insulate the victim from *hypothermia* with dry clothes and waterproof coverings, and then wrap him in closed-cell foam pads in the stretcher. Vietnam-style body bags or neoprene exposure bags of waterproof material have been used to good advantage to protect and warm the victim and keep him dry during the usually long and slow evacuation. Space blankets, while popular, seem to offer only the same protection and warmth as plastic sheeting.

Warm food and drinks (carried in thermoses) considerably help warm conscious patients in the early stages of hypothermia, as does skin-to-skin contact in a Polarguard or synthetic pile sleeping bag (down is ob-

viously not useful in wet conditions). More on hypothermia in the
following chapter on medical considerations.

Protecting the subject's face, hands, arms, and legs from injury, and
administrating first aid (with sterile, dry bandages) are problems which
must be managed smoothly in dark, cold, muddy conditions. The key to
rescue work in caves is to streamline and simplify the medical kit and all
related gear as much as possible, and to do the same for all technique.

In Sequoia-Kings Canyon Parks Cave. *Photo David DeMarais*

Repackaging is crucial, and must be thought out ahead of time. Small, lightweight, watertight containers are essential. Soft waterproof blitz packs without pockets that could catch in crawlways and of a smaller size than usual (or repacked into several units) may be necessary. An I.V. unit may not be realistical in tight passages. Some rethinking of surface medical and rescue procedures is mandatory.

The technical equipment for cave SAR is often the same as for cliff evacuations. One basic difference is the use of non-stretch caving rope. All ropes stretch, but caving rope is designed not to absorb energy under loading nor to provide a dynamic belay. Caving involves only a minimum of climbing but frequent ascending and descending on fixed ropes, where stretch is a real nuisance. Pigeon Mountain Industries, Inc. (PMI) rope stretches 2%, versus almost 50% for a laid mountain rope like Goldline. All lead climbing, however, should be done on regular climbing ropes capable of absorbing the impact of a leader fall.

Personal lighting devices are as important to a caver as a swami belt or harness to a climber. The great cave light debate is a classic one among cavers. Each team member must carry a twenty-four-hour supply of light from a helmet-mounted lamp, either carbide or electric, and extra parts and batteries. A carbide lamp uses an acetylene generator that drips water onto calcium carbide crystals to produce a gas that escapes through a burner tip, where it is lit by a striker and its flame amplified by a metal reflector. The flame is a hazard, and can quickly burn nylon ropes, harnesses, or clothes. Most carbide lamps last three or four hours per filling. Extra carbide should be carried in a plastic bottle or other waterproof container. Carbide lamps are still the most traditional and reliable, though electric lamps are gaining acceptance (especially in Britain). Many cavers carry one of each type.

Electric lamps have become more reliable with the development of lead-acid batteries. The most durable are those used by professional miners. The two lamps of that sort most favored by cavers are the Kohler Wheat Lamp and the Mountain Safety Research (in Seattle) lamp, both with lead-acid batteries. Both are fairly expensive — over $80 for lamp, battery, and recharger (either AC for home or DC for charging from a car). The MSR model has the added advantage of windows with float balls that indicate the specific gravity of the acid. The Justrite electric headlamp is operated by four regular alkaline D-cell batteries, and is popular among recreational cavers. Keep in mind that any long caving trip or rescue will most likely require a change of batteries; have plenty available. Lithium batteries, while a much longer and cheaper source of power (over the long run), should be carefully managed in caves as they have been known to explode when wet.

There is also a hazard from battery acid in lead-acid batteries — the acid will instantly severely damage nylon ropes and slings. The damage is very hard to see until it is too late. Electric miner's lamps can spill acid out the vent holes while crawling on one's side. There are more reports of rope, equipment, and body injury from spilled battery acid than from carbide flame damage and burns. The use of polyester slings and harnesses (manufactured by Troll Products) is recommended.

Around Christmas 1977, a group of cavers was descending into a 350-meter Mexican free-fall pit. As the third person rappelled into the pit, the sheath of the rappel rope parted about 30 meters from the top. Luckily the core held and the sheath slipped less than a meter down the rope. The caver completed the rappel to the bottom and the rope was pulled up and retied. The damaged section was preserved and a test a few days later proved that the nylon had been injured by battery acid from a cave light. The only visible damage was a slight discoloration of the rope's nylon yarns. At the damaged spot the nylon could be pulled apart with a few fingers. Somehow a small amount of acid had been spilled in the trunk of the caver's car when the rest of the equipment was piled on top of the rope.

In addition to the primary light source, two independent sources should be carried by each team member, say another headlamp or a waterproof flashlight with spare batteries and bulb, and waterproof matches and candles. The caver must be able to find, operate, and repair these in total darkness.

Unique caving equipment has evolved for vertical rope work. This includes carabiner brake bars, rappel racks, figure eight descending rings, whale's tails, and rappel horns. The brake bar rack is by far the most common. Most of the descending devices are used to increase or reduce friction during long descents, lest the caver gain speed on the way down. Failure to use these variable friction devices has caused problems in some of the 200 to 300-meter rappels climbers have made on rescues in Yosemite.

Cavers have assembled a remarkably diverse body of technique for *ascending* the huge drops encountered in big caves. One of the most memorable methods was a rope ascender powered by a small gasoline engine which straps onto the user (not too good in an energy crisis). Other possibilities are covered in Chapter 13 and in the references listed. Many cavers avoid using Jumars or similar ascenders due to their low breaking strength and the probability of mud caking the cam teeth, causing the ascender to slip.

Tyrolean during Soldier's Cave rescue. *Photo James Steinberg*

The Gibbs ascender, specifically designed for caving, is the most popular ascending device. It is rugged, simple, and works under icy, wet, and muddy conditions if used properly, and its ample rope channel accepts ropes enlarged by the accumulation of mud. The non-spring-loaded Gibbs will follow along on a rope as the climber moves up because the cam action is not spring-loaded, although a spring is optional on the latest model. It has readily been adapted for use in other types of SAR work and on expeditions using fixed ropes because of its strength and sure grip on muddy ropes.

For pitches less than twenty meters, the steel cable ladder is much more efficient as an ascending tool. The aircraft-quality cable and duraluminum steps make these ladders light and without stretch. But their low tensile strength (generally only 300 kilograms) necessitates a full belay whenever they are used, now standard practice in North America and Britain. Ladders are commonly available in ten-meter lengths linked together for longer pitches, and roll up for carrying and storage. The cave SAR cache should stock enough ladders to fix the short drops found along probable rescue routes underground.

If the cave's geography is known, try to plan ahead what equipment will be used at which points in the cave, and send it into the passageway in roughly that order. If a perusal of the cave topo map (Fig. 25.1) reveals three major drops of 30, 65, and 40 meters, then have ropes of roughly that length sent into the cave in that order if a variety of lengths are available. Short ladders are saved for the known and unknown brief drops. If the cave is unknown, then it is probably easier to take long lengths of rope and cut off pieces (or leave whole ropes) as necessary, fixing them in place and continuing.

On rappels and ascents of standing ropes, be certain that the belay rope attached to the caver does not become entangled with the standing rope or progress will halt. And avoid bouncing on the ropes — the anchors are often questionable and there is almost no stretch in caving rope to absorb the load.

Other equipment needed for cave SAR includes a good helmet with a chin strap and a headlamp attachment. Sturdy, warm clothes, gloves, food, water, and other gear sufficient for a twenty-four-hour stay underground should always be carried, along with the usual carabiners, large-mouthed rescue pulleys (the light climbing ones do not accept muddy ropes), slings, runners, large bolts, and a specially modified medical kit. Other basic team gear includes a Neill Robertson style litter, one that can be dragged (e.g., Stokes litter or even a drag sheet made out of an old conveyor belt or such), an exposure bag, a team EMT kit, field telephones, maps, and related hardware.

Clothing needs include wool (not cotton) long underwear tops and possibly bottoms, heavy but loose overalls that allow mobility, wool shirt, wool socks and sturdy lug-soled boots (Vietnam jungle boots are light, cheap, and drain water), and light leather and cloth gloves to protect and keep the mud off of hands for delicate moves. Wetsuits are common in wet cave travel if the cavers' stay will be a long one (over three or four hours). The thinner, lightweight suits are far more flexible and long sleeves are highly restrictive. Synthetic pile sweaters are warm when wet but collect mud and become heavy in wet caves. Goretex gear tends to leak when dirty, and is far too expensive for caving. Cheap raingear under the overalls works best. Essentially clothing should be disposable — the latest in caving fashion is still more or less army surplus. Zippers are the first thing to go in clothes due to mud, corrosion, and freezing. A toothbrush and water (forget the toothpaste) help loosen them.

Because caves often house streams carrying meltwater from above that is colder than the mean temperature inside, hypothermia in the cold and wet conditions is a constant threat, especially in the Northeast. Dress appropriately. Caving harnesses and slings should be made of polyester if available, due to its high resistance to acid damage, marginal strength loss when wet, and low stretch (as noted in the chapter on ropes).

Raising and lowering technique is much the same for cave as for big wall rescues, and often includes the use of a Maasdam rope puller. Power winches generally are not employed underground, nor is a helicopter hoist (it's pretty rough flying in caves . . .). Cave rescue folk, however, should know about working in and around helicopters and other types of aircraft, because of their advantages for transporting rescue teams and victims.

The Stokes litter and the Neill Robertson stretcher are the most common litters for cave rescue work, although British and European cavers have developed some intriguing litters of their own. One ingenious example is designed for moving a victim through water-filled passages, and comes complete with an attached breathing system. The most current and most definitive source of cave SAR information is the *Handbook of Cave Rescue Operations*, edited by Daniel I. Smith and the National Cave Rescue Commission of the National Speleological Society.

Other unique technique includes covering a waterfall with sheets of polyvinyl so that a victim can be hauled up without getting soaked, and temporarily diverting, pumping, and damming water to assist in operations.

Accounts of actual rescues illustrate both proper and unsuccessful responses to particular SAR situations. Two edifying cases follow.

In West Virginia, three cavers were negotiating a mapped cave and descending a ten-meter drop. A rope was rigged, and one of the group rappelled down. The rope broke as the second man descended and he fell, fracturing both ankles and suffering possible spinal injuries. The third caver found his way out of the cave and went for help.

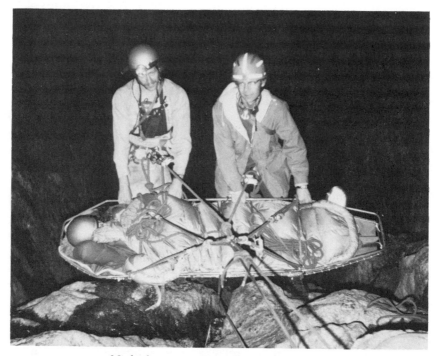

Night lowering. *Photo Jon Kaunupace*

First notice was given to rescue teams at 2 P.M. As few local cavers had been trained in rescue procedures, active cavers responded to the call. Special rescue equipment like a Stokes litter, flexible ladders, and so on was unavailable. Several non-caver EMTs entered the cave with the rescue party at 5 P.M. The EMTs immediately began having difficulties traveling through the cave because of the discomforting environment and their unfamiliarity with caving technique. A physician without caving experience arrived and had even more trouble adjusting to the psychological stress of the tense, dark, unknown situation and topography.

The victim was initially rigged to a backboard in such a way that he would have slid down off of it during the vertical lift. Fortunately this gap in training and field practice was recognized and corrected before any serious damage was done. The medical personnel ended up largely concerned with maintaining their own composure instead of monitoring and caring for the patient. Consequently, the victim's legs brushed both the ceiling and rescuers on a few occasions, painfully converting a closed fracture of one ankle into an open fracture. The patient was finally extracted from the cave at 2 A.M., somewhat worse for the trip out.

In SAR work, we all live in glass houses. Honest, frank evaluations of SAR events are essential. According to a report on this rescue, "All such problems resulted from the lack of underground knowledge on the part of the medical personnel, rather than from improper treatment. Obviously, when underground, standard (surface rescue) techniques need modification."

Another example of cave rescue occurred in Lost Soldier's Cave in Sequoia/Kings Canyon National Park, California. Lost Soldier's Cave consists of around 1000 meters of interconnecting passages and rooms reaching a depth of about 100 meters below the cave entrance. In January 1976 a group of five cavers checked out for a day trip. At 3 P.M., after being in the cave for almost three hours, one of the party members fell three meters and injured his lower back. There was only one route out, through some 130 meters of passages involving two vertical raisings of 10 and 20 meters. Some of the passages were only 30 centimeters wide.

When the initial call came in, Paul Fodor, who had participated in prior rescues in this cave, was briefed over the telephone at home. As he was running out the door, Paul spied a piece of plywood his children were using as a teeter-totter. On a whim he threw it in the back of his truck, thinking it might come in handy later on.

The dozen personnel assembled were either trained cave rescuers or volunteer cavers. An FM radio communication system was set up in the cave during the operation, and worked so well that there were no communication problems. Usually field telephones are installed for cave rescues, necessitating the stringing of wire all through the cave. As the rescue team made its way toward the victim, it quickly discovered that a regular evacuation backboard would not fit through the first narrowing of the passageway. Fodor, who had anticipated this, returned to his truck, grabbed the liberated teeter-totter, a saw, and a brace and bit, and reentered the cave.

The teeter-totter was cut down to the smallest possible backboard that would fit the victim. The brace and bit was brandished to drill tie-down holes for webbing, and the victim was laced onto the backboard. Medication for pain was given, but intravenous administration was not begun because the victim was in very stable condition, with no apparent internal bleeding or manifestations of shock. The I.V. was also deemed impractical in view of the need to keep the bag elevated and the needle in place in the tortuous passageways.

At two of the most constricted sections, the subject had to be removed from the backboard and slid through the crawlway as carefully as possible. A chest harness was tied on to facilitate movement, allowing him to be both pushed and pulled, but he still experienced extreme pain despite the administration of adequate morphine. When the victim was off the backboard, movement was restricted to about ten centimeters per push, interrupted by rests. At times, radio communication was necessary between the rescuers at his head and those at his feet, as the passageway was so tight they could not talk through the two-meter gap. At the first vertical lift, the victim was restrapped onto a conventional backboard and raised by a 3:1 pulley system. The anchors for the pulley rigging and two directionals were tied-off natural formations (speleothems), in some places backed up by climbing nuts. An EMT monitored the victim every step of the way.

The second vertical raising was accomplished with a similar raising system located outside the cave near the entrance, where it was easier to set up and work from safe anchors. The victim was literally pulled right out of the cave into the waiting ambulance, over twelve hours after the accident. The hospital diagnosis revealed no further injuries from mishandling despite high potential for mishap. Patient, skilled team effort performed an intricate extrication in good style.

This second example is only a brief description of one successful operation. In general rock technique for raising and lowering victims, constructing self-equalized anchors, and managing ropes and belays applies to cave SAR work with some modification. Since caves are alien environments requiring considerable skill to negotiate, the details of cave rescue work are best left to publications on the subject and, more importantly, to local or national cave rescue personnel and teams capable of training interested SAR groups.

Cave rescue organizations and operations both have their share of all-too-common SAR problems: command conflicts, late notification, late arrival, credibility gaps between actual and theorized abilities of groups and individuals, equipment malfunction, lack of training and so on. But qualified and experienced personnel are available. The Cave Rescue Communications Network (CRCN), for example, operates in Virginia, West Virginia, North Carolina, and Tennessee and takes calls for rescue assistance in order to dispatch local resources to the scene. The CRCN address is P.O. Box 3063, Charlottesville, VA 22903.

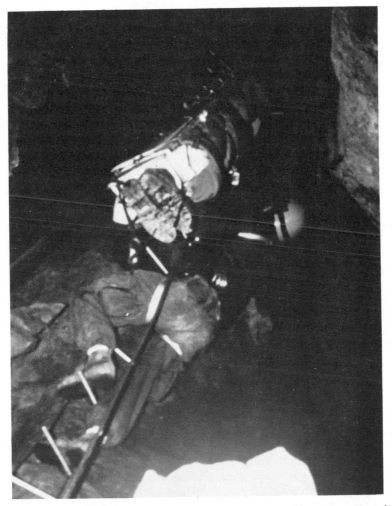

Ascending 20-meter pitch during Soldier's Cave rescue. *Photo James Steinberg*

Information about cave search and rescue resources (or any other kind of SAR resources or assistance) is available on a twenty-four-hour basis from the U.S. Air Force Rescue Coordination Center located at Scott Air Force Base in Illinois. The center has a toll-free (800) number and should be contacted by the local official with legal responsibility for search and rescue. The Scott team cannot direct local or state organizations to do anything, but serves as an invaluable coordination center for connecting local needs and scattered specialized resources.

The National Cave Rescue Commission (NCRC) of the NSS is comprised of a national commissioner and regional directors responsible for developing and carrying out NSS policy on cave rescue. The commission (c/o National Speological Society, 1 Cave Avenue, Huntsville, AL 35810) maintains a resource file of trained rescue personnel and technical equipment organized by region, and keeps an inventory of its own specialized gear. The NCRC also provides liaison between state and local authorities and caving organizations, sets rescue team standards, and offers a curriculum on cave rescue operations. Their annual cave rescue seminar is well attended and changes location each year; recently it has been offered in New York, Texas, and Tennessee. Occasional regional seminars and some local training sessions are also arranged.

Two other useful resources offer a mail-order service for caving publications and equipment: Speleobooks, P.O. Box 12334, Albuquerque, NM 87105; and Bob and Bob's, P.O. Box 441, Lewisburg, WV 24981.

Remember — caves are a world apart from surface settings and present very difficult rescue situations at best. Training and skilled personnel must be cultivated in order to have any chance of a successful SAR operation underground. Happy spelunking!

BIBLIOGRAPHY

CHAPTER TWENTY-FIVE

BARLOW, ROBERT, AND VINES, TOM. *Hazards and Rescue Problems in the Cave Environment.* La Jolla, CA,: NASAR paper 77-1019, 1977.
BLUE WATER, LTD. *Product Catalog.* Fort Lauderdale, Fla., n.d.

HALLIDAY, WILLIAM R., M.D. *American Caves and Caving*. New York: Harper Row, 1974.

MONTGOMERY, NED R. *Single Rope Techniques*. Broadway, N.S.W. Australia: Sydney Speleological Society, 1977.

OWENS, GARY. "A Vertical Caver Looks at Ascending Safety," *Off Belay*, August 1975, pp. 12-15.

SMITH, DANIEL J., ED. *Handbook of Cave Rescue Operations*. Huntsville, Ala.: National Speleological Society. 1978.

THRUN, ROBERT. *Prusiking*. Huntsville, Ala.: National Speleological Society, 1977.

26 | Field Medical Considerations

THE VAST MAJORITY of this book is concerned with three core elements of search and rescue: locating, reaching, and evacuating someone from dangerous circumstances in a wild environment of one sort or another. Yet psychological and medical stabilization of the victim, the fourth core element, may be *the* most important one. Avoiding the complication of extant injuries is a major facet of stabilization. Victim evacuation by moving the injured inappropriately or prematurely, or by convincing the weary or distraught to walk or rappel down terrain they feel reluctant to negotiate is not sensitive SAR management and may seriously upset the equilibrium achieved in the situation thus far. Thus, discussion of stabilization in a SAR event not only focuses on the medical considerations but also on the general management and decision-making strategy.

Fortunately there are many well-written works on field recognition and treatment of specific diseases and injuries penned by physicians with solid outdoor experience. A number of these works are listed in the bibliography for this chapter. Thus these pages do not constitute an attempt at a field medical textbook or a course on crisis intervention but instead a look at the evolution of technique for the problems of diagnosis, treatment, and handling of victims in serious SAR situations.

The environs of SAR work are generally unstable and uncontrollable, and present patient handling complications beyond the obvious problems introduced by the isolation from immediate care and transport. Objective concerns like the response of victims and SAR personnel to all

Climber rescued off the face of Half Dome, Yosemite.

of the above factors collaborate to produce complex and volatile predicaments.

Wilderness Medicine Training

SAR medical personnel must not limit their training to medicine. Experience indicates that many of the best wilderness medicine practitioners were trained as Emergency Medical Technicians (EMTs) after or in conjunction with mastery of the skills of wilderness travel and survival, climbing, skiing, or paddling. Persons schooled in specialty sports readily adapt to the requirements of performing first and second aid in a vast spectrum of circumstances — in a waterfall, a tight squeeze in a dark cave, a blizzard at 4300 meters.

The difficulties of reaching someone in need always become painfully apparent after the first fifteen minutes of running or scrambling up a trail or talus slope carrying rescue equipment, personal gear, and the substantial EMT bag. The access skills become more complicated and essential as the talus or trail grows steeper and the weather erratic, culminating in the sophisticated art of hard technical climbing. If it's winter, dark, or stormy the confidence gained through recreational and SAR experience in similar surroundings may well determine the success or failure of the operation, rather than advanced medical expertise.

The medical training necessary to best complement field skills varies. My own crash training program in administering injectable medicines is not recommended. It involved giving an injection to an injured climber sequestered on an imaginary ledge the night after I had studiously injected sterile water into well-behaved oranges for half an hour, and then injected more of the stuff into the head nurse. Hopefully that program has come a long way since then.

One cannot become overtrained in emergency field medicine. There will, however, always be field limitations on the application of technical knowledge due to a lack of equipment or environmental restrictions. The ability to read EKG strips from a heart monitor will help an EMT recognize and treat cardiac problems, but the available treatment will most likely be CPR rather than cardiac drugs and defibrillation.

Emergency Medical Technician, ParaMedic, and Pre-Hospital Technician programs and registration and certification in national medical organizations vary from state to state. In some states membership in national organizations is not recognized in lieu of state certification.

Find out what the state requirements are and exactly what is offered in terms of training in the area. Talk with local SAR EMTs for advice. The general guideline is to get as much training as possible, but to adapt it to use in your personal specialty.

Ideally any SAR team member should be prepared to handle any field situation. Realistically it is wise to select and refine medical technique and equipment for those injuries and circumstances one is most likely to encounter. Fractures of all types, bleeding, internal injuries, excessive heat and cold injuries, diabetic coma and insulin shock, blisters, high altitude effects, and heart disease, in decreasing order, are the most common SAR medical problems in wilderness areas.

In Yosemite we found that someone with EMT-1 certification (about 80 hours of training) who had completed a specialized NPS Park Medic Program offered through a local hospital (125 hours) was well prepared to manage the demands of first and second aid during rescue events. The park's program provided the background and experience necessary to administer injectable medicines and various intravenous fluids. It also required 40 hours of emergency room experience in a county hospital, insuring practice in patient assessment as well as application and refinement of diagnostic and treatment technique. Some Valley EMTs continued their training by completing a 200-hour advanced cardiopulmonary care course, qualifying them to perform heart defibrillation, read electrocardiograms, and administer advanced cardiovascular drugs.

Medical personnel trained in this manner were able to manage and stabilize injuries until the victim reached the hospital. However, it became necessary for the SAR team to modify EMT field equipment and change some procedures taught in the hospital. More on these adaptations later.

The Field Medical Kit

After a dramatic rise in backcountry SAR in Yosemite in the late sixties it became apparent that a complete artificial environment for victims and rescuers must be transported by the hasty teams: food, shelter, warmth or coolness, and water. Initially the field unit often forgot a sleeping bag to put the patient in or down clothing for the rescuers. Environmental factors may extend the predicted time frame for completion of an operation as well as complicate medical diagnosis and treatment, so survival technique must be second nature for field personnel. It became necessary to broaden the perspective on SAR logistics, and to devise a more universal system of hasty and secondary equipment and support.

The first EMT kit employed in Yosemite operations was a large internal frame rucksack that served as the repository for any piece of equipment someone thought should be along. The crew was set for anything from hypothermia to snake bites to delivering babies underwater. Since the kit contained everything except a foldable helicopter it weighed about 25 kilograms, was virtually without organization, and had no surplus space. We had to dump it out on a ledge and rummage through stuff bags and plastic boxes blowing away in the wind. As it was too heavy we started cannibalizing it when a call came in by dumping its contents on the rescue cache floor and taking whatever seemed appropriate. Meanwhile at the accident scene, when it turned out that the victim had a scalp wound that only *looked* bad and the real problem was two broken legs, the correct equipment was never present and had to be blithely improvised from tree branches or pack parts. This carnival procedure was not too professional.

Organizing an evacuation on Mt. Rainier. *Photo Dick Martin*

Eventually, after enough experience and careful observation of what items were consistently in demand, the crew evolved a core kit. Were two bottles of oxygen mandatory on *every* rescue? Since traumatic injuries to limbs and internal organs were the most common ailments, why was a complete obstetrics kit carried? The SAR crew prioritized the kit according to the types of medical emergencies most likely to be encountered in descending order of probability, as noted above.

A smaller, more pragmatic field EMT kit emerged from this process, cased in a medium-sized pack with an internal frame. The kit was opened like a suitcase by placing it on its back and unzipping one side, and was rebuilt internally to prominently display the equipment in large pockets and stuff sacks. The pack also worked admirably while hanging from a tree or a set of bolts on a cliff. Adequate space was left in the pack to add personal or additional medical gear as the situation required. The first design was realistically considered a working model for field testing, and in fact its contents did change numerous times.

After six months of field trial in this form it was found that despite the room for personal gear the kit was still being carried as a second pack by one of the hasty team members. We decided to pare it down to a smaller kit organized in modules that could be divided among rescuers. This kit is the one presently in use in Yosemite. It contains the items in the accompanying lists.

DIAGNOSTIC MODULE
Scissors
Blood pressure cuff
Stethoscope
Watch with sweep second hand
Penlight
Hemostat
2 Thermometers (clinical & hypothermia)
2 Pr. tweezers
3 Airways (adult, child, and pedi)
1 Bulb syringe
1 50 cc suction syringe and catheter

INTRAVENOUS MODULE
2 1000 cc bags lactated Ringer's
1 500 cc bag 5% dextrose in water

2 Macro solution sets
1 Pedi solution set
2 20-gauge catheter needles
2 18-ga. catheter needles
2 16-ga. catheter needles
2 14-ga. catheter needles
2 19-ga. butterfly needles
2 21-ga. butterfly needles
1 Roll 13mm tape
5 Gauze pads, 5x5mm
10 Band-Aids
10 Alcohol swabs
4 Towelettes
3 Tourniquets

TRAUMA & DRESSING MODULE
2 Triangular bandages
2 Kerlix
4 Kling
6 Surgipads, 20x19cm
3 Rolls of tape
1 Ace bandage
1 Betadine scrub
3 Swabs
6 Towelettes
10 Gauze pads, 10x10mm
10 Band-Aids
2 Steri-strips, 13x100mm
2 Steri-strips, 6x75mm
1 Pr. bandage scissors
10 Ammonia inhalents
1 25x75cm large trauma dressing in pack

SPLINTS
2 Full-leg air splints
1 Arm air splint
1 Ankle air splint
1 Wrist air splint
1 Wire ladder splint

1 Towel for cervical collar
Trauma dressing

DRUG MODULE
Injectable:
2 Meperidine HCL (Demerol) 100 mg.
1 Benadryl 50 mg.
1 Xylocaine (Lidocaine) 100 mg.
2 Narlozone (Narcan) 0.4 mg.
2 Epinephrine (adrenalin) 1:1000 1 mg.
1 Valium 10 mg.
1 25 g. dextrose in 50 cc preloaded syringe
2 Bicarbonate preload
Neosporin ointment
Syringes & needles:
   3 3 cc with needles
   2 1 cc with needles
5 Alcohol swabs

ORAL:
15 Tablets aspirin
10 Tablets Seconal 100 mg.
10 Tablets Dexadrine 5 mg.
10 Tablets Codeine
20 Salt tablets
20 Lomotil tablets
Syrup of Ipecac
Activated charcoal

SIGNAL & SURVIVAL MODULE
Penguin flare gun and three flares
Orange hand-held smoke flare
Military day/night flare
Signal mirror
Whistle
Compass
Knife
Matches
Pencil and pad

Yellow plastic tube tent
2 Space blankets or nylon waterproof tarps
Maps
Toilet paper

One D tank of O_2, which at a constant flow rate of 4 liters per minute will last for about 100 minutes, became the focus of a separate small kit. An oxygen mask and nasal cannula reside there along with three sizes of oral airways, a bulb syringe, and an oxygen tube to fit the small hand resuscitator or Ambu bag, in case the oxygen runs out and the patient has to be hand-ventilated. Two more oxygen bottles are kept strapped onto a Kelty backpack frame along with a positive pressure resuscitator.

Other medical gear such as a Greene splint, Scoop splint, and Hare traction splint, hangs on the same wall as the EMT and oxygen kits, so that everything is in plain view and theoretically nothing will be forgotten.

Two blitz team packs hang near the EMT gear. They contain the following items, listed on a tag wired onto each pack to avoid confusion.

BLITZ PACK #1
Main pack contains:
1 11mm 50-meter rope
1 Swami belt
1 Hammer & holster
1 Pr. aid slings
1 Pr. Jumars
6 Short slings
2 Long slings
3 Prusiks
Nut rack: 1 ea Hex 1-10
            1 ea Stopper 2-8
Bong rack: 1 ea 63, 75, 100cm
CONTENTS OF TOP POCKETS (top flap
    pocket is open & empty; inner
    flap pocket contains these
    items):
1 Belay seat
1 Knife
1 Disposable space blanket

1 Disposable storm shelter
1 Pk. matches in case
3 Penguin aerial flares & launcher
1 Penguin orange smoke
1 Whistle
2 Pulleys
1 Monocular
1 5-watt radio battery
"THIS PACK CONTAINS:
NO water
NO headlamp
NO helmet
NO radio harness"
(Sign taped on pack)

BLITZ PACK #2
Main pack contains:
1 9mm 50-meter rope
1 Swami belt
32 Free carabiners
1 Hammer & holster
3 Prusiks
4 Short slings
2 Long slings
1 Pr. Jumars
1 Bolt kit: 2 holders, 2 drifts, 4
   drills, 6 bolts, 6 hangers
1 Pin rack: 1 ea angle 13-50 cm, 1
   Leeper, 4 long Lost Arrows, 4
   short Lost Arrows
1 Knife blade
1 Sky hook
CONTENTS OF TOP POCKETS (these
   items in inner flap pocket; outer
   flap pocket is open & empty):
1 Belay seat
1 Disposable space blanket
1 Disposable storm shelter

1 Match case (full)
1 Day/night flare
1 Whistle
1 Knife
1 5-watt radio battery
1 Signal mirror
"THIS PACK CONTAINS:
NO water
NO headlamp
NO helmet
NO radio harness"
(Sign taped on pack)

The concept of firehouse response for the blitz or hasty team is simple. When notification comes in of a suspected medical problem, two or perhaps three rescuers are immediately dispatched with the two blitz packs and the EMT kit. Even if there is someone at the scene with a radio to convey information the EMT responds quickly, physically and technologically prepared to reach the victim and begin patient evaluation while the assessment and planning of the full rescue and evacuation effort takes place.

Once the hasty team reaches the victim, the examination results are communicated to the support team and doctors by radio, and additional supplies — more I.V. fluids, oxygen, whatever — are quickly moved to the scene by appropriate means. Planning for the evacuation phase and mobilizing supplemental rescuers and gear continues.

This EMT kit may not be entirely suitable in remote areas or on expedition climbs, where medical equipment must be stockpiled at caches or camps. Given helicopters or other rapid transport, reasonably accessible replacement equipment, and the rapid availability of SAR personnel, the medical kit organization presented here works extremely well in fairly centralized districts.

One July 4 two climbers were beginning the second pitch of the classic Steck-Salathé route (Grade V, 5.9) on Sentinel Rock in Yosemite Valley. As one climber began to lead the second pitch, a rock the size of a bowling ball dropped out of nowhere and struck the belayer in the right leg, breaking his right femur just above the knee. The lead climber made his friend as comfortable as possible on a ledge about one by two meters, rappelled down, and ran for help.

Stabilizing a climber who took a 120-meter fall when his rappel anchor broke. *Photo Tim Setnicka*

An initial blitz team of four rescuers and the reporting climber was sent in motion about twenty minutes after his report. The team consisted of three climbing EMTs and a superb climber. The partner of the injured climber was a medical student who gave an excellent diagnosis, so a traction splint was carried in addition to the standard EMT kit described above. Only basic personal gear, bivouac gear, and ascending and climbing gear was carried. The approach to the base of the climb involved fourth-class (easy roped) climbing up three rock ramps after ascending a substantial talus slope situated about three kilometers up an established trail.

The start of the climb was gained in about one hour. Three rescuers immediately jumared up the rope left in place by the reporting climber during his descent. They found the ledge was barely large enough for the injured climber to lie on, and that his broken leg was supported out in space by a short webbing runner. One rescuer bypassed the injured man and climbed above to position anchors for lowering the victim in a litter when the time came. The other two rescuers assessed the injuries and began putting a traction splint on the leg, all while hanging free on Jumars around the injured party.

Free-hanging EMTs on Jumars splinting leg on face of Sentinel Rock. *Photo Bev Johnson*

A larger support team left the rescue cache about thirty minutes after the blitz team, supplied with a Stokes litter and additional equipment. By that time a request had been placed through Scott Air Force Base in Illinois for a military helicopter, specifically one with winch capability from nearby LeMoore Naval Air Station. A plan evolved to place the injured climber in a Stokes litter, lower him 50 meters to the top of the ramps, move him out as far as possible toward the edge, and have the Navy UH-1N helicopter pick him up with its hoist. Aerial evacuation would foreclose the need for an all-night lowering operation down the ramp system and talus slope, a proceeding that would be extremely difficult, medically counterproductive for the victim, and dangerous for the rescuers.

Before any treatment or stabilization of the obvious injuries (the broken leg and some serious lacerations) was begun, a complete body survey and a patient history were performed as best possible under the circumstances. This examination included a check that the climber had an open airway, was breathing well, had good circulation, and was in stable condition and not likely to suddenly lapse into shock. Special attention was paid to potential head, neck, and back maladies, along with a thorough survey of the chest and abdomen for internal injuries. Vital signs were taken (pulse, respiration rate, blood pressure, so on) and transmitted by radio to a consulting doctor at a nearby hospital.

Injectable Demerol, an analgesic medication, was recommended by the physician but vigorously declined by the climber, who was coping with his pain admirably and was barely in shock. Administering intravenous fluid was considered by the EMTs but the oncoming darkness and problems of managing an I.V. throughout the complex evacuation argued against this treatment, especially in light of the very stable condition of the victim. Some risk was involved but the decision against an I.V. was made in order to assure minimum delays in getting the climber down the rock face and into the helicopter and hospital as swiftly as possible.

The broken leg was immobilized in the traction splint after about fifteen minutes of examination and preparation. By that time two separate sets of anchor points had been established and the litter was hauled up to the ledge and secured. The friction lowering system was clipped into the two anchors, and the victim was slowly eased into the litter. One rescuer transferred his anchor system from the ledge to the litter in order to guide the litter down, correct any difficulties (such as rope hang-ups on flakes), and monitor the patient. The other two rescuers rearranged their tie-ins and became independent belayers, one for each of the two litter lowering ropes. This was all accomplished while the rescuers were hanging free in étriers (webbing foot slings) from nuts and ropes anchored above.

The litter was lowered to the ramp, moved out to the edge while still on belay, and hoisted by the Navy helicopter's winch. The victim was in the medical clinic just over four hours after the accident occurred. The traction splint and a few dressings comprised the total medical treatment required due to the superb mental and physical condition of the injured climber. At his request, no pain medication was given at any point and he never succumbed to shock. Only the most basic EMT technique was necessary in this case, when all went smoothly. But what if bad weather or darkness had caught the operation? Or the Navy helicopter was not available? Or the fracture was compounded by poor litter attendance? Contingency plans must always be meticulous in detail, yet realistic.

Field Medical Notes

The idea of requisite modifications of standard EMT training, experience, skills, and equipment for wilderness SAR work has been broached. There is a great deal more to be said about that subject, but much of it almost instantly descends into highly technical and controversial discussion of specific field practices in certain environmental conditions — when to use diuretics to treat Acute Mountain Sickness or pulmonary edema, for instance. Touching on these subjects and treatments is impossible without fuller explanation of the whole complex of factors affecting any one perceived injury. This takes much more expertise and space than is available to a non-physician EMT SAR manager like myself. No effort is made here to delve into most wilderness medicine topics. Many of the most useful general articles and symposia proceedings are listed in the bibliography for this chapter.

There are, however, a number of medical concerns in SAR work that have been overlooked by the YOSAR team over the years. Some of them are briefly presented below, not so much in an effort to teach about them as to realert rescue personnel to their presence so that further awareness and training can take place. Some of these concerns — like frostbite and AMS and hypothermia — also affect rescue workers during operations, and so are hastily covered to reemphasize their importance. Far more detailed and comprehensive readings are available. Study them. Seek out as much training as possible and a few highly competent physicians to guide the team on medical issues.

Blood Pressure

Some medical procedures work better in the field than others. Trying to take a blood pressure (BP) under extreme conditions, say from a hypothermic snowshoer lying in powder snow during a storm, is difficult verging on impossible. It became apparent that it was better to palpate a blood pressure if there was trouble hearing a regular BP. The technique is uncomplicated. Place the blood pressure cuff in the normal position on the arm and pump it up well past the point where the needle of the dial stops moving with the pulse, usually between 150 and 200mm Hg. Instead of placing the diaphragm of the stethoscope over the brachial artery in front of the elbow, place one or two fingers (not a thumb, because you may read your own pulse) over it. Slowly let the air out of the BP inflation bulb. When you feel a pulse, read the pressure, which will be the systolic. One cannot get a diastolic with this method. The BP is reported as "145, palpated." This technique makes taking a BP less complicated, and still provides a reference point for monitoring a patient.

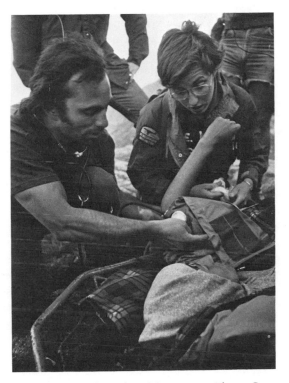

Taking blood pressure in the White Mountains. *Photo George Bellerose*

Falls or Severe Trauma

In treating any injury associated with a fall or other severe trauma, the Yosemite SAR team now *always* puts a cervical collar on the patient. Hidden cervical spinal injuries often occur during injury to the head. A surprising number of basal skull fractures are present in victims who remain conscious, operate normally, and complain about other more painful injuries. On at least three occasions in recent years in Yosemite basal skull fractures were diagnosed and treated at the hospital but were not recognized and stabilized in the field. Fortunately no medical complications resulted, although a change in first aid procedure did — a collar automatically goes on anyone involved in a fall or other obvious trauma to the entire body.

Internal Injuries

Internal injuries initially went undetected during treatment of climbing injuries in Yosemite. The spleen is the most likely organ to be ruptured during a fall, with the liver as runner up. A severely ruptured internal organ generates obvious pain. An I.V. is almost always necessary, because blood is lost from the circulatory system into body cavities. Life-threatening internal injuries may not be obvious in a semiconscious patient or one suffering great pain or severe bleeding. Thus a more analytical examination with the basic EMT kit equipment is essential.

The abdomen is bordered on the top by the diaphragm, on the bottom by the pubis, and, for our purposes, has the navel (umbilicus) in the center. This area can be divided into four quadrants, using the umbilicus as the center and drawing perpendicular horizontal and vertical axes through it (Fig. 26.1). The terms *right upper, right lower, left upper*, and *left lower* identify the quadrants from the patient's perspective.

Organs in the abdomen are classified as *solid* and *hollow*. The liver, pancreas, spleen, and kidney are solid organs, while the stomach, gall bladder, colon, intestine, urinary bladder, and appendix are considered hollow. The solid organs are more prone to rupture and bleeding upon impact. Hollow organs may rupture from trauma and cause severe infection. The likelihood of rupture of solid organs is as follows: the spleen first, then the liver, and finally the kidneys; the pancreas rarely ruptures.

Possible damage to the diaphragm should be considered during the patient examination, as it could cause additional abdominal injuries. This is especially true for chest injuries located between the 5th and 9th intercostal spaces (the muscles between all pairs of the 5th through 9th ribs).

To assess abdominal injuries, first rule out any spinal injury. If a person is unconscious, in severe shock, or feels no pain, *do not* begin to palpate (press down on) the abdominal region. This could cause additional damage.

If spinal, chest, and abdominal injury seem absent, begin the assessment by looking at the abdomen. Check for any asymmetry, extension or distention, wounds, drainage, or other abnormal signs. If damage to internal organs has occurred, internal bleeding may begin, causing an abdominal color change as the blood and fluid flows into spaces between organs.

Other symptoms that may be observed in the patient include pain (note location and severity), nausea or vomiting, localized tenderness, and guarding, the involuntary tightening of muscles into a hard protective shield over an injured area. A complete abdominal examination includes a systematic palpation of each quadrant.

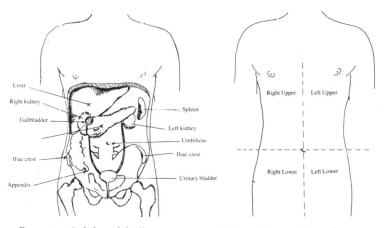

Fig. 26.1 Solid and hollow organs and the abdominal quadrants.

Pain or tenderness in the right upper quadrant without recent injury usually denotes a gall bladder or liver abnormality. Pain there caused by trauma usually suggests damage to the liver, which may be indicated by a Kerr sign, i.e., referred pain in the right shoulder. Pain referred to the shoulders can be the result of anything that irritates the diaphragm (blood or infection) because of the peculiar innervation of the diaphragm. Pain near the back often accompanies damage to the right kidney. Kidney problems are also recognized by blood in the urine and pain in the testicles. Tenderness and pain in the left upper quadrant usually means damage to the spleen, which may have a referred pain in the left shoulder. On rare occasions, the pancreas is injured.

In the lower right quadrant, pain without trauma suggests appendicitis. This is further indicated by rebound pain created by the quick release of pressure created by pressing down on the area. However, rebound pain can accompany any kind of generalized abdominal inflammation. It is an important sign that something significant is going on in the abdomen.

The left lower quadrant is mostly intestine, so pain in this area could indicate a tear of either the large or small intestine. Misinterpretation is certainly possible, as many organs overlap from one quadrant to another.

Finally, it is important to check for a pelvic bone fracture. This is not an abdominal injury, but can be easily checked at the same time the abdomen is surveyed. A fracture of this type is very serious because any displacement may cause abdominal injuries, as well as damage to the veins, arteries, and nerves below or inside the pelvis. Pelvic injuries should be suspected whenever a victim is more comfortable with his legs apart or his knees bent, and experiences considerable pain when his legs are moved together. Also, the patient will usually complain of pain if the surveyor gently places his hands on the illiac crests, the two hip bones next to the skin, and *gently* applies pressure.

The point is to recognize that *something* is abnormal in the abdominal region, rather than exactly which organ or bone. Treatment is relatively simple: stabilize the fracture and replace fluids by I.V. as necessary, to prevent hypovolemic shock caused by internal bleeding. Treatment may also include fluids by mouth and narcotic drugs, but this should be approved by a physician. Narcotics decrease respiration, and make it difficult to evaluate and monitor the patient's condition. Exceptions include long bivouacs or painful evacuations, such as by litter. An EMT cannot directly stop internal bleeding; surgery is required. In sum, make a conscious effort to detect and treat internal injuries along with the more obvious and oftentimes less severe superficial injuries.

Perhaps even more serious than trauma-related injuries are those problems associated with cold or altitude including hypothermia, frostbite, and acute mountain sickness.

Hypothermia

Hypothermia commences whenever the body loses heat faster than it can produce it. There are numerous situations which create the conditions necessary for hypothermia. They are often subtle in nature and creep up on the unwary. River rescue, for instance, during the early summer when the air temperature is above 32°C but the water temperature is around 10°C always produces the initial stages of hypothermia if quick action is not taken. The combination of fast water and the effects of water-immersion hypothermia can drown even a strong swimmer in a short period of exposure. Likewise, classic "English rain" conditions of 5°C and raining are very conducive to rapid loss of body heat.

Hypothermia occurs in stages illuminated in the accompanying table.

Table 23

The Stages and Physical Effects of Hypothermia

FIRST STAGE:	37-35°C (98-95°F)
	● Violent, uncontrollable shivering; fatigue; chills; clumsiness; impaired use of fingers and hands.
SECOND STAGE:	35-32°C (95-90°F)
	● Numb fingers and toes; rigid muscles; obvious gross muscular incoordination.
	● Impaired speech; disorientation; amnesia; apathy.
	● Note: shivering may stop.
THIRD STAGE:	32-28°C (90-82°F)
	● Semiconsciousness; slow respiration; blue skin; weak pulse; cardiac arrhythmia; severe muscular incoordination; irrationality; dilatation of pupils.
DEATH:	28-25°C (82-78°F)
	● Unconsciousness; cardiac arrest.

The prevention of hypothermia centers around guarding against heat loss from the body (through warm clothes and adequate shelter), and increasing heat production by and input into the body (via warm fluids, food, and exercise). This sounds simple but is challenging in adverse temperature and weather conditions.

Treatment of a hypothermia victim includes halting body heat loss and providing mechanisms for internal heat production. The first stage of hypothermia may be reversed by replacing wet clothes with dry, warm ones and introducing hot fluids, like cocoa or soup. In the second stage, the body cannot generate enough heat on its own and needs heat from other sources, a fire or the warmth of an unclad, non-hypothermic body stuffed in a dry sleeping bag with the unclad victim and surrounded by sufficient insulation. Direct skin-to-skin contact is the key. As the subject recovers, hot food and fluids can be fed to him to increase heat production.

Third-stage treatment is more difficult because external body warmth may not be enough to revive him, and he cannot be given warm fluids or food. Since the core temperature of the body is down to 32°C (90°F), all metabolic processes including breathing, heart rate, and brain functions are slowed down. Rapid rewarming by immersion in hot water or even sudden entrance into an overheated cabin can produce shock, causing irregular heartbeats and rates, and possibly halting cardiac output, resulting in death.

On Mt. Rainier. *Photo Dick Martin*

In field conditions rapid rewarming of a third-stage hypothermia victim should be avoided. Rapid rewarming or the introduction of hot fluids can force the cold blood in the extremities back into circulation through the core, further lowering the core temperature. The guideline in the field for the decision between rewarming or not is consciousness — if the patient is unconscious, he should be littered out to a hospital immediately without any further delay. If the patient has some gross muscle coordination and is conscious, and the party has the strength and manpower to carry him out, then he should be rewarmed. The whole party's safety must be considered in a decision of this sort, as overextension of the rescuers in a brutal storm could endanger their lives.

Field rewarming of a moderate hypothermic patient is facilitated by the introduction of hot drinks with a high caloric content. Coffee and tea, due to their caffeine content, are diuretics and do not contribute much liquid; they should be avoided. Active exercising and flexing of muscles helps rewarm a mild hypothermic case. If victim rewarming in sleeping bag or hydraulic sarong is chosen, carefully remove all wet clothes and replace them with dry ones before easing him into the bag. Remove any restrictive clothes or jewelry. Monitor a littered patient's progress continuously as snow accumulation, tight litter straps, and inactivity can encourage body cooling, especially of extremities and splinted fractures. If he is shivering then he is telling you he is cold. Special hypothermia thermometers that read from 75-105°F are available from the eminent mountaineer and high altitude researcher Dr. Charles S. Houston, 77 Ledge Road, Burlington, VT 05401. At press date they are $3.75 each, postpaid. These notes on treatment sketch only the most basic procedures. A great deal of research and writing on hypothermia has been generated in recent years — consult it.

Lastly keep in mind the motto that people are never cold and dead, only warm and dead. Rewarm and resuscitate all hypothermics. Massachusetts General Hospital in Boston had a case not too long ago of a patient who was brought in with a core temperature of 17°C (64°F) and no ECG — but who lived. Don't give up.

One solution to the problem of rewarming hypothermic travelers was developed by members of the Bellingham Mountain Rescue Council in the state of Washington. Treating hypothermia victims is a major concern for SAR organizations in the Pacific Northwest, and frustration over the lack of a good field method led the BMRC to begin work on what was later dubbed their *hydraulic sarong*. The sarong (after a Malaysian garment) is a large (50cm by 115cm) piece of heavy cloth which is wrapped around the patient's midsection and chest and secured with Velcro tabs. Fairly rigid vinyl I.V. tubing (0.95cm inside diameter) is woven back and forth within it, similar to coils in old auto radiators. The joints are bonded with PVC (polyvinyl chloride) cement. The tubing is attached to a small hand bilge pump with a large orifice, which draws water into the tubing from a pot of snow and ice heated over a standard mountaineering stove. The hot water surrounds the body and warms its core, which is able to gradually absorb the heat. The sarong weighs only 1.5kg, and is relatively easy to carry.

The BMRC sarong was first used in December, 1971 on a boy lost while hunting. He had an armpit temperature of 25.5°C (78°F) when found, and had become comatose and begun convulsing. The sarong treatment was started at 5:00 A.M. and continued for three hours, raising his armpit temperature to 27.5°C (81°F). By this time an electric generator and electric blanket had been carried in by support rescuers. These replaced the sarong and continued warming the victim to 32.5°C (90°F) by 10 A.M. He was eventually evacuated and, after a stay in the hospital, recovered with no permanent side effects.

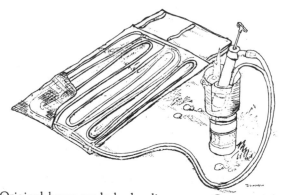

Fig. 26.2 Original home-made hydraulic sarong. Commercial models are now available. Courtesy of *Off Belay.*

British researcher L.G. Pugh has indicated that it takes 578 kilocalories to raise the core temperature of a 70kg person from a hypothermic state of 30°C (86°F) to a normal temperature of 37°C (98.6°F). Tests have shown that, using a standard SVEA 123 stove and Sigg cookset as a heat source, the sarong can deliver 2.5 kilocalories per minute; therefore, just under four hours of sarong treatment would be required in this example. Although the theoretical danger of circulatory collapse during rapid rewarming has been postulated, experience has indicated that this is not a problem for adults who have been hypothermic for a relatively short period of time. Significant shift or deficit of body fluid will not occur during a few hours of mild or second-stage hypothermia, and dilation of the vascular bed of the skin is nearly impossible until the core temperature has risen. However, the patient must be conscious and have some gross motor coordination for the sarong to be considered at all.

A commercially made hydraulic sarong incorporating the same principle of circulating warm fluid around the victim is manufactured by Energy Systems Corporation, 1 Pine Street, Nashua, New Hampshire 03060. This Warm-Rite model uses a catalytic, batteryless generator that produces both heat and electricity. The heat is transferred to a liquid (ethylene glycol) pumped into a full body liner filled with tubing. Electricity made during the process powers the pump. The temperature can be easily regulated by controls but must be carefully monitored to avoid overheating the patient. The Appalachian Mountain Club camp at Pinkham Notch, N.H. has one of these left attached to a packframe in the rescue cache. The power unit is small, 20x18x23 centimeters, and complete with fuel cell and liner weighs only eight kilograms. The generator has been adapted to clip directly onto the midsection of a Stokes litter frame. The unit is compact, lightweight, and a potential lifesaver. Thus far the AMC has only used it as a *preventative measure* during cold weather litter evacuations of victims with other ailments. It does work well for this purpose.

Many wilderness medical authorities argue that use of the hydraulic sarong is not an effective way of treating severe cases of hypothermia in the field because the rewarming occurs from the surface and not the core. The core can be rewarmed with hospital technology and monitoring not available in the field. However the effect can be approximated by rewarming with heat or *hot oxygen* introduced through the breathing passages. This technique has been employed most frequently in Scotland and Wales, with one of the first documented procedures appearing in the *Scottish Medical Journal* in 1971 (vol. 17:83-91, by Lloyd, Conliffe, Orgel, and Walker).

This procedure is still controversial but has been used in field applications with success. One of the major difficulties is locating a hot oxygen unit that will prove reliable in the field. A commercial model was briefly manufactured but was discontinued due to mounting insurance and liability pressures. Fortunately Hal Dunn (Alpine Rescue Team, c/o Colorado Search and Rescue Board, 2415 Maplewood Avenue, Littleton, CO 80121) designed and built an inexpensive field unit.

It is simply a reaction chamber through which oxygen passes on its way from the cylinder to the mask or cannula. The reaction between soda lime and injected carbon dioxide gas produces heat and moisture, both absorbed by the oxygen. The temperature at the mask ranges between 38-52°C (100-125°F), depending upon ambient temperature, length of tubing of the mask, insulation, and other factors. Breathing hot oxygen is described as being similar to breathing the air in a sauna. The specifics of construction, design, and use are available from Hal Dunn. Some critics feel that warmed oxygen treatment results in too much condensation in the lungs, however. Remember if a hot oxygen system is not available, mouth-to-mouth resuscitation provides warm air as well as oxygen to a patient — and it is always on hand. Do not get carried away with technological wizardry that may not prove reliable in field conditions.

Frostbite

Frostbite is another cold injury with severe repercussions if not checked and treated early. Frostbite occurs when the tissues in the body freeze, and ice crystals form from water obtained from inter- and intracellular spaces, killing the cells. Only a very rudimentary discussion follows. Be aware that the cold and altitude injuries mentioned in these pages affect *rescuers* as well as rescuees.

There are three general degrees of frostbite: frostnip, superficial frostbite, and severe or deep frostbite.

Frostnip usually occurs in the tips of the ears, nose, fingers, toes, and on the cheeks. It appears as a sudden whitening of the skin and is not accompanied by pain. Usually someone else notices it before the victim. If its presence is recognized early, there is usually little damage done. Treatment is immediate rewarming of the area by covering it with a wool hat or scarf, blowing warm breath on it, or going inside a warm room. Do not rub anything on frostnipped skin, especially snow. As circulation returns, there is usually a tingling sensation. The skin may turn red, eventually flaking off superficial layers of skin. Use an informal buddy system to stay aware of your own and another's exposure to windchill and cold.

Superficial frostbite is more serious. Affected areas have a white, waxy appearance, and are firm to the touch. Immediate rewarming of the affected area should be begun as soon as possible by removing boots and gently massaging feet for example, and climbing into an insulated sleeping bag. As the area rewarms it may turn a mottled blue or purple and may swell. Pain or a stinging sensation may occur due to nerve damage.

Deep frostbite occurs when frostnip or superficial frostbite goes undetected. Deep frostbite is an extremely serious injury. Major areas of tissue have been frozen and killed, and may lead to infection and amputation. The frozen areas appear cold, pale, solid, and hard. The damage can be compounded by rough handling, which tears and causes further trauma to the tissues.

Field treatment is straightforward but tricky. If the frozen area has been thawed or partially thawed by the time the victim is located it should be maintained in a thawed state. Do not attempt to refreeze or cool down the tissue. Thawing frozen areas is performed in a water bath of about 38-41°C (100-105°F). If possible suspend the frozen parts in the water. No weight-bearing pressure should be allowed. Do not attempt to thaw directly in front of an open heat source like a campfire as the area is insensitive, numb, and easily burned. The temperature of the water bath should remain constant, so relatively large quantities of warm water must be made available and a thermometer used. Several large pots and stoves with high heat output help. Thawing continues until the frozen area flushes red or goes blue. Usually severe pain and even shock accompanies the rewarming process, so be prepared to manage these conditions, as well as the threat of infection. Once thawed the frozen parts need to be protected from weight-bearing pressures and activities such as walking or skiing. Wrap the injured areas in soft, sterile, bulky cotton and dressings to aid healing and insure immobilization, and raise the body part. Soak the injury daily in a warm germicidal soap and water solution. Make every effort to avoid rupturing blisters. Smoking must be prohibited.

The tricky part of frostbite treatment is the decision of whether or not to rewarm. If a helicopter or evacuation team can be relied upon to have the victim off to hospital care soon and the expected time of arrival is within an hour or two, do not try to heat up a whole watershed's worth of snow on mountain stoves to rewarm someone's feet in a mountain tent. A severe case of frostbite in a backcountry cabin in a storm generates no choice but to proceed with rewarming. But if you are in a snowcave at 4700m on Denali during a storm and evacuation means helping someone down to a helispot when the storm clears, and his feet are starting to thaw while waiting, the decision is more difficult. The conventional wisdom is once the frozen area is thawed, do not refreeze, and do not thaw unless continual warmth and litter evacuation are available. It may be necessary to prevent thawing in order for the injured to walk out to the road for hours or even days. Once thawing occurs the intense pain prohibits self-evacuation and may gravely endanger the rest of the party, especially on technical terrain. Very strong pain killers — aspirin, codeine, and morphine — will probably be necessary to enable a casualty to walk out. Be certain to have them in sufficient supply.

Evacuation after plane crash. *Photo National Park Service*

Acute Mountain Sickness

Any time one goes "to altitude," that is 2400-3000m (8,000-10,000') or higher, the resulting decreased atmospheric pressure forces certain physiological changes to take place to insure that the body gets enough oxygen. Each person responds differently to these changes, which often produce adverse side effects known collectively as altitude sickness or, more recently, as Acute Mountain Sickness (AMS).

For the purposes of discussion it is useful to combine three separate problems, as the treatments and symptoms are largely the same for all three for SAR personnel and mountaineers. Dr. Peter Hackett, a leader in the study of AMS through his medical work in Nepal and affiliation with the Himalayan Rescue Association, has written a small but important booklet, *Mountain Sickness: Prevention, Recognition, and Treatment* (published by and available from Mountain Travel, Inc., 1398 Solano Ave., Albany, CA 94706). Hackett's book should be required reading for *anyone* going to altitude. It refers to the three elements of AMS as acute mountain sickness, high altitude pulmonary edema, and cerebral edema.

Acute mountain sickness usually initially takes the form of a headache. Depending upon the individual other symptoms including insomnia, loss of appetite, vomiting, cough, shortness of breath, irregular breathing, tightness in chest, loss of coordination, swelling around eyes and of the face, general weakness, and reduced urine output are signs of AMS. Treatment of mild cases of AMS is straightforward: stop and rest an extra day or night to help the acclimatization process. If the symptoms do not disappear then rapid descent is necessary, usually 150 to 300 meters of elevation change. Reascent can take place after a brief period of rest at the lower altitude.

High Altitude Pulmonary Edema (HAPE) is the collection of non-infection-related fluid in the lungs. The earliest sign is a persistent cough; gurgling sounds heard when an ear is pressed to the chest and the spitting of red sputum are also prominent symptoms.

Cerebral edema, the excessive accumulation of fluids between the brain and the skull and the resultant pressure, is difficult to diagnose. Headaches, uncertain balance, and labored breathing suggest incipient HAPE.

If any of these symptoms appear, usually upon the onset of a headache, they should be closely monitored. Compare the breathing, pulse, disposition, balance, agility, and so on of the suspect to someone healthy. If there is some question as to whether or not the suspect should descend, give these two tests. The first is the classic heel-to-toe walk along a straight line that many law enforcement agencies once used to test for drunken driving. Mild AMS cases can usually walk along a three- or four-meter line without falling or wildly waving their arms for balance. Not so for more serious ones.

The Romberg test for loss of coordination consists of having the suspect simply stand at attention with his eyes closed while someone's arms or members of the group surround him so he knows he will not fall. In 10 or 15 seconds an AMS case will not be able to stand still, and will sway or even fall. If the suspect fails these tests he must descend immediately.

AMS can be divided into three stages: mild, moderate, and severe. *Mild AMS* is characterized by slight headache, some insomnia and loss of appetite, and shortness of breath when exercising. Treatment revolves around awareness of the potential problems. Stop, rest an extra night or day, and sleep and eat well. If symptoms do not disappear, descend and rest for one or more days at a lower altitude until noticeable improvement transpires.

In *moderate AMS* the same symptoms are more intense, and may include reduced urine output. If a day of rest produces no improvement, descend with the victim immediately. Remember that the sooner the descent, the more rapid the recovery, and that descent does not necessarily mean the end of the trip if acclimatization improves.

In *severe AMS* the rapid onset of pulmonary and cerebral edema occurs, and death may quickly follow. Early symptoms for HAPE include but are not limited to breathlessness both during exertion and at rest, increased respiration and heart rate (up 50-100% of normal at sea level), a dry or wet cough, and rales (gurgling) in the chest. Cerebral edema's presence is partially indicated by loss of coordination, determined by the two tests mentioned above.

Hackett advises the mountaineer and SAR team member that, "The point to remember is that the distinction between one and the other is not really important for their significance is the same — death may be only hours away, and immediate action is indicated." What is the immediate action for companions or a rescue party? Hackett lists three treatments: 1) descend, 2) descend, 3) descend! Pretty clear. Make sure that anyone with AMS symptoms is not left alone at camp or allowed to descend alone as deterioration may result in his incapacitation and inability to negotiate even gentle terrain.

With regard to drugs, "There are no medications which we recommend routinely for prevention of AMS. Indeed, we feel strongly that medication for this purpose may be harmful, both because of side effects, and giving one [sic] a false sense of security." But, in emergency circumstances certain medications may be necessary, although their use is controversial at best.

Hackett lists ten drugs he considers useful in treatment of AMS, including oxygen, Diamox, Tylenol, aspirin, codeine, Decadron, Valium, Lasix, morphine, and Phenergan. Most of these are prescription drugs and must be used under a doctor's or paramedic's (or EMT's) supervision. Disadvantages and contraindications accompany the benefits of their use. Most of these drugs are carried in the medical kit of NPS rangers on extended patrols at altitude, e.g., in Mt. McKinley National

Park. Bottled oxygen units are also routinely carried on SAR events at altitude.

The key, of course, is prevention of AMS through a gradual ascent, while preventing dehydration and avoiding overexertion and metabolic starvation by providing sufficient calories. Search and rescue groups face special problems of acclimatization, for they are routinely picked up relatively low and flown up to altitude by plane or helo. In the American West it is common to drive above 3000m to begin a trip or SAR event. One of the classic mountaineering sins — quick gain in altitude with little exertion — is therefore commonplace, increasing the probability of rescuers suffering AMS symptoms.

Because AMS normally takes at least 24 hours to develop, a very rapid rescue at altitude by unacclimatized personnel is possible, though not without risk. Reinhold Messner and Peter Habeler, the Tyrolean superalpinists, have planned several recent successful ascents of 8000m Himalayan peaks (Hidden Peak, Everest, and Nanga Parbat) on the assumption that a superbly conditioned climber can climb high and return fast enough to avoid AMS problems by simply finishing and descending before their onset. If the operation is going to be an extended one, rescuers may have to be landed low and walk up in order to begin acclimatization.

Rescues are better performed at altitude by climbers already there or ones who have been at altitude recently (within the last month at most). It appears that one loses the accumulated red blood cells that enable additional oxygen to be carried through the bloodstream at the same rate that they are originally acquired during acclimatization. Research suggests that the body usually adapts to a particular elevation in about two weeks; after that, little improvement is noted. Therefore, someone who was at altitude within the last fortnight and was there long enough for the body to at least begin acclimatization, can probably return suddenly to that elevation with a higher than average probability of avoiding acute AMS symptoms. Every individual responds to altitude differently, and does not know how until he or she has ventured there. If one has had problems in the past at a certain elevation, then it is quite likely that he or she will experience difficulties again upon return there. Anyone with a record of a bout with pneumonia or other respiratory problems within the past several years, or who is under the age of 25, is especially prone to pulmonary edema.

SAR personnel and team leaders should carefully assess their own and others rates of adaptation to altitude, and take this into account during callout. Multi-day training climbs reveal how one's body performs. Likewise, alternative transportation and operations plans should be considered if the event unfolds on high, flat terrain with relatively few easy, steep descent routes. If a helo lands a team on a plateau at 4000m, there will be little recourse for a rescuer or rescuee with sudden AMS symptoms other than helo evacuation, and no escape in a storm.

In sum, 1) know how you and others perform at altitude; 2) take this into account when planning a trip or event; 3) watch others carefully for symptoms when at altitude — loss of balance, cough, increased respiratory rate, loss of appetite; 4) proceed at an appropriate rate of ascent and rest when necessary; and 5) descend immediately if any abnormalities develop.

In sum SAR field medicine is highly complex and requires considerable study and practice. It is wise to completely rethink the medical field kit and methods for SAR events in all manner of terrain. One watchword to keep in mind is a traditional one — KISS, Keep It Simple, Stupid! If the field team cannot logistically support a medical decision — e.g., rewarming a patient that will have to be lowered 300 meters down an active icefall during a storm — then other alternatives must be considered. Keep the safety of the SAR crew in mind at all times so that only one victim needs attention.

Half Dome rescue, 1934. *Photo Ralph H. Anderson, National Park Service archives.*

BIBLIOGRAPHY

CHAPTER TWENTY-SIX

ABRAMOWICZ, MARK, M.D. "Treatment of Frostbite," *The Medical Letter*, 1976.

AMERICAN ACADEMY OF ORTHOPAEDIC SURGEONS. *Emergency Care and Transportation of the Sick and Injured.* Chicago: American Academy of Orthopaedic Surgeons, 1976.

ARNOLD, JOHN W., AND DAYTON, LYNN B. "Hydraulic Sarong," *Off Belay* 21 (June 1975):2-4.

CLARKE, C., WARD, M., AND WILLIAMS, E. EDS. *Mountain Medicine and Physiology.* London: The Alpine Club, 1975.

DUNN, HAL. *Treatment of Hypothermia by Heated Oxygen.* No further publisher's data.

HACKETT, DR. PETER. *Mountain Sickness—Prevention, Recognition and Treatment.* Albany, Ca.: Mountain Travel, Inc., 1978.

HOUSTON, DR. C. "Altitude Illness — 1976 Version," *American Alpine Journal*, vol. 20, no. 2, 1976.

LATHROP, THEODORE G., M.D. *Hypothermia, Killer of the Unprepared.* Portland, Oregon: The Mazamas, 1970.

MILLS, WILLIAM, M.D. "Out in the Cold," *Emergency Medicine*, New York, 1976.

MOUNTAIN MEDICINE SYMPOSIUM. *Proceedings.* Yosemite, Ca.: The Yosemite Institute, 1976.

MOUNTAIN MEDICINE SYMPOSIUM. "Summary of Treatment of the Cold Injured Patient," Seattle, 1976.

NOTO, JAMES V. "Psychological First Aid," *Emergency*, vol. 10, no. 11 (November 1978):63-65.

RESNIK, H.L.P., AND RUBEN, HARVEY L. EDS. *Emergency Psychiatric Care: The Management of Mental Health Crisis.* Bowie, Md.: Charles Press Publishing, 1975.

SMUTEK, RAY ED. *Mountain Medicine 1. Off Belay* Reprint Series. Renton, Wa.: *Off Belay* magazine, 1979.

STEELE, PETER, M.D. *Medical Care for Mountain Climbers.* London: William Heineman Medical Books, 1970.

WARD, MICHAEL, M.D. "Frostbite," *Mountain Medicine and Physiology*, London: R. & C. Moore and Company, 1970.

WASHBURN, B. *Frostbite.* Boston: Museum of Science, 1975.

WILKERSON, J.A., M.D. *Medicine for Mountaineering.* 2d ed. Seattle: The Mountaineers, 1973.

Final Thoughts: Back to the Real World

HUEY HELICOPTERS AND HYDRAULIC SARONGS are handy and fun, but everything has to be kept in perspective. The hundreds of pages of text and myriad illustrations in this book depicting all kinds of ideas and implements that lend credence as well as drama can, in some cases, overemphasize and glorify search and rescue. SAR field activities are generally exciting, but the emphasis should be on the SAR event that did *not* take place or an event where the scope and complexity was minimized by the astute, immediate actions of the victims. The best SAR event never occurs — it is only heard as a story in the inn after an epic on the walls or whitewater standing waves that eventually turned out fine, without injury — one exciting enough to weave a good tale and to provide a little understanding.

For anyone with more than a passing interest in SAR a crucial fifth core element must emerge in our thinking and philosophy. This element, *preventative search and rescue* (PSAR), should really be introduced before the other four: locate, reach, treat, and evacuate. The use of PSAR to prevent and minimize as many potentially dangerous situations as possible through education and training should be one of the main objectives of SAR work. The optimal SAR team activity is sitting around the rescue cache playing checkers, if PSAR is taken seriously and the need for rescues diminishes. While field operations have positive elements, they are a response to a mistake or problem that most of the time did not have to happen.

"Serve Him Right." From *Mountaineering* volume of the Badminton Library of Sports

Preventative SAR requires a perspective difficult to develop. The attitudes and skills that are the essential tools and outlooks for anyone entering a wilderness situation are the foundation of PSAR. Most experienced wilderness users have evolved a personal commitment to safe, careful, and rational wilderness use based on their own early mistakes and problem solving in a broad range of wild environments: winter storms above timberline, flash floods in desert canyons, 300-meter ascents through waterfalls out of Mexican caves. This commitment is demonstrated as a balance of skills, attitudes, awareness, and education that gives the backcountry wanderer or SAR team member a superior chance of avoiding major problems and extracting himself from minor ones with little or no assistance. This commitment helps prevent minor mishaps from compounding themselves into major Greek tragedies.

Two examples help illustrate the point. One early May in Yosemite, cries for help were heard from the Nose route on El Capitan. It had been raining and snowing continuously for about fifteen hours. Two climbers were spotted on Camp IV ledge about 300 meters up the face. Communications were difficult due to the storm but the cry "Hypothermia!" was distinctly heard. A rescue was immediately started.

Fortunately a helicopter was able to pendulum a haul sack containing food, water, warm clothes, and a two-way radio to the climbers via a complex and highly hazardous maneuver. If this had been unsuccessful the plan was to either lower a rescuer down from the top of El Cap over 300 meters to Camp IV or to lower one of the climbers onto some small ledges in a different area of the face somewhat more accessible. Fortunately neither of these plans had to be implemented.

By radio the two asked how long the storm was predicted to continue and advised that they could possibly finish the climb if it stopped raining soon. They added that they would be okay since we provided them with warm clothing. At the time of this rescue effort there were at least six other parties on harder routes on El Cap, yet none of them required any assistance. When asked why they did not rappel off, they admitted knowing about the Rohrer rappel route but one of them had lost a rope to the Stove Legs Crack while rappelling off the same route at an earlier point in his climbing career. They simply were afraid to chance it.

The pair passed the night in relative comfort. With the radio and the aid of a telescope the SAR crew talked them down the rappel route the following day, a nine-hour project. Once on the ground the pair agreed that their predicament was due to a lack of proper clothing. Theirs were classic mistakes: they did not have a tube tent, rain gear, or a bivouac sack and were wearing only light cotton clothing. All were inexcusable miscalculations on an undertaking of that caliber. Not attempting to rappel off on their own when they knew about the perfectly adequate rappel route and choosing to call for a rescue were virtually criminal. The two were precisely correct when they stated that the helicopter crew was in far more danger than they were during the hover and pendulum operation. The cost of the rescue — $3,291.50.

This rescue is comparable to an incident late in July of the same year on the same climb at approximately the same elevation on El Cap. About ten pitches up a climber took a long leader fall and sustained some reasonably serious injuries, the worst of which was later diagnosed as a ruptured spleen. He and his partner got themselves down off the climb and to the hospital with no fanfare, completely unassisted. A nurse asked the injured climber why he had not called for a rescue and he replied, "I was responsible for getting myself up there and I was responsible for getting myself down."

What is the difference between these two similar incidents? The first rescue was totally unnecessary, the second was not a rescue at all but could easily have launched a justifiable big-wall operation, were it not for the competence of the climbers.

Rick LaValla of the Washington State Department of Emergency Services and Gene Fear of the Survival Education Association have studied what type of recreational user takes to the wilderness and why things go wrong there for him. They concluded that the average SAR victim is a composite outdoorsperson, a combination of part climber, fisherman, hunter, skier, camper, hiker, and backpacker all blended into one. He or she usually does not practice any one sport especially well, but joins in a multitude of activities to varying degrees. Most wilderness users reside in densely populated areas, travel relatively far for seasonal recreation, and have a reasonable amount of time and money to spend on these pursuits. Usually too much faith is placed in material equipment advances and the latest mechanical devices, considered essential items. Sadly, this description seems to fit most of us reasonably well today.

Further study of experienced wilderness users by LaValla and Fear revealed that they had acquired individualized additional knowledge in five general categories over and above that of the average wilderness recreationist. These five categories are:

1) Self first aid — knowledge and preparation for first and second aid for injuries;
2) Survival knowledge — how to protect and provide for oneself and partners in an emergency of any sort;
3) Navigation — how to use a compass and knowledge of where and how to travel safely;
4) Wilderness travel — technique of eating, sleeping, and traveling in various environments; and
5) Wilderness specialty skills — specific knowledge about and technique of particular outdoor endeavors like skiing, hiking, and paddling.

But simply gaining additional factual knowledge in wilderness skills is seldom enough. Knowing how to apply this information for self-help is the key to autonomy and safety. Knowing how to climb El Cap is not necessarily enough to keep folks out of trouble. The difference between the two incidents mentioned above is one of attitude, preparedness, and expertise.

Exactly how one goes about learning self-preservation methods is clear though not trivial. If you are a climber, study and practice the tricks revealed in Bill March's little book *Modern Rope Techniques in Mountaineering*. Hikers can turn to books like Craig Patterson's *Mountain Wilderness Survival* or Gene Fear's *Surviving the Unexpected Wilderness Emergency*. But more than reading, consciously *practicing* these basic skills in situ is the key. If out ski touring, spend one night away from the safety of a tent in a snow cave dug with the tail of a ski. You will not only learn a lot about constructing snow holes but will also probably never leave the shovel at home again!

For those of us involved in SAR on a regular basis, because we purposely are part of a SAR organization, there is an additional burden — one of style and ethics. We must control technology, not be enslaved to it. A great deal of this book has dealt with technology of all kinds, in what has almost become the *technological imperative* of SAR. Too many rescue teams view highly sophisticated gadgetry as the panacea to cure all ills. Access to the most modern equipment does not prove to be the universal antidote to accident and injury. Know the state of the art, what equipment is available, and help provide a sound philosophical framework to guide the future of SAR work.

But in the harsh realities of the real world, good judgment dictates that more technology is not the answer, at least not by itself. We should not let the helicopter separate us from the basic technique of movement in the wilderness: climbing, staying physically fit, preparing to survive the unanticipated bivouac. Technology separates us from these fundamental human skills as old as the species. As professionals we must take pride in the fact that we performed a large-scale raising operation without placing a single bolt, or that by carrying the litter a little farther we avoided the scars of a hacked-out helispot. It is more admirable to walk than to fly. The burden of style and ethics is always with us. Often the manner in which goals and objectives are reached is *the* distinction between a professional performer or organization and an ineffective one.

Cigar shop wall, Clearwater, Florida. *Photo Kenneth Andrasko*

There is a final sobering thought about wilderness SAR. The practice of rescue is a duel with death. Saving lives suggests that they are lost as well. As a result, SAR is the elemental, emotional art of action in the face of danger. Earlier I wrote of some general technique and guidelines along these lines, but here I am referring to the possibility that you or another SAR person may be killed or injured. Search and rescue is a noble and holy pursuit, when one considers that a human being is purposely going out of his way to sweat, toil, and sacrifice to help another, often unknown person in need. There is, however, a significant gap between noble philosophy and the stark realism of death.

I immediately think of Jack Dorn, a local Yosemite climber who worked for the park's concessionaire off and on so he could remain in the Valley and climb. As a member of Camp 4 (now known officially as Sunnyside Campground), the traditional unruly home of climbers in the Valley, Jack learned the predominant lifestyle there of surviving in the Valley by causing a minimum of bureaucratic friction. Jack was interested in being a member of the volunteer rescue group in Camp 4. He missed a number of rescues because he was out climbing, but finally got his chance during one stormy spring period when it had been raining and snowing steadily for a day.

Three rescues developed almost simultaneously and all involved long walk-ups in foul, sleeting weather. Jack was part of a group sent to hike up to the Valley rim in the early morning hours by the Yosemite Falls trail, a freeway by local standards. When his party of six stopped in the sleet to take a break at one point, Jack was nowhere to be found. When it became light, the team found Jack's body at the base of some rock slabs 200 meters below the trail. For unknown reasons — probably a combination of wet moss, fogging glasses, and an instant of carelessness — Jack had stepped off the trail and slid down the slabs to his death.

The two climbers Dorn was walking up to rescue were safely pulled off the rock early in the morning. Their story was all too familiar — both were local employees who worked in the area and were new climbers. They had plenty of time to observe the spring weather patterns but still chose not to take any survival gear between them except one thin raincoat. They were doing a long climb which neither had been on before. Lastly, it appeared that they had sufficient gear with them to rescue themselves. All of the noble idealism of SAR melted down to a puddle of nothing at all when measured against the situation in which Jack Dorn lost his life. It was a tragic waste. Somehow it seemed to many that the two climbers were guilty of manslaughter.

Aside from the moral and sometimes financial burden that a person may have to carry with him because he was rescued is a larger and perhaps more important reason for any wilderness user to squarely assume personal responsibility for traveling and playing in the wilds safely. If this individual awareness and commitment to self-help and safety does not become manifest in each of us, we jeopardize what Galen Rowell describes as "the most basic of wilderness values, the right to risk life and limb. . . ." Wilderness use is one of the freest and most unregulated forms of activity available today in an increasingly centralized and bureaucratic world.

The federal government is required by law to assist anyone asking for help. The type of response depends on the individual situation, but there will always be a response of some sort. The cost of these searches and rescues is paid totally by tax dollars, and as yet has not been passed along to the rescuee. Worse yet is when someone yelling for help is really crying "wolf." We all still have to pay for the helicopter ride. When a rescuer is killed or injured the cost is immeasurable.

This situation has to change. Unthinking and unaware individuals are causing unnecessary risks to lives and property as well as costing all taxpayers money. They will be responsible for new restrictions that will unjustly affect all wilderness users. I am gravely concerned about this inequity and the effects it will likely cause in our bureaucracy. Traditional responses have been mandatory registration and the closing of some routes to climbing. I personally realize the ineffectiveness of both measures. Closed routes force climbers into secrecy or other areas nearby. Simple registration gives us accurate records of ascents but little more. These traditional solutions act only to encumber the wilderness user and the bureaucracy with more restrictions and regulations.

The ultimate solution is to move the moral burden of responsibility and financial accountability back to the wilderness user. In European countries the local alpine clubs have insurance that might well provide models with application in the U.S. The end result must be that each of us be held responsible for our own actions while in the wilderness, just as we are held responsible for our actions while driving on a highway. The cost and burden of negligence should not have to be carried by the taxpayer and federal government any longer. If self-contained parties do not develop, parties will be contained by regulations.

BIBLIOGRAPHY

FINAL THOUGHTS

MARCH, BILL. *Improvised Techniques In Mountain Rescue.* England: Jacobean Press, Ltd., n.d.
MARCH, BILL. *Modern Rope Techniques in Mountaineering.* 2d ed. rev. Manchester, Eng.: Acerone Press, 1976.
ROWELL, GALEN. "On Safety and Wilderness," *Sierra,* November-December 1977, pp. 43-44.

Index

The Appalachian Mountain Club And Its Activities

The Appalachian Mountain Club is a non-profit volunteer organization of over 25,000 members. Centered in the northeastern United States with headquarters in Boston, its membership is worldwide. The A.M.C. was founded in 1876, the oldest and largest organization of its kind in America. Its existence has been committed to conserving, developing and managing dispersed outdoor recreational opportunities for the public in the northeast and its efforts in the past have endowed it with a significant public trust and its volunteers and staff today maintain that tradition.

Ten regional chapters from Maine to Pennsylvania, some sixty committees and hundreds of volunteers supported by a dedicated professional staff join in administering the Club's wide-ranging programs. Besides volunteer organized and led expeditions, these include research, backcountry management, trail and shelter construction and maintenance, conservation and outdoor education. The Club operates a unique system of eight alpine huts in the White Mountains, a base camp and public information center at Pinkham Notch, N.H., a new public service facility in the Catskill Mountains of New York, five full service camps, four self-service camps and nine campgrounds, all open to the public. Its Boston headquarters houses not only a public information center but the largest mountaineering library and research facility in the U.S. The Club also conducts leadership workshops, mountain search and rescue, and a youth opportunity program for disadvantaged urban young people. The Club publishes guidebooks, maps and America's oldest mountaineering journal — *APPALACHIA*.

As an organization providing information, leadership, hospitality, food and lodging to more than a half million hikers, canoeists, ski tourers and other lovers of the outdoors every year, the Appalachian Mountain Club endeavors to promote wise planning for and use of the backcountry — its rivers, forests, mountains and lakes — and has committed itself to working cooperatively with other managers and recreational users in this effort.

We invite you to join and share in the benefits of membership. Membership brings a subscription to the monthly bulletin *APPALACHIA*; discounts on publications and at the huts and camps managed by the Club; notices of trips and programs; and association with chapters and their meetings and activities. Most important, membership offers the opportunity to support and share in the major public service efforts of the Club.

You are welcome to become as active in the AMC as you wish, or you may elect to become a quiet contributor.

The Club invites the membership of all those who share a love of the woods and mountains and wish to support their protection. Membership is open to the general public upon completion of an application form and payment of an initiation fee and annual dues. Information on membership as well as the names and addresses of the secretaries of local chapters may be obtained by writing to: The Appalachian Mountain Club, 5 Joy Street, Boston Massachusetts 02108, or calling during business hours 617-523-0636.